THE COLD OF MAY DAY MONDAY

THE COLD OF MAY DAY MONDAY

AN APPROACH TO IRISH LITERARY HISTORY

ROBERT ANTHONY WELCH

OXFORD

UNIVERSITY PRESS

OXFORD
UNIVERSITY PRESS

Great Clarendon Street, Oxford, OX2 6DP,
United Kingdom

Oxford University Press is a department of the University of Oxford.
It furthers the University's objective of excellence in research, scholarship,
and education by publishing worldwide. Oxford is a registered trade mark of
Oxford University Press in the UK and in certain other countries

First Edition published in 2014

Impression: 1

Published in the United States of America by Oxford University Press
198 Madison Avenue, New York, NY 10016, United States of America

British Library Cataloguing in Publication Data
Data available

Library of Congress Control Number: 2013950550

ISBN 978-0-19-968684-1

Printed in Great Britain by
Clays Ltd, St Ives plc

To Pino and Giusi Serpillo

Acknowledgements

My thanks to Pino and Giusi Serpillo of Sassari, without whose friendship and guidance this book would not have been written. And to Professor Aldo Morace, Dean of Faculty at the University of Sassari where the lectures in which this book has its origin were delivered. My thanks to the Librarian and staff of the university libraries at the University of Ulster and at Sassari; and to my colleagues in the University of Ulster who gave me their support while I was Dean of the Faculty of Arts from 2000 to 2008, and afterwards when I enjoyed a sabbatical before taking retirement. A special word of gratitude to Professor Gerry McKenna MRIA, who, while Vice-Chancellor, gave forceful encouragement to research in the Arts and strengthened my resolve to continue to write and research while enmeshed in administration. I thank him for his friendship since then, and for his solicitude.

I am greatly indebted to Jacqueline Baker, Senior Commissioning Editor at Oxford University Press, for her faith in this not altogether typical book; and to the anonymous readers for the Press, all of whose comments have been incorporated, and whose thoughtful considerations have enhanced the final work. My thanks to Jonathan Williams, my agent, for his advice and careful guidance.

My thanks to Professor Roy Spence, and to Mr Mark Taylor, Mr Colm Harvey, Dr Peter Gallagher, and the medical and nursing staff at the Causeway, Mater, and Royal Victoria Hospitals; to Dr David Conkey at Laurel House, Antrim Hospital, and to the great nursing team there. It lifts the heart and the spirit to see such dedication and humanity in action, day in, day out.

This is hopelessly inadequate but I will say it anyhow: thank you to my wife Angela for your love over forty and more years, and to our children and their partners: Rachel and Richard; Killian and Imali; Tiernán and Lauren. And my thanks and love to our dead son, Egan, who is always with us, and to his fiancée, Charlotte Moffett. This book, like everything I have written since his death by drowning in the river Bann in 2007, is driven by him, and by his great spirit.

Robert Anthony Welch

Coleraine
January 2012

Contents

Introduction

This book has its origin in a lecture series given at the University of Sassari in Sardinia when I was an Italian-government Visiting Professor at that university in March and April 2009. The invitation to take up this position was extended by my friend and colleague, Professor Giuseppe Serpillo, of the Dipartmento di Teorie e Richerche dei Sistemi Culturali, who has done as much as anyone in Italy to advance and deepen knowledge and appreciation of the literature of Ireland in that country and in Sardinia. Professor Aldo Morace, Dean of the Facolta di Lettere e Filosofia, also put himself out to ensure that the appointment went smoothly. I want to thank both Professor Serpillo and Professor Morace for their warm hospitality during my time at Sassari. They went to great trouble to ensure that my stay was comfortable and enjoyable.

The association between the University of Sassari and my own university, the University of Ulster, is a long-standing one, going back as far as 1988 when we began, under the ERASMUS scheme of the European Union, to exchange students and enhance staff contacts. This link has, unlike many such, been extremely productive, leading to numerous conferences and research collaborations on Irish and Italian literature and culture. The leading presence here was always Professor Serpillo, a true academic, an outstanding critic of Irish writing, and one of the finest translators of Irish poetry into Italian.

My task, as Visiting Professor, was to deliver a series of lectures on the history and culture of Irish literature, which would give, in as much as it lay within my power, an extended account of that literature (in other words, not concentrating exclusively on the last few centuries), by taking the story back to the cultural mind-set from which it emerged in the early periods of the Celtic era. This approach meant that an attempt needed to be made to take account of the mythology, folklore, and legendary materials of early Irish culture, and the circumstances in which these foundational layers were formed. Such a contextualizing principle underlies all this history: the literature is constantly related to political and economic environments and to larger cultural patterns.

The aim was to keep the narrative as simple as possible, bearing in mind that the students to whom these lectures were given were working in a second language. Professor Serpillo and I helped them to understand more fully what was being said by his translating my lectures, paragraph by paragraph, as I gave them. They were not read lectures; they were delivered with the minimum of notes, which made Professor Serpillo's task all the greater. As ever, he undertook this exhausting regime with his usual scruple and enthusiasm.

It was also necessary to base this approach to an Irish literary history on a smallish number of texts, which the students could read without too much difficulty, but which would, at the same time, take them to the heart of the historical and cultural issues in any of the periods being dealt with. This meant that the choice of illustrative texts had to be highly selective. It would not be possible for the students to cope with discussion of more than three or four texts in any one lecture. This approach has, to a significant extent, been carried over into this book: each chapter has a small number of key texts, on which the discussion of the history and progress of the literature is based. This makes it possible for the reader to use this book as a basic introduction to the history of Irish writing of all periods on the basis of a relatively small number of texts. This has meant that I have concentrated on themes, issues, and larger patterns, rather than on dry chronology; but it also allows for deep and strategic analysis of major work. With such an approach the selection of texts and authors to be treated for the lectures and for this book had, necessarily, to be very rigorous. Such an exiguous set of choices has involved, in the modern period (from about 1890 onwards), some hard decisions about whom to include as exemplary of major shifts and tendencies. There will be absences here that will surprise some readers, but the alternative—dreary plodding through a list of authors so as not to exclude or offend anyone (especially the prickly living)—would have not served the main outline of the story well. And, in any case, the tedium in so many literary histories, when they encounter the quandary of dealing with living authors, arises because the easiest line is often taken, and as many as possible of the living are named, in order to avoid giving offence.

However, when I look back, on the final chapter in particular, which concerns itself with living and contemporary writing, my conscience is stricken that so many have been, it may seem brutally, excluded from sustained discussion and appraisal. In particular I am exercised by the short shrift given to poets such as Brian Coffey, Paula Meehan, Medbh McGuckian, Paul Durcan, Michael Davitt, Tom Paulin, Thomas McCarthy, Michael Longley, Eiléan Ní Chuilleanáin, Greg Delanty, John F. Deane, Theo Dorgan, Patrick Galvin, Vona Groarke; novelists such as Benedict Kiely, Dermot Healy, Colm Tóibín, Joseph O'Connor, Colum McCann, William Trevor, Glenn Patterson, Robert McLiam Wilson, Anne Haverty, David Park; and playwrights such as Tom Murphy, Billy Roche, Vincent Woods, Thomas Kilroy. But the very rehearsal of such a (by no means exclusive) list reveals only that the contemporary scene must necessarily be truncated in a historical account of the entire tradition. My choice of authors to consider at some length was driven by my own taste and reading, but also by a more determining factor: I wanted to choose living authors whose work would reveal connections with, or sharp disjunctions from, the traditions of Irish literary experience as outlined in this book. Others will tackle this problem differently. And yet, there are pangs of regret and the worse torment of remorse: I have just read McCann's brilliant last novel, Tóibín's magnificent short stories that align him with the masters, Leontia Flynn's most recent collection, and I am rebuked.

While this book has its origin in that series of lectures given in March/April 2009 for students on an undergraduate degree programme, it is my hope that the approach adopted here will appeal to the ordinary reader who is curious about the history of one of the great literatures of the world, not least because the concentration on getting the right text to illustrate a certain period or theme or issue allows the reader to branch out from that point, if he or she so wishes, to look at other works by the same author, or to extend his or her reading based on the clues and directions provided in the commentary.

I wish to thank the students at the University of Sassari for their patience and their amazing responsiveness to these talks. Irish literature, as much as any literature, is based on the emotional response of highly developed intelligences to the often raw sorrow of event, historical cruelty, and misfortune. There were occasions when I gave these lectures that I was moved close to tears not just by my redis-covering in the lecture room the brilliance and unrelenting focus the writers bring to their subject matter, but also by the quick receptivity the Sardinian students displayed when it came to matters of feeling, and in understanding a culture very different from theirs, but with many and surprising connections and parallels.

I

Ancient Things

I rish is a Celtic language, and Irish literature, in the Irish language, is the oldest vernacular literature in Europe. The Celts, it is now agreed, did not arrive in Ireland until around 300 BC. This is very late, when it is recalled that Ireland had been settled for five thousand years or so before that time. It is almost as if the Celts were amongst the last to discover Ireland, as they say about Christopher Columbus's discovery of America.

It would be inaccurate to identify the Celts as a people or a race; instead, they were a widely dispersed cultural grouping, showing a remarkable uniformity in their life-patterns and forms of belief. They were all over Europe. Lyon in France is named after the deity known in Irish as Lugh, the Celtic Apollo; Vienna recalls the personage who evolved into Fionn in the Irish Ossianic cycle of tales; the Shannon and the Seine are named after the same female entity, Sequana. The Celts got to Asia Minor (modern-day Turkey); they sacked Rome; they were in Gaul (France) and Spain (one of the legendary invaders of Ireland was called Míl Espáine, Spanish Míl), Germany, and, of course, Britain and Ireland. Wherever evidence of their presence is found, no matter how far apart these evidences may lie, a very close kinship can be seen in the artefacts they made, the way they buried their dead, the kind of sacrifical rituals they performed, and how they engaged in warfare and combat. Their belief-system was complex, involving deities with overlapping and manifold functions, not unlike that which is found in Hinduism. As with Hinduism, where the Brahminical caste supported and administered the institutions of religion, in the Celtic world there were the druids, who discharged similar functions and enjoyed a correspondingly high status. There are indeed affinities between the Celtic world and that of the Indian subcontinent, which is not surprising when it is considered that the Celtic languages and many of those in India belong to the same vast Indo-European family. The word 'brahmin', for example, is cognate with the Irish word 'breitheamh', meaning a judge. It may also be that, given that Ireland and India are located at the extremities of the Indo-European continuum, their cultures preserve closer ties and similarities than might be expected, seeing as communities at the far reaches of a shared spectrum of human endeavour and expression tend to be conservative, and to hold on to older forms of life and behaviour. Scholars agree that Irish culture has, in its earlier forms, a conservative and even archaic tendency, and I know that many Indian scholars would also say that India too exhibits such a cast of mind. I would go further and say that Ireland still, to this day, retains something of this archaizing and conservative ethos, a mentality that, perhaps, can cause an awful lot of bother when it moves into the political arena.

When the Celts arrived in Ireland they brought with them an Iron Age culture, known as the La Tène culture after a famous site in Switzerland where a sacrificial trove of chariots and armour was found. They fought from chariots, and they cut the heads off their defeated enemies and wore them as trophies around their waists. Conall Cernach, an Ulster warrior, and a version of the horned deity Cernunnos (the horned or peaked one), who appears on the famous Gundestrup cauldron found in Denmark, boasted that he never slept without the head of a man from Connacht under his knee. They were known and feared as great fighters, and would go naked into battle. It was said of them that they were afraid of nothing, except the possibility that the sky might fall.

There were people (or rather peoples) in Ireland when the Celts showed up. We know very little of these communities, other than what can be gleaned from archaeology, and hesitantly inferred from early Irish mythology, legend, and whatever survives in folklore, which, it is now accepted, may be more than used to be thought was the case. These peoples built, over time, what we now call Newgrange on the banks of the river Boyne; they built Navan fort, known in Irish as Emain Macha, outside Armagh; and were responsible for many other tumuli throughout Ireland, including one overlooking the Bann at Mountsandel near Coleraine, the river up which it is probable that the very first settlers came, in around 5000 BC. To give some perspective, this would have been some two thousand years before the time

that the story of Gilgamesh, the world's first epic tale (that we know of),
was composed, in the Sumerian language, in that part of the world we
now know as Iraq. The Pyramid of Cheops is another two thousand
years away; and Homer will not begin to recite the *Iliad* for another four
thousand years.

We know that the peoples that preceded the Celts took the burial of
their dead very seriously, and that they perceived human existence as
being part of a cycle that involved it with the changes of the seasons
and the continuous variation between day and night. That much is
clearly evident from the archaeological evidence at Newgrange and
other places. At Newgrange the architecture is such that the interior of
the tumulus is lit up when the sun rises at the winter solstice. A thin
shaft of light, made all the more luminous by the surrounding darkness,
comes through the aperture at the entrance, shoots along a dark and
narrow passageway into the pitch dark of the central chamber with
its huge engraved stones, and gradually lights up the circular stone
enclosure as the radiance grows. The archaeologist Michael J. Kelly,
who excavated the tumulus in the 1960s, used to tell his students at
Cork (of whom I was occasionally one, sitting in on his lectures with
his permission) about the shock and wonder he experienced when first
he saw this amazing sight.

The Celts gained ascendency over whomever were there before
them. We do not know if this was done by force, or whether there was
some kind of peaceful accommodation and amalgamation of traditions.
Knowing what we do about our species, however, it is doubtful if
there was an easy accord. Yet the Celts appear not to have been racially
triumphalist, and the literature they evolved in due course in Ireland
has many stories of the peoples of Ireland, different invasions and
settlements, and a complex awareness of the diversity of origins of all
the island's constituent human traces.

The Celts were polymorphic. That is to say, they held a complex
view of reality, whereby single entities, their gods for instance, were
not confined to one role, and different fields of reference and frameworks of association could intermingle and interpenetrate. Their
mythology, which naturally reflected their religious outlook, they
brought with them, and any rites and ceremonials would have been
carried out by the druidic caste, an institution in place across the full
extent of the Celtic world, from Ireland to Tomis (where Ovid, the

Roman poet, was exiled amongst the Getics, a Celtic people), and across the Black Sea to Asia Minor.

This multi-locational mythology they adapted to what they found before them in Ireland, so that in Irish mythology (or rather that branch of Celtic myth which developed in Ireland) places like Newgrange became associated with the Celtic deities. Newgrange, called Brú na Bóinne in Irish (the fortress of the Boyne), became the habitation of the Dagda, the Good God, an Irish god of gods, comparable to Krishna in Hinduism. Beneath the tumulus he has his cauldron of never-to-be-diminished beer, which he dispenses to the Irish dead for all eternity. Or at least that is the case in one version. The river they called the Boyne, An Bhóinn, from Bo-Ann ('White Cow'), once again linking an Indo-European figure with local specifics: this personage is clearly a version of the same archetypal pattern that is reflected in Indra, the cow-goddess who gives her name to India.

The Celts took this transposition and adaptation much further. They not only associated the previous inhabitants of the island, and their monuments, with their own deities; they also reconstructed their own mythology to give the predecessors very significant roles in legends that embodied a continuously changing world-view as they settled in Ireland. The inhabitants of Newgrange they called the Tuatha Dé Danann, the peoples of the goddess Danu (who, in another location, gives her name to the Danube). When the Milesians, the people of Míl Espáine (by whom they meant themselves, the Celtic Irish), came to Ireland, they said that the Tuatha Dé Danann went underground to live in the tumuli and earthworks that the Celts knew had been built by those who were there before them. The Tuatha Dé Danann then became a deified people, the gods of the Irish, and eventually evolved into the *sídhe*, the fairies of folklore.

This complex process of adaptation and amalgamation was probably effected by the Celtic mythographers, the druids or a related learned class, who would have been the antecedents of the poetic hierarchy, the *filid*. However this unification of myth and local specifics was managed, it did take place, and it is, in its way, a powerful instance of the Celtic instinct towards cultural cohesion and coherence. This creative act, which probably took a century or more to bring about, laid a groundwork for a complex of legend and myth which lies at the heart of Irish literature, the Irish world-view, and Irish patterns of belief. The Tuatha Dé, the Celtic invention which put the ancient inhabitants of the island into the picture, haunt Irish literature with their abiding presence. Their magic lured Yeats, and many others, among them Lady Gregory, George Russell, George Moore, Patrick Pearse (to mention some of those who were in thrall to them in the early twentieth century), down to Thomas Kinsella, Ciaran Carson, Paul Muldoon, Medbh McGuckian (to bring us down to the century's end, and beyond). Names such as Lugh, Oengus, Manannán Mac Lir, the Morrigán, Fand—all still resonate.

One effect this incorporation of the monuments and earthworks of the previous inhabitants into the legends and myths of the Irish Celts had was to render the landscape of Ireland, in its mythologized aspect, animate with significance. The landscape was a place that could be read. It had a complicated network of interwoven story that made it numinous and mysterious. The landscape held within itself its secrets; beneath, there was an otherworld, to which access could be gained through certain places, locations of awe and terror. Kings were inaugurated on these sacred sites, because through these places there could be gained some kind of contact with the force of the land itself, the presiding tutelary deity, always female. Tara, for example, was the place where the high king of Ireland was inaugurated from early Celtic times in a ritual that, from what is known of it, reflected ancient Indo-European practices. It seems to have involved a symbolic mating of the intended king with the tutelary goddess. The king, in what was clearly some kind of shamanistic performance, assumed bull-form (it has been suggested that he put on the bloody skin of a freshly killed animal), in which shape he slept with the goddess, who in turn endowed him with otherworldly power.

Because the landscape was full of story, a branch of learning evolved which specialized in the lore of place. This form of literature (as it developed, the material mostly was encapsulated in verse) became known as the *dindshenchas*, the knowledge of the meaning of place, and it was a body of work that was obligatory study in the schools of poetic learning. Every place of any importance (and some with none) had its legend, which told how the place got its name, something Brian Friel makes hilarious but devastating use of in a famous passage about the origin of a crossroads called Tobair Vree in *Translations* (1980). It turns out that it means 'the well of Brian', because a man by the name of Brian who had a huge growth on his face came every day to the well and washed in it, believing that it was blessed and that he would be

cured. The growth remained and one day Brian was found drowned
in the well. The well wasn't at the crossroads, and it has since dried
up, so, the native translator asks, what is the point of preserving a
name that reflects an insignificant tale that scarcely anyone remembers? So much for the pieties of tradition and the lore of place.

The evolution of dindshenchas, the incorporation of the earlier
culture into the Celtic network of mythology while at the same time
implicating the old knowledge into the landscape, reveals a major
preoccupation in Irish literary culture: a deep-rooted concern with
origins. Irish people have always been (still are) preoccupied with
where someone comes from, to whom he or she is related, how places
got their names. This obsession with origins may well reflect the fact
that way back in Celtic times it was not at all clear who the Irish were,
where they came from, what their relationship was or should be with
whomever was there before them. This tangle of uncertainty influenced the polymorphic nature of Irish myth, and it also led to the
creation of what has been called synthetic history, the creation of
origin tales to explain why such and such a person came to be in a
specific place, or why a certain dynasty should be where it is. In other
words, knowing the answer you want to get, you set out to invent
a history that will fit in with where you want to end up. It may be
said, perhaps, that an obsession with origins reflects a deep-seated
doubt about the possibility of establishing any degree of certainty at
all in such matters.

However that may be, the observation that the Cork short-story
writer and literary historian Frank O'Connor made about one of the
dominant traits in Irish literature remains true: it has what he called a
tendency towards 'the backward look'. This takes various forms: the
search for the origin, a feeling for the archaic, and a general sense that
long ago things were a hell of a lot better than they are now, or if they
weren't, then they were at least a lot more interesting.

Much of what has been said about Irish literature and the mentalities
to which it gives expression is encapsulated in a folktale about the Hag
of Beare which was recorded by one of the collectors for the Irish
Folklore Commission.[1] Although the recording was made in the
twentieth century, the tale is, as Gearóid Ó Crualaoich has said,
primordial. It takes us right back to beginnings, to origins. The Hag
is associated, though not exclusively, with Beare Island off Castletown-
beare in west Cork. Stories about her are to be found all over Ireland

and Gaelic Scotland, and she is frequently described as residing at places as widely dispersed as the stories about her are. She is, in effect, a tutelary goddess of the land of Ireland, and indeed Scotland, and can manifest her presence at any location in the Gaelic world.

The story in question is called 'The Hag of Beare and the Cold of May Day Monday'. It was collected in County Mayo, and this is where the Hag is in the story, although as it opens we are told that she was very old, and that she had travelled nearly the length and breadth of Ireland. She had a herd of cows with her, and goats too sometimes, as well as sheep. She was always moving with her animals, from county to county, we are told. The Hag is in nature, and of nature; the natural world is in her care, and that world is Ireland. Although she is always moving, in keeping with her multi-locational and polymorphic functions, she does stay a long time when she comes to Nephin mountain in County Mayo, as the pasture there, at the foot of the mountain, is very good. Nephin is a mountain with many otherworld associations.

A local man wants to hear stories from the Hag, because he understands that she is a source of all kinds of old knowledge. He comes to her and asks her if she can tell him what happened on a day, many years before, when it became intensely cold, even though it was the first day of summer, May Day. Although she is very old she cannot recall that time, and tells him to go to an ancient Eagle who lives in the ruins of a forge. He may be able to tell the enquirer about the day of terrible cold. The man finds the Eagle, who says that he has been in the forge for seven hundred years. He goes on: 'This anvil that was in the forge was new and the peak that it had then was as thick as any peak that was ever on any anvil. When I used to eat my food I used to rub my beak on the peak of the anvil, on both sides . . . in order to clean my beak. The peak now, today, is so worn and slender from my rubbing my beak on it after my meals for so long that it is as thin as a pin.'

But even though he has been there this length of time he has no recollection of the cold that came on May Day Monday. The Eagle tells the man to go to the Otter of the Rock to see if he can tell him what he wants to know. The Otter has been on the rock for five hundred years, and he has it worn down so deeply that no trace of him can be seen from any side when he is lying in the hole he has made in the stone, but even *he* can give no account of the cold of May Day Monday. The only chance the man has of finding out what he wants is to go to the Half-Blind Salmon of Assaroe on the Erne, and if the Salmon cannot help, then no account of the day will be had anywhere.

He finds the Salmon, who can tell him what it was like to experience the cold of that day:

> I was here in the same place I am now . . . and I leaped up out of the water to catch a fly. And in between my leaping and my landing back in the water there came such thick ice on the river here that it held me up when I fell back. I stayed there, fallen back on the ice, until a seagull came and took the eye out of my head. And blood came out of my head, from the socket of the eye, and the blood melted the ice and I went down again into the water. And that is the cold that was there on May Day Monday.

We are here on the edge of primordial time. We are also in a world where the forces of nature, its colossal energies, are very much in evidence. The ice of the Ice Age comes so fast that a waterfall (Assaroe, in Irish Eas Rua, 'red waterfall', red being the colour of the underworld) freezes over in less than a second. The tale reminds us of the literally awful powers that are in the world around us, that we take for granted, and that we abuse at our peril. This realm, the one to which the Hag gives entrance, is one where destruction and creation, death and life, are not separable. The deadly attack of the seagull is what allows the Salmon to go back to his living element. The Hag presides over these mysteries. She is also, as is revealed in many of the stories about her, someone you take great care not to cross; if you do, her retribution is fierce and implacable, because we are not dealing with human motive, causality, or intellection.

We are dealing with what Shakespeare called, in *The Winter's Tale*, 'great creating nature' (IV. iv. 86). She is ancient, implicated in the hidden significances of the land of Ireland; she is yet another variation of the entity with whom the king is mated at his inauguration. She knows the secrets of time—that it is only human invention, and that concepts of beginning and end dissolve in the infinite nano-second that is her domain. She is ancient, but she is also ever-young, and can reveal herself in her astonishing female beauty as she pleases. She is everywhere in Irish literature, from a seventh-century poem explicitly about her, to variations of her as Róisín Dubh, Cathleen Ni Houlihan, Síle Ní Ghadhra in Gaelic poetry and in Irish poetry and drama in English. J. J. Callanan, James Clarence Mangan, Samuel Ferguson, W. B. Yeats, Lady Gregory, Austin Clarke, Anthony Cronin, Brendan

Behan, John Montague, Seamus Heaney, Paul Muldoon, Ciaran Carson, Nuala Ní Dhomhnaill—all paid homage to this entity, as did Robert Graves, who built a whole poetic theology around her in *The White Goddess* (1961). Even Samuel Beckett knew her and feared her. She appears in those short love poems, frantic with longing, which he wrote, but also in her hellish hag-form in the desperate and atrocious couplings that surface regularly in his terrible fictions. It might even be possible to suggest, somewhat mischievously, that Beckett himself became a kind of version of her nibs.

When the Celtic Irish wrote their (invented) histories of the coming to Ireland of the sons of Míl Espáine, the Milesians, they adjusted their mythology to existing conditions, creating an otherworldly network out of known sacred places. They brought the concept of the tutelary goddess (one of whose manifestations was the Hag) with them and gave her manifold habitations all over the island, and in Scotland. However, she was probably there before them anyway, in that she is a universal archetype, so that what almost certainly occurred was the renewal of basic patterns in a different and conducive context.

The druidic institution would have been the means whereby these adjustments were managed and embedded in the newly evolving mindset. The Celts have, said Jorge Luis Borges, the Argentinian fabulist, in a lecture of 1963, a startling propensity for the founding and maintenance of academies of learning and poetry.[2] He is referring to the druidic institutions and their remote descendants, the bardic academies of Ireland in the late Middle Ages. Poetry, as a branch of knowledge rather than as a form of entertainment, has a very high value in Irish tradition. Poetry is the means of coming into contact, through highly worked and potent use of language, with those energies over which the Hag presides. Not only that: poetry is a means whereby those energies can be harnessed for the good of the chieftain and the realm; poetry in this conception is a civic act, a mentality that to this day informs most of what Seamus Heaney has written. If there is not the order of poetry and the poetic academy (and originally the druidic academy), then the hag energy may well fly loose. Academies are required because the energies they seek to bring to order are powerful, with the potential to destroy if not subjected to rule and government.

In the eleventh-century *Lebor Gabála Érenn* ('The Book of Invasions'), which tells the invented stories of the different invasions of

Ireland down to the Milesians, the first of the Irish to put his foot on
the land of Ireland is the poet Amergin, whose name means wonderful
creation. He then utters his famous hymn, which unites nature, human
perception, language, energy, force, conflict, and beauty into one
forceful declaration. At the same time it asserts the potency of poetry
to be the means whereby we can experience the huge energies of
nature in a way that can bring about some small understanding of
them. Irish literary tradition, in the hymn of Amergin, is making it
very clear that poetry, and the institution of poetry, is of primary
importance in human society, that it speaks of ancient and original
things:

> I am the wind on the sea;
> I am the wave of the sea;
> I am the bull of seven battles;
> I am the eagle on the rock;
> I am a flash from the sun;
> I am the most beautiful of plants;
> I am a strong wild boar;
> I am a salmon in the water;
> I am a lake in the plain;
> I am the word of knowledge;
> I am the head of the spear in battle.[3]

This is a literature with a long history, and, like other literatures (the
literature of India for instance), it is written in a number of languages.
Irish writers are well known today across the world, and Ireland is
proud of the fact that, in the twentieth century, four of her writers
have been awarded the Nobel Prize for Literature: W. B. Yeats,
George Bernard Shaw, Samuel Beckett, and Seamus Heaney. She is
also very much aware, in a kind of grim satisfaction, that other writers,
just as great as these, have been overlooked by the Swedish Academy:
James Joyce, for instance; Brian Friel; Máirtín Ó Cadhain.

That last name will bring many readers up short. Who? Ó Cadhain was
a writer of fiction in the Irish language who was born and reared in the
Connemara Gaeltacht (the Gaeltachtaí are the remaining Irish-speaking
areas of Ireland, situated mostly along the western seaboard), joined the
Irish Republican Army (IRA) in the 1930s, was imprisoned by the Irish
state, and eventually became Professor of Irish at Trinity College, Dublin.
He also wrote one of the essential books of Irish literature of any period,
Cré na Cille ('Churchyard Clay', 1948), a work of fiction to set alongside

Joyce's *Ulysses* (1922) or Jonathan Swift's *Gulliver's Travels* (1726). But the mention of this book brings us back to the question of the languages of Irish literature. Ó Cadhain's work is very little known outside Ireland for two reasons. The first reason, obviously, is because he wrote in Irish. But the second introduces a whole different set of considerations. Ó Cadhain put all kinds of constraints on his literary executors, among which is an injunction against the translation of his masterpiece (and of course he knew it was one—all true writers can tell when they have produced the goods) into English. He wanted his work to be read in his native language by Irish readers because he was convinced that the central issue in Irish life and culture was that of the language and the very likely extinction of Irish by its more powerful kinsman in the family of Indo-European languages, English. Ó Cadhain was a republican, and remained one all his life, so that English, like Irish, was more to him than just a means of communication: it was the symbol of the sovereign power that had retained supremacy over Ireland for many centuries, and to his mind this dominion was far from ended. He was, also, all too aware that *Cré na Cille* was well beyond the capacity of most readers of Irish, something that sorely grieved him. The language of his novel is only a heightened and more eloquent form of the language that was spoken in his native part of Connemara, just west of Spiddal, ten miles or so from Galway city, when he was a child in the 1920s. If there was, he ardently believed, any hope for his country, then its people had, somehow, to recover the richness that the Irish language contained. It was, as Father Peter O'Leary put it in the early twentieth century, an armoury of the spirit. Without it, without the capacity to read easily what he had laboured to produce, then the country was a cipher, a ghostly ruin, a dereliction.

Hopeless, hopeless idealism, some might say fanaticism even. English is the language that the Irish speak. Many say that they write it with extraordinary style: think of the cadences of Edmund Burke, bristling with startling realizations of the pressure of truth; or the vast lexicons of Joyce's *Finnegans Wake*, where, as somebody once put it, Joyce took an Irish revenge on the English language. English was the language that the four Nobel Laureates wrote (or write) in. (We should also recall that Beckett wrote a good deal of his work initially in French.) But Ó Cadhain's lonely insistence will not and should not go away. Irish has been the language of Irish literature for close on two thousand years, and that literature is of great significance.

That the language of Irish literature is now, primarily, English is a fact that should give us pause. That language shift was not an act of nature. It was a matter of policy on the part of a British administration, as it sought to subject Ireland to its rule, for hundreds of years, and eventually a decision by the Irish themselves. Now, most Irish people are foreigners to their own tongue, one of the reasons, perhaps, why Irish writers write English with ferocity, edge, and style. Style is not namby-pamby tomfoolery, it is not ease; style is collected force, relentless precision, absolute concentration. It is what Yeats has when he writes 'Byzantium'; or what John Banville has, in his taut recoveries of the capacity syntax has to awaken realizations with the force of something like truth.

Irish and English are not, of course, the only two languages of Irish literature: there is a significant body of work in Hiberno-Latin. Irish ecclesiastics in colleges of devotion and learning on the Continent, from St Gall to Bobbio, Salamanca, Louvain, Rome, and Paris, wrote primarily in Latin; and they were practising an art and linguistic skill that had evolved in the Irish monasteries at home from around AD 550 onwards. Irish hagiography, in the Irish monasteries at home and abroad, was mostly in Latin. The Latinist tradition was not, however, exclusively the domain of clerics. Maghnus Ó Domhnaill wrote a life of Columcille in his castle at Lifford, County Donegal in 1532. John Lynch's *Cambrensis Eversus* (1662) was a rebuttal of the lies and misrepresentations about the Irish perpetrated by the British author Giraldus Cambrensis, as far back as 1188 and recycled on a regular basis by anti-Irish commentators since that time whenever it was convenient to propagate unflattering views of the country, its people, and their habits. There is hardly an anti-Irish stereotype that does not have its origin in Giraldus's innocent-sounding *Topographica Hibernica*, from their drunkenness and lasciviousness, to their tendency towards blind and uncritical loyalty to their chieftains, who are, in Giraldus's caricature, mostly villainous wretches. Irish Latin culture continued into the eighteenth and nineteenth centuries, in debased form admittedly, and into the hedge schools that survived right up to the Famine of the 1840s and a little beyond.

As well as Latin writing, there is a small but interesting body of literature in Middle English and Norman French composed in the Pale, the anglified area around Dublin (which tended to expand and contract according to the intensity or otherwise of British resolve to extirpate native custom and culture) and in or near Kilkenny. The Kilkenny pieces include the sensual and playful *The Land of Cockaigne*, a poem that praises the pleasures of eating, drinking, and sex. The sex has an added frisson in that it involves copulation between the monks and nuns of two (conveniently adjacent) convents. John Montague had great fun translating parts of this poem for *The Faber Book of Irish Verse* (1974), which he edited. Temperament, and perhaps experience (if *Company*, 2001, a memoir which includes an account of Montague's amours in the United States in the 1960s is to be credited, and why would it not?) fitted him uniquely for this task. The following is a brief extract, in the original Middle English, which describes how the monks and the nuns disport themselves stark naked in a river of sweet milk:

> The yung monkes that hi seeth:
> Hi doth ham vp and forth hi fleeth,
> And commith to the nunnes anon,
> And euch monke him taketh on,
> And snellich berith forth har prei
> To the mochil grei abbei
> And techith the nunnes an oreisun
> With iambleue vp and dun.[4]

In the extract 'hi' is 'they'; 'snellich' is 'quickly'; 'prei' is 'prey'; 'oreisun' is 'prayer'; 'iambleue' is 'jumping' or 'jiggling'. Enough said.

2

Iron Age Martial Arts
and Christian Scribes

There are descriptions of the Celts and their culture in a number of Latin texts, the best known being the accounts of Diodorus Siculus and Tacitus. Furthermore, Julius Caesar's *De Bello Gallico* includes a description of druidism as he encountered it amongst the continental Celts of Gaul. But by far the fullest account we have of the Celts and their world comes from early Irish literature. We witness the Iron Age Celts in these stories: we see them at war, we get some understanding of their belief systems, we are given insight into their way of life. Kingship is crucial to the order and structure of this society. The druidic institution is the means by which the elites are informed as to whether or not they are in harmony with the forces of the natural world. There are divination practices to assist in interpreting the signals that nature is constantly emitting about the necessary balances to be observed between her realm and that of human action and motive. Magic is used to try to correct imbalances when they occur. Fosterage is a common practice, where a child is sent to another chieftain to be raised, thereby lessening the chance of conflict arising between the two septs involved in this arrangement. Such mitigations are essential in warlike societies. Equally important, of course, is proficiency in fighting.

It would appear that there were schools of martial arts, to which young men, even children, were sent to be trained. The great hero of the Ulster sagas, Cú Chulainn ('the Hound of Culann') was sent to Scotland to be trained there by a woman, known as Scáthach ('the Shadowy One').

Women, it seems, were far from being regarded merely as chattels, adornments to life, or objects of sexual gratification. Many stories reflect their standing in society, none more so than *Táin Bó Cúailgne*

('The Cattle Raid of Cooley'), where Queen Medb of Connacht insists on the invasion of Ulster so she can get her hands on the famous Brown Bull of Cooley. Medb (meaning intoxication) leads the aggressor army herself, along with her somewhat subdued consort Ailell, and takes control of all negotiations and strategy. Deirdre, in the famous story *Longes mac nUislenn* ('The Exile of the Sons of Uisliu'), a pre-tale to the *Táin*, explaining why certain Ulstermen are among the Connacht forces, is another wilful creature. She insists on having the man she loves, Naoise, even though the high king Conchobor has reserved her for himself since she was a baby; in following her own will she accomplishes the doom that the druid Cathbach predicted for her when she was born.

Always, in these stories reflecting the lives led by the Celts of the Iron Age, there is the otherworld, a hinterland to all action, and from which come, on a frequent basis, emissaries and messages; and to which, from time to time also, those who live what are recognizable human lives are taken or gain access. There are stories of cattle raids (this seems to have been a very popular pursuit, a means of swift enrichment while at the same time impoverishing your enemy), such as the *Táin*; exiles, as in the Deirdre story; wooings; elopements; destructions of places; deaths and slayings; conceptions and births; sieges; caves; and so on. In the twelfth-century manuscript collection the *Book of Leinster*, there are some twenty categories of tale, grouped according to themes such as those listed.

There is, however, another way in which the stories of early Irish literature are categorized, a method first evolved, in part, by the nineteenth-century scholar, native speaker of Irish, and son of a storyteller and scribe from County Clare, Eugene O'Curry.[1] This groups the tales into four cycles: the mythological cycle, dealing with the Tuatha Dé Danann and their interactions with the beings of this world; the king cycle, dealing with stories of kings and the ancestry of dynastic families; the Fionn or Ossianic cycle, concerned with the doings of Fionn, his band of warriors, the Fianna, and his son Oisín (whence Ossianic, another name used for this cycle); and the Ulster cycle, concerned with the Ulaid, the people of Ulster, and their territorial battles. These categories drift into one another, in that mythic elements surface in all types of tale; and Fionn is himself a figure who has powerful mythological resonances.

The Ulster cycle is the corpus of tales which gives the fullest picture of the Iron Age Celts and their ways of life. It also contains the masterpiece of early Irish narrative art, the *Táin Bó Cúailgne*, and the heroic deeds of the great Ulster hero, Cú Chulainn. As is often the case in early storytelling of many traditions, the figure destined to live a heroic life undergoes a name-change. In Cú Chulainn's case his birth-name was Setanta, connecting him with the Setantii, a British tribe, and we are told that his earthly father was a Briton. He had an other-world father as well, none other than Lug Lámfhada, 'Lug of the Long Hand', the Irish sun-god, who gives his name to Lúnasa, the month of August. This mixed ancestry is of significance as the action of the *Táin* unfolds.

Cú Chulainn acquires his heroic name because one day, as a child, he is playing hurling with an iron ball on the plain before Emain Macha, seat of the Ulaid (and a pre-Celtic tumulus), when he ventures, unwittingly, close to the forge of Culann the smith. Culann's hound attacks him, and as it does Setanta throws the iron ball at the dog with such force that it smashes through the animal's throat and out the back of its neck. Culann, when he sees the hound dead, is distraught, and complains to the boy that he has no way now of defending his forge. The boy says he will take on that function: hence Cú Chulainn, the hound of Culann.

When Medb of Connacht hears of the prowess of the great Brown Bull of Cooley, nothing will satisfy her until she has him for herself. She is in bed with her spouse Ailell, talking about this, when she tells him that she is ready to invade Ulster to get what she wants. He meekly tries to remonstrate with her but she is not to be put off. Medb is more than just a wilful Iron Age Lady Bracknell; she is in fact a version of the Hag, and has a destructive, as well as a creative, nurturing mode. With her name carrying connotations of intoxica-tion, she is the drink given symbolically to the king when he is inaugurated, and she is the entity with which he mates. Her name connects her to 'mead'. She is, writes P. L. Henry, 'the goddess who dispenses the drink of sovereignty' from the otherworld.[2] She surfaces, with a wild irruptive force, in Mercutio's extraordinary speech about Queen Mab in Shakespeare's *Romeo and Juliet*, clear testimony to the survival of what the Welsh poet David Jones called a Celtic substratum in the cultures of Ireland and Britain.[3] And near to a quaintly (but also ominously) named hamlet in Kinross in Scotland, Rumbling Bridge, is a mountain called Seemab, where she surfaces again. As with all creatures of Celtic myth, she is multi-locational and polymorphic.

The Connacht forces move north-east towards the passes into Ulster. The men of Ulster are under a curse laid on them by Macha (another version of the Hag) because of the way they abused her when she was pregnant. The effects of this malediction are that every time Ulster is under threat, its men are laid low with the symptoms of childbirth, the so-called *couvade*. They cannot move in the throes of their agony. Cú Chulainn is not affected by the curse, because he is not from Ulster; he (the mortal part of his paternity anyway) is British. If, to this day, you go to the bottom of the Newtownards Road in Belfast, which is on the threshold of a loyalist stronghold, you will see a mural of Cú Chulainn, standing guard, as in ancient times, over the true-blue Ulster territory, a British enclave, which he is protecting from Irish incursion. Celtic myth continues to be capable of manifold adaptations.

If Cú Chulainn is free of the curse of Macha, he is on his own against the mighty forces led by Medb. These include the Ulster warrior Fergus and a number of his followers, who are estranged from the Ulster king Conchobor because of his betrayal of a trust in relation to the safety he promised the sons of Uisliu. These men, because they are now on the attacking side, are not affected by the curse. Even though Cú Chulainn is on his own, he is equal to the task. In fact, so effective is he at mass slaughter that at one point Fergus negotiates with him an agreement whereby he will engage in single combat, day after day, with the best of the Connacht fighters.

The *Táin* is not a unified text. It survives in different rescensions or versions in manuscripts from different periods, reflecting various styles and tastes, and dynastic priorities that would affect the way the tale was assembled and the materials presented. It is composite, varied, and diverse. The style is sometimes terse and fierce; sometimes it is elaborate, baroque, and full of fancy rhetorical flourishes. There are mysterious and obscure passages of verse which are more like incantation, written in archaic Irish; and there is a good deal of topographical lore, explaining the names of places in the tradition of the dindshenchas, and connecting location with events in what was, obviously, a dynastic conflict of major consequence. And yet it is now generally agreed that this assembly of tales and lore and magic is a masterpiece of European narrative. It has found, in Ciaran Carson, its most recent translator, someone of whom it might be said that he was born for the task. Carson, an Ulsterman, is a poet of exceptional range and power, who, in his own work, unites eloquence with a steely vernacular edge. In the following extract Fergus, the estranged Ulsterman, negotiates terms of single combat with Cú Chulainn. He is accompanied by Etarcomol, a hothead, who is to fight Cú Chulainn the following day, but cannot contain himself: 'Etarcomol stayed behind, staring at Cú Chulainn. "What are you looking at?" said Cú Chulainn. "You", said Etarcomol.'

After further such terse and violent exchanges Etarcomol goes off, intending to come back the next day, but he cannot stop himself, and turns his chariot around, so that the left side faces Cú Chulainn, a sign of pure aggression which has to be responded to; the fight is on: '"I don't want this", said Cú Chulainn, "though you've asked for it". "But you must do it", said Etarcomol. Cú Chulainn cut the sod from under his feet and he fell over with the sod on his belly.'

Cú Chulainn tries to persuade Etarcomol to leave, but the other is intent on a fight to the death. 'Either I take your head', he says, 'or leave you mine.' And so it goes on until eventually Cú Chulainn, growing sick of the other's obstinacy, brings his sword down 'through the crown of his head and split[s] him to the navel'.[4]

This raw bleak power, this relish in the brutality of combat, the coolness with which violence is recounted, gives the *Táin* a great deal of its energy. These are headhunters, warriors, fierce men in the grip of loyalty to territory, to a force from which they cannot draw back. A woman's implacable certainty of will is at the back of it, but this woman is not just a woman; she is also an embodiment of that which in human nature makes us want, sometimes, to fight to the death. The *Táin* brings those things in us to the narrative and does not gloss them over. This, it says to us, is what we can be like. And how good would you be in such a circumstance? This terrible question lies at the heart of why this text commands our (sometimes alarmed) attention. There are times when the fight is on, and it is not possible to escape from it, try as you might.

The scribe (possibly a monk called Aedh mac Crimthainn) who compiled the rescension of the *Táin* in the twelfth-century *Book of Leinster* wrote a disparaging and perhaps worried note at the end of his laborious task, in Latin, in which he says that he does not accept this history or rather fantasy; some things in it, he says, are the lies of demons, while others are poetical figments; 'some things seem like the truth, while others are for the delectation of idiots.'[5] He is well aware that this material recalls a pagan, pre-Christian Ireland. He is making this record in a script that came to Ireland with the introduction of Latin and with Christianity, and here he is using the art of writing, almost certainly in a monastery (probably Holy Cross in County Tipperary), to record a world that it was the church's mission to replace. But it was all a long time ago, even back then, and it would be safe to assume that whatever demonic powers may have animated Medb and her like would by now have been tamed by the sanctity of the church and the message of Christ.

Christianity came to Ireland around the middle of the fifth century (the traditional date for the start of Patrick's mission is 432). It would have taken, even allowing for the possibility that there was, as tradition holds, a remarkably swift embedding of Christianity, at least fifty years for Christian institutions, such as monasteries and places of learning, to establish themselves. It would have taken perhaps another fifty years for the fledging church to become confident enough to allow the new art of writing to be used to begin to record the ancient stories of the old days. That would mean that the *Táin*, the stories of the Ulster cycle, and many of the tales from the other groups of sagas (apart from the Fionn cycle, which on the whole seems to have been composed at a later date) would have begun to be written down, at the earliest, around 550, by which time the world that they describe was already six hundred years in the past. It is not surprising that Frank O'Connor described the 'backward look' as a dominant feature of Irish literature, when you consider that at the very start they were looking back to what was, to them, an ancient world. And they were putting that world into books.

The Irish have always been a bookish people, and the making of books was of great significance if what happened in the past was not to be forgotten, and that was important so that you could tell others and yourself who you were and the kind of people you came from. There is, in fact, a story about how the *Táin* was recovered. It is in the *Book of Leinster* and is called *On the Recovery of the 'Táin'*; in it two poets, Emine and Muirgen, set off to Italy, where they believe that a book, called the *Cuilmenn*, which contains the *Táin*, has been taken. This *Cuilmenn* ('Book Written on Skin') is one of the famous lost books of Ireland. There is great concern amongst the learned classes that such a major portion of Ireland's heritage and its history may be lost, and these two have been sent by a high conclave of Ireland's scholars to find the lost book and, in particular, the story of the *Táin*, only bits of which survive in the recollections of the assembled sages. On the way they come upon the grave of Fergus in Connacht. Emine goes off to find a place to stay for the night, while Muirgen sits at the gravestone and chants a poem to the dead Fergus. A mist descends and in it the ghost of Fergus comes out of the realm of the dead and dictates to the poet the entire story of the *Táin*, which is now known to be authentic, because it has come from one of the participants, and from the dead.

The Irish monasteries were places of learning and piety which also took great care to preserve the materials of native culture. This is less surprising than it might seem at first, in that it is now generally accepted that there was effected, in the early days of the Christian mission, a significant degree of accommodation between the new institution and that of the religious system that preceded it, that of the druids. This explains the rapid acceptance of the new faith, and the quite remarkable extent of the effort of cultural preservation upon which the early Irish church embarked. The Irish took to books with immense enthusiasm because they allowed a means whereby the old ways could be preserved.

It may be reasonable to infer that from around 600 the materials of Irish literature and legend began to be put into books in the monasteries. It would be a difficult matter, however, to identify what is the most ancient extant Irish book. O'Curry, in one of his lectures on the manuscript materials of Irish literature entitled 'Of the Earliest Existing Manuscripts' (delivered, as all his foundational lectures were, under the auspices of Blessed John Henry Cardinal Newman, founding Rector of the Catholic University of Ireland, this one on 15 March 1855), avoids the issue as to which is the earliest of all the manuscripts, and returns to the *Cuilmenn*, the ancient lost book, which he has discussed in an earlier talk. He tells us of Dallán Forgaill, and his successor as chief poet of Ireland, Senchán Torpéist, who sent out the two young poets, Muirgen and Emine, to find the precious text. O'Curry is himself, of course, in the long tradition of Irish learning, and his scholarship, deep as it is, is inclined towards story, rather than the dry rehearsal of fact, or arid speculation.

Most of the stories and poetry of early Irish literature are preserved in large codices, or collections of disparate materials, compiled under ecclesiastical patronage in the eleventh and twelfth centuries. These anthologies of all kinds of writings were made by copying from other and older sources, so that, while these books are late, considering the antiquity of the tradition they were preserving, they contain some very old texts along with others of much more recent composition. Such an admixture, where newer composition can be found alongside much older text, can feature in a rescension of a specific story. Sometimes the impulse seems to have been to assemble as much as could be found from various sources, without seeking to discriminate as between which texts seem to belong to the older strata of a tale, and which were adventitious additions.

Rescensions of the *Táin* are to be found in the eleventh-century *Book of the Dun Cow* (in Irish *Lebor na hUidre*, so called because the vellum it was written on was reputedly bound in hide from a brown cow) and the *Book of Leinster*, formerly known in Irish as *Lebor na Nuachongbála*. There are other sources, and different versions. The tracking of the various scribal interventions, and the analysis and dating of the different textual levels is a considerably complex matter, for the *Táin* and for many other texts. What is abundantly clear is that there was an extremely evolved literary and antiquarian culture in the ecclesiastical academies of early Christian Ireland. They were also places of outstanding devotion and piety.

Columcille (in English, St Columba, d. 597), the celebrated patron saint of Derry, founded a church there and at many other locations in the northern part of Ireland. He established the monastery at Iona off the coast of Scotland, and it was almost certainly here that the *Book of Kells* was compiled and inscribed in the eighth or ninth century. The Columban church, named after him, spread its influence not only all over Ireland, but throughout Scotland and England. The monastery at Lindisfarne, for example, where the *Lindisfarne Gospels* were compiled and illustrated, was a Columban establishment. Columcille was renowned not only for his piety but for his irascibility, and it is said that, having fallen out with local dynastic chieftains in the north, he left Ireland for Iona, vowing never to return. In doing this, he set a pattern whereby Ireland is left by the man of learning and faith so he might spread the gospel as a kind of penance and offering to Christ in atonement for some sin, or in a spirit of self-denial. He became the exemplar of the *peregrinatus*, the wanderer for Christ, a road taken by a great many Irish men and women of God over the centuries. These included, in the early Middle Ages, St Columbanus, who founded the monastery at Bobbio, as well as foundations at Luxeuil and Fontaine. St Killian founded Würzburg, and St Gall founded the monastery named after him in St Gallen, Switzerland.

Many poems are ascribed to Columcille in the manuscripts, and, while it is almost certain that none of them are actually by him, it is clear that his life provided an inspiration that devotional poets wished to be associated with. The following is from an invocation to the Blessed Virgin:

> Queen of all who hold sway,
> Pray for us, so that through your
> Grace and chastity, our misery
> And sin may be no more.[6]

An especially interesting example of the accommodations made between pagan belief systems and Christianity is a poem which the scholar Kuno Meyer dated to the tenth century. In this poem the Hag of Beare (Cailleach Bhéara), that figure out of a primordial world who embodies the creative and destructive forces of nature, is reimagined as an old woman, looking back at her pagan and sensual youth, with a mixture of repentance and of regret that those days are gone. It has been suggested that this version of her casts her as a nun (*cailleach* can mean a nun), now retired to a monastery, so she can atone for her past misdeeds. Whatever one's thoughts about this interpretation, the poem is far from being a Christian rejection of paganism in favour of a life of devotion. What it does is realize the tensions between these two value systems in verse that is cast as the speech of a woman in whom they are exercising their contradictory impulses:

> The tide has gone out in me
> As with the sea; age has yellowed
> My skin, and though it makes me sad
> I still take pleasure in food.
>
> Look at these arms now, all bony
> And thin. One time the art they practised
> Was pleasure, as they encircled
> The necks of great kings.
>
> Look at these arms now, all bony
> And thin. It would not be
> Worth my while these days to put
> Them around good-looking men.[7]

The German scholar Kuno Meyer was, in the early twentieth century, one of the first to recognize the unique qualities of this poem, and it was he too that first drew the world's attention to a body of poetry in early Irish literature that is, without doubt, one of the glories of

European culture. These are the early Irish nature lyrics. Often very short and haiku-like, these poems were frequently written, almost as exclamations of delight, in the margins of manuscript copies of the Bible or some other devotional or pietistic text. They are pure exultations of the spirit, leaps of the heart in response to the beauty of the world. They come out of an intensely religious sensibility, in that in them the creation is seen as proclaiming the glory of God, but there is nothing religiose about them. This is the blackbird, as he was heard singing over Belfast Lough:

> The small bird
> Lets out a whistle
> From the tip
> Of a clean
> Yellow beak.
> The note goes out
> Over Belfast Lough—
> A blackbird sings
> From a branch
> Of yellow flowers.[8]

3

Reciting from the Finger-Ends:
The Bards and Ossian

It is generally agreed that the Bardic Schools of poetry, as they are called, evolved over a long period, from at least the beginning of the Christian era, and that they had their origins in the druidic institutions of early Celtic times. The poet, in ancient Ireland, was held in awe, not just because he insisted upon it (unlike some of his contemporary descendants), but because of the powers he was thought to command. He (and while there were women poets, it seems to have been a predominantly male profession, so it was mostly 'he') retained much of the dignity accorded to the druidic caste. The Old Irish word for poet is *fili*, a word cognate with Sanskrit *velos*, and it means the one who sees, and therefore associates poetry with a visionary activity. The term 'bardic' requires a little explanation. There is an Irish word 'bard', but it referred to a much less august personage than that implied by the term 'fili'. The bard was a reciter of the works of others, or a composer of ephemeral verses of various kinds. It is odd that this term should have been brought into use in English to describe what were actually 'filid' (the plural of 'fili'), and probably came about through a mis-apprehension, a failure to recognize, in translation, the crucial hier-archical distinctions involved in the two words, and which were essential to the bardic institution.

The poet was feared and respected. He enjoyed high prestige in Gaelic society, because he was the one who held open the connections with the powers of nature. He was involved in all the crucial cer-emonials and functions of kingship. He wrote the inauguration poems for his chief (who would also, in most cases, be his patron), in which he called upon the forces of the natural world to bless the incoming ruler, and bring him prosperity, success in battle, and the consequence of such success, peace. The poems would also remind the ruler that he had to pay attention to the forces that determined his good or ill fortune, and would, effectively, be a means of reinforcing the central role of the poet himself, because his art was the means whereby the king could gain knowledge of what nature had in store for him, and indeed how his behaviour might modify or adjust his fate. The poet was a diviner, and a prophet, and would lose no opportunity of letting his patron know that the energies his poetry had to deal with were the same as those that informed all of life, visible and invisible. He would admonish the ruler and patron to keep a strict observance of the laws of hierarchy, custom, and rank; these were the conventions that ensured a king's continuance in power, and to do anything that would disrupt them would create untold damage and disorder. Of course these laws, which sustained kingship and rule, were the same laws over which the poet presided, and which also sustained him and his office. It was, in essence, a magical role, and one that guarded its secrets, the sources of its power, jealously.

It is for this reason, perhaps, that we know relatively little about the details of the training and discipline to which a candidate for the profession would have to subject himself. They kept this secret knowledge to themselves. We know even less about the theoretical or philosophical concepts that would have underpinned this training. Undoubtedly there were such, but they do not seem ever to have been stabilized into a systematic intellectual framework, unlike, say, the Indian traditions of linguistic knowledge, which evolved highly sophisticated structural frameworks of grammar, aesthetics, and thought-processes at a very early stage, around five or six hundred years before Christ. But Indian linguistic and poetic philosophy, and aesthetics, were written down, and entered the Indian tradition of manuscript transmission, while the Irish poets seem to have relied heavily on the oral imparting of bardic knowledge and tradition. The secrecy and intimacy of this means of passing on wisdom and technique seem, again, to have been influenced by the druidic associations this caste inherited and cultivated.

It is not, however, as if we know nothing about their training and mentality. It is known, for instance, that bardic training went on for as many as twelve years. A candidate for the poetic profession would enter the bardic academy aged 10 or 11. Very often he would be a member of a family known as professors of the art of poetry; there are in fact dynasties of poets. Among the great poetic families are the following: the O'Dalys, the McNamees, the McAwards (or Wards, now a common itinerant name in Ireland, a fact that tells its own story), the Higgenses (from Ó hUiginn, originally a Scandinavian name, so the caste was not exclusively retained for the 'native' Irish, seeing as Gaelic tradition is always uncertain as to what that is), the O'Husseys, the McGowrans, the Agnews, the O'Clerys. Each of these families would have its own school into which it would accept candidates in what would have been a highly selective process.

There they studied through autumn into spring. We know something of what it was they studied: the ancient stories of Ireland; mythology; histories of dynasties and kingships; genealogy (since it would become necessary, in due course, to trace a patron's lineage back to one of the ancient settlers in Ireland, and thence to Noah after the Flood); dindshenchas (the lore of place, since it was essential to be able to connect actual locations to the vast tapestry of legend and story that had evolved about the Irish landscape); the Bible; Latin; and exemplary poems by their illustrious predecessors. They studied language. The highly imaginative and brilliant reconstruction of bardic linguistic thinking presented by Robert Graves in *The White Goddess* is not any longer easily dismissed as febrile raving. Graves may well have gained access, through the force of his own poetic insight, into some central conceptualizations in bardic thought about letters and the alphabet and their connection to the natural world. Furthermore, his daring speculations about ogam writing (a form of runic script cut into stone, and pre-dating the adoption of the Latin alphabet in Ireland) and its relationship with the Irish alphabet as it evolved, and the mentalities revealed in that relationship, are exhilarating, to say the least, and are, at long last, receiving serious consideration from some Celtic scholars.

However, it has to be said, the hard evidence for what lay behind Irish linguistic thought is scarce enough. There survive what are called the Bardic Grammatical Tracts. These are texts that, it appears, were studied in the Bardic Schools. They are crammed with rules and regulations about practical matters of grammar and prosody: you can do this; you can't do that. A certain set of consonants can rhyme together, as certain vowels can assonate with each other; there are families of related sounds. The consonant 's', for some reason, is regarded as sterile, and should rhyme only with itself. This kind of classification intrigues, as it undoubtedly intrigued Graves, in that there lurks behind such an impulse a sense that these particles are animate with life, and that that life has categories within it in which these particles group forcefully together through some form of familial kinship. No less an authority than Rudolf Thurneysen, the great German Celticist and grammarian, noted this tendency to attribute animate qualities to particles of language in the bardic tracts in a review article in *Zeitschrift für celtische Philologie*, and he is quoted, with unerring instinct, by Frank O'Connor in *The Backward Look*. Thurneysen says that the 'Irishman sees the grammatical schemas as concrete realities', citing such a capacity as giving solidity to the intellectual force of Eriugena (*c*.810–*c*.877), the Irish philosopher at the court of Charles the Bald in France.[1]

It is clear that the bards studied language very closely, and that they had a strong sense that it held an enormous power, the power to change reality. It became then a crucial part of their training to know how to order it by understanding its forms, usages, and traditions. But we are still, it is generally agreed, very much in the dark as to the particulars of how they encountered that body of knowledge, and what that body of knowledge was. We are told that, for example, there were seven grades of poet. The highest accomplishments were attained when the poet became capable of, among other things, divination and spontaneous and sudden insight. Such powers seem to be implied in the ancient texts relating to poetic training, such as the eighth-century *Uraicecht na Ríar*. A high level of proficiency was reached when a certain form of recitation became possible, known as 'dichetal do chennaib', reciting from the finger-ends. This reference to recital and the use of the fingers as part of some rite seems to indicate a stage in development and training of skill and instinct where divination became possible through a combination of language and digital movements. I have seen the poet Michael Harnett, whether consciously or not I do not know, recite poetry while at the same time making odd movements with his fingers. Another stage appears to have been reached when the poet acquired 'imbas forosnai', a manifestation that enlightens, clearly another activity connected to divination. A further key attainment was regarded as 'teinm laegda', the chewing into the marrow, again related to prophecy and foretelling, and reminiscent of what was told about Fionn mac Cumhail, whereby he could attain knowledge of secret and future things by chewing into the bone of his

thumb.[2] The highest rank in the bardic order was that of *ollam*, meaning
something like 'manifold in accomplishments', and this is the term used
in modern Irish for the rank of professor in Irish universities, a complimentary adaptation it would be tempting to comment upon. There
appear to have been gradations within this highest rank, in that there was
a personage known as the *ard-ollam*, the supreme 'ollam' on the island of
Ireland. It is not known how such persons were selected.

There is a very moving story which comes from the period when
the Bardic Schools are well into their decline. Mícheál Ó Cléirigh, of
the O'Clery bardic family, and one of the Four Masters, who compiled, with others, the famous *Annála Ríoghachta Éireann* ('The Annals
of the Kingdom of Ireland') at Bundrowse in County Leitrim, having
completed his task on 10 August 1636, and having made four copies of
the vast work, took one of these with him on horseback to north
Tipperary, so that it could be ratified by someone called Flann Mac
Aodhagáin. Mac Aodhagáin (McEgan) was ard-ollam, and, clearly,
Ó Cléirigh wanted his ultimate imprimatur, so that the work, an
enormous effort which sought to amalgamate as much as possible of
the annalistic records pertaining to all periods of Irish history, might be
relied upon by future generations to be as faithful as possible to the
Irish interpretation of the island's traditions. Ó Cléirigh has a clear
sense that what he is doing is of the utmost significance, given that
the world of the bardic academies, which produced the likes of Mac
Aodhagáin and of Ó Cléirigh himself, is heading for extinction.
It appears that the man Ó Cléirigh travelled over 150 miles, along
seventeenth-century highways, to seek authorization from was the
last to hold the title of 'ard-ollam'. By this time, the Bardic Schools
had been in existence for well over a thousand years. In a few decades
in the seventeenth century they were, to all intents and purposes,
rendered extinct.

The bards enjoyed their period of greatest ascendancy from around
1200 to 1600. They standardized the language of poetry and evolved
a highly stylized artistry of expression, where every syllable was strictly
counted and balanced against other syllables. Rhyme and assonance
developed extraordinary complexity, so that each quatrain of what
they termed *dán dírech* ('straight verse') became a dense orchestration
of varied but echoing sounds. The technique is breathtaking in its
brilliant energy of interconnecting linguistic awareness, where sonic
sameness and difference are set off against each other, only to be

justified in the harmonics that evolve in a metric system that implicates virtually every particle of the language in the interwoven aural pattern. This is Irish written as a classical language, where the virtues are dignity, strict observance of form, elaborately worked technique, and convention.

They are said to have composed in the dark, and to have put a stone on their stomachs as they formulated their elaborate verses. The poems were recited orally, by the poet himself or by a performer, sometimes known as a *reacaire* (or indeed 'bard', as explained already), and would have been chanted to the harp or other musical accompaniment. Again, we know little of what this music for poetic accompaniment was like, in that Irish music as it has come down to us comprises the songs and airs of the people, and records made from the eighteenth century onwards are of music primarily meant for solo performance, especially on the harp. Clearly the musical background to these recitations must have been a vital element in the overall artistic effect.

One distinguished commentator after another has expressed varying degrees of bafflement and frustration at what they tend to agree is a sterility in bardic poetry. Osborn Bergin, who did more than anyone else to bring this tradition to light, by editing some of its greatest texts and by his critical commentaries on those texts, expresses reservations about a poetic tradition that seemed to him to have stultified over centuries, and which appeared to prize metrical proficiency above personal emotion or what we would now think of as literary values. Others, such as D. A. Binchy, Risteárd A. Breatnach, or Seán Ó Tuama, would, with varying degrees of qualification and demurral, concur with Bergin's judgement. They all would make exceptions, and point to masterpieces of poetic achievement, such as Muireadhach Albanach's poem on his dead wife, Ó Maoilchiaráin's heart-breaking elegy for his dead son, or Gofraidh Fionn Ó Dálaigh's poem on a child born in prison, but they would agree that it seems as if bardic poetry took a major branch of Irish literature into a dead end, where it repined for hundreds of years.

Now, one is not so sure. We are less certain of the absolute validity of, for example, emotion as an element in literary appreciation. Or it may be better to put it another way, and say that being engaged with works composed in the intense form of language that poetry is may involve many kinds of intellectual, psychic, and affective responses, of which emotion is only one. Or it may be that emotion itself is a much wider range of varied impulses and reactions than the perhaps narrow straits of personal feeling allow. We cannot be sure of what was shared in the dining hall or recital room when a bardic poet brought forth, out of his brain, to accompaniment, the newly composed but entirely conventional verses that would make all that was taking place in that moment, for that chieftain, or that chieftain's wife or relations, vibrate in concordance and relationship with the entire past of Ireland, and with the Irish language itself. They were who they were in that moment because of the continuity of the language, its absolute insistence on the permanence of its forms. Bardic poetry is the poetry of language itself.

Amongst the bodies of knowledge that had to be mastered in the Bardic Schools were the stories now classified into the four cycles of tales: the Ulster, the Ossianic, the kings, and the mythological cycles. An ollam had to know some 450 tales from these cycles, that is, know them so he could recite them in full, as needed. Any one of these could take many hours to recite, sometimes across four or five evenings. We now know that there is nothing exceptional in these attainments—a tribe in the Ob basin of Siberia have shamans who recite their epics, which extend, in the narration, across ten or more nights—and yet it is still impressive that the human mind, in the tradition of oral narrative, can retain a whole compendium of complex storylines and structures in their entirety, without deviating, in essentials, from one narration to the next.

It was necessary for the bard to be familiar with these materials because they were an important branch of Irish learning, but they were also a significant source of parable and illustration, which he could apply to current situations and circumstances. Amongst the store of legend and myth that he would have memorized, certainly from the twelfth century onwards, was the Fionn or Ossianic cycle. From around this time it appears that the Ossianic lore entered the bardic canon of Irish literary heritage.

This tale cycle is one of the cornerstones of Irish tradition, in Irish and in English. It was the first to come to the attention of the wider literary world in the fabrications James Macpherson from Scotland created in the late eighteenth century, which he based, loosely and inaccurately, on versions of tales from the cycle he found in the Scottish Highlands. The tales of Fionn and his warrior-band, the Fianna, are spread all over the Gaelic-speaking world, and that, of course, as in the case of the tales of the Hag of Beare, includes Scotland. Indeed, a bardic poet from, say, Cork could, in the fifteenth century, travel to Scotland and find professional employment, so closely related were their cultural environments. So it would have been the case, as is now recognized, that Macpherson did encounter in the Highlands the tales of Fionn and Oisín (or Ossian); his Fingal and Temora are curious distortions of Fionn and Tara ('Temair' in Middle Irish); and he does respond to a romantic spirit in the Ossianic cycle. But Macpherson's strange and rhapsodic 'measured prose' (his term) creates a cloudy and obscure world in which bards come and go, winds blow, there are terrible and heroic battles, girls faint all over the place, and Cú Chulainn turns up in the wrong cycle. It sounds like great fun, but it is actually horrifically tedious to read. Samuel Johnson, who had a superb instinct for what was genuine or false in anything, people or literature, knew the Macpherson *Ossian* for what it was—an imposture.

Tales of Fionn (which means 'white' or 'shining'), it is generally agreed, were a feature of Irish literary narration from the early Celtic era. He was a version of the sun-god in his ancient Indo-European origins, and was, like Cernunnos, transformed, in the stories that grew up about him, into a quasi-divine human, or a quasi-human deity. While there are one or two references in sources that date from the early Middle Ages to early tales of Fionn, it appears that his lore remained in the realm of oral narration until much later than was the case with, for example, the Ulster tales. It was not until the twelfth and thirteenth centuries that his stories began to be assembled in the codices, at which time they seem to have been, in their redactions, a response to a taste for romantic narration that had a European dimension, exemplified, in very different ways, by Jean de Meung's *Romaunt de la Rose*, or in England by the author of *Sir Gawain and the Green Knight*.

The Ossianic tales and poems (many of the later tales, or 'lays' as they were sometimes called in English, are in verse) tell of the exploits of Fionn and the Fianna, who live outside the norms of society and yet retain deep attachments to it. They move about all over Ireland and Scotland. They have various encampments or sites that they visit, many of which have stories linked to them from the mythological cycle, and are also to be found in the dindshenchas. One of these is Ben Bulben, outside present-day Sligo, beneath which W. B. Yeats is buried.

That mountain is among their favourite hunting places, and the stories have it that a door swings open in the rock of that eminence through which access can be gained to the otherworld. It is on that mountain, too, that Diarmuid Ó Duibhne dies at the end of the story of Diarmuid and Gráinne, known as *Tóraigheacht Dhiarmada ocus Ghráinne* ('The Pursuit of Diarmuid and Gráinne'). The beautiful Gráinne, in an Ossianic version of the Ulster Deirdre story, is destined to be married to the aged Fionn, but elopes with Diarmuid, with whom she has fallen in love. Fionn's implacable rage does not ever relent, and he pursues them all over the Gaelic world, while they seek shelter wherever they can find it, often in the open, or in the portal dolmens in the Irish landscape, some of which are known in folklore to this day as the beds of Diarmuid and Gráinne. Eventually Diarmuid is gored by the boar he is hunting on Ben Bulben, and is lying wounded when Fionn comes upon him. Diarmuid begs his old enemy for a drink of water, which would save him. Fionn goes to a nearby well and cups some water in his hands, but three times he lets it fall through his fingers on the way back to Diarmuid, who dies. The stone door in the cliff opens and Diarmuid is drawn into the otherworld of ancient Celtic myth and the Tuatha Dé Danann.

The Fionn tales are set in the time of the high king Cormac mac Airt, who, tradition has it, reigned during the third century AD. The Fianna, in spite of their nomadic way of life, are deeply involved with the structures of power, so that they are summoned to assist the high king whenever the sovereignty of Ireland is under threat, something that frequently happens in these tales. Invaders come, in various stories, from all over the world, from Scythia, for example, or from the East; the country is sometimes held in thrall by giants; or Fionn's intervention is required to disable the powers of the otherworld. The Fianna, for the most part, live in nature, and are a band of legitimized outlaws. Much of the lays, or poetry, of the cycle praises the beauty of the natural world, and to some extent this body of verse inherits the responsiveness to the particularities of nature from the early monastic lyrics: birdsong, the sound of water, the leaves on the trees, flowers, the barking of hounds in the pursuit of the hunt. These natural phenomena and many more are brilliantly evoked, in prose and verse of startling freshness. The thrill of being in nature, relishing its delight and variety, is a constant theme in this work. For example, there is a poem that describes those things that gave Fionn most pleasure, and it is dense with specific and localized instances: sleeping near a waterfall, listening to the lowing of cattle, the sound of waters on Sliabh Mis, the burst of song from the blackbird of Leitir Laoi. The word which opens the line in which the blackbird is lovingly recalled captures, astonishingly, in its own music, and in the abrupt incursion it makes into the syllabic rhythms of the line, the birdsong that it re-creates, with heartbreaking beauty and accuracy. The word is 'sgaltarnach', the line 'Sgaltarnach luin Leitreach Laoi'. Even readers who know no Irish will get some sense of the absolute rightness of that word for the amazing aural shock you get every time you hear the abrupt beauty of a blackbird in full throat breaking the silence.

A constant theme in the Fionn cycle is the clashes (but also the accommodations made) between pagan tradition and Christian piety. In the *Acallam na Senórach* ('The Colloquy of the Ancients'), Oisín, the son of Fionn, and another warrior of the Fianna, Caoilte mac Rónáin, survive into the Christian era along with a small band of followers, where they encounter St Patrick. The *Acallam*, compiled in the twelfth century, is frequently thought to be more than a mere assembly of tales by a scribe or scribes; it looks rather more like a literary creation in its own right, based on a variety of sources, including early folklore and oral tradition. The old warriors are ancient now, and at first they terrify the Christians: they are very tall, and are accompanied by great wolf-hounds. But Patrick baptizes the old men, at which flocks of demons rush out of their bodies. When they have eaten and drunk together, Patrick begins to ask Caoilte (the first to meet him) about the times of Fionn. How they survived this great stretch of time is not explained in the *Acallam*; in folk tradition they have spent the two hundred years between the time of Fionn and that of Patrick in the otherworld, but here they are just very old, and have the aspect of giants from ancient time. Such tales, of giants once inhabiting the earth in a human era antecedent to our own, are very common in the literature and folktales of the world, as Doris Lessing acknowledges in her works of science fiction, themselves full of an ancient wisdom. Caoilte begins to unfold the stories of the places of Ireland and Scotland, and their links to Fionn and the Fianna. Patrick delights in these tales, and gets his scribe, Brogan, to write them down, thus encapsulating, in this brief narrative stroke, the process whereby the pre-Christian lore of Ireland was preserved in the books which monastic learning made possible.

The Fianna are named after the word for 'hunt', *fian*, and hunting the wild spaces of the country is an activity in which a great deal of time is spent. Often Fionn sits on a high point above the pursuit, his heart filled with joy at the sound of the hounds and the belling of stags and deer. At one point in the *Acallam*, Patrick asks Caoilte where in Ireland or Scotland did the Fianna find the best hunting, and he is told that the place was the isle of Arran, off the Scottish coast. In describing it, Caoilte leaves the prose, rapturous enough in conveying the delights of Arran, to go into verse, which in part reads:

> Nervous deer were on her hills,
> luscious blackberries amidst her waving grasses,
> cold water in her streams,
> her dark oaks thick with acorns.
>
> Greyhounds and hunting dogs were there,
> blueberries, and sloes on the blackthorn,
> lodges backed up close to the woodland,
> deer at pasture in the oak groves.

One of the central texts of Irish literature is the *Duanaire Finn* ('The Poem-Book of Fionn'), compiled in a manuscript in Ostend in 1627 by a scribe called Aodh Ó Dochartaigh for a Somhairle Mac Domhnaill, an officer in the Spanish army in the Netherlands at the time. The poetry was for the entertainment of Mac Domhnaill, one of the McDonnells of Antrim, who would have held sway for centuries over the seaways between Ireland and Scotland. That the stories of Fionn were being set down for him, in exile, from manuscripts in Louvain, tells its own story of loss and displacement, and it may not be romanticizing Mac Dómhnaill too much to see him as one of the Fianna left behind in a changed world, like the revenants of Patrician Ireland in the *Acallam*, looking back on the days that are gone. Because, by the 1620s, bardic Ireland was in its death-throes, the Fianna were a symbol of her condition, and Ireland had begun to be undone.

4

The Undoing of Ireland:
Conquest and Reconquest

There is an old rhyme which goes: 'At Baginbun, Ireland was lost and won.' Baginbun, in County Wexford, was where the Normans first came ashore in 1169, and where the Norman Invasion of Ireland began. The history of this conquest is a hopelessly tangled affair, involving dynastic conflicts in Ireland, a papal bull from the only English pope ever to assume the Holy See, abductions, banishments, and the English king Henry II. Dermot MacMurrough, king of Leinster, at enmity with the Irish high king, Rory O'Connor, and Tiernan O'Rourke of Breffny (present-day Longford, more or less), whose wife he had abducted, sought assistance from Henry in 1166. Henry had, already, through the efforts of John of Salisbury, who visited Pope Adrian IV in 1156, been given authority to invade Ireland and subdue its church and its institutions of governance to the rules and practices of Rome. A papal bull, called *Laudabiliter*, was issued to confirm this authority, although the authenticity of this bull has sometimes been called into question. What is strange to us is the idea of the Pope giving the lordship of Ireland to Henry II, which is what he did, whereby Henry held his authority under the sponsorship of Rome. This may be explained by the curious fact that, from the time of the Emperor Constantine, all the islands of Europe were regarded, in Rome, as being under the rule of the Pope, so that when Adrian made what is called his 'donation' to Henry, he was merely carrying out a duty, long neglected, of bringing Ireland, a territory constantly beset by violent clashes between rival dynasties, into some kind of conformity with the rest of Europe. He was, at the same time, facilitating the future ambitions of a contentious man, Dermot of Leinster.

Having sought, and gained, Henry's consent, MacMurrough approached Norman lords in Bristol, in particular Richard FitzGilbert de Clare, the earl of Pembroke (known as Strongbow in reference to his proficiency with the longbow), to assist him, letting them know he was acting under the writ issued by the king. And so it began, with Strongbow himself going to Ireland in 1170, when he married Eva, MacMurrough's daughter, who had been promised him as part of the deal, as well as the kingship of Leinster on her father's death.

Henry, it appears, did not trust Strongbow, and feared the establishment of a rival Norman kingdom in Ireland, over which he held 'lordship' by papal authority. He arrived himself in 1171, securing the allegiance of the Norman lords by then established in Ireland and many of the native chieftains. A synod at Cashel accepted the ordinances and practices of the Roman church.

However, these Norman settlers very quickly accommodated themselves to the Irish way of life, and this because the 'Irish way of life', if it may be called such, had retained a remarkable ability to hold fast to its essential features across, by this stage, seven or eight hundred years, while at the same time showing an equally adaptable capacity to change and to modify itself. Christianity had, in the fourth and fifth centuries, been incorporated into the institutions and observances of Celtic Ireland to create a vibrant, dynamic, and missionary church throughout the Dark Ages; and now, in the twelfth century, the Norman feudal social framework seemed easily to translate itself into ancient concepts of kingship and loyalty that were the cornerstones of Irish Celtic society. So much so that Giraldus Cambrensis ('Gerald of Wales'), who visited Ireland with King John, Henry's son, in 1184, complained, in his *Expugnatio Hiberniae* ('The Conquest of Ireland') of 1189, that the settlers have become, in the famous phrase, 'more Irish than the Irish themselves', and this less than twenty years after the first Normans landed.

The Normans brought with them a style of architecture that has left its mark on the Irish landscape in the form of the severe, four-square keeps to be found all over the island, one of which W. B. Yeats converted for use as a house in the early twentieth century; and their influence is to be found in the designs of the convents and monasteries founded by European orders of friars, monks, and nuns, such as the Cistercians. They also brought with them the conventions, behaviours, and emotions associated with the cult of love known as 'courtly love', *amour courtois*. This elaborate set of ritualized patterns, in which a lover courts a high-born lady, usually already married, attains (or does not attain) his objective, suffers the maladies of the lovelorn, engages in a whole system of hidden communication where a glance or the lifting of an eyebrow can unleash a tearing rush of erotic fervour, enters Gaelic poetic tradition, to create a remarkable and cultivated body of courtly verse known as the *dánta grádha*. These poems are written, characteristically, by aristocrats, sometimes of Norman descent, from around 1200 to 1650; they make use of slightly loosened versions of the high bardic style, so that the outcome is a superb example of the capacity Irish literary culture has to absorb and transform new styles and attitudes. Not least among the qualities of this poetry is a worldly and sardonic air, so that often to the intense and interior world of erotic longing is brought what the contemporary poet Augustus Young has called a 'scholastic sting' in the 'lyrical tail'. Young's own scorpion bite is evident in his versions of these poems, published in 1975. These are, without doubt, the best translations of these elegant and tough courtly poems yet made:

> Keep to yourself your kisses,
> woman, you're wasted on me;
> delfwhite teeth, what a pity
> I've lost my taste completely.
>
> Since I stole from a man's wife
> a kiss too good to be true,
> my lips are dead to this life;
> I can't taste anyone new.[1]

It is not known who wrote this poem, but it could well have been someone of Norman descent. In any case, the world it evokes is that of the Provençal troubadours and their conventions, with a toughened Irish edge. But if the Normans brought the Europe of the Angevin monarchs, the Plantagenet kings, and the crusades into contact with Ireland, Giraldus was also right, in that the Normans became entirely involved with the Ireland that evolved from the twelfth century to the sixteenth. The Burkes, the Fitzgeralds, the Lacys, the Roches, the Nugents were Norman families, all of whom had, at different times, their own bardic poets, and who, for entertainment, would have listened to the stories of Cú Chulainn or of Fionn.

In the 1570s Tadhg Dall Ó Huiginn, one of the greatest of the later bards, wrote a poem for a Seán MacWilliam Burke, in which he asserts the right of the Burkes to ownership of the land of Ireland. Ó Huiginn connects the Burkes with Charlemagne, claiming that they descend from him, and he also associates the family with William the Conqueror, saying that from this genealogy came 'he who took London from the hands of the Saxons'. This poem begins with the line: 'Fearann cloidhimh críoch Bhanbha'—('Banba [Ireland] as a territory is swordland')—that is, there is no inheritance that is sure other than that gained by violence. Therefore, Ó Huiginn's strange and desperate poem goes on to say, no man has any claim to this land, not even someone who might assert hereditary rights going back to the Milesian invaders. The only lawful right to ownership of this territory is that maintained by strength of arms. He then proceeds to interpret the legendary history of Ireland, involving the Tuatha Dé Danann and the Sons of Míl themselves, in the light of this doctrine, that force overrules all.[2]

This attitude of Tadhg Dall's has sometimes been seen as illustrating the institutionalized nature of the bardic function, that this is an order that will adapt what it says to whatever circumstances prevail, so that if the patron happens to be a Norman, over whose Gaelic purity of lineage there might be some question, then it is a simple matter to get over this difficulty by saying that lineage does not matter at all, unless, as in the case of this MacWilliam Burke, the legacy is one of violence, which is what is called for now. However, it may well be that Ó Huiginn's frame of mind, here as in other of his poems, reflects not so much the time-serving nature of the bard for hire to anyone who will pay, as the altered circumstances of his own time. He is writing poems to Burkes and also to O'Rourkes and O'Haras, but he is doing so at a time when the world from which he came, and that continues for a time to sustain him, is going under. The period during which he wrote, from around 1570 to 1590, was when Elizabeth I was engaged in bringing to conclusion the work begun by her father Henry VIII, the subjection of Ireland to English rule, once and for all. This was a Tudor Re-conquest of Ireland, a renewal of an authority claimed over the country since the time of Henry II, but now, ironically, prosecuted not to bring Ireland into conformity with Rome but the opposite, to establish the English Protestant Reformation and Settlement in Ireland, and so protect Britain from possible danger through alliances that could (and would) be made between Irish chieftains and the Catholic monarchies of Spain and Rome. Her determination, to create a Protestant Empire based in Britain could, many of the bards realized (and certainly among them Tadhg Dall), be opposed only with force.

Elizabeth reinstituted the procedure initiated by Henry VIII, known as 'surrender and regrant', whereby an Irish chieftain, submitting himself to the queen, and swearing loyalty to her, would be given the lands he claimed were his under patent from the throne, if she was convinced by his renunciation of past errant ways. Rival claimants to Irish territories exploited this opportunity for their own advancement, and swearing loyalty to the British sovereign became a convenient way of getting rid of troublesome opposition from relatives who would argue right of succession. And, of course, even when such avowals were made, they were often not kept; and furthermore, the consequences of this appeal to a remote authority in London were very often yet more wars, complicated alliances and negotiations with one-time enemies or neighbouring chieftains; then pleadings to the English authorities in Ireland to make intercession or take sides. In general, it might be said that Elizabethan policy in Ireland created confusion and havoc, by design or not, so that Ó Huiginn's despairing urgings that all that matters, where territory and rights of ownership are in question, is force, reflects a dreary and bloody actuality. In 1567 a Donnell O'Connor submitted to Queen Elizabeth I at Hampton Court, recognizing her as 'his sovereign Lady, acknowledging that both he and his ancestors had long lived in an uncivil, rude and barbarous fashion', and imploring her that 'he be henceforth reputed as an Englishmen [sic]'. However, when he returned, he found that he continued to be harried by the O'Donnells, who traditionally had a levy from him, and when he appealed to Robert Cecil in England he found that Henry Sidney (father of the poet Sir Philip Sidney) was to look into O'Donnell's claims, with the intention of making sure that the crown got money from the two of them. Then O'Connor raided O'Donnell's castle at Bundrowse, and O'Donnell in turn invaded Sligo, plundering his enemy's lands. It is a messy business.[3]

One of the major poems of this angry confusion is Tadhg Dall's, known by its first line: 'D'fhior chogaidh comhailtear síothcháin' ('To the man of war peace is observed'). It is addressed to Brian na Múrtha O'Rourke (Brian O'Rourke of the Destructions), head of the O'Rourke sept, and knighted by Henry Sidney in 1567, who found him 'the proudest man that ever I delt with in Irelande'. Tadhg Dall's advice is unambiguous: fight, because that is the only way you will be allowed to live in peace. There can be, he says, no treaty with the English:

> If any Irish warrior think it politic
> to pacify the English, remember this:
> your best bet is to spend your time
> tearing them to pieces.[4]

There is more than just implacable hate in Tadhg Dall's verses: these are the utterances of a man who knows his own survival and that of the way of life of the many generations that have preceded him in his poetic office are at stake. His language, his office, his authority, his learning: these things will count for nothing in the wilderness that awaits him and his kind. He is perfectly clear in his mind that the order he embodies has endured for a millennium and a half, and that it will almost certainly go under. For the next two hundred years one Gaelic poet after another will return to the same theme and the same emotions: anger, sorrow, vain hope, the longing for deliverance through a strong leader ready for war against a mighty and seemingly insuperable power.

And O'Rourke? What happened to him? He went to Scotland in 1591, seeking assistance from James VI, and bearing gifts (including four big Irish hounds), but he was extradited by James at Elizabeth's insistence, brought to London, and locked up in the Tower. He was sentenced to execution at Tyburn as a rebel and a traitor. It appears, from an account of the hanging of an Irish rebel in Francis Bacon's essay 'On Custom' who is almost certainly O'Rourke, that he requested to be hanged in the Irish fashion with a withe made from willow, rather than with a hempen rope. He was granted his wish.

One of the figures from this period who holds a dominant position in Irish historical memory is the enigmatic Hugh O'Neill, earl of Tyrone. Tradition has it that the young O'Neill was fostered, not in the Irish fashion to a relative or a strategic ally in a neighbouring territory, but in the Pale, in a house under the direct patronage of Sir Henry Sidney. It used to be fancifully asserted that he was brought up at Penshurst Keat, no less, where the Sidney family had their seat, with its big house and magnificent gardens, celebrated in a famous elegy by Ben Jonson, but this has been shown not to have been the case. O'Neill's title, earl of Tyrone, was one he held under patent from the crown, signalling his compliance, in the early part of his career when he returned to Ulster, with English authority and custom. In a complex series of shifts and manoeuvres, involving allegiance to the Catholic church, advantages over rival chieftains, enmities created by a sexual liaison and elopement with Mabel Bagenal (daughter of Sir Nicholas, marshal of Elizabeth's army in Ireland), and negotiations with Philip of Spain, O'Neill moved into outright rebellion, perhaps seeing himself as the Irish leader of a holy war against a heretical England, which he knew would have widespread support in Catholic Europe. In 1598 he inflicted a major defeat on the English forces at the Battle of the Yellow Ford, where Sir Henry Bagenal (Mabel's brother, and now marshal of the army in Ireland, succeeding his father) was killed. Seeking to consolidate this victory, and to extend his authority, O'Neill, with his allies, campaigned west into Connacht and south into Munster, driving out the settlers Elizabeth had planted in lands confiscated from the Irish and pillaging the territories of those Irish in league with the crown. It was during this campaign in Munster that the residence of the English poet Edmund Spenser at Kilcolman Castle, outside Buttevant, was burned down, with Spenser himself losing a son in the flames (according to Ben Jonson), and having to flee to Cork and thence to London, where he died shortly afterwards.

On this campaign into Munster, O'Neill was joined by, amongst others of his allies, Hugh Maguire of Fermanagh, subject of one of the most famous poems in Irish literature through its translation in the nineteenth century by James Clarence Mangan. Entitled, in Mangan's version, 'O'Hussey's Ode to the Maguire', it is by Maguire's bardic poet Eochaidh Ó hEodhasa. The poet is in Fermanagh, thinking of the dangers his chieftain is exposed to in the south. It is winter, the night is bitterly cold, and the poet anxiously considers what it must be like for his patron to endure such extreme conditions out in the open, fighting, making war against the enemies of Ireland:

> This night is too cold for Hugh,
> the heavy rain makes me sad;
> I pity him, my closest friend,
> who must endure this bitter cold.[5]

When Maguire was made chieftain of his sept in 1589, Ó hEodhasa's inaugural ode welcomed his accession, saying that he would wash Ireland in English blood. Now, on his winter campaign, Maguire gets solace from the burning ruins of the settlers and their sympathizers which he leaves in his wake in his career through Munster. And it is not just Maguire who takes comfort in this destruction; his poet finds relief in thinking of it also, how the chieftain's face is warmed in the cold night by the tossing masses of flames pouring from the sides of burning castles:

> But the tossing winds of fire
> pluming from the sides of white
> stone-walled castles, warm
> that clear distinctive face of his.

Mangan's translation of this poem of intense focus, constrained anger, and exultation in destruction moves into another sphere altogether, but one not unrelated to the original impetus for the poem. Mangan made his version two-and-a-half centuries later, in 1846, at the time of the Great Famine, and his reanimation of Ó hEodhasa is charged with Mangan's distress at the state of the country, mixed with his own anger and sorrow and his yearning for some violent cessation to sufferings long endured and seemingly without prospect of relief. Here is Mangan's whirling adaptation of the first four lines above:

> Where is my chief, my master, this bleak night, mavrone?
> O cold, cold, miserably cold is this bleak night for Hugh!
> Its showery, arrowy, speary sleet pierceth one thro' and thro',
> Pierceth one to the very bone.
>
> Rolls real thunder? Or was that red vivid light
> Only a meteor? I scarce know; but through the midnight dim
> The pitiless ice-wind streams. Except the hate that persecutes him,
> Nothing hath crueler venomy might.[6]

The hate that 'persecutes' Maguire is nowhere in the Irish, of course, but here Mangan is translating the hatred that rises in him when he thinks of the imperial policy that is letting hundreds of thousands of people starve to death while vast quantities of food are being exported from Irish ports, into imagery he is taking from Elizabethan Ireland, and converting it by means of his own nationalist (and humanitarian) rage into a fiery, unsettled, ranging rhythmic energy.

But back to the seventeenth century, and O'Neill and his war against the English. After the earl of Essex failed to subdue him (a debacle that ended in a parley midstream in a river outside Dundalk, and which led to Essex's own ruin), Elizabeth sent Charles Blount, Lord Mountjoy, to face O'Neill. Mountjoy, a formidable soldier (and a patron of the poet Samuel Daniel), defeated O'Neill and his allies at the Battle of Kinsale in 1601, one of those dates (like 1690 and the Boyne, or 1798 and the United Irish rebellion, or 1916) that mark a turning-point in Irish history. Kinsale is the beginning of the end of the Gaelic order that had its origins in the accommodations made between pagan Celtic Ireland and Christianity in the fifth century, and the poets and chroniclers knew it.

O'Neill, survivor that he was, tried to salvage some of his fortunes by offering submission to Elizabeth, but she was having none of it. His submission was accepted by Mountjoy in 1603 a few days after the queen had died, a piece of information carefully withheld from him at the time. Eventually, harried by the English administration in Ulster (which passed him over for office), and compromised by his own and his allies' negotiations with Spain and with Rome, he left Ireland in 1607, along with others, including Rory O'Donnell, son of Red Hugh, his son-in-law and brother-in-arms at Kinsale. He did not return and is buried in the church of San Pietro Montorio on the Janiculum Hill in Rome. A poem by Eoghan Ruadh Mac an Bhaird, bardic poet to the O'Donnells, describes Nualaidh, Rory's sister, lamenting over the tomb in the floor of the church. This poem, in Irish beginning 'A bhean fuair faill ar an bhfeart', was translated into what he called a 'transmagnificanbandancial elegy' by Mangan in the early 1840s. The translation contains the following remarkable lines, built out of a phrase of Mac an Bhaird's, which Mangan had from a literal translation provided for him by the scholar Eugene O'Curry: 'Theirs were not souls wherein dull Time | Could domicile decay or house | Decrepitude!'[7]

Meanwhile the lands the princes of Tyrconnel and of Tyrone had left were being handed over to English or Scottish planters by James I, Elizabeth's successor, in a system of resettlement he already had some experience of as James VI of Scotland, when he removed the traditional landowners of the Isle of Lewis, replacing them with persons of his own choosing.

The Annals of the Four Masters, written in the 1630s by Mícheál Ó Cléirigh and his associates, move into threnody when they come to describe the Flight of the Earls, saying that the day that the Irish princes left Lough Swilly for the European mainland was one of the saddest days for Ireland that ever had been. The princes meant to return, of course, and O'Neill never ceased urging Ireland's case in Rome, but it was not to be. The Flight was indeed an extraordinary event. The poet, playwright, and scholar Seán Ó Tuama, in his lectures on Gaelic literature at University College, Cork, used to point this out to his students in the 1960s. Think, he would say, think about what happened: the major leaders of the Irish cause leaving their own lands and their own people. It was, he would say, a very strange thing to do, and would ask his students to consider if they had ever heard of anything like this happening anywhere else. It was, he thought, probably quite unusual, and saying this (in Irish) he would look out of the diamond-paned windows of the stone-walled lecture theatre, while his students would think of Kinsale, and what was lost.

At the beginning of the seventeenth century there was Kinsale; towards the end, in 1690, there was the Battle of the Boyne. And in between all manner of turbulence. In the early seventeenth century Ó hEodhasa writes of his foreboding about Maguire, his chieftain; towards the end, Dáibhí Ó Bruadair writes in disgust that he would be better off as an idiot and a churl for all the good his learning and his study of the craft of poetry has done him. If he were an idiot, then he would be accepted by the ignoramuses now in power:

> What a pity I'm not an idiot
> though I know it's a terrible thing,
> because then I'd be well in
> with all the thickheads.[8]

Ó Bruadair's life and work (he was born in around 1625 and died in 1698) provide a unique and Gaelic perspective on the upheavals that took place in seventeenth-century Ireland, from the rebellion of 1641—driven by protest at the seizure of lands from the native Irish—to Oliver Cromwell's campaign in Ireland in 1649/50, which ruthlessly suppressed Catholic and Royalist resistance to the English parliament, to the War of the Two Kings (James II and William of Orange) culminating at the Boyne, which settled the Protestant supremacy in Ireland for over a hundred years. Poems that Ó Bruadair wrote after 1690, in particular 'An Longbhriseadh' ('The Ship-wreck'), express his characteristic mix of rage and despair at his own and his country's downfall, as he sees it. Ó Bruadair is sick at heart, not just because of English oppressions or the 'curse of Cromwell'; he is crazed with anger and frustration at the dissensions among the Irish themselves, and the readiness of the lower orders of the native stock (the 'catheads' as he call them) to run to those in power, seeking their own advantage, ready to forswear any trust or loyalty. In this mood he concludes 'The Shipwreck', saying that he will, now that the country has lost any sense of itself, write no more for the people of Ireland:

> I thought that in freedom I'd be easy and graceful,
> a steward to someone, or even a provost,
> but now I'm reduced to wearing raggy old shoes
> I'll stop all this writing on behalf of the Irish.[9]

Another voice from the seventeenth century that demands to be heard, even in so selective a history as this, is that of an individual about whom Ó Bruadair himself wrote a panegyric on 16 May 1682. The person in question is Geoffrey Keating, the historian, chronicler, and poet who, in his *Foras Feasa ar Éirinn* ('Groundwork of Knowledge Concerning Ireland') defended the Irish against the detractions of Giraldus and his Elizabethan successors, amongst whom was the poet Spenser. Ó Bruadair, using a severe bardic poetic form (unlike in 'The Shipwreck', where he uses a rolling accentual metre to emphasize the slackness of the time he has come to, which also gives a pounding vehemence to his virulence), praises Keating's faithfulness to what he regards as the 'real' story of Ireland. The poem is called 'Searc na Suadh' ('Love of Sages'), and was occasioned by a namesake of Keating's, John Keating, Lord Chief Justice of Ireland, acquitting, at Limerick, certain Catholic 'gentlemen' of being involved in complicity with the 'Popish Plot', a piece of black propaganda which alleged a Catholic conspiracy to assassinate Charles II. It will be evident from this how immersed Ó Bruadair's mentality and emotions were with the state of Ireland and of Britain at the time, and how it seemed right to him to connect John Keating's resolve to pay attention to actuality and not be distracted by rumour and faction, with the rigour and fidelity of his namesake, Geoffrey. He writes:

> Geoffrey Keating, fruit of the tree of wisdom
> is the man whose code I value most of all:
> from obscurity he brought forth the true story of Ireland,
> and cleared a straight road through the dark.[10]

Keating completed his history some fifty years before, at around 1634, and it had been circulating in manuscript from that time. The fact that this great work of Irish literature was not printed in Irish until 1811 (and then only in part) tells its own story about Ireland's culture in the seventeenth century, especially when one considers how much that century was one in which the printed book became the medium through which all kinds of interests throughout Europe communicated their convictions and values.

Not long after Kinsale and the Flight of the Earls, Keating was in Bordeaux, studying for his doctorate in divinity. While there, he writes the poem which begins 'Óm sceol ar ardmhagh Fáil', a cry of agony (one of the great many that are to pierce Irish literature for the next two hundred years) at the tidings he receives of the state of things back home:

> Distracted with grieving for Ireland sleep leaves me,
> And I am tortured forever by the state of her faithful people.[11]

The last word on the distressful state of Ireland, and on the fate of her learned classes, must go Aodhagán Ó Rathaille, whose poetry embodies the devastating consequences of the Boyne defeat. Ó Rathaille's family held lands in the Sliabh Luachra district in the borderlands between north-west Cork and Kerry under the Brownes, viscounts of Kenmare. The Brownes were Jacobites, that is, supporters of King James, and were, therefore, on the losing side in the war with William of Orange, now William III. Their lands were confiscated, which meant that the Ó Rathaille family were also shown the road. Ó Rathaille tells, in various heartbreaking poems, how he is reduced in fortune, at one point recounting, in shame and rage, how he has had to eat dogfish and periwinkle on the west Kerry coast, where he has been forced to take refuge.

The political reality, underpinned by the series of legal enactments known as the Penal Laws in the 1690s and beyond, behind these poems of Ó Rathaille was that the Catholic population of Ireland, greatly in the majority, was reduced to supplicant status. Irish Catholics could not hold public office, they could not maintain schools, they could not send their children abroad to be educated (in effect depriving them of university education, because Trinity College, Dublin, was a Protestant stronghold), nor, famously, could they own a horse worth more than five pounds, since such an animal could be used for military purposes. There were, as ever, ways and means of getting around this draconian legislation, as did, for example, Daniel O'Connell's family in Caherdaniel in County Kerry, but the brute fact was that such a body of discriminatory law existed, and was often mercilessly enforced. These laws affected most grievously those whom they were designed to ensnare, the Catholic landed classes, from whom opposition and rebellion were mostly to be feared. Such were the Brownes, from whom the Ó Rathailles leased their lands; and such indeed were the Ó Rathailles themselves.

Browne's lands were taken over by people whom Ó Rathaille considered upstarts, creatures of low breeding and cunning who creep into the places and houses of their betters, who make the necessary avowals of loyalty to the authorities, and who are ready to renounce the Catholic religion. Many of those who served as officers in the army of King James II (among them his outstanding commander Patrick Sarsfield) left Ireland to take service and commission in the forces of the Catholic monarchs of Europe. These were known as 'The Wild Geese'. These soldiers hoped that they would return, serving behind a Stuart king, James or his son, to reinstate the (as they saw him) rightful monarch, usurped by the Orange interloper, 'King Billy'. The Jacobites who remained at home looked with anticipation to such a triumphant return. The poets gave expression to these hopes in a genre of poem known as the *aisling*, or vision-poem, and Ó Rathaille is one of the finest practitioners of this form.

In the aisling a beautiful woman comes to the poet, who is often asleep out of doors, in the natural world; she reveals who she is, Éire, or Aoibheall (goddess of north Munster, but also a version of the sovereignty goddess, the Hag), Cathleen Ni Houlihan, or a number of other personalities, all in effect the same at root. She then tells the poet that she is in thrall to a foreign master (often described as an ugly, misshapen boor), but that the Stuart is coming from across the sea to free her. The poet awakes to the reality that the Old Pretender is still to arrive, that his condition remains as it was, and that the waiting must go on. There were rumours of a Jacobite invasion in 1708/9, and it

appears that some of Ó Rathaille's masterpieces in the aisling form
were written at around that time, including 'Gile na Gile' ('Brightness
of Brightness'), a poem of headlong energy and tremulous anxiety,
conveyed in an onward rhythmic pulse that communicates anticipation mixed with fear:

> Brightness of brightness I saw in the lonely byways,
> crystallized crystal was the green of her two clear eyes,
> sweeter than sweet was her voice not hoarsened by age
> while the red and the white contended in her beautiful features.

Ó Rathaille's last poem was the magisterial and terrifying 'Cabhair Ní
Ghoirfead' ('No Help I'll Call'). Written probably in 1729, the year of
his death, and the year too in which Raghnall MacCarthy, the last of
the Jacobite nobility in Sliabh Luachra, died, this poem is one of the
fiercest in Irish literature, a tradition in which rage is given its room.
Now that the last of the MacCarthys to hold allegiance to the old cause
is gone, there is no point, any longer, Ó Rathaille declares, in asking
anyone for help, or torturing yourself with the futility of hope. No,
best now that the 'dragons of the Lee' (the MacCarthys) are gone, to
hope for nothing more than death, because at least in death he will be
able to be amongst those whom his fathers followed before Christ was
lifted up on the Cross. It is not any thought of heaven that gives him
consolation, or of the resurrection, but being again amongst those he
loves to distraction, his princes:

> I'll stop it all now, it won't be long before I'm dead
> Since the dragons of the Lee have been destroyed;
> I'll follow to the grave those whom all the brave admired,
> The princes my ancestors were servants to before Our Saviour died.[12]

This is a poem of exceptional power, possibly because it achieves a rare
combination of personal energy and emotion with a responsiveness to
public circumstances and political reality. This fusing of the public and
the private spheres in a coherence of artistic energy is a quality that
characterizes some of the best poetry in the Irish tradition, in works like
Ó hEodhasa's Hugh Maguire poem; Ó Bruadair's 'Shipwreck'; any
number of Yeats's poems, but especially perhaps 'Easter 1916'; Seamus
Heaney's poems in *North* (1975); Anthony Cronin's sonnets in *The End
of the Modern World* (1989); and Ciaran Carson's *Belfast Confetti* (1989).

Ó Rathaille's defiance, his despair, his unswerving loyalty to his tradition, stand, in the early decades of the eighteenth century, the century of the flourishing of Anglo-Ireland, of the great houses at Powerscourt and Lissadell, of Georgian Dublin, of Swift and Burke and Sheridan, as a rebuke, a kind of icon of something implacable in Irish history that would not be obliterated, even though his own dereliction made him long for that condition. He is everywhere in twentieth-century Irish literature, in Yeats and James Stephens, Frank O'Connor, Thomas Kinsella, Michael Hartnett, and even, I believe, in Samuel Beckett, in the frantic raving voices of his old men who wander the roads of a baffling country.

5

Ireland: A Colony?

Edmund Spenser, Elizabethan poet and celebrant of the Virgin Queen in *The Faerie Queene* (1590–6), was also the person who, perhaps more than anyone else, was responsible for setting down some of the dominant attitudes of what would later be called the colonial mind-set. His *A View of the Present State of Ireland* was written, probably, around 1596, but remained unpublished until 1633, when it was issued with some similar appraisals of Ireland by Sir James Ware as *Ancient Irish Histories*. By this time it had already achieved notoriety, and Spenser's views were attacked by Keating, who almost certainly read it in manuscript, in his *Foras Feasa*, written in the early 1630s. A more comprehensive depiction of the colonial mentality could scarcely be imagined than that which Spenser provides in his dialogue between two Englishmen, Irenius and Eudoxus. It shows how it is a necessary prejudice in the mind of the person who colonizes others that he should regard them as subhuman. He must view their culture and language as barbarous customs, which have to be rooted out. They, the colonized, are seen as wild, lecherous, filthy, and out of control, so that the colonizer has no option but to impose order upon them if he is to carry out his duty as a civilized creature and a God-fearing man. The religious practices of the colonized have to be seen as blasphemous and idolatrous. In fact, it is very hard to know if it is going to be possible at all to bring such uncouth creatures into anything remotely resembling proper governance, and it may be that there is nothing else for it but to exterminate them all.

The prose in which Spenser writes this tract is astonishingly horrible (bearing in mind the fluency and sweetness of much of his verse), a gnarled, deformed, and hectic tirade, where anxiety and loathing frequently submerge the thinking, so that it is often very difficult to follow the run of the sentences. They are jammed with detail, nervous asides, insults, exordia, as Spenser tries to make his way through the wilderness that his mental landscape becomes when he is trying to explain what Ireland is, to himself as much as to anyone else. It is a classic of colonial nightmare, in a way the originating text for all the many writings devoted to race-hatred. Spenser is in reality what Mr Kurtz became in Joseph Conrad's fictional account of this phenomenon, *Heart of Darkness* (1902).

One truly ghastly and virtually incoherent passage describes what may be done to try to constrain those creatures which the colonial, the Englishman, has been condemned to master. The natives cannot be allowed to intermingle with the civilized. If they are to live, if there is no possibility of their extinction (by far the best course of action), then they should be kept apart in a separate place, and in such a manner that they are continually under surveillance. If they are not strictly guarded at all times, then they will establish contact with those whom it has not been possible to quarantine, and undermine, through collusion and intrigue, the security you have taken such trouble to erect. We are, of course, witnessing in this terrified mental state, in its hysterias and hatreds, the envisaging of that apotheosis of all security measures, the concentration camp. The construction of such places, or places like them, is the solution towards which the colonial mind inevitably gravitates: you cannot trust the natives not to kill you as you lie in your bed or as you play with your children; therefore you must lock them up, and eventually you must kill them. And this is the conclusion Spenser reaches in his dialogue, or at least it is one of his solutions, because the argument is contradictory and often hard to follow, in its extreme shifts, passions, and evasions. Here is a brief extract from the passage dealing with the sequestration of the Irish, and their dispersal, whereby they can be kept away from their leaders who are always all too ready to foment rebellion:

they will privilie relieve theyr frendes that are foorthe; they will send the enemye secrett advertisement of all their purposes and journeyes which they meane to make upon them, yea and to betraye the forte it selfe, by discovery of all her defects and disadvauntages (yf any be) to the cutting of all theyr throates. For avoiding wherof and many other inconveniences, I wish that they should be carried farre from thence into some other partes...[1]

And now the frantic rhetoric swings round again to go back over what it has said, but introducing different emphases and arguments: it is a tissue of incoherent hatred.

At one point in the dialogue Irenius (meaning 'Irish-based', and for whom read Spenser) explains to his interlocutor that there 'is amongst the Irish a certayne kind of people called Bards, which are to them insteede of poetts'.[2] Now Spenser goes on to outline how truly dangerous these bards are, because they encourage their auditors to engage in all kinds of mischief and wrongdoing by praising such actions by those for whom they write their poems. Here we have Spenser making it quite explicit that poetry, which should, to his mind, conduce to virtue and make men try to behave more honourably, is, amongst the Irish, used for exactly the opposite purpose: to get men, especially the young, to behave as louts, thieves, rapists, and arsonists.

He cites, as an example, how one of the bards praised a certain 'notorious theif and wicked outlawe'. He does not say who this is, but he could easily be thinking of the famous rebel Brian O'Rourke of the Destructions, and the poetry written to him by Tadhg Dall Ó Huiginn, which does indeed urge O'Rourke on to ruthless slaughter of the enemies of Ireland. Of this outlaw the bard, according to Spenser, said:

that he was none of those idell milk-sops that was brought up by the fire side, but that most of his dayes he spent in armes and valyaunt enterprises; that he did never eate his meate before he had wonne it with his swoorde; that he was not slugging all night in a cabin under his mantel, but used commonly to keepe others wakin to defend theyr lives, and did light his candell at the flames of theyr howses to leade him in the darkeness . . .

Irenius's companion is suitably appalled at this, but then goes on to ask if there is any 'arte' in these writings, to which the reply is yes, there is, and Irenius (Spenser), we learn, has had various pieces translated for him. But his clear view is that such 'good grace' and 'comliness' as he found in them was used to make the vice and wickedness which they advocate all the more attractive, a perversion of the nature of creativity itself. This 'evill custome' needs, he says 'reformation', by which he means not just that it should be reformed, but that it needs the Protestant Reformation itself.

I have gone back to Spenser's tract because it is, in many respects, the founding document of British colonialism, not just for Ireland, but as a historical phenomenon that would have a world-wide extent and an imperial destiny. His epic poem of imperial dominion and triumph, *The Faerie Queene*, was dedicated to Elizabeth I, and on the title-page she is hailed as a 'magnificent Empresse', and queen of France and Virginia (named after her) as well as of Ireland and England. There is no doubt but that in Spenser's mind the reformation of Ireland, its anglicization and conversion, was to be a prelude to the establishment of a Protestant Empire in Europe and in the New World.

As the seventeenth century wore on, and as Catholic Ireland endured defeats, suppression, dispossession, and the enactment of the Penal Laws which created a Protestant Ascendancy, it might seem as if the colonial objective, of bringing Ireland under what was thought of as the civilized rule of the crown and parliament, was being achieved. Her bardic academies, so deeply distrusted by Spenser, had either disappeared or were functioning in reduced circumstances in out-of-the-way places (such as west Clare or The Fews in south Armagh). As was the case with Aodhagán Ó Rathaille and his patrons, Catholics were removed from their lands, sometimes with the assistance of legal procedure, where relatives who had conformed to the established church, the Church of Ireland, were deemed legitimate inheritors. Catholics could not, of course, sit in parliament, neither in Westminster nor in the Irish parliament in Dublin.

But, to put it mildly, the colonial situation is a complex and contradictory one, for all concerned, colonizers and colonized. As Ó Bruadair and Ó Rathaille and their Jacobite patrons were beginning, in the early 1690s, to endure the consequences of the so-called Glorious Revolution of 1688 (which set James aside and enthroned William of Orange), and of the Battle of the Boyne, a young member of what would become known as the Protestant Ascendancy was beginning to make a name for himself. This was Jonathan Swift.

One of his first poems was an 'Ode to the King: On his Irish Expedition', in praise of William and of his valorous actions in Ireland, where, he writes, 'Treason there in Person seems to stand, | And Rebel is the growth and manufacture of the Land.'[3] Swift was to become less certain in his allegiance to the crown and deeply questioning of the right of the English parliament to make legislation that was binding in Ireland. But that said, it does very little to convey what lies at the heart of Swift's tortured and furious writings, not just on Ireland but on other subjects as well. However, Ireland, and her relations with England, the injustices visited on her as a lesser realm in what should be, in Swift's view, a truly United Kingdom, underlies a great deal of what he wrote.

When Swift returned, reluctantly, to Ireland in 1714 to take up the Deanship of St Patrick's Cathedral in Dublin, he found himself in a position where he was able to observe the way power could operate at a distance, in London, and pay scant regard to the consequences of the decisions it made about Ireland in Ireland itself. Although one might say that Swift was himself a member of the Ascendancy, he now found himself in a situation where he could see that those in power and authority more often than not discharged their functions with indifference or even contempt towards those who had the misfortune to have to live through the actualities created by executive decision. He was being taught what it was like to be on the receiving end of the colonial system. How is it, he once wrote, that I am less of a free man when I cross the Irish Sea than I am when I am on the other side of that narrow stretch of water? In *The Drapier's Letters*, written in the 1720s, while he was also at work on *Gulliver's Travels*, he pretends to be an honest draper, arguing the case for Ireland having the right to be able to legislate for itself. The immediate cause for these writings was the granting of a patent to a certain William Wood to mint halfpence for Ireland, but the main issue was the indignity and contempt visited heedlessly upon the Irish Protestants by a British administration, when, the Draper says, they are and ought to be as free a people as their brethren in England.

It was the casualness of power, its brutal indifference, its inhumanity, that aroused what Swift called, in the epitaph he wrote for himself, and which is engraved in marble on a wall of St Patrick's Cathedral, his 'saevo indignatio', his savage indignation. This we see all through *Gulliver's Travels* (1726). And while there is no point in trying to find precise correspondences between all the places Gulliver travels to and contemporary England and Ireland (though some do exist), it is impossible to disentangle that work from the attitudes he had formed about how the powerful attain office and keep it, how they behave towards each other and to their subordinates, how they crave money and satisfaction, how they develop their talent for cruelty, how greedy they are. As an Englishman (he always regarded himself as such) who was also Irish, Swift was, as an Irishman, subject to the whims of

England, and the horrific consequences of indifferent executive power and decision.

Here is Gulliver, the decent, honest-to-God Englishman, attempting to explain to his master, the horse, in the section called 'A Voyage to the Houyhnhnms' (where the horses are in the ascendant over the humans, the Yahoos), what a chief minister of state is like in England. This, in its artful irony (where Gulliver is, in all cack-handed sincerity, trying to explain what political actuality is like as power is sought and dispensed), is written by someone who has watched, with an outsider's edgy attentiveness, the secret machinations of those who are on the inside of the structures of authority. The rage that informs this writing is that of the dependant, and of someone who has been made to feel that he is such:

> a first or chief minister of state . . . was a creature wholly exempt from joy and grief, love and hatred, pity and anger; at least makes use of no other passions but a violent desire of wealth, power, and titles; that he applies his words to all uses, except to the indication of his mind; that he never tells a truth, but with an intent that you should take it for a lie; nor a lie but with a design that you should take it for a truth; that those he speaks worst of behind their backs are in the surest way to preferment; and whenever he begins to praise you to others or to yourself, you are from that day forlorn. The worst mark you can receive is a promise, especially when it is confirmed with an oath; after which every man retires, and gives over all hopes.[4]

This is more than just an astute awareness of the hidden manoeuvres that the maintaining of power necessitates; there is, here, an understanding of what it is like to look on those who are in a position to determine, without a thought, how you live (and indeed if you are going to have a life at all), while you are excluded from any possibility of having a say in what they think or do. It is strange to say this, but there is, emotionally speaking, not a great deal of distance between Swift's horror at what an indifferent system can do to those who are powerless, and Ó Rathaille's despair at the end of his life when he knows that there is no use any longer in seeking assistance in a world that has become alien and fierce. And yet Swift is at the heart of the colony, dean of St Patrick's, respected in London and Dublin, while Ó Rathaille is a victim at the margins. Except that Swift is also the Draper, and *Gulliver's Travels* was printed as if it had been written by one Lemuel Gulliver, a surgeon and a ship's captain. The pseudonyms were necessary because what the Draper wrote would, he foresaw correctly, be regarded as seditious, and the tale that Gulliver tells does not spare the English administration.

In 1729, the year in which Ó Rathaille died, Swift issued, anonymously, one of the most horrific texts in all Irish literature, *A Modest Proposal*. When Swift wrote this pamphlet there had been three years of famine, and the proposer opens by describing how the roads are thronged with beggars and the starving. Swift is here writing about the ordinary people of the country, the Catholics, many of whom became destitute as the Penal Laws took effect and their one-time landlords, who would more often than not have been Catholics like themselves, were dispossessed. With those gone from whom they would have had work and access to a bit of land, the *fodhaoine* ('under-people', as they were known in Irish) would frequently have no option but to take to the roads. The highways would have been crowded with wandering beggars and tramps, women and men, and in many cases numbers of children trailing along behind them, crying with the hunger.

Famine was a continuous reality for the poor throughout the eighteenth and nineteenth centuries, not just in Ireland but throughout Britain and Europe. What made Ireland more vulnerable to its effects, perhaps, was the fact that many of the landlord class were absentees; that is, they left their estates under the management of an agent at home while they lived in London and in Dublin on the proceeds forwarded to them from the rents taken up on their behalf from a peasantry whom they did not know and whose lives, on the whole, meant nothing to them. It was a recipe for disaster, corruption, bribery, and sharp practice. The land agent is a demonized figure in Irish fiction of the eighteenth and nineteenth centuries, and with good reason. As is the absentee landlord, whose demands for money from home, to sustain a lifestyle light years away from the brute horrors their luxury inflicted on those whose labour ensured its continuance, were unceasing.

Swift's proposer has a solution to the problem of the country being overpopulated with beggars and their children, and that is that the children should be eaten. His proposal is advanced with a very serious analysis of the statistics and circumstances that occasion what, he admits, is an unusual recommendation, but then, he is careful to point out, his remedy is solely for 'this one individual Kingdom of Ireland, and for no other that ever was, is, or I think ever can be upon

Earth'. According to the proposer's chilling computations, something like three-fifths of the people of Ireland are destitute, which means that the children they will produce cannot be fed. In which case, the humane and the economical thing to do is to feed them from the breast, and at no additional cost, to the point where they became fat enough to eat, when they will then contribute to the prosperity of the country while at the same time solving an intractable problem. Swift's humanitarian rage drives the maddened and distraught irony that animates every step of the argument the proposer makes, every detail of his recommendation:

I have been assured by a very knowing American of my acquaintance in London; that a young healthy child, well nursed, at a year old, is a most delicious, nourishing, and wholesome food; whether stewed, roasted, baked, or boiled; and, I make no doubt, that it will equally serve in a fricasie or ragout. I do therefore humbly offer it to public consideration . . . that [the children] be offered in sale to the persons of quality and fortune, through the kingdom; always advising the mother to let them suck plentifully in the last month, so as to render them plump, and fat for a good table. A child will make two dishes at an entertainment for friends; and when the family dines alone, the fore or hind quarter will make a reasonable dish; and seasoned with a little pepper or salt, will be very good boiled on the fourth day, especially in winter.[5]

This is truly a savage indignation. The culinary details, the home economics, carry the stress of a mind driven to total outrage at what he sees being done to poor people. And Swift explicitly brings England before the tribunal of his accusation. At one point the proposer says that this idea of his will not, in any way, disoblige England, because the meat from children cannot easily be exported, because it is too tender to be kept a long time in salt. Therefore it cannot be exported to the English market and there compete favourably with English produce, to the detriment of that economy. But Swift then says, since he has mentioned salt, that he could name a country that would be 'glad to eat up our whole nation without it'. He doesn't name this country, but it is perfectly clear which one it is, the one so careful to protect its own interests even though the kingdom is supposed to be united.

In some later nationalist commentary Swift is thought of as a patriot and as a father of a separatist approach to Irish affairs. The story is more complicated than that, of course, in that Swift was primarily driven to outrage at the subjections visited on his own Protestant people.

However, it is clear that the scope of his sorrow and pity extended beyond sectarian boundaries, and that he was driven to write by the fierce contradictions that lie at the heart of colonial actuality.

In 1729, the same year in which Swift published *A Modest Proposal*, Edmund Burke was born in Dublin to a Protestant father and a Catholic mother, a Nagle from County Cork, which latter was a part of the world where he spent a number of childhood years. This unusual background was to produce one of the finest and most exacting examples of the conservative intelligence, an Irish conservative intelligence, dealing with the contradictions of the colonial reality, although Burke himself would have steadfastly rejected that Ireland was, or should be regarded as, a colony of the larger island. If Swift finds himself in a situation where he feels compelled to attack the brutal indifference of England to Ireland and Irish interests, Burke is the supreme apologist for the security that established order can bring, and that order proceeds from the structures of power and authority, with which one interferes at great peril. There is no greater advocate than Burke for the sacredness and awe which anything but the striving and restless mind should accord to institutions of long continuance; nor is there anyone who argues with such a passion and a force as he does for the validity and efficacy of the unity of the kingdoms of Great Britain and Ireland.

Towards the end of his life, in a letter to Thomas Keogh, written from The Gregories, his house in Beaconsfield, Buckinghamshire, in November 1796, he tells his correspondent that he is only too aware of the 'distracted state' of Ireland. For years now Burke has been warning of the dangers of rebellion, and there is no doubt but that he had his finger on the pulse of the agitations as they were mounting in Ireland in the wake of the French Revolution. In his letter he describes his personal attitude towards issues of what we would now call identity and his sense of belonging to both England and to Ireland: 'Considering as I do England as my country, of long habit, of obligation, and of establishment, and that my primary duties are hers, I cannot conceive how a man can be a genuine Englishman, without being at the same time a true Irishman. . . . I think the same sentiments ought to be reciprocal on the part of Ireland, and if possible with much stronger reason.'[6]

Burke goes on to say how afflicted he is to see that a 'small faction' should now, in Ireland, arrogate to itself to be 'the whole of that great kingdom'. He is here writing about the United Irishmen, the revolutionary, republican, and separatist organization, one of whose leaders is Wolfe Tone (whom Burke has met), and whose dictum was that England was the never-failing source of all Ireland's woes. In 1796, the year in which he wrote this letter, the United Irishmen were preparing themselves for the rebellion of 1798, a prospect that Burke greatly feared, as he feared all revolutionary turbulence. And Tone, in the month after Burke wrote this letter, would lead an abortive French revolutionary fleet into Bantry Bay in Cork.

Burke's fear of revolution was based on a genuine terror of what men may be capable of when they are released from what he would regard as the necessary constraints of custom, reverence, order, and religion. For him the crown, the established church, and parliament, in their annexations and mutuality, evolved over a long period of time, were the basis of social cohesion and indeed of human happiness. In this unity and accord, Ireland and England should be as one, and anyone or anything that would usurp that unity was guilty of a crime against humanity and against nature, because such cohesions as the British constitution had evolved were themselves organic products of human civilization: the state for Burke, as Yeats reminds us, was like a tree, long-rooted, steadfast, vigorous, varied and diverse, yet retaining all the different branches in a consistent and beautiful order.

Burke's thinking about the order and integrity of the British constitution has its fullest exposition in his magnificent *Reflections on the Revolution in France*, with the subtitle 'and the proceedings of certain societies in London relative to that event', published in 1790. This is by way of being a letter (an extremely long one) in reply to a young Frenchman who has written to Burke, asking his opinion on recent events in France. There has been an address, recently, in commemoration of the Glorious Revolution in England (which supplanted the Catholic James II) of one hundred years before, delivered in London at the dissenting church in Old Jewry in the City. The speech was by the Welshman Richard Price, a revolutionary sympathizer, who sought to connect the French Revolution with the British change of monarch in 1688, saying that this underlined the British right to choose by whom they should be governed, and to set aside, if they wished, hereditary claims and succession. The Williamite accession is, as we have seen, crucial to the history of Ireland, in that it was the means whereby the Protestants, or rather the established church, ensured a supremacy over

Catholics. For Burke, therefore, it was the action that ensured that his mother's family and that of his wife (a Nugent and a Catholic) would have against them a discriminatory system of legislation that went a long way to ensure that they were second-class citizens; or at least, if such disadvantage were to be resisted, such resistance would take strenuous effort, ingenuity, and endless manoeuvre and compromise. It could be argued, perhaps, that the ceaseless shiftings and flexibility of Burke's anxious, restless, and capacious intellect owe much to an inheritance of subtle realignments and adaptations to circumstance that a legacy of survival as Catholics in a hostile milieu would have fostered in his mother's people.

Whatever about all that, Burke attacks Price's (to his mind) superficial interpretation of the Williamite succession, turning the revolutionary argument completely on its head in a prose ablaze with passion and reverence. No, he writes, it is not like this at all, it is not as if the Glorious Revolution usurped anything; rather was it the opposite. William ensured the continuity of ancient rights and privileges by overthrowing an authority that was itself lawless and innovatory. He saved the precious institutions of the church by reuniting the monarchy with the ecclesiastical reform established by the past energy of faith in England, thereby securing a maintenance of order that was the only sure guarantor of liberty and peace, both public and private. It is, he asserts, a puny exhibitionism of intellect that imagines that there is or can be such a thing as the rights of individuals, taken singly, and in separation from the incorporation they receive in society along with the rights of others; and those others include not just those who are living, but also all the great concourse of the dead whose memory we should honour. The 'rights of man', as expounded by the French innovators, is shallow ignorance, careless of the intricate nature of what it is to be human, a condition wherein rights and freedoms undergo all kinds of 'refraction and reflection'. Hence Burke's use of the word 'reflections' in the title of his work; he is not just referring to his thoughts or ruminations on an event, he is indicating that what he is trying to write engages with the whole intricate and complex apparatus of the human mind and emotion as it experiences and creates value, and as it is attached to things like the family, trust, love, God, and tradition.

The British Constitution is a living thing incorporating all who give it their allegiance, as Burke does his. In the letter to Keogh quoted above he refers to his primary duties as being owed to England, which is where he lives, but reciprocal duties should be discharged by Irish people living in Ireland towards their sister country, and by the English towards the Irish. Burke's is an idealistic vision, created by a consciousness of how vulnerable the type of compact and confederacy he envisages is to partiality, narrowness, and the strivings of those who put their own vanity before their duty. His is a curiously Catholic type of Britishness, even though he is always anxious to acknowledge and defend the Protestant love of liberty he saw in America, whose rights he also defended.

Burke, so strong was his love of the secure though flexible constitution of the British state, hated faction, which he saw as the precursor of rebellion. And he came to see, to his dismay, the Protestant Ascendancy in Ireland as such a faction, within the larger incorporation of the body politic. In the 1790s, in the wake of the revolution in France, Burke saw that there were great dangers in a failure to conciliate the Catholics of Ireland. There had been some relaxation of the Penal Laws in the 1780s, after the Irish parliament of Henry Grattan had won a measure of legislative independence from Westminster, but the danger, as Burke saw it, was that if the Catholics, whose temperaments would be naturally inclined to loyalty to the institutions of state, were not granted full participation in British liberties and freedoms, then they would fall into the arms of the Dissenters, a republican breed, and eager for the disruption of what he would call 'traditionary' rights.

But Burke was aware that these arguments of his were falling on deaf ears. There was not an accord between the English and the Irish legislatures, such as he had envisioned; and there certainly was no accord between the Protestant Ascendancy in Ireland and the Catholic majority. The representatives of the latter (whose Catholic Action Committee had for secretary none other than the United Irishman Wolfe Tone) were growing more fractious as conciliation seemed to grow more difficult of attainment, while the Irish Protestants appeared to want to hang on to their supremacy to the bitter end. It was in this context that Burke wrote in 1793 to his son Richard, who had been active in seeking equal rights for Catholics, about the Ascendancy. It is, he says, no more and no less than a resolve, on the part of Protestants, to maintain their dominion over the great majority of their fellow-countrymen, an abomination which involves, on the part of the

Protestants, 'pride and dominion', and on the Catholic side 'subservi-
ency and contempt'.

And it is not as if this 'persecuting faction' (this is what he calls them)
even knows anything about the theological reasons why it should
delimit the freedoms of their fellow-countrymen. They care nothing
about such refinements. In the old days, Burke says, when people
persecuted others, they had at least some sort of belief in a dogma or a
set of maxims to which they wanted to convert those who were in
error, as would be the case, for example, with Spenser, although Burke
does not mention this keystone of English colonialism in Ireland. No,
this lot are a faction who

would render millions of mankind miserable,—some millions of the race co-
existent with themselves, and many millions in their succession, without
knowing, or so much as pretending to ascertain, the doctrines of their own
school . . . the errors which the persons in such a faction fall into are not those
that are natural to human imbecility, nor is the least mixture of mistaken
kindness to mankind an ingredient in the severities they inflict. The whole is
nothing but pure and perfect malice. It is, indeed, a perfection in that kind
belonging to beings of a higher order than man, and to them we ought to
leave it.[7]

The perfection which, Burke is saying, in the contorted prose he is
writing here, the Ascendancy have attained belongs to beings of a
higher order than mankind, who can achieve a purity of malice. He is
talking about Lucifer and Beelzebub, and is saying that these Irish
Protestants have become demonic, a line of thinking that goes from
here right through to the demonized landlords of Sheridan Le Fanu
and Bram Stoker in *Uncle Silas* (1864) and *Dracula* (1897).

The failure of the Irish Protestants to conciliate the Catholics, and
the broader failure in Britain, as a whole, to release Catholics from
their disadvantages will not have the effect of protecting the interests of
those who confess the established faith. It will, Burke argues, drive
Catholics and Dissenters alike into the clutches of those who profess a
new and godless religion based on the rights proclaimed in the French
Revolution, a conversion that will compel its adherents to fury and
destruction of all that the Constitution of England and Ireland was
created to sustain: humanity, kindness, religion.

It is in despair that Burke writes to his son. He has little hope that
the unity that should involve the two kingdoms of Britain into an

incorporated mutuality will materialize, and is all too aware that his worst fears, of outright rebellion and the ripping apart of the fabric of peaceable life that will accompany it, will be realized. He was right. Differing views in Ireland were to consolidate into factions, a word and a concept deeply hated by Burke (perhaps in recall of the so-called faction fights in the countryside in pre- (Great) Famine Ireland, when rival gangs with old feuds would meet up on Fair Days and at other times to settle scores with extreme, and sometimes deadly, violence). These factions included: the Irish Protestants of the established church; the Dissenters; the Orange Order (founded at Loughgall, County Armagh, in 1795); the Catholic secret societies (Defenders, Ribbonmen, Whiteboys); the United Irishmen; the Catholic Committee; and so on and so forth.

In that letter of his of 17 November 1796, just before Tone is in Bantry Bay with an armed force of *sans-culotte* Frenchmen, Burke writes about the current disturbances. Tender to the last to the religion of his mother and wife, he maintains that the deepest roots of the present discontents do not originate with the Catholics:

there is, and ever has been, a strong republican Protestant faction in Ireland, which has persecuted the Catholics as long as persecution would answer their purpose, and now the same faction would dupe them to become accomplices in effectuating the same purposes; and thus either by tyranny or seduction would accomplish their ruin. It was with grief I saw last year with the Catholic delegates a gentleman, who was not of their religion, or united to them in any avowable bond of public interest, acting as their secretary, in their most confidential concerns.

This man, he has found out, was engaged in correspondence with known traitors, and acting in concert with enemies of all government and religion. This Jacobin was (although he is not named in the letter) clearly none other than Wolfe Tone, who, as Burke was writing, was in France, making final preparations, with the Directory in Paris, for an invasion of Ireland.

The invasion failed, owing to bad weather conditions, but there was a rising in 1798, by which time Burke was dead, of stomach cancer and, almost certainly, of grief over the death of Richard, his son. The rising was fiercely put down, and it was followed by the Act of Union, abolishing the parliament in Dublin. It was as if the English government was saying to Ireland: seeing as it is perfectly clear you cannot control your own affairs, then it is best to make an end of any pretence of legislative competence on your part, and deal with matters directly from here. It was not the last time there was to be direct rule over Britain's Irish territories. The Act of Union was not that union of minds and hearts that animated Burke's most passionate writings. What the Union of 1800 did was to affirm Ireland's subaltern status as a dependent colony. The woe of her new subjection issues in the sorrowful tones and cadences of the forlorn *Irish Melodies* of Thomas Moore at the beginning of the new century.

6

Romantic Ireland?

The strenuous prose and supreme oratorical skills of Edmund Burke, the witty alertness of the drama of Richard Brinsley Sheridan, are, to a significant degree, driven by questions of Anglo-Irish identity as these were surfacing in the latter part of the eighteenth century. Sheridan's drama in *The Rivals* (1775) and *The School for Scandal* (1777) exposed the follies of polite society to an icy satire that brought an Irish coldness to bear on the frantic agitations of a world driven by the desire for status, wealth, and the superficialities of acquisition and being well thought of. Burke concerned himself with questions of authority and of power. Sheridan and Burke are political writers, in the sense that they are occupied with those things that affect the social condition of men and women, how they live, and how they feel about how they live. Both men entered the political sphere, and immersed themselves in the world of political decision, and in the circumstances under which such decision and the interventions of power become necessary. They are examples of Irish political ability and intelligence operating at the heart of British public life, of which there are a great many other instances in the eighteenth and nineteenth centuries. The barrister John Philpot Curran comes to mind, as do Arthur Wellesley, the duke of Wellington, victor at Waterloo and prime minister; John Wilson Croker, secretary to the Admiralty; Robert Stewart, Lord Castlereagh, foreign secretary; and the Liberator, Daniel O'Connell.

However, apparently far removed from the hectic excitements, panics, and brief triumphs of political action was another dimension of Irish (or perhaps Celtic) culture. This surfaced in Scotland, at Moffat in Lanarkshire, where a young man called James Macpherson described to John Home, the poet and author of a popular tragedy called *Douglas*, ancient epic poetry in Gaelic which he claimed to know a good deal about. Home was fired up by Macpherson's account of this verse (his tragedy was based on a ballad, and there was a growing enthusiasm for authentic works of British 'genius', a word frequently used in this context), and he urged Macpherson to translate the epic material so it could be made accessible to a wider literary world. It turned out that that world was more than ready for what Macpherson promulgated as the rough utterances of Scottish heroic epic. Re-enter Oisín, son of Fionn mac Cumhail of the Fianna, save that now he was called Ossian. Fionn became Fingal, and the title of the first of these Ossianic productions was *Fingal, an Ancient Epic Poem in Six Books* (1763).

The volume met with great success: the characters of the Fionn cycle were promiscuously mixed in with other personages from other cycles and the whole lot tricked out in the dark, heavy robes of late eighteenth-century yearning for a wild Celtic realm where desire and action were unconfined by the needs of politics and the threats of violent change.

There is no need to dwell on the Macpherson controversy, save to say that the appetite which these poems catered for reflected a wider cultural turn towards folklore, indigenous material, the ancient: Macpherson called his first major Ossianic work an 'Ancient' epic poem, clearly divining the taste for such things. When Thomas Percy issued his collection of the ballad poetry of England in 1765, he was careful to entitle it *Reliques of Ancient English Poetry*. Percy's work had a profound influence on English and Irish Romanticism, with writers as different as Wordsworth, Coleridge, Keats, and Samuel Ferguson making striking use of the narrative ballad form.

Alongside this rediscovery of 'ancient things' in literature and oral culture, there was an interest in 'antiquities', and a fashion for antiquarianism developed in the Irish and British leisured classes. Prominent amongst antiquarians in Ireland were General Charles Vallancey, Sylvester O'Halloran, and Joseph Cooper Walker. Vallancey's theories about Ireland and the Irish are bold, to say the least. He believed that the Irish language was Phoenician in origin, and that it was 'masculine and nervous' in its nature, making it capable of complexity and abstract subtlety. The fact that he did not know the language did not deter him from these and like assertions. However, Vallancey, an English military man and an engineer (who oversaw the reconstruction of Charles Fort at Kinsale), was keen to advance the claims of Ireland as an ancient and venerable civilization, and, along with others, formed a Hibernian Antiquarian Society, which had, amongst its objectives, the study of Irish cultural tradition and the establishing of reliable scholarly procedures to ensure, in so far as that was possible, an exact body of knowledge about the Irish past, its literature, language, and other heritages. Walker, Vallancey, and O'Halloran in particular, were incensed at the assertions made by Macpherson, who sought to claim the tales of Ossian for Scotland, cutting Ireland out of the picture; and even going further than that, maintaining that Ireland's literary tradition was of far less account and much less venerable than that of Scotland.

The Royal Irish Academy, founded in 1785, was dedicated to the 'cultivation of Science, Polite Literature and Antiquities'. It evolved from the Hibernian Antiquarian Society, and a stimulus for its foundation was the setting straight of the record that the Macpherson issue had blurred. How may a true record of ancient culture be established, and what might have been the actual relationships between Ireland and its sister island in the early phases of their histories? It will be evident from this that the pursuit of exact knowledge of Irish civilization was not without its political dimension in Georgian Ireland, and in the Dublin of Grattan's parliament. Most of these scientifically minded antiquarians were Protestant, and it is evident that their interest in the origins of Irish cultural life was more than an amateur curiosity; their enquiries were involved with their own sense of who they were, and what part they might play in a united kingdom in which they hoped their role would not be a marginal one.

When she issued her *Reliques of Irish Poetry* in 1789, Charlotte Brooke explicitly addressed this issue in the preface she wrote for her anthology. She says that 'we are too little known to our noble neighbour of Britain', and that were the two kingdoms better known to each other, they would be firmer friends. Poetry may act as a higher form of language between the two, thereby opening up possibilities of more mutually immersive communion. The language she uses is flowery, a bit sentimental, but there is no doubt whatsoever about its sincerity: 'The British muse is not yet informed that she has an elder sister in this isle; let us then introduce them to each other! together let them walk abroad from their bowers, sweet ambassadresses of cordial union between two countries that seem formed by nature to be joined by every bond of interest, and of amity.'[1]

The language is fascinating. It is deeply feminized, as if to say that the feminine impulse will be one that may act as an emollient between two cultures that have, somehow, grown away from what they should really be like, into a hostile abrasiveness. They are formed by nature to be in concord, so that their dissensions are unnatural. And yet, keeping Macpherson's outrageous claims in mind, Brooke is at pains to point out that Irish literature is much older than that of Britain, and therefore, she trusts that she is doing an 'acceptable service' to her country ('my country' is the phrase she uses) 'to rescue from oblivion a few of the invaluable reliques of her ancient genius'. Patriotism, antiquarianism, mutual understanding, retrieval, ancientness, relics, reliques, genius, spirit: all are invoked in this fluent if emotional writing. She is clearly echoing Thomas Percy, by whom her work was encouraged: he had by then become bishop of Dromore in County Down. But while he accomplished a significant feat of scholarship in bringing the English ballad to the attention of the world of learning and the reading public, Charlotte Brooke's achievement, for all the mildness evinced in the manner in which she lays out her prospectus in the preface, was, in its way, much more demanding because of the labour involved, in learning the language and in coming to grips with a literary culture very different from that with which she was familiar.

Charlotte Brooke, a fairly remote antecedent of the well-known Brookeborough family in County Fermanagh, was born in Rantavan, County Cavan, daughter of the sentimental novelist and pamphleteer Henry Brooke, to whom she was devoted. She even says, in the preface to the *Reliques*, that she should, probably, have remained in the attractive shades of obscurity, rather than seeking the clamour and attention of publication, in honour of the memory and out of respect for the 'superior genius' of a dear father, now dead. She was encouraged into print by the group of antiquarians active in the newly formed Royal Irish Academy, Joseph Cooper Walker, O'Halloran, Vallancey, and Charles O'Conor (the last, as a Catholic, being granted honorary membership), not least because she had studied Irish very carefully and knew a good deal about its literary tradition. Her love of Irish literature began, we are told, when, as a girl, she heard a labourer on the family lands in County Kildare read poems from a manuscript during a break from work to an audience of farmhands. She gained enough mastery of Irish to be able to appreciate the subtleties of its verse, and writes with an enthusiasm, obviously informed by precise understanding, of the effects that it can create, linguistically and emotionally. This 'neglected language' has 'various and comprehensive powers', so that it can be 'pathetic' and simple, it can have 'force of expression', 'sublime dignity', and 'rapid energy'. This analysis is worlds away from the rhapsodic speculations about this 'neglected language', however well meant, of Vallancey.

In order that there be no ambiguity about the authenticity of the material upon which Charlotte Brooke's translations are based, she printed, at the back of her volume, the originals of her versions. Interestingly, the poems she chose come from a variety of genres. There are poems from the Ossianic or Fionn cycle (Macpherson had claimed that the Fionn tales were exclusively Scottish) and the Ulster cycle; there are love poems and songs; and there are what she calls Odes and Elegies, poems of praise and laments. It is, in fact, the first anthology of printed Gaelic verse ever assembled, and it is an astonishing achievement for someone who, by culture and upbringing, was outside the Gaelic literary tradition. Nothing that her father wrote, either his supposedly Jacobite play *Gustavus Vasa* (1739) or the novel *The Fool of Quality* (1765–70), comes anywhere near what his daughter did, in significance and originality. And that is because, in the *Reliques*, Irish literary tradition, a tradition that extends back to the Iron Age Celts and possibly further, makes its first authoritative appearance in English. Charlotte Brooke is well aware of the importance of what she is doing, which is one of the reasons why, aside from her feeling that, out of respect for her father's achievements, she should avoid advancing herself, she is only too aware that she may be inadequate to the task.

Her translations are dimmed over with a fug of late eighteenth-century poetic diction, a striving for sublimity or for sentimental effect. In spite of the fact that her work was undertaken, in part, to assert the claims of Ireland to a poetic supremacy over that in Scottish Gaelic (Macpherson's claim which outraged the Irish antiquaries), nevertheless the heavy pall of Ossian's brooding clouds falls over Charlotte Brooke's versions. Ossian, in its Scottish strain, was a kind of literary infection that transmitted itself all over the place, even amongst the Irish. This is Charlotte Brooke's translation of one of the *dánta grádha*, which in the original is marked by the characteristics of irony, terseness, and restraint typical of the poetry in this genre:

Daughter of Owen! behold my grief
Look soft pity's dear relief!
Oh! let the beams of those life-giving eyes
Bid my fainting heart arise,
And, from the now-opening grave,
The faithful lover save![2]

It would be pointless to belittle the quality of this writing as verse. No, what matters about Brooke's work here, and throughout her versions, is the effort that has been expended in trying to make Irish poetry resonate with something of its energy in eighteenth-century English. That English is confined by the high rhapsodic style thought suitable by early Romanticism to convey ancient passions, legendary feelings, and also by Brooke's own limitations as a poet, but the writing is infused with the intensity of her appreciation and enthusiasm for a literary tradition she admires, and which she is convinced matters greatly to civilization. Two lines of a version she made of a poem from a late rescension of the Deirdre story from the Ulster cycle are sonorous with reverence for the world of Irish storytelling, manuscripts, the bardic poets, and the old mythologies. The lines are from Deirdre's lament for the sons of Uisliu: 'No more his dark-red shield shall Ainle wield! | No more shall Naoise thunder o'er the field!'[3]

This is Romantic Ireland, but it is 'no more'. And yet Charlotte Brooke is seeking to revivify, through her interpretations and translations, what has been lost. Oblivion is a Romantic concept in itself, and these poets, in their obscure antiquity, are attractive because they have about them the mystery of the dead and gone.

Charlotte Brooke published her *Reliques* in 1789, the year of Revolution. In 1798, the year of rebellion in Ireland, Maria Edgeworth, another devoted daughter (her father, Richard Lovell Edgeworth, the writer and improving landlord, was described devastatingly by Byron as the worst type of bore, the energetic sort), was working on *Castle Rackrent*, a novel of the Anglo-Irish Ascendancy and of the 'Big House'. Maria Edgeworth's novel laid the foundations for a whole sub-genre of Irish fiction that was to have a very significant longevity, extending from her depictions of the degeneration of an Irish (too Irish) family, which is also Anglo-Irish in some way, the Rackrents, down through Le Fanu and many others to Somerville and Ross, Molly Keane, John Banville, and Seamus Deane, to name just these. But complex as many of these depictions of gentility going down and going off the rails are, not many of them have the ambiguity and resonance that the founding novel in this style has.

It is, to some degree, a Romantic novel, in that she writes about an Ireland of the good old/bad old days, before 1782, Grattan's parliament, and the year in which the Edgeworths returned to Ireland to take up the responsibilities of running their estate at Edgeworthstown, after Richard Lovell had spent years in England imbibing the spirits of benevolence and enlightenment in the company of the likes of Josiah Wedgwood and Erasmus Darwin. She achieves a breakthrough in the creation of the character of the narrator, the old retainer Thady Quirk, 'honest Thady', a kind of Romantic figure in himself, an Irish version of the creatures of the land and the environment to be found in Wordsworth's poems of the Lake District. Maria Edgeworth's impulse is in part anthropological, in that it has set itself an objective that was to become a perennial feature of Irish literature in English: the desire to inform English readers of what their fellow-citizens of the united kingdom were truly like, so that a better understanding of Irish ways of life and manners of thought could be had across the water. Hence the footnotes that bedeck the text, and the glossary of Hiberno-English words that comes at the end.

She wants, also, to give some idea of Irish speech, thinking that it will entertain her readership with its quaintness and authenticity, as the dialect of the Scottish poet Robert Burns had done, and as had various stage-Irish characters on the London stage. The difference with Edgeworth's version of Hiberno-English, however, is how accurate it is, so that Thady's locutions and syntax come off the page with the immediacy and concreteness of something carefully observed and thought about. Here is how Thady speaks to the reader and introduces himself: 'Having, out of friendship for the family, upon whose estate, praised be Heaven! I and mine have lived rent-free, time out of mind, voluntarily undertaken to publish the Memoirs of the Rackrent Family . . . .'[4]

Almost immediately he tells us that he is known as 'honest Thady' in the family, although he is now known as 'poor Thady', because he wears a long greatcoat in every season, a sign of poverty and of the old ways. However, at this point Edgeworth interjects the first of her notes, to tell us that this cloak is actually the ancient mantle of the Irish, described by Spenser, the garb of the rebel and the outlaw. Edgeworth, in other words, as soon as Thady starts talking, has him say things that put us on our guard. But it is not the case either that she reveals him as two-faced and a secret colluder in the downfall of the Rackrents: the story is nowhere near as explicit, or perhaps as obvious, as that.

We learn from Thady that the Rackrents were originally not called that at all. They were known as O'Shaughlin, clearly a Gaelic (and a Catholic) name. However, they stood in line to inherit when a Sir Tallyhoo Rackrent died in a hunting accident, except that the inheritor, a Sir Patrick, had to comply with a 'condition' which he 'took sadly to heart', but came to think better of what he had to do in time. Edgeworth does not tell us explicitly what this condition was, but it is clear that Sir Patrick had to convert to the reformed faith and take the oath of allegiance along with the name Rackrent. He was, in other words, a Jacobite who took his chances and swallowed his pride in order to get hold of the family lands. Thady tells us that this was in his grandfather's day, so that the time-scale here, seeing as the novel is set before 1782, takes us back to the 1720s or '30s, when Ó Rathaille was put out of his lands in north Cork by the likes of Sir Patrick, and Swift was writing his frantic proposal in response to the derelict condition of the country.

Sir Patrick, it turns out, swallows more than his pride. He was taught to drink by his father, who had the shakes, and he himself gets these as well, and worse, and dies. The stories of Sir Patrick's successors are all relayed to us through Thady, whose account, warm and apparently uncritical, reveals a dynasty of wasters, obsessives, sadists, alcoholics, and incompetents, until we arrive at the final stages of the story, when Thady's son, through a labyrinth of mortgages, jointures, wills, and codicils to wills, has engineered himself into a position where he has almost entire ownership of the house and lands, eventually putting the last of the Rackrents, Sir Condy, out of the house and into the Lodge.

Sir Condy tries to model himself on Sir Patrick, and succeeds. Alcoholism works its poison on him as well, and he eventually signs over the last of the estate (apart from a jointure, settled on Sir Condy and his estranged wife) in a peculiar scene, during which Thady is reduced to tears to see his old master manipulated by his clever son Jason, a lawyer. Edgeworth makes the scene all the more affecting when she describes the ruined and drunken man filling a glass for Thady and bringing it to his lips, a drink Thady declines. Edgeworth tells us, in an afterword as 'Editor', that all the features in the tale were 'taken from the life', and the scene of Sir Condy's undoing has the mark of something actually observed, or if not, very vividly relayed to her and her father: the frantic pouring of the drink, the kindness to others that often characterizes alcoholics, the despair at seeing a life go out of control. There is a Romantic abandon in the Rackrents; they belong to an ancient feudal world, to which Thady is, to some degree, attached. But their world is gone. Jason, as the story ends, is, Thady tells us, in dispute with Sir Condy's wife over the jointure, Sir Condy having died from an alcoholic seizure. He does not know what to say about this legal wrangle: 'I'll say nothing; it would be a folly to be getting myself ill-will in my old age.'

This is a baffling and, to an extent, terrible story about 'old' Ireland. Nothing is what it seems. Thady himself, and his son Jason, we assume, must be converts to the reformed faith: Thady, we notice, has dropped the 'Mac' (he has a niece, Judy, who has retained it, who once might have married Sir Condy, the equivalent of his going native), and Jason could not practise law if he were Catholic. Edgeworth has littered the novel with puzzles and clues to which there are no answers. The only consolation, as she keeps on telling her readers, is that all of this is a long time ago. Now, in 1800, when she published, there is a Union to be enacted. But even here she has her doubts: will the Union 'hasten or retard the melioration of this country?' Is it really all over with the old Romantic Ireland that plays such havoc with people's lives? *Castle Rackrent* is a strange and despairing book, which carries in its narrative the strong inference that there is no solution to be found to what has racked the Rackrents. It is a story of, as Seamus Deane has said, 'startling incoherence', as was Spenser's *View*, two hundred years before and the founding text of colonial Ireland, the first authority to which Edgeworth refers in her sad tale that is 'hard to read', a phrase Spenser uses to describe icons of moral disgrace in Book III of *The Faerie Queene*.[5] What are we to make of her last sentence, which is in the form of a double question: 'Did the Warwickshire militia, who were chiefly artisans, teach the Irish to drink beer? or did they learn from the Irish to drink whiskey?'

As if to say that the Irish may never be able to stop doing what they are condemned to do, that is, destroy themselves through their lack of control. And it may even be worse than this, in that their fatal lack of discipline, because it appeals to our baser instincts, will become a virus that will get into those whose responsibility it is to control the spread of such contagion. We are, as with Spenser, once more in the presence of the fear the colonial has that those whom he colonizes may take over him and his property, along with his women and children, changing what he loves into what he abhors. *Castle Rackrent* is not an 'enjoyable literary experience' (are there ever such things? one might ask): it is a hard read.

Richard Lovell Edgeworth in August 1798 mustered a force of yeomanry to march against the French who had landed at Killala and who established a short-lived Republic of Connacht. And while the insurgents spared the Edgeworth estate in County Longford, nevertheless it is quite clear that he and his daughter had reasons why they might welcome a union of Ireland and Britain. But of course there were others of their class who thought very differently of revolution— that it heralded a new world of equality and enlightenment, and a return to authentic humanity, a humanity repressed by the artificial structures of a heartless and exploitative society driven by the greed and selfishness of those who wield power. This ideology, a Jacobin ideology, drove the activists of the United Irish rebellion. Among these were the brothers Thomas Addis Emmet and Robert Emmet. Thomas Addis befriended at Trinity College, Dublin, a fellow-student there, Thomas Moore, a Catholic, who wanted to join the United Irishmen. Catholics were allowed to enter Trinity as a result of a recent easing of the strictures of the Penal Laws. It appears that Emmet, who had been asked to do this by Thomas's mother, took the young Moore for a walk in the country and urged him to keep himself out of danger by not formally becoming a member of the society, now proscribed by the government. Moore retired to the dark recesses of the library founded by Narcissus Marsh, adjacent to St Patrick's Cathedral, to concentrate on his first work, a translation of poems attributed to the Greek poet Anacreon, *The Odes of Anacreon* (1800).

These translations are now largely overlooked as lax fancies, mildly erotic musings, empty mellifluousness. Not so: they are extraordinarily fluent evocations of a world of dalliance and pleasure. They are Romantic in the sense that they create a world of suspended life, a kind of sweet dying, that is an aspect of the Romantic imagination, one associated with a tendency in John Keats, a tendency that Keats resists, creating the tensions of the later poet's great odes. The interesting thing about Moore's *Anacreon* was that, though written at a time of extreme civil and military turmoil in Ireland, the poems seem to inhabit a sphere of longing and intoxication very far removed from the pitchcaps which were put upon the rebelling 'croppies' in

Wexford; and the hangings, drawings, and quarterings with which the 1798 rising was put down:

> Give me the harp of epic song,
> Which Homer's finger thrill'd along;
> But tear away the sanguine string
> For war is not the theme I bring.
> Proclaim the laws of festal rite,
> I'm monarch of the board tonight . . . .

Moore wishes to portray, in lines that anticipate a later poem of Yeats, 'All the happy heaven of love, | These elect of Cupid prove.'[6]

Whatever about the wishes expressed in these brilliant translations for a timeless realm of sustained and infinitely prolonged pleasure, their perfect pitch and fluency cannot have been acquired without much labour, which in itself must have involved a significant transmutation, in Moore's psychology, of the fear and confusion he would have felt as his friends put themselves in danger for a cause he had wanted to serve. A great many of the Anacreontic poems celebrate the joys of drink, and Moore's praise of drunkenness reads as a kind of sensual rebuke to the grim fear of alcohol that features in *Castle Rackrent*. It is as if Anacreon Moore is saying, yes, we know the Irish drink, but so did the poet from Teos in Asia Minor, so did all the Greeks, and life can contain this joy and not be destroyed by it. Not only that, it can be a spur to poetry itself: 'When I drink, I feel, I feel, | Visions of poetic zeal' (Ode XLIX). Moore is here giving expression to one of the obsessions of Romanticism, that which had to do with drink and narcotics, and their supposedly liberating effect on the mind. But there is also an Irish context in which his extolling of the drunk acquires a different resonance when one keeps in mind the stereotype of the Irish as uncontrolled addicts.

The *Anacreon* enjoyed much success, and Moore, now removed to London, acquired a reputation on account of its scandalous liberties. The Prince of Wales, the future George IV, loved it and allowed the volume to be dedicated to him. The Prince's mistress, the much-fêted (and Irish) Mrs Fitzherbert, became one of Moore's subscribers, along with a group of London notables. Moore had become, with amazing speed, a much-sought-after guest in liberal circles sympathetic to Ireland and, to some extent, to the ideals of the French Revolution.

Moore was a great entertainer, and a fine singer with an affecting and emotional style of delivery. His musical abilities were a key factor

in the most successful of all his undertakings, *The Irish Melodies*
(1808–34). His success in establishing himself so quickly must be an
example of one of the most rapid ascents to prominence of any poet.
Charm was a factor, evidently, a kind of innate goodness and innocence (mixed with perhaps not a little mischief), his own quite
extraordinary poetic gift, but also something else, a readiness in London and in England for something Irish, wild, Romantic, full of feeling
and sentiment. He was what *Ossian* had been before him, what the
'age demanded', in the phrase of Ezra Pound. This is in no way to
belittle what this man of prodigious poetic energy achieved.

While he was a student at Trinity, Moore came upon the first
volume of Edward Bunting's *General Collection of the Ancient Music of
Ireland* (1796), based upon airs transcribed from the harpers (some of
them aged over 100) at the Belfast Harp Festival of 1792, a festival
sponsored by radical Presbyterians who were interested in Gaelic
culture as well as in French ideas. Wolfe Tone was present at this
assembly, but was not impressed by the music: 'Strum, strum, and be
hanged', he wrote in his diary. However, in spite of his impatience, the
Belfast United Irishmen clearly linked republicanism with Irish culture. This association was not lost on the young Moore, and he and a
friend, Edward Hudson, would play Bunting's airs, on one occasion
impressing Robert Emmet with a fiery tune, 'The Red Fox', causing
him to exclaim that he wished he were at the head of an armed force
marching to it.

It does not seem to be absolutely clear where the idea for a collection of songs by Moore based on traditional Irish airs first came from,
but certainly a factor in his undertaking the *Irish Melodies* was the
appearance of Sydney Owenson's (later Lady Morgan) *Twelve Original
Hibernian Melodies* (1805), in which she set her own words to Irish
tunes. She also made, with her wild good looks, her singing, and her
playing on the harp, a big impression on London society. Her novel of
1806, *The Wild Irish Girl*, captured the stereotype she had conjured up,
and gave it a location in the west of Ireland, all swirling clouds,
pinnacled castles, absentee landlords, decent Catholics, and atmosphere. The clouds of Ossian are still very much the backdrop. And
there are footnotes crammed with antiquarian detail, ensuring that the
reader remains in no doubt about the longevity of Irish cultural
tradition and the veracity of her account of it.

But it was to be Moore's moment. William Power, a music publisher in Dublin, with his brother James in London, agreed to issue a volume of Irish songs, and secured the agreement of Sir John Stevenson, choirmaster at St Patrick's Cathedral, to arrange the music to the lyrics that Moore would provide. It may well be that it was William Power who suggested to Stevenson that he contact Moore to see if he were willing to undertake the work. However, the Powers contracted with Moore that he would perform the songs in highly select venues in London and Dublin, making best use of his new and very influential contacts, to publicize the songs.

In a letter to Stevenson, written in 1807, as work was going forward for the first number of the *Melodies*, Moore says that he will give his best efforts to what Sir John has proposed, because the undertaking is what he calls 'truly national'.[7] He says this not just because he hopes that the songs will draw attention to Ireland and Ireland's plight, but also because he believes that somehow the Irish character is most fully given expression to in music, and it will be his task, if he can manage it, to find utterances that will somehow convey that elusive thing, the essence of the national identity, what Thomas Davis would later call the 'spirit of the nation'. He must, he says, 'feel and understand that rapid fluctuation of spirits, that unaccountable mixture of gloom and levity, which composes the character of my countrymen, and has deeply tinged their music. Even in their liveliest strains we find some melancholy note intrude—some minor third or flat seventh—which throws its shade as it passes.' This melancholy strain he directly associated with what he called 'the wrongs which lie' upon a 'lively temperament' (the Irish) as it seeks to shake off these injustices, or forget them.

There is a more personal emotional pressure also at work on the sorrowful beauty Moore was to construct in the word-harmonies of the *Melodies*, the memory of the United Irishmen Rebellion, the execution and deportation of his friends, and the recollection too of Robert Emmet's pyrrhic insurrection of 1803, his public hanging in Thomas Street near where Moore's parents lived, and his beheading afterwards. These men, the men of 1798, never lost their glory for Moore; they were, he said, the 'ultimi Romanorum', the last of the Romans, and he never failed to honour their memory.[8] It would be hard to think of a position more opposed to that of Burke, who feared republicanism, Roman or otherwise.

'Oh! Breathe Not His Name' is Moore's elegy-song for his friend Robert Emmet, for whom he and Edward Hudson (deported to Australia for his part in the rebellion) played 'The Red Fox' from Bunting. Emmet's famous speech from the dock, after his sentence was handed down, had asked that his epitaph not be written until his country 'takes her place among the nations of the earth', and asked the world, movingly, for 'the charity of its silence'. Moore's song keeps faith with his friend's injunction, and makes an elegy out of the saying of nothing. Emmet's name must not be said yet, and there is a sense, conveyed in the plaintive, flowing sadness of the perfectly cadenced words, that this may never be:

> Oh! breathe not his name, let it sleep in the shade,
> Where cold and unhonour'd his relics are laid:
> Sad, silent, and dark be the tears that we shed,
> As the night-dew that falls on the grass o'er his head.
>
> But the night-dew that falls, though in silence it weeps,
> Shall brighten with verdure the grave where he sleeps;
> And the tear that we shed, though in secret it rolls,
> Shall long keep his memory green in our souls.

The sorrow will continually sustain itself on the memory, the memory deriving itself from the sorrow. The whole thing is an etherized stasis, prolonging itself indefinitely on itself, as it renews itself from itself. This is a strange accomplishment, but it perfectly accords with Emmet's wish, creating an eloquence out of silence.

Many of these songs create similar effects: Romantic silence, suffering, eloquent, non-progressive grace. They realize a kind of 'hemiplegia' (a word Joyce would use a hundred years later when he tried to describe the psychic condition of the Dublin he was writing about) of feeling that seeks to convey the melancholy of having to bear the consciousness of wrongs having been done from which there seems to be no escape, neither from the consciousness of the injustice nor from the wrongs themselves. This is the nightmare that has to be gone through by those who are colonized. It is the nightmare of history from which Stephen Dedalus is trying to awake in James Joyce's *Ulysses* (1922). Joyce was a great admirer of Moore and of the *Irish Melodies*, recognizing in them one of the most eloquent expressions of the incommunicable grief that consciousness of victimage brings, as well as hopeless longing, remote fury, and the sublimation of frustration into dangerous and ungoverned cravings. These moods Joyce captured in his own very Moore-like poems, *Chamber Music* (1907), and he was himself a fine interpreter in performance of the *Melodies*, being possessed of a tenor voice so good that he did think for a time of making a career as a singer.

But Moore should not be thought of as entirely 'hemiplegic'. This fluent, concussive eloquence of his had its political edge, which was not lost on many reviewers. In 1810, when the third number of the *Melodies* appeared, it contained a piece that returned to the founding text of all Anglo-Irish cultural and colonial relations, Spenser's *View*. He goes directly back to the passage where Spenser is castigating the bards for promoting vice by urging rebellion and war against the English, and quotes him in a footnote. Moore's song 'Oh! Blame Not the Bard' is an intriguing rejoinder to Spenser's dismissal of the poetry of the bards. Written to the air of 'Kitty Tyrell', a composition of the harper Turlough O'Carolan (1670–1738) which was taken down by Bunting, it is a jaunty piece, with a driving, complex rhythm. Moore tells us in a footnote that it acts as an apology on behalf of those snarled at by Spenser, but the manoeuvre has a twist. The apology is for not being seditious enough. Do not blame the bard, Moore says, if he turns to 'Pleasure' (thinking of his own reputation as the Anacreontic poet). The lax strings on his harp should urge to martial action instead of doing what it does, just sighing the slack joys of 'desire'. But the pride is gone, the spirit that in the past would never yield is broken, because to love Ireland is now treachery, and to defend her means execution. To be Irish now, and to make any progress under the Union, it is necessary to betray all that your people have believed in, a clear reference to the Penal Laws and the discrimination practised against Catholics. The very means by which an Irishman can now advance implies the destruction of his country; he must light his progress from a torch that is lit from the bonfire of his own values. But, Moore goes on, in the arching rhythms of O'Carolan's planxty, gaiety strangely mixing with sorrow and dread, we shall never forget, we shall always honour the name of our country, and always recall the wrongs done. Memory will triumph over circumstance, we will at least have our grief; *that* cannot be taken from us. And so strong is this grief that we (the Irish, represented by the Bard now singing Moore's song, by Moore himself) will make even those who subject us, our 'Masters', weep with pity, even as they hammer the rivets into the chains that bind us. It is, by any standards, a highly charged political poem and song, ferocious, direct, unapologetic, and doing the very thing, but in an elegant early nineteenth-century manner, sugared over with the appearance of soft sentiment and harmless charm, that Spenser accused the bards of. This is nationalism, romanticized; it is rebellion made affecting; it is victimage recognized for what it can do to the will, making it pliant to opportunity, eager to inform and betray. It also relishes, and knows that it is doing so, the sharp toxic sweetness of submission and regret; it knows the attractions of self-abasement. The song is a Romantic evocation of the sorrows of the colonized, and it is no accident that its presiding genius (or daemon) is none other than the 'Undertaker' himself, Edmund Spenser:

> But alas for his country!—her pride is gone by,
>   And that spirit is broken, which never would bend;
> O'er the ruin her children in secret must sigh,
>   For 'tis treason to love her, and death to defend.
> Unpriz'd are her sons, till they've learn'd to betray;
>   Undistinguish'd they live, if they shame not their sires;
> And the torch, that would light them thro' dignity's way,
>   Must be caught from the pile where their country expires!

As Maria Edgeworth had shown, not more than a few years before this song appeared in 1810, it is possible to 'shame' your ancestors, as the Rackrents had done, and still live not only 'undistinguished' but in disgrace and self-defeating obsession.

Moore romanticized Ireland's cause. The accounts that survive of his live performances testify to the electrifying effect his emotional renditions of his own songs had upon his auditors. They would also be alert to the recent history of Ireland, of failed rebellion, of Catholic demands for equality, all issues that work upon the emotional fields the songs evoke. The later nineteenth century and the twentieth have tended to see Moore as a time-pleaser, a self-satisfied purveyor of cloying national sentiment to a liberal establishment that relished incendiary ideas rendered anodyne and saccharine by a watered-down version of Irish music. This is entirely unfair. Moore's Ireland is Romantic certainly, but it carries with it an unsubdued loyalty to the ideals of the United Irishmen, and a proud, though not completely well-informed, awareness of the longevity of Irish literary and musical traditions.

One of the remarkable (and unread) poems of the nineteenth century is Moore's Romantic, sprawling epic *Lallah Rookh* (1817), hugely popular in its day. It is a poem of Oriental exoticism into which are woven Moore's continuing fidelity to his dead friend Robert Emmet, who figures as Hafed, an Iranian Gheber, with Lallah Rookh suggesting Sarah Curran; Iran stands for Erin, while a character called the Veiled Prophet has insinuations of Daniel O'Connell, whom Moore deeply distrusted as a demagogue and inflamer of multitudes. The Orientalist background romanticizes Ireland's situation, giving it remoteness, mystery, and the opportunity for flights of complex fancy which could swoop opportunistically on political implications and jar the reader's nerves with a thrill of recognition mixed with the dangers associated with what is strange and alien.

From Vallancey and others there had evolved the notion that the Irish had an Oriental pedigree, a factor that made them all the more remote from the supposed solidity of the English and their pragmatic fixations with money, laws, and responsibility. Moore took this notion and made it the basis for an elaborate tapestry of stories in his epic, as if returning the Irish temperament to its origin in the mysteries of the East, while at the same time never forgetting for a moment the juridical inequalities that kept the Irish subject to a people so much less imaginative than they, or so the inverted stereotype went.

Moore was greatly admired, and by none more so perhaps than George Gordon, Lord Byron, who gave Moore his 'Memoirs' (later burned in the office of the publisher John Murray in London at the request of Byron's family), and who dedicated his own Oriental poem *The Corsair* to him in 1814. In this dedication he writes, to Moore, that he knows that his friend is himself working on a poem whose scene is to be set in the Orient. There, he says, 'the wrongs of your own country, the magnificent and fiery spirit of her sons, the beauty and feeling of her daughters, may be found. . . . Your imagination will create a warmer sun, and less clouded sky; but wildness, tenderness, and originality are part of your national claim of oriental descent, to which you have already thus far proved your title more clearly than the most zealous of your country's antiquarians.' The Irish are beginning to be perceived as the Orientals of Europe, and *Lallah Rookh* is seen by Byron, no doubt echoing Moore's own ambition, as an act of imaginative transformation, in which the mental labour of the poetic will connects Ireland, the Irish, and the country's circumstance to a vast world of feeling that is not circumscribed by the ordinances of British law and its discriminations. *Lallah Rookh* takes the issues that lie at the heart of the troubled relations between England and Ireland and weaves them into a great exotic tapestry, crammed with all kinds of details culled from a breathtaking variety of sources. Moore's scholarship and learning are impressive, but even more striking is how unbookish the ceaseless flood of imagery is, how fluently he manages to present the themes of oppression and freedom in a continuously shifting flow of realization that is itself a defiance of the spirit.

There are fire-worshippers, panthers that raid the shores of Lebanon, harems, angelic spirits; the scenes and illustrations move all over the Middle and Far East, from Cyprus to Kandahar, to the Nile, to Kabul, Kashmir, Shiraz, and to Shah Jehan's garden, called the Shalimar, on the plains outside Delhi. It is clear that Moore put his heart and soul into this, now utterly neglected, poem, possibly the most significant of the Irish nineteenth century. Moore's Orient is a lifting up of Irish distress and wrong, sharply felt by him, out of the immediate circumstances of Anglo-Irish politics, so that they become transfused by the brilliant irradiations of a mind so lucent and inventive that its action is itself an indication that nothing can imprison it, or stop its force of realization. The poem is a poem that proclaims its freedom even as it rehearses the wrongs that rivet chains into the mind. It is a work that involved immense labour and must have exacted a great emotional price. The following lines describe a Feast of the Roses held in Kashmir, at which two lovers are to be reunited after sad separation:

> The board was spread with fruits and wine,
> With grapes of gold, like those that shine
> On Casbin's hills;—pomegranates full
> Of melting sweetness, and the pears
> And sunniest apples that Kabul
> In all its thousand gardens bears.
> Plantains, the golden and the green,
> Malaya's nectar'd mangusteen;
> Prunes of Bokhara, and sweet nuts
> From the far groves of Samarkand,
> And Basra dates, and apricots,
> Seed of the sun, from Iran's land;
> With rich conserve of Visna cherries,

> Of orange flowers, and of those berries
> That, wild and fresh, the young gazelles
> Feed on in Iraq's rocky dells.[9]

And he is to start on the wine yet, the reds from Shiraz, the whites ('bright dew | from vineyards of the Green-Sea gushing'), the amber-hued sweet wines from Rosolli. Abundance, excess, drink, a 'genial deluge', as if to give a counter-stroke to the memories of famine, the starving beggars of Swift, the drunken wasters of Maria Edgeworth, the wretches who crawled out of holes and crevices in the aftermath of the suppression of the rebellion in Munster during Spenser's early years in Ireland, their mouths green from eating grass and shamrock. Might it not be argued that Moore's Romantic Ireland, transported to the Far East, is a kind of antidote to the toxins of hate and memory on which the colonial and the colonized thrive? Is it not surely the case that the reason Moore was so well liked was not because he was a 'well-pleased pleaser' (Joyce's devastating phrase for the self-satisfied Richard Irvine Best in *Ulysses*[10]), but because he was a genuinely good man, who did not betray friends, and who did not betray his country?

7

The Folk Tradition

While Moore was getting himself known in the London of the early years of the nineteenth century, cultivating the good opinions of the Prince of Wales, Lord Moira, and Richard Brinsley Sheridan, another poet, Brian Merriman, was trying to attract pupils to a new school he had set up in Limerick city, a school for mathematics. In around 1802 Merriman had moved from Feakle, County Clare, into the town, hoping, one presumes, to enjoy a better standard of living than he had in the country, where he had been a farmer and had kept a hedge school. In the Ordnance Survey Letters for Clare, written by John O'Donovan while he was in the field working for the Survey in the 1830s, we are told that Merriman removed to Limerick because he was worried that his two beautiful daughters would be abducted on account of their looks and their relative wealth. Precious little is known about Merriman other than a few bare facts, and O'Donovan's strange story. What we do know for certain is that he wrote, sometime around 1780, one of the most remarkable poems in Irish, *Cúirt an Mheán Oíche* ('The Midnight Court'), the last major Gaelic poem before the revival of Irish in the twentieth century.

The poem opens in the aisling format, that convention where the poet falls asleep in the countryside and is granted a vision of Ireland in female form, who looks forward to the return of the Stuart and her freedom from the bondage she has to endure from the stranger, England. The aisling form is connected to the legends associated with the tutelary goddesses, the sovereignty archetype, and the Hag, who, as in the stories of the Hag of Beare, can be both young and old, beautiful and horrifying, and also capable of shifting between these manifestations.

Merriman's poem makes full use of the amplitude of possibility surrounding this figure for his own satiric and comic purposes. He, Merriman, falls asleep, and is visited by a gigantic hag,

> Broad-arsed and big-bellied, built like a tank,
> And angry as thunder from shoulder to shank.[1]

This monster is five or six yards or more in height. She is filthy and bad-featured, and has come to make sure that Merriman will attend a court, presided over by Aoibheall, another version of the Hag, and goddess of Thomond, who has her fort or rath at Craglee, in County Clare. The court is a court of love, convened to hear complaints by the women of Ireland against the men, who, cowed by the church or fearful of poverty, are resisting marriage and sex.

One of the complainants is a girl who has married an old, worn-out, jaded creature for the financial security he can bring her, except that she has to endure a frigid and joyless bed, when her blood longs for excitement and satisfaction:

> Attractive and bright, with an amiable heart,
> This lady was skilled in the amorous art;
> She'd work through the night, and she liked it a lot,
> For she'd give the right fellow as good as she got,
> And urging him on with her murmurs and sighs,
> She would stretch at her ease, with a gleam in her eyes.

Merriman's *Cúirt* is a one-thousand line triumph of bawdy rhetoric, wit, and satire, which also recognizes something very disturbing that is at work in contemporary Irish life: the fact that in a world where poverty is the ever-present condition of existence, getting married and having children is a thing not to be taken for granted. The sexual frustration of the juicy young thing married to a dried-out old prune may be funny, but her erotic longing is also nightmarish, in that it is a yearning for what cannot easily be had in a life where money, and the keeping of it, matters greatly, because without it you will starve. The longing for sexual pleasure and orgasm is hilarious because it is so dreadfully irrelevant. Children are a heartbreak in a world where starvation is the norm, and in such a context marriage can become a terrifying prospect.

This lack of sexual pleasure and satisfaction is, strangely enough, why Ireland has produced some of the finest folk love songs in the world. The longing fills the absence of the actual thing in real life. Merriman's poem went directly into the folk tradition, and it would, all through the terrible misery of nineteenth-century Gaelic Ireland, have been recited at night around firesides, with the children out of the way, and probably the women too, as the men, many of them bachelors, enjoyed what Timothy Buckley, the Tailor from Gougane Barra in west Cork, would call in the 1930s and '40s 'wan grand dirty night'.

When *Lallah Rookh* was published, there would have been firesides all over the Irish countryside where not only poems such as Merriman's *Cúirt* would be recited, but also stories told of Fionn and Oisín, Cú Chulainn, the Hag of Beare, the Tuatha Dé Danann, and songs would have been sung as well: love songs, songs about local events, comical songs, laments, as well as songs about religious subjects. The musical tradition would still be vigorous, and although there would have been fewer wandering harpers than would have been the case fifty years before (the numbers of the surviving Catholic landowning gentry having declined still further as the eighteenth century wore on), there were still itinerant musicians walking the roads, some of them now tinkers who could hammer together a fiddle out of tin.

We are, effectively, talking about the dispersal of a highly literary and indeed hierarchical cultural tradition amongst the ordinary people, the hewers of wood and drawers of water. But this extension of an intensely cultivated, and frequently esoteric literary culture into the peasantry, while it involved a decline of sorts, nevertheless was a factor in the creation of one of the significant folk cultures of the world. The speech of, say, the Blasketman Tomás Ó Criomhthain (1856–1937), who wrote *An tOileánach* ('The Islandman'), was, it has been remarked by a number of those who knew him well, highly self-conscious and indeed literary, capable of great eloquence, pithy exactitude, careful finesse and restraint. His linguistic resource, while remarkable, was not uncommon, and it will have had its origins in the contact the speech and oral culture of ordinary people had with the literary inheritance the language carried with it.

The permeation of the oral culture of ordinary people by elements of the learned traditions of the bards, the storytellers, and the topographers was effected too by the descent into the labouring classes of many who would have held a much higher rank in the older scheme of things. Eoghan Rua Ó Súilleabháin (1748–84), for example, the most musical and exquisite of all the practitioners of the aisling genre, between spells as a hedge-schoolmaster and a time in the British navy, worked as a 'spailpín', an itinerant labourer. In one poem, he dispenses with his customary ethereal music to address his friend the blacksmith Séamas Mac Gearailt, requesting him to make a spade that will stand him in good stead in the work he now finds he has to do:

> When you're done my spade will be tricked out nicely and trim,
> And even though I've always had a yen for the books
> I'll not stop till I heft my implement right up to Galway,
> Where daily I'll get my sixpence and something to eat.[2]

There is, just, the faintest suggestion, in the skirling irony of the song, that the spade might be capable of being put to uses other than farm or labouring work, which is why it is quite important that it be made soundly and well. If, says Ó Súilleabháin, he gets tired out from the drudgery, he may be able to amuse the ganger with the stories of Troy, Samson, Achilles, Deirdre, or of Fionn. When the day's work is over, he says, he and Séamas will meet up in the tavern, and he will spend every last halfpenny he has earned on whiskey and ale.

It was some such itinerant labourer that Charlotte Brooke encountered on her father's land, reading aloud from a manuscript during a break for food, the other workers sitting around, all ears for the ancient stories. This rural recitation was to set her on the journey that led to the *Reliques*. In the same year that *Lallah Rookh* was published, 1817, Mícheál Óg Ó Longáin, one of the most learned of the later scribes, began working for Bishop John Murphy in the city of Cork, copying manuscripts, assisted by his sons, and glad not to have to turn his hand to navvying and working for day wages.

Ó Súilleabháin, Ó Longáin, and many others like them, men of education and some learning, were now part of the huge and growing population of the rural Irish poor. It was a tragedy for them, of course, and they never ceased to think that they were cast into a situation way beneath their dignity, but their stories and their songs and poems went into the already extremely rich folk culture of the people, making it even more self-consciously artistic and deliberate in its effects. It may be said, without exaggeration, that after Merriman, while the Gaelic literary tradition in its formal manifestation went into decline, there began to develop, based on cultural strata that had been in existence for over a thousand years, a folk and oral tradition of truly impressive range and sophistication. It seems as if Irish literary and linguistic culture has the capacity, at times of dereliction and decline, to find new modes of expression, where the ancient energies get rechannelled into different directions and new forms. Irish folk culture is recognized as one of the finest manifestations of the folk mind to be found anywhere in the world, and attracted scholars from Scandinavia, Germany, and France from the middle of the nineteenth century, eager to investigate what they recognized as an important strand of Indo-European ethnological heritage.

Moore's *Melodies* had some kind of vestigial contact with folk tradition, in that the airs the songs were based upon came out of Bunting's collections (the 1796 volume was revised and expanded in 1809, and was followed by two others), which themselves were based on transcriptions made in Belfast and in the field. The collection of folklore and folk-song was becoming widespread across Europe in the early nineteenth century, with Jakob and Wilhelm Grimm publishing their *Kinder- und Hausmarchen* ('Children's and Household Tales') in 1812. A young Corkman, Thomas Crofton Croker, published an account of a *caoineadh* (an, often spontaneous, Gaelic funeral elegy recited over the body of the dead person) which he heard at a funeral in Gougane Barra in west Cork. This led to his being invited to London by Thomas Moore, where he was encouraged to begin collecting in a serious and methodical way. His field-work resulted in *Researches in the South of Ireland* (1824), the first body of collected Irish folk materials. Its significance was quickly recognized by the Grimm brothers, who translated parts of it into German in 1826.

Croker now turned his attention to the folk-song tradition of Munster, writing, in 1826, to a young poet from Cork, J. J. Callanan, to ask him if he would assist in his next projected undertaking, a *Minstrelsy of the South of Ireland*. Callanan, himself engaged in field-work at the time in Bantry, wrote back to say he could not become involved with Croker's undertaking because he himself was preparing something along the same lines, a collection he was going to call *Munster Melodies*. The instinct to guard jealously territory that might prove lucrative (look at how successful Moore had been with Irish material, Callanan would be thinking, and he wasn't even in touch with the real thing) is all too pathetically in evidence, as well as a readiness to imitate what tortured him with its success: he would do for Munster faithfully what Moore had failed to do for Ireland.

As it happened, nothing came of the Munster Melodies project, save for a few translations from Callanan's hand, one of them a masterpiece, 'The Outlaw of Loch Lene'. Callanan's poem-translation is very free with its original. In a sense what he does is to create a new piece that floats out of the mysterious erotic turbulence of the folk-song he worked from, a new poem that is begotten by the imaginative sympathy he has with the feverish world of longing that the Irish song conjures in its strange landscapes, its wildness, its outlandishness:

'Tis down by the lake where the wild tree fringes its sides,
The maid of my heart, my fair one of heaven resides:—
I think as at eve she wanders its mazes along,
The birds go to sleep by the sweet wild twist of her song.[3]

Croker heard the caoineadh, the keen, at Gougane Barra in 1813, when he was 15, and it made a profound impression on him, as it did on J. M. Synge, when he heard it on the Aran Islands ninety years later. As Croker and Callanan conducted their field excursions into west Cork, searching for the survivals of what they would call the Irish minstrelsy, amongst the repertoire of recitations, poems, songs, and stories that many *seanchaithe* ('storytellers') would have in their memories was the most famous of all the Munster keens, that of Eibhlín Dubh Ní Chonaill on her husband Art Ó Laoghaire.

This caoineadh, which appears to have had its origin in the actual keen made by Eibhlín Dubh over her dead husband, entered Irish folk tradition, from which it was collected. It seems that the first transcription was made as early as 1800 from Norry Singleton, a woman who was a professional keener herself. The events that the keen recounts occurred in 1773. Eibhlín Dubh's husband, Art Ó Laoghaire, had been a captain in the Hungarian Hussars, and so one of the 'Wild Geese', except that in Art's case he returned, and became notorious in County Cork for his recklessness and violence. He wore a sword in public, something banned under the Penal Laws, and generally behaved in a manner likely to draw attention to himself. Eibhlín Dubh, of the O'Connell family in Derrynane, County Kerry (Daniel O'Connell was her nephew), married him against her family's wishes; they wanted a quiet life, and had little time for ostentatious and provocative behaviour such as Art's.

Trouble arrived soon enough. Art fell out with one Abraham Morris, high sheriff of Cork, his mare beating Morris's at races in

Macroom. Morris, invoking the Penal Law where a Protestant could buy any horse from a Catholic for five pounds, tried to get Ó Laoghaire's horse from him, but was refused. Art went on the run, but was eventually set upon by Morris and his men at Carraig an Ime, and shot dead. The mare that was the subject of the dispute galloped back to the family home, and, according to the caoineadh, Eibhlín mounted her and rode to where her husband lay on the road, covered in gore. She tells us in the keen that she got down on her knees and drank his blood.

This caoineadh is a perfect example of the integration of an oral folk tradition of keening (where the qualities of the dead person are recalled, his or her achievements remembered, and the sorrow of the mourners at the death and the funeral expressed) with a highly dramatic and rhetorical set of consciously poetic (but nonetheless effective for that) flourishes. The man comes before us in all his vigour and strength, while the speed and eloquence of Eibhlín's Dubh's words are driven by passion and love. Her rage at those who have felled her man is startling and full of power, but most affecting of all are the heart-smitten memories she has of him when he first took her breath away:

> You are my love forever!
> The day I saw you,
> By the end wall of the market house,
> My eye observed you,
> My heart warmed for you,
> I escaped from my father with you,
> A long way from home with you.[4]

Thomas Crofton Croker went into the field to collect folk materials; so did J. J. Callanan; so too did the poet and translator Edward Walsh, who grew up in Millstreet, County Cork, and made excursions into the countryside to collect poems, stories, and songs. In the north a hedge-schoolmaster called Patrick Lynch collected words and airs for Bunting, who continued to record as much as he could of Irish musical heritage from the people. The Ulster Gaelic Society, founded in Belfast in 1830, had in its membership the young Samuel Ferguson, who set to work translating Irish poems and songs from James Hardiman's *Irish Minstrelsy*, published in 1831. One of Hardiman's assistants at the Public Record Office in Dublin, where Hardiman was employed, was the scribe and scholar John O'Donovan, who went on to work on the Ordnance Survey, contributing information on place-lore based on research undertaken in the field by himself and others. The Ordnance Survey had a Topographical Section, presided over by George Petrie, himself a scholar of music, folklore, and architecture, and it was for this section that O'Donovan worked, as did James Clarence Mangan, Samuel Ferguson, W. F. Wakeman, and others. The collection of folklore, the understanding of place-names, the 'bringing back to the light of intellectual day the already recorded facts, by which the people of Ireland will be able to live back in the land they live in, with as ample and as interesting a field of retrospective enjoyment as any of the nations around us' (in Samuel Ferguson's elegant and Burke-like phraseology), was a major cultural undertaking by the 1840s.[5] And central to this enterprise was the recovery of the folk culture of the people. Petrie continued in the tradition established by Bunting, and went on to produce a two-volume *Ancient Music of Ireland* (1855–1882); Walsh and Ferguson explored the tradition of folk poetry, in particular the love songs.

In many of these there is an emotional directness, and a frank urgency of passion. They often deal with extremities of grief and sadness at love denied or unrequited. One of them, translated by Ferguson in 1834, is the famous love song 'An Clár Bog Déil' ('The Bare Deal Board'). It is a young man's song, in which the lover wishes that he were in Cashel of Munster with his girl, even if beneath them they only had the bare deal board as a bed. In a wild frenzy of sorrow he says that he would prefer to be dead than to be as he is, wandering the roads of Ireland, distracted without her:

I'd wed you without herds, without money, or rich array,
And I'd wed you on a dewy morning at day-dawn grey.
My bitter woe it is, love, that we are not far away
In Cashel town, though the bare deal board were our marriage bed this day.[6]

This is Ferguson's version of the first verse, the long sprawl of the final line opening out to waywardness and longing, a kind of floating searching of the possibility of capturing, rhythmically, the shifting turbulence of grief. Walsh, who translated a different version of this song in his *Irish Popular Songs* of 1847, has the final verse as follows: 'Alas! that I did not early die before the day | That saw me here, from my bosom's dear far, far away'.[7]

Both Ferguson and Walsh are trying to get out of the straitjacket of their given poetic conventions to attain some kind of freedom and energy commensurate with what they can see in the original songs, but it is difficult for them. The last two lines of the Irish are something like the following: 'It is my venomous sorrow that I wasn't left down in the earth | Before I was driven out into the barren places, and my love left behind.' It is going to take some fifty years before poetic convention in English is ready to accommodate this kind of wild utterance, and even then not without some difficulty in comprehension, as in J. M. Synge's often misunderstood linguistic strangeness and range.

These songs, in their longing for the far realms of feeling, for open wild spaces, for the secrecies of woodland, the freedom of the open road, reflect the confinements of a society reduced by legal constraint and by the moral authority of a Catholic church, the influence of which was increasing over the course of the nineteenth century. Catholic Emancipation, through the agitations of O'Connell, was achieved in 1829, but well before that date the church had become a steadying force with its emphasis on the values of family, good order, progress, and the curtailment of instinct in the service of civic virtue. This controlling presence is to be seen in Merriman's *Cúirt*: sexual passion must needs be subdued to economic reality; marriage is something to be gone into only if it can be afforded. There can be no doubt but that these constraints, backed up by the moral imperatives of the church, themselves deriving their authority from the Vatican and its interpretation of the Ten Commandments, were accepted by many Catholics, who were seeking to break free from the miserable shackles of poverty and hunger. But, as is often the case where emotional constriction is in place, the imagination broke free, to create some extraordinarily powerful poems and songs of passion and yearning.

Here is a song, 'An Seanduine' ('The Old Man'), apparently sung to the air of the Scottish tune 'The Campbells are Coming', in which a young girl gives vent to the rage she feels at having yielded to her parents and a trickster of a priest when they persuaded her to marry an old man for his money and the security and content it brought to all concerned, other than herself:

> If I found my old fella drowned in a boghole,
> I'd bring him back home and there I would wake him,
> Then I'd lock up the door and pocket the key,
> And I'd take myself off with the virile young lads.[8]

There is a reckless humour in this, of course, but in many of the songs where the young lover expresses his or her feelings there is abandon, extreme emotion, and the evocation of an existence where all the normal constraints are set aside:

> A bed of rushes lay beneath me last night
> And I pushed them away with the heat of the day.
> My love came to me and laid by my side;
> We were shoulder to shoulder, mouth on mouth.[9]

This is the famous 'Mo Bhrón ar an bhFarraige' ('My Grief on the Sea'), collected by Douglas Hyde in his *Love Songs of Connacht* (1893), a volume that was to have a profound and far-reaching effect on the poetry and fiction of the revival of Irish literature that took place at the end of the nineteenth century. Immediately following this, in Hyde's collection, is another famous love song, 'An Draighneán Donn' ('The Blackthorn Tree'), which embodies the world of strangeness and intense feeling that is so marked a feature of these songs.

It is the song of a girl who has been abandoned because her family had not the money for a suitable dowry. Now a prostitute, she sits drinking with men, all of whom think she is theirs when she is with them, whereas her mind cannot stop racing on the man she loves:

> A hundred men think I am theirs when I drink ale with them,
> But they all recede from me when I think of you and me talking,
> Your body smoother than the silk on Slievenamon,
> And my love like the flower on the dark blackthorn.

The air for this song was taken down by Bunting, and his collaborator Patrick Lynch also transcribed some of the verses. Hyde's version, as printed in his collection, does not have a couple of heartbreaking verses at the end, where the girl, in some kind of wild phantasmagoria, begs the boy whom she loves to take her with him. He, she tells us, was the only man she has ever really made love to ('the only one to whom I gave my secret'); he must take her even though she has nothing, no money, no cattle; she is not, she tells him, pregnant ('I have no little child under my girdle'); if he does not take her she is done for: 'If you won't take me I'll not live a year from today.'[10]

It is not impossible that Hyde chose not to print verses such as these, or it may be that the version he heard did not have them, but Hyde's collection, whatever the adjustments and elisions he may silently have made to his texts, opened up a new world of feeling for Yeats, Lady Gregory, Synge, James Joyce, and many others as well: Joseph

Campbell, Padraic Colum, Patrick Pearse. Yeats said that Hyde's *Love Songs* brought a new power into literature, and likened his versions to what he called 'thrusts of power' in the phrase of Flaubert.[11]

Hyde (1860–1949), from Frenchpark, County Roscommon, was the son of a Church of Ireland clergyman. He learned Irish in his local area, and went on to devote his life to its preservation and to scholarship in Gaelic literature and folklore. *Beside the Fire* (1890) was a collection of tales, taken down from oral narration, printed with translations on the pages facing the Irish. In 1893 he became president of the newly founded Gaelic League, set up to preserve and, wherever it had fallen into disuse, revive the Irish language. He was, like many at this time in Ireland, a convinced cultural nationalist, arguing for the abandonment of English mores and even codes of dress, championing the wearing of Irish tweed, the support of Irish-made goods, and the avoidance of foreign imports, especially if they came from England.

As is clearly evident from the scholarly introduction to *Beside the Fire*, where Hyde gives an account of ethnological scholarship in Ireland from the time of Crofton Croker, together with evaluations of his work and that of his successors, Patrick Kennedy, Lady Wilde, and Jeremiah Curtin, and from the wonderfully informed commentary he provides for the folk materials in the *Love Songs*, he is a reliable and scrupulous folklorist.

The effect the recovery of folklore had on Irish literature in the latter part of the nineteenth century was to compel many writers and artists into a deep examination of questions of identity. Yeats, Lady Gregory, Joseph Campbell, and many others discovered, among the Irish country people, stories and poems that seemed to bring them into a living relationship with some of the deepest strata of European culture itself. So that, instead of the west of Ireland being a marginalized and peripheral place, it seemed to be turning out that it retained access to some of the mother lodes of the ancient world. To Yeats, for instance, the Fionn stories and those to do with Oisín brought him right back into the most central preoccupations of the European mind, which had to do with nature, human behaviour towards it, the supernatural and our relation to it, and, most importantly perhaps, the kind of emotion aroused by works of human creativity in poetry and storytelling.

What also attracted were those things in folklore which seemed strange to the cultivated mind: a flexibility about time and space and the relations between them, and a readiness to bring into poetry and song sudden shifts of thought, abrupt surges of feeling that tended to extremity and lack of control. In a curious way Macpherson had, over a hundred years before, intuited these qualities, and tried to render them in prose hectic with emotional strain and reach, but his style and sensibility could cope with these intimations only by melodrama and exclamatory invocations of something cloudy and weird. Now, at the end of the nineteenth century, as the world was entering into a phase of chaotic disturbance and revelation of a kind not seen before, the radical surges of Irish folkloric power had a correspondence in the gaps that were becoming apparent in the human psyche itself.

An interesting example of the strong influence of folk tradition is to be found in the work of Joseph Campbell from Belfast. Campbell, the son of a building contractor, became enthused by Gaelic poetry and song, and by the nationalist cause. He went into the field and collected in Ulster and in Connacht, finding the famous air 'My Lagan Love' in Fanad in the north of Donegal in the early years of the twentieth century. Curiously, this was a song in English, taken down from a man who had it from his father, who got it from a sapper on the Ordnance Survey in the 1830s or '40s. The song and the air have an unearthly beauty: 'Where Lagan stream sings lullaby, | There blows a lily fair; | The twilight gleam is in her eye, | The night is on her hair.'

One suspects that a little doctoring has gone into these lyrics: the twilight gleam in the girl's eye is a little redolent of a fervour for folkish things that might have more to do with the Malone Road than Fanad; nevertheless, it would be callow to take away too much from the mood the song unravels, and the way the words, in their fluent melancholy, make a perfect weave with the sorrowful and glorious tune. Another, just as interesting piece from Campbell is a translation or version of a love song he had from Mícheál Mac Rudhraighe in County Mayo called 'The Little Yellow Road', the air of which is one of the greatest of the slow tunes of Ireland. The song has the startling specifics and emotional immediacy of the love-song tradition, well conveyed in Campbell's verse with its swift transitions:

> I travelled west
> By the little yellow road
> In the hope I might see
> Where my secret abode.

> White were her two breasts,
> Red her hair,
> Guiding the cow
> And the weaned calf, her care.

The song progresses into despair and distraction, ending up with the lover drinking, drinking with anyone who comes, buying for everyone: 'I pay, I pay, | And I pay for two.'[12] All caution and carefulness about money is thrown to the winds; what matters is the sorrow, and the feeling of it, and the thrill that the oblivion of alcohol can bring as the emotion sinks into the torment in which it delights. Songs such as these are often sung by men who are not entirely sober, their voices driving against the words as they try to realize the feeling they evoke. I have heard such passionate declamations in Kruger's pub in Ballyferriter, County Kerry, and once, remarkably, by Darach Ó Catháin in the Victoria pub in Leeds, a city where Darach worked on buildingsites in the 1970s. Listening to him, in the company of the poet Pearse Hutchinson, I knew I was listening to something that went back two thousand years. This was before we were asked to leave because the landlord didn't want 'any of that Pakistani singing'.

Despite making a couple of attempts to learn the language, Yeats did not know Irish, but he recognized in its folk and mythological traditions a source of enormous power. Their effect on his poetic development cannot be overestimated. He learned from the song tradition and the mode of declamation he found in the *sean-nós* ('old ways') style of singing a quality of passionate urgency, a commitment to embodying in the words the emotions evoked, that he sought to re-create in his verse. At a *feis* (a Gaelic cultural festival) in Galway in the 1890s he was riveted by the energy of the delivery of a traditional song, by the way in which the singer seemed to be possessed by the world that came into being as he sang. The integration of words, feeling, and rhythm achieved by the best sean-nós performers became an exemplar, even though Yeats had no ear for music. It was the dramatic realization of emotion, the complete surrender involved, which attracted him to this style.

A poem like 'He Wishes his Beloved Were Dead', from Yeats's collection *The Wind Among the Reeds* (1899), incorporates in its syntax, rhythmic force, and imagery a great deal from the Irish folk-song tradition, in particular the extremities of some of the love songs. The poem is all one sentence, a ferocious onward rush, out of life and into the complete world of the poem, which is a world of love and total feeling. It would be better if the woman he loves were dead, the speaker says, because then she would come to him, a thing she will not or cannot do in the grim actuality that is life this side of the grave. The model behind this poem may well be Edward Walsh's translation of 'Táim Sínte ar do Thuamba' ('I am Stretched on your Grave') from his *Irish Popular Songs*, but there are many such songs where death is longed for as a realm where love can be free of the shackles that bind it in the world of dowries and farming and common sense. In Walsh's original the boy is stretched out on his girl's grave; he smells of the earth, and has taken on the colour of the sun and the wind. He wants to die and assume the form of a ghostly wind so he can flow down to meet her shade on the wide plains. Walsh translates: 'On the wings of the whirlwind | In the wild wastes you'll meet me.'

Yeats twists the idea to his own preoccupations. The girl is not dead, but very much trapped in the concerns of life that keep her from the speaker. If she were dead, and a ghost, then she would come to him and be kind to him:

> Were you but lying cold and dead,
> And lights were paling out of the West,
> You would come hither, and bend your head,
> And I would lay my head on your breast;
> And you would murmur tender words,
> Forgiving me, because you were dead...[13]

The word 'paling' has a touch of Pre-Raphaelite ethereality about it, but there is no doubt but that the whole poem comes out of the 'West', the Ireland of the love songs, and the stories that Yeats and Lady Gregory were beginning, in the 1890s, to gather in the Galway countryside. Yeats is becoming a major modern poet by means of his ability to connect with the folk culture of the people, the legends and mythologies still to be found in their tales, and the passionate syntax evident in the songs they declaimed and in the way they spoke English as well as Irish, full of drama, energy, and even sometimes violence. The Yeats poem ends: 'O would, beloved, that you lay | Under the dock-leaves in the ground, | While lights were paling one by one.'

The real triumph in these lines is not the 'beloved' or the repeated 'paling'; it lies in the 'dock-leaves' that come straight from the folk culture, the real thing. All the dispersed sorrow and vague longing of Thomas Moore is here focused by a specific image of weeds growing on the grave of someone loved to distraction. A great modern poet is on his way by means of the ancient things that are to hand and which are still being transmitted, and to which his astonishingly open emotional apparatus is receptive.

James Joyce makes brilliant use of folk tradition and song in the short story that concludes *Dubliners* (1914), 'The Dead', written in 1907. The bumptious and vainglorious Gabriel Conroy gives a speech after a New Year dinner on the Feast of Epiphany at his maiden aunts' house in Dublin. At the end of the evening his sexual desire for his wife Gretta becomes inflamed as he sees her listening attentively to a rendering of the song 'The Lass of Aughrim'. He sentimentalizes her reaction and imagines that she shares his longings, which he hopes she will gratify when they get back to their hotel. It turns out, however, that her mind and feelings have been elsewhere, back in the west in Galway where she comes from; she has been thinking of the boy she once loved, a Michael Furey, who used to sing that song for her. He had, she tells Gabriel, a beautiful voice and would have been a singer but for his poor health. Gabriel is now outraged by jealous lust but probes yet more into the story of Michael Furey. It turns out that he is dead, and that the night before Gretta left Galway as a young girl to come to a convent school in Dublin, her boy threw gravel against her window. It is pouring with rain and she cannot see who it is, so she goes down to find Michael Furey standing in the rain 'at the end of the wall where there was a tree'. She implores him to go home out of the rain but he tells her that he does not want to live now that she is going away. She has been gone only a week when he dies, and he was buried in Oughterard, where his people came from.

The story is straight from the scenarios we see described so often in Gaelic love song: the lover out in the weather, choosing death rather than life; the girl away, kept secure in the normality of the ordinary world; the lover rejoining the non-human world of nature. Meanwhile Gabriel, a west Briton according to the nationalist Miss Ivors, is outside all this, and as the story closes he realizes how remote he is from the 'west', the world of the dead, far across the 'dark mutinous Shannon waves', the world with which Gretta is still intimately involved.[14]

The strange thing is that the story of Gretta and the boy who loved her is based on a similar event in the girlhood of Joyce's wife, Nora Barnacle, who herself came from the Irish country people, and whose odd name is a translation of the Gaelic Ó Cadhain. Joyce returned to the theme, which obviously meant a great deal to him (the last pages of 'The Dead' are as emotionally powerful as anything in Irish writing), in a short poem of 1913, 'She Weeps Over Rahoon' (Rahoon is the graveyard in Galway where Nora's early love, Michael Bodkin, is buried). Despite all the circumstantial biographical correspondences, the poem is a deeply affecting variation on the classic themes of Gaelic love song:

> Rain on Rahoon falls softly, softly falling,
> Where my dark lover lies.
> Sad is his voice that calls me, sadly calling,
> At grey moonrise.[15]

The line passes on, surprisingly, to Samuel Beckett in a short poem of the late 1940s, no doubt influenced by this very poem, where the same mood prevails, apart from a caustic shift in the last line:

> I would like my love to die
> and the rain to be raining on the graveyard
> and on me walking the streets
> mourning her who thought she loved me.[16]

8

Famine

In 1997 I was asked by the George Moore Society in Claremorris, County Mayo, to give a lecture to their annual summer school, not this time on Moore (which I had done before) but on the Great Famine. The year 1997 was the 150th anniversary of 'Black '47', according to many the worst year of the Famine that started in 1845 and continued to 1850. I gave the lecture on a stiflingly hot night in August in an upstairs room in a public house on the main street. The room was packed. Mayo is a place where the memories of the Famine are still very strong, it having been one of the worst-afflicted areas during the catastrophe. It is from that time that the saying comes: 'Mayo, God help us!'

I gave the worst lecture of my life, or so it felt to me. My hosts said, no, that it was very challenging, most interesting. My theme was 'Famine and the Mechanics of Hate', and I tried to show that the experience of destitution and hunger can and does lead to hatred: self-hate for being a victim (if such you are), or a survivor, when many others have not lived; hatred of those whom you think (or know) have reduced you to victimage, or afflicted you with the guilt of being alive when so many others have died. As I worked through my explanations, and talked about the various literary texts I had selected, the thought began to dawn on me that here I was, a complacent analyst, advancing my theories of collective memory and how suffering can lead to brutality and rage, speaking like a vainglorious fool (a Gabriel Conroy) to direct descendants of people who had been through what I was now indulging in the luxury of having ideas about. I became deeply ashamed and wanted to be anywhere else other than that room above the pub looking out on the square of Claremorris town. I began to perspire, and I could feel my face slick with sweat.

Famine is a terrifying subject. One hundred and fifty years after the Great Irish Famine I do not think it was an excess of sensitivity or an over-exercised scrupulous conscience that afflicted me with terror and panic that night in Claremorris. I think that, even then, all that time later, it was not possible easily to speak about something so dreadful amongst those whose ancestors knew what the real thing was like: what it felt like to be reduced to utter misery and powerlessness, when you might do anything at all to be able to continue to live. I longed, that night, for silence, to be silent. But I went on; there was no other option.

I suppose it should be said that in the scales of human atrocity the Great Famine does not weigh in as one of the real heavyweights. Since the middle of the nineteenth century there have been appalling dev-astations of inhuman brutality and hatred: genocides, holocausts, mass slaughters, incarcerations of whole peoples, incalculable carnage car-ried out in the name of valour and bravery, extinctions of whole cities in the name of peace and peace-making, legalized killings in so-called liberal societies. By comparison with these (and the atrocities are deliberately not named, in that to do so would dishonour those who are sent to their deaths often through our indifference or slackness of will), an over-insistence on Irish grievance in relation to wrongs done could easily seem not just uninformed but disproportionate, lacking in realism, ignorant, self-obsessed, as Louis MacNeice pointed out in his *Autumn Journal* (1939).

And yet. No other event in Irish history had such devastating effect. It changed the country out of all recognition. George Petrie, in the introduction to his *Collection of the Ancient Music of Ireland*, written in 1855, only five years after the Famine had ended, in trying to describe the change that has come over the Irish countryside because of the disaster, speaks of the terrible silence that has settled on the land: '"The land of song" [Moore's phrase] was no longer tuneful; or, if a human sound met the traveller's ear, it was only that of the feeble and despairing wail for the dead. This awful, unwonted silence, which, during the famine and subsequent years, almost everywhere prevailed . . . gave [Irish people] . . . a [deep] feeling of desolation.'[1]

Silence, the inability to articulate the quality of the distress that has been undergone, is constantly referred to in accounts of the Famine, fictional or actual. The pre-Famine world and that which came into being after the disaster were entirely different realities. Before the

Famine, in spite of Kinsale, Cromwell, the Boyne, the Penal Laws, the starving multitudes of Swift's day, the savage putting down of the United Irish rebellion, there were still the remnants of a Gaelic community. There was song and music. Alongside the poverty, a subsistence scratched from tiny patches of land leased to labourers in lieu of payment for work on the estates of the landlords, there was still in existence a vibrant social and cultural life. The potato, especially the 'lumper' or horse potato, because it cropped so luxuriantly even on poor soil allowed people to feed themselves from very little land, and it meant that any other produce they could cultivate was sold to make up in cash the shortfall in rent not met by their labour. This was a precarious and fragile economic arrangement, and once the potato crop failed there was total disaster in a population that had mushroomed to 8 million, at least doubling in size within a century, because of the seemingly magical nutritive properties of a single crop.

A few grim facts and statistics: in these years, 1845–50, over a million people died from starvation, typhoid, and cholera; another million left Ireland. In the following decades two further million were to leave, fleeing a land they had, many of them, come to believe was cursed. People stopped speaking Irish, opting for bad English. Irish was associated with death, the old ways, the bad times, 'an drochshaol' in Gaelic. It was regarded as unlucky to speak Irish, and it became a badge of disgrace and destitution. What centuries of English policy had not succeeded in doing, the Irish people themselves, as part of their instinct to adapt and survive in a world where Irish was seen to be a sign of defeat, carried out: they stopped speaking their own tongue.

A new Ireland was coming into being—anglophone, watchful, distrustful, suspicious of the English yet sycophantic to them, utterly dismissive of anything that did not yield cash. All that on the one hand, but on the other there were militant nationalism, implacable Irish rage, the Fenians, the murders in the Phoenix Park in 1882, when Chief Secretary Lord Frederick Cavendish was killed, and an Irish revivalist movement. Ireland's 'split little pee', in Joyce's phrase in *Finnegans Wake*, was forming, but the division at the source was the Famine, and along with it the governance and economic structures that had created the circumstances where such a disaster could take place. The Famine remains the decisive event in modern Irish experience, with the possible exception of the Easter Rising. Lady Gregory described it and the loss of the Irish language as the two great landslips in Irish life. She is right about this, save that the one landslide created the other. The hurtling battery of harsh economic reality did not just send people fleeing to the ships at Queenstown and Derry; it also smashed into those secret places in the psyche where language, and one's at-home-ness in it, reside, so that the sooner you left its miseries behind you, the better, even if you had to put up with being mocked because of your brogue for a century to come. And even if you had to struggle with the feeling that perhaps you had no language to speak of worthy of the name.

There has been a (to some degree understandable) tendency amongst Irish historians to resist the traditional interpretation of the Famine as the example, *par excellence*, of the indifferent cruelty of perfidious Albion towards its sister kingdom. This is understandable because there was a desire, amongst revisionist historians, to resist the comfort and assurance to be gained from blame, the satisfaction to be derived from a supposedly righteous anger. It is always very conveni-ent to have something monstrous to accuse someone else of, not least because accusation offers welcome release from the unease of self-scrutiny. Historians wishing to revise the 'England bad–Ireland good' approach to the Famine have emphasized the economic circumstances of the disaster, the importance of the ideology of free-market eco-nomics (whereby it was deemed inadvisable to interfere with the free play of the forces of supply and demand), and the perilous explosion in the numbers of the underclass and the labouring poor, all of which, the revisionists argued, combined to make the catastrophe unavoidable.

It is important to be as dispassionate as possible about the Famine and the structures of authority and economics in which it took place. When the potato blight struck in 1845 it reduced yield by two-thirds. By November it was clear that a major disaster had arrived. A deputation from Young Ireland, a nationalist movement founded by Thomas Davis, and which published the influential newspaper *The Nation*, went in that month to Dublin Castle, seat of authority in Ireland, with a list of demands. The group was headed by Daniel O'Connell, the Liberator, now engaged in a campaign to repeal the Act of Union. They presented their petition which detailed measures that, they argued, the Lord Lieutenant, Lord Heytesbury, should put in place to deal with the crisis. These included the cessation of all food exports, the closure of distilleries (to conserve grain), employment schemes and relief procedures, and the opening of food depots to feed the starving. O'Connell then went to the Mansion House to present the petition in person to Heytesbury, whom he found cold, curt, and monosyllabic. The Lord Lieutenant made a prepared statement, which he read, and gave assurances that the government was most concerned.

The government was a Tory one, headed by Sir Robert Peel (O'Connell supported the liberal Whig opposition, led by Lord John Russell, friend of Thomas Moore and grandfather of the twentieth-century philosopher Bertrand Russell), and Peel saw a political opportunity in the Famine. It could provide him with an impeccable reason for the repeal of the Corn Laws. The Corn Laws imposed a tax on imported grain, thereby inhibiting free trade, very dear to Tory ideology, then as now. So, instead of stopping the export of grain from Ireland, and again constraining the free market, he repealed the Corn Laws and opened up trade in grain, which he and his advisers believed would have the effect of allowing plenty of American corn and meal into Ireland, and indeed Britain, itself suffering the effects of the potato blight, though on nothing like the scale of what was taking place in Ireland.

This is a perfect example of economic ideology going entirely adrift from actuality. The brute fact was that the Irish poor never *bought* any farm produce; they *sold* it to pay that portion of the rent not covered by their physical labour. These rents, often for no more than a strip of land at the edge of a field, the landlords (or their dreaded agents) could set as they pleased, demand being so great, and the market dictating the level up to which rents could be racked. There were no rights to fair rent or security of tenure; rack-renting was normal practice. The Indian meal (or maize) from America was, to a starving tenantry with not a shilling to spare, as unattainable as gold-dust unless it were to be handed out free. Furthermore, to add another twist to the knife, the repeal of the Corn Laws reduced the price of the grain these miserable creatures had to sell, thereby driving them even deeper into want.

Peel did introduce some successful measures. He got the famous Barings Bank to buy, in today's money, something like £25 million worth of grain and set up a commission to distribute it to counter the damage being done by greedy rural hucksters who were creating food monopolies and cartels to inflate prices. The destitute should still, Peel thought, pay for their food wherever possible, and to that end public-works schemes were set up, which built roads into the bogs, created bridges over streams, constructed sea walls, harbours, and piers. Many of these were left unfinished; some of the roads into the bogs were roads to nowhere. It was believed that if money were to become available, through honest work, then food would flow to it, in obedience to the irresistible magnetism of market forces.

However, the public-works schemes were to be financed not just by government money—that would be to fly in the face of the free-market ideology—but jointly by the Treasury and contributions made by the landlords of a given locality. Some landlords and their agents made the subventions, but many either could not or would not put their hands into their own pockets to save a ravaged underclass who were now not just a nuisance but a rebuke. Irish property, it was being said by government, should pay for Irish poverty. Under these circumstances it would be a very attractive proposition to get the peasants off the land so they would no longer be the responsibility of those who owned it.

Government came to the rescue of the landed classes, and in March 1846 legislation was introduced at Westminster whereby landlords could either make contributions to the relief schemes, or assist their tenants in leaving the land and making payment towards the cost of transporting them to America or other shores. Thus a new market opportunity opened up: the lucrative activity of shipping human cargo at very low cost to the new world where there was a demand for cheap labour in the cities. Conditions were mostly vile on these so-called 'coffin ships', and many died on the voyage across the ocean. In *Star of the Sea*, Joseph O'Connor's outstanding 'Famine novel' of 2002, the captain of a ship, in the steerage of which Irish emigrants are crammed, remarks in a diary that he keeps how so many of the overcrowded wretches die, and notices too that there is a greater than usual number of sharks around the ship, a consequence of the many burials at sea.

It is a strange fact of Irish literary history that in the contemporary fiction and prose of the 1840s and 1850s there is very little writing of any force that deals with the actualities of Famine. Apart from one or two notable exceptions, it took over a hundred years for the literary imagination to come to terms with the central catastrophe of modern Irish history. One of the exceptions was the ravaged mind of James Clarence Mangan (1803–49), drug addict, alcoholic, and someone who was mentally unstable and who possibly suffered from a schizoid affective disorder. He was also a poet of genius, and an outstanding, if unruly, translator from Irish, German, and other languages, including Persian.

He made versions of Hafiz, the Persian poet, only to say that they were 'half his'. In an autobiographical sketch he once described his personality as 'Protean', and perhaps it was this vulnerable and unsettled quality that enabled him, unlike so many of his contemporaries, to write about the horror of Famine in a manner that registers profound emotional shock while at the same time retaining artistic control.

Mangan's Famine poems come out of the human suffering caused by the indifference of administrative systems, government ideology, and free-market economics. Peel's bill, which facilitated the removal of the indigent from the land, was enacted in March 1846. The following month Mangan published two devastating poems. 'Siberia' is a keen of despairing indignation at official policy, its cold-heartedness, and uncaring brutality. The metaphor is of ice-locked impotence, useless rage, silence, fear:

> In Siberia's wastes
>   The Ice-wind's breath
> Woundeth like the toothèd steel;
>   Lost Siberia doth reveal
> Only blight and death.[2]

Here, in this Siberia that is Famine Ireland, the exile is adrift from life and meaning in a place of ice and silence. You cannot curse the causer of your torment, the 'Czar', because the tongue in your head is split by the cold:

> Therefore, in those wastes
>   None curse the Czar.
> Each man's tongue is cloven by
>   The North Blast, who heweth nigh
> With sharp scymitar.

The companion piece to this poem, which was first published in the *The Nation* of 18 April, alongside accounts of the numbers of the dead in Limerick and other places, was called 'To the Ingleeze [English] Khafir, Calling Himself Djaun Bool [John Bull] Djenkinson', and it is supposedly written by a personage called 'Meer Djafrit' (Mere Chaff Writ), as if to say that the author is mere chaff, of no account, therefore it is of little import if such as he lives or dies. He and those like him are the husks of the grain that are filling the ships that leave Ireland's harbours. The poem is a scream of visceral hate, with a purity of rage

that reminds one of Ó Bruadair or Ó Rathaille. Rage is certainly
something that Irish poetry does exceptionally well:

> I hate thee, Djaun Bool
> Worse then Marid or Afrit,
> Or corpse-eating ghoul!
> I hate thee like sin
> For thy mop of hair
> Thy snub nose and bald chin
> And thy turkey-cock air.

Mangan himself, it may be said, was a Famine victim. Weakened by his
addictions, he contracted cholera, which reached epidemic propor-
tions during the Famine, and died in the Meath Hospital in Dublin on
20 June 1849. The cause of death was noted as starvation.

These two poems by Mangan show how his mind worked tangen-
tially, how he comes around to writing what he needs to write by
indirection, whether through metaphor or caricature, savage humour,
weird despair. He is perhaps, after Moore, the most significant Irish
poet between Brian Merriman and W. B. Yeats, because the cast of his
personality, the mode of his perception, was such that he was capable
of registering the shocks and brutalities of contemporary history and at
the same time of finding images, fancies, sleights of hand, characters,
rhetoric that answered in their strangeness and indeed extremity the
terrors and humiliations visited on an Ireland that experienced the
indifference of Empire in its time of need. The effect on Mangan's
personality seems to have been devastating, but he was one of those to
whom it is given to know in the core of their being the way things are
in society and in the human spirit at any given time. Mostly such
victims are destroyed by what they know (as indeed Mangan eventually was), but Mangan, fluent poet that he was, and fluid personality,
realized in himself a shifting void of baffled terror that allowed him to
create a language (or languages) for atrocity. It is not for nothing that
he has a poem, supposedly a translation from the Arabic, called 'The
Howling Song of Al-Mohara'.

Mangan's Famine poems appeared in April 1846. The following
month William Carleton began to publish, serially, in the *Dublin
University Magazine*, his flawed Famine masterpiece *The Black Prophet*,
which ran until December. Carleton (1794–1869) was born into an
Irish-speaking Catholic family in Clogher, County Tyrone. At one

point he seemed to have been destined for the priesthood, but he tells us in his autobiography that on his way to the classical schools in Munster he had a nightmare of a ferocious bull (is this Adrian IV's papal bull obscurely surfacing?) which he took as a portent, warning him to change his course. He turned back to Clogher where he resumed his athletic pursuits, attended the hedge school where he also did a bit of teaching, and joined the Ribbonmen, one of the Catholic secret societies that organized agrarian violence and attacked landlords and their agents. In his twenties he left Tyrone, putting his revolutionary ways behind him, and made his way to Dublin to seek fame as a writer. He converted to the Church of Ireland and started writing for the Revd Caesar Otway's *Christian Examiner* sketches and tales based on his own first-hand knowledge of Irish country life (Yeats, in a memorable phrase, called this searing immediacy of Carleton's a 'fiery shorthand'). Carleton evokes a pre-Famine world of wakes, funerals, pilgrimages, hedge schools, faction-fighting, drinking, singing, and dancing; but, while he credits the devotion and piety of the 'peasantry', he is, at the same time, careful to point out the evils of attachment to Rome and its errors, and is eager to drive home the argument that, while the Irish peasant may be attractive in his naivety and innocence, his allegiance to Catholicism makes him infantile and idiotic in a world where it is essential to modernize and leave behind superstition and idolatry, quaint though they may be in retrospect. Carleton is yet another example of the divided mind of the colonized wanting to be the colonial.

By the time he came to write *The Black Prophet*, Carleton had established himself as the most authoritative delineator of Irish country life, capturing, however disparagingly at times, its traits, customs, and its English speech, wild and eloquent with its strange and colourful distortions caused by the continual and only half-repressed presence of Irish. In *The Black Prophet*, based, not on the contemporary catastrophe, but on Carleton's own personal recollections of the earlier Famines of 1817 (the year of *Lallah Rookh*) and 1822, he evokes, as the central character the prophet of the title, the so-called 'prophecy man', a figure who was common in rural Ireland of pre-Famine times. These men, sinister creatures, much feared and respected, wandered the country making prophecies, often foretelling the ruin of England because of its Protestantism, based, they would say (though often in much less decorous terms) on the sexual rapacity of Henry VIII. There would be natural disasters, including famine, God's punishment on those who sinned amongst the indigenous Irish as well as the landed classes; but these apocalyptic events would herald a new dawn of Catholicism and a return to the one true faith of Rome.

The novel is a confused mess. Sprawling, complicated, with a plot full of hidden identities, deceit, boxes of crucial papers stolen away, the story is to be followed only with great difficulty. There are huge and billowing stretches of cloudy rhodomontade, atmospheric descriptions of lowering landscapes, terrible unnatural heat; and moving through all this is the presiding embodiment of catastrophe and doom, the prophecy man, Donnel Dhu, Black Donnel. He, it turns out, is a murderer, and has assumed the role of prophet as a disguise so that he can incriminate the Daltons, an idealized family totally innocent of any wrongdoing. In spite of its shortcomings, however, the novel, with its terrible visions of all-engulfing devastation, the credulous servility of the people to the priests, the treachery and guile, the heartbroken evocations of suffering and death, creates a psychic landscape of nightmarish and obsessive force. The nightmare was Carleton's own.

As he wrote and published his novel, in the second half of 1847, he would be all too aware that, had he stayed in Clogher, he would be going through something very like the horror he evokes. He is not a famine victim because he has left the world that would have exposed him to that fate and chosen instead a life in Dublin, publishing his work in the Unionist and Tory journal the *Dublin University Magazine*, thinking of himself as British. And yet the British church and state, to which he has given his allegiance, fail to take decisive action in the face of Irish distress. Carleton's identification with the institutions of the Union is absolute; therefore the people he describes in his nightmarish book are victims because they have attached themselves to popery, superstition, drink. They are guilty of ineffectuality and so deserve their misery. Driving through the scenes of human suffering and dereliction he creates is an element of hopeless accusation; these people are victims because they have deserved to be. The prose itself is destabilized by self-hate. Carleton cannot help but pity those who are subjected to hunger, but he cannot abide the impulse of that pity. It is as if the things that are closest to him, the things that call forth his love (and Carleton's nature is a loving one), are those very things he has to come to hate.

There is a scene in which the writing seems to come apart before our very eyes as these two impulses, of love and hate, pity and rage,

collide. A woman and her three children are lying dying or dead in a
hovel by the roadside. A Father Hanratty rides past and notices that the
cabin is occupied, which it should not be, the previous occupants
having died of typhoid fever. The priest goes in, and exclaims: 'Great
God, guide and support me in this trying scene!' This is of course
stagey, melodramatic, discomfiting. Carleton perseveres, and tries to
give the reader a Famine interior:

There lay in the woman's eyes—between her hurt and painful eyebrows, over
her shrunken forehead, upon her sharp cheekbones, and along the ridge of her
thin wasted nose—there lay upon her skeleton arms, pointed elbows, and
long-jointed fingers, a frightful expression, at once uniform and varied, that
spoke of gaunt and yellow famine in all its most hideous horrors. Her eyeballs
protruded even to sharpness, and as she glanced about her with a half-
conscious and half-instinctive look, there seemed a fierce demand in her eye
that would have been painful were it not that it was occasionally tamed down
into something mournful and imploring by a recollection of the helpless
beings about her . . . [3]

Carleton goes on to say that she has sunk to a 'mere condition' of
animal life. The writing is incoherent. What lies on this woman's body
is an 'expression' of famine that is, bafflingly, 'uniform and varied'. He
cannot write this scene, he gesticulates at it, trying to rouse emotion,
including his own. Appallingly, the dying woman is dead to his
sympathy. The syntax is unsteady and unstable because his own attitude suffers from the same vacancy as does his prose.

   This critique of this passage is not in any way to demean what Carleton
was trying to do; indeed, the very instability of the writing is testament to
his integrity as an author: he cannot cope with the huge tensions that are
in collision here, and he cannot disguise his failure. In spite of the literary
inadequacy there is a huge honesty at work. The priest, Carleton tells us,
bends down over the woman when he sees she is trying to say something.
He brings his ear near to her mouth and hears her saying one word, very
faintly. The word is 'hunger'. This is not English; it is not possible to say
that noun in English and make anything like normal sense: 'the hunger'
would be possible, or 'we're hungry'. What Carleton is actually thinking
of is the Irish word 'ocras', and it is possible in Irish to use a noun like this,
without article or verb, and it increases the emphasis and urgency. That is
the word Father Hanratty would have heard. The vast majority of those
who perished in the Famine were (often monoglot) Irish-speakers. The

language was a badge of death, subjection, powerlessness. And it was the world from which Carleton had come.

When he published the novel in book form in Belfast in 1847, Carleton dedicated it to Lord John Russell, now Whig prime minister, having succeeded Sir Robert Peel. He is quite direct in the dedication. The book was written, he says, 'to awaken those who legislate for us into something like a humane perception of a calamity that has been almost perennial in this country', pointing out that the famine he is writing about was based on those he had witnessed as a young man. There was little chance that he would succeed in awakening perception that might lead to action. Russell's Whig administration, if anything even more attached to free-market economics than Peel's, stopped the public-works schemes, fearing the creation of a culture of dependency. Russell revised the measure whereby the Treasury matched local money from the landed classes for relief schemes, by introducing a Labour Rate Act, which issued the Treasury co-financing money as loans to the landlords, to be repaid by those who took them out. What this meant was that these grants, which under Peel were financed by the taxpayers of the Union as a whole, were now to be entirely paid for by those holding the land. The Union of Great Britain and Ireland did not exist when it came to Irish distress.

The repeal of the Act of Union was a cause taken up by the aging Daniel O'Connell, and the advanced nationalists of Young Ireland, such as Thomas Davis, John Mitchel (friend and biographer of Mangan), and Charles Gavan Duffy, but after these measures of Russell's Whig government some of the Tory Unionist class also began to think that, as Sir Samuel Ferguson put it, 'the disadvantages of the Imperial connection greatly outweigh any advantages'. Ferguson himself, Tory, Northern Unionist, future president of the Royal Irish Academy, joined a grouping of the landed and establishment interest known as the Protestant Repeal Association. He argued that British government policy, as it was now evolving, would have the effect of 'plebeianizing' the country, of destroying those very people of rank, wealth, and responsibility on whom Ireland would need to depend for leadership. In many ways Ferguson was absolutely correct: the economic policies of the British administration in the Famine years did as much (and perhaps more) to lay waste the status and privilege of the Irish landed Ascendancy as did the land agitations from the late 1850s onwards.

The trigger for this move on Ferguson's part seems to have been a comment in a debate at Westminster during which demands were made for more direct intervention to alleviate the situation in Ireland, where hundreds of thousands were dying, while at the same time ships laden with food produce were leaving Irish harbours for the London, Bristol, and Liverpool markets. In exasperation at the seemingly never-ending pleas for assistance from the Irish, one MP stood up and said, 'if Nigger were not Nigger Irishman would be Nigger'.[4] A racial slur, of course, but the comment, ignorant and mindless as it is, takes us into the vile arena where power converts to oppression and where those who wield authority begin to experience a disgust at those who are subject to them. We are into a place where a mechanics of hatred, driven in part by self-hate, starts to operate. Friedrich Engels, after a visit to Ireland in 1856, wrote to Karl Marx as follows: 'Here one can already observe that the so-called liberty of English citizens is based on the oppression of the colonies', in which he sees Ireland as the exemplar of all colonial oppression.[5] 'Niggers', those black slaves burnt to cinders in the sugar plantations of the West Indies, and the Irish are, at some level, indeed interchangeable.

This perception outraged Ferguson, as we saw, and it also outraged John Mitchel, the firebrand revolutionary and editor of *The Nation*, who was transported to Van Diemen's Land as a felon and rebel. In *The Last Conquest of Ireland (Perhaps)* (1861), written after he had made his escape to America, Mitchel recalls defending indigent people in the Ardara and Glenties area of south Donegal who were being prosecuted for trespass because they gathered seaweed for manure and for food from seashores on the estate of the Marquess of Conyingham. 'Can you', Mitchel asks rhetorically, 'picture in your mind a race of white men reduced to this condition? White men! Yes, of the highest and purest blood and breed of men.'[6] It is conceivable that blacks might be subjected in this way, but white Irish? How can that be? We are in a terrible part of the human spirit here, a logical consequence of the 'cash-nexus' (a phrase Mitchel actually uses), where the only thing that matters is the monetary value attached to things and to people. If a creature is of little value (a black slave, an Irish navvy) it hardly matters what you do with him or her; and if they are a bother and an obstacle, then it is better that they die, as quickly as possible, and in as great a number as may be achieved.

Mitchel's outraged humanity sent him into a Carlylean rage when he contemplated the injustices done to the Irish, but, in a strange and horrific mutation, when he escaped from Van Diemen's Land and made his way to America, he supported the cause of slavery, and in a paper he set up in New York in the 1850s called *The Citizen* he unleashed his racist venom against the 'fat', 'lazy Negroes' of America. He becomes locked in the mechanics of hate. Experience of deprivation and humiliation becomes exorcised by visiting it on others. We act out what has been done to us on a new set of victims. To be Irish is to learn intimately, because you are subjected to them, the methods of contempt and disdain; you then practise these same learnings on those who may be below you, and you also rehearse how it may be possible to treat those who once were over you just as you have been treated. It is, as Thomas Kilroy brilliantly puts it in *Doublecross* (1986), his play for the Field Day Theatre Company, a 'double cross', in which hate, a cross to be carried, creates mirror images of itself to perpetuate its angry insistence, each one begetting the other in a ceaseless cycle of continually renewing rage. Famine had to issue in violence. The Fenians were formed, in Ireland and America in the 1850s, from which grew the Irish Republican Brotherhood; from that came Sinn Féin and the IRA, the Easter Rising, Civil War, the Treaty, and the 'Troubles' of the twentieth century.

Irish life and culture is everywhere impregnated with the consciousness of famine. It surfaces in Lucky's speech in Beckett's *Waiting for Godot* (1954), a whirlwind of confusion and distressed memory: 'the skull the skull the skull the skull in Connemara in spite of the tennis the labours abandoned left unfinished graver still abode of stones in a word I resume alas alas abandoned unfinished the skull the skull in Connemara in spite of the tennis the skull alas the stones...'[7]

The Famine memory is throughout the poetry of Nuala Ní Dhomhnaill, a contemporary poet who writes in Irish, and who remains profoundly in touch with the deepest strata of folklore and myth in Irish literature while at the same time responding to the anxieties that have arisen with materialism, greed, and the never-satisfied need to consume. This is from a poem called 'Dípfríos' ('Deepfreeze'), from *Feis* (1991):

> Treasure trove of household needs, healing well
> of our ancestral hunger which does not increase,
> nor does it disappear. We adore its horn
> of plenty, no limit to its cold streams

> of honey and cream, peaches, apples,
> Irish stew, french fries, rump
> of beef already minced,
> puddings, cakes, and two whole sheep.[8]

But perhaps some of the most haunting memories of Ireland's Great Famine occur in the work of one of the greatest of modern American novelists, Cormac McCarthy, who is, of course, of Irish extraction. In all his fiction there is the keenest delineation of what it is to be ravenously hungry, and with that an almost sensuous satisfaction in describing the pleasures of eating and cooking, and of satisfying the cravings of hunger. But there are also the most horrific accounts of what it is to be driven to eat anything, because it becomes necessary to do so, or because the corruption of deprivation has worked its way into the soul to such an extent that the eating of what is normally forbidden becomes a craving in itself.

In an early novel, *Outer Dark* (1968), a girl in a remote Appalachian outback in the early twentieth century gives birth to a son who has been fathered by her brother. The brother dumps the child, who is then found by a tinker; meanwhile the girl, who has been fooled into thinking that her child is dead, finds out that she has been deceived by the boy's father and sets out to find her baby. Her brother then sets out after her, and the novel tells the tale of their strange adventures in a feral world, where men and women are outside any forms of convention or restraint. It is a place of savagery, appetite, and unremitting hunger and need. At one point the brother, Culla Holme, is rescued from drowning by a small gang of wild rednecks, filthy, violent, menacing. They are sitting around a campfire in the woods, and over the flames a stew of some appalling meat is being cooked. They offer Holme some of this terrible food, and he, in spite of his fierce hunger, cannot swallow the foul mess. The suggestion is there that what they are eating is human flesh, that he has fallen among cannibals. This hint is confirmed at the end of the novel when Holme comes upon the same wild bunch again. They have found and hanged the tinker, and the child, disfigured in some accident, is manhandled amongst them. The gang leader, 'the man', asks Holme to pass him the child, which he does. Holme tells them that his sister would take the child back and look after him, but it is no use. 'The man' has his own intention:

Even the mute one stirred. The man took hold of the child and lifted it up. It was watching the fire. Holme saw the blade wink in the light like a long cat's eye slant and malevolent and a dark smile erupted on the child's throat and went all broken down the front of it. The child made no sound. It hung there with its one eye glazing over like a wet stone and the black blood pumping down its naked belly. The mute one knelt forward. He was drooling and making little whimpering noises in his throat. He knelt with his hands outstretched and his nostrils rimpled delicately. The man handed him the child and he seized it up, looked once at Holme with witless eyes, and buried his moaning face in its throat.[9]

'Rimpled'. Appetite as inhuman craving, total transgression, hunger so extreme and ravenous that it breaks through one of the ultimate human taboos. It is possible, McCarthy is implying, to get to a state where you will eat anything.

Cannibalism is also a theme in McCarthy's apocalyptic novel *The Road* (2006), where a father and son wander through a post-nuclear landscape, seeking bits and scraps to eat, and trying to evade the marauding gangs of human flesh-eaters. The scene is America, cities destroyed, trees blackened, and the landscape turned to dust and mud, an 'ashen scabland'. Father and son make their way through this wasteland, heading towards the sea, scavenging what they can, fearful that what little they have will be taken from them or that they will be slaughtered for food. It is a wasted America, but it is also a landscape of Famine, of the wretches who wander the roads in Carleton's writings, or the famished creatures who haunt Swift's nightmare satires or Lucky's manic ravings; it carries in its implications the memory of Ó Rathaille on the wild and starved roads of west Kerry, houseless and ravenous, so hungry that he is reduced to eating raw dogfish and periwinkle. *The Road* is a deeply Irish book, with a deeply troubled memory-bank of deprivation, just as McCarthy is a profoundly Irish as well as an American writer.

9

New Departures

In 1904, looking back at the Famine, Michael Davitt wrote in *The Fall of Feudalism in Ireland*:

There is possibly no chapter in the wide records of human suffering and wrongs so full of shame...as that which tells us of...a million people—including, presumably, two hundred thousand adult men—lying down to die in a land out of which forty-five millions' worth of food was being exported in one year alone, for rent—the product of their own toil—and making no effort...to assert even the animal's right to existence.[1]

Were these people men at all? Davitt goes on to wonder; how could they have meekly accepted death without protest or insurrection? This is, of course, how the mechanics of historical guilt and its thirst for self-accusation function: you hate your own people, you hate yourself, you hate those who make you hate yourself. Shame deepens into self-disgust, which in its turn begets a craving for the blind satisfactions of rage against those you accuse, including yourself, and this drives the appetite into a longing for submission, alcohol, amnesia.

Davitt was the son of a tenant farmer in County Mayo who grew up in industrial Lancashire in England where he lost his right arm in a cotton mill at the age of 11. He joined the Fenians and was imprisoned for gun-running. In 1878, in America, he and John Devoy, a Fenian resident in the United States, agreed on what they called a New Departure, where the cause of Irish independence was to be linked with the securing of justice for the Irish tenant farmer. They went to France, to seek the agreement of the leadership of the Fenians, the Irish Republican Brotherhood, for this alliance of interests, and met, amongst others, the novelist Charles J. Kickham (1828–82), author of the highly emotive *Knocknagow* (1879), a fierce attack on the heartlessness of the landlord system. Kickham would not hear of any deviation from the pure revolutionary cause. He made use of an ear-trumpet, which, in the course of the conversation, he set aside in a gesture of impatience and intransigence.

Davitt and Devoy, again in France, arranged to meet Charles Stewart Parnell, and with him they had greater success in forging a confederacy. While remaining, it seems, characteristically remote and ambiguously non-committal, Parnell nevertheless gave the two Fenians to understand that in certain circumstances he would not be opposed to physical force to achieve the aim of self-government. Furthermore, though a landlord himself, the conditions for poor tenant farmers in the late 1870s were such that Parnell found himself moving into ever closer accord with the views of the Fenians, which were that Irish land should be for the Irish people, the tenant farmers and the labouring agricultural poor.

What was happening in these years, in fact, was that the whole miserable business of Famine was repeating itself yet again. The potato crop failed between 1877 and 1879; the prices available for farm produce were plummeting (the result, it appears, of American com-petition) in Britain as well as Ireland, which meant that there was less demand for Irish migrant workers on English or Scottish farms (which had been a valuable source of income in Ireland for twenty years or so); impoverished tenants started borrowing from moneylenders or 'gom-been men' at rates they could not afford to repay; and meanwhile, land forsaken by the indigent, or from which they were evicted, was being taken over, as ever, by those who had managed to squirrel money away. A 'new departure' was needed, and this alliance of Fenianism and Parnellite politics gave rise to the Land League and the Land War, with Parnell president of the League. Devoy was able to promise the support of the American Fenians for this movement, which had for objective that the land of Ireland should belong to its people.

The 1880s was a decade of intense political activity and social unrest, as Parnell led a constitutional movement for independence and Home Rule, allied to a campaign for reform of the land system, which made strategic use of tactics that moved at times very close to armed action. At the same time he was brilliantly gearing the Irish Parliamentary Party at Westminster into an effective political machine, one capable of exploiting divisions between British interests at Westminster and precarious electoral majorities there to the benefit of the Irish cause.

The old nationalist diehard Lady Wilde, 'Speranza', mother of Oscar, described Parnell in these years as a 'man of destiny' who was capable of breaking the fetters of Ireland that bound her in submission to England. 'Speranza' (Jane Francesca Elgee) was an exceptional woman who tends to be overshadowed by her shatteringly gifted son, and her controversial and famous husband, the surgeon, archaeologist, and folklorist Sir William Wilde.

Jane Elgee was a nationalist firebrand, sharing the extreme revolutionary views of John Mitchel, who took over as editor of *The Nation* in 1847 when Charles Gavan Duffy was interned. She wrote a pamphlet, *Jacta Alea Est* ('The Die is Cast'), in which she called for war to commence if England did not bring forward fair proposals for an independent Ireland. A great deal of her poetry, for *The Nation* and elsewhere, is in a similar vein, and she wrote an elegy for William Carleton, praising his huge sympathies with the Irish people and his allegiance to them. There is a very late pamphlet of hers, which is held in the Library of Congress in Washington (it appears not to be in the British Library), called *The American Irish*, which is startling in its ferocity. These are the kinds of views that Oscar Fingal O'Flahertie Wills Wilde (the Macpherson shades, tinged with Lady Morgan, continue to lower) grew up with. From internal evidence, this pamphlet, published as an appendix to Horace Wyndham's *Life* of 1951, can be dated to the late 1870s–early 1880s.

In the pamphlet Speranza points out that the Irish in America now number many millions, that they have taken their concept of liberty from the American republican ideal, and that they have retained an affection for the 'old country' which seems to grow stronger for its being an attachment in exile. Lady Wilde even, at one point, imagines an invasion of Ireland by the Irish Americans in order to annex the island to the United States in a federal union. The long attrition between Ireland and her neighbour has exhausted Irish energy and endeavour, but it must cease: 'Other nations have had their seven years war, or thirty years war, but Ireland has carried on an utterly unavailing war of seven hundred years.... Disaffection is not an evil where wrongs exist, it is the lever of progress, but incoherent disaffection only scatters and weakens the energies of a people.'[2]

Lady Wilde goes on in this pamphlet to categorize the English as a stolid people, lacking in imagination, and in this she is echoing the kind of simplistic distinctions made by Matthew Arnold in his Oxford lectures on Celtic literature in 1866: the Celts were dreamy, free of the so-called 'despotism of fact', whereas the Saxons were practical and down to earth, ideal as shopkeepers and bureaucrats. Lady Wilde writes of the 'round, stolid English head, and pale cold eyes . . . a people made for commerce and industry'. This is shallow, of course, and tawdry, but it marks an extremity of nationalist ideology: these are exactly the views fanatic nationalists, of whatever ilk, are drawn to as they try to find justifications for their racial intolerance. The mechanism here is not that far removed from that operating in the mind and feelings of such as John Mitchel and James Clarence Mangan.

What effect such ideas had on her son Oscar is hard to fathom, but they would certainly have had some impact, even in reaction. There is a sense in which Oscar Wilde loved English life and society, and that he revelled in the status he enjoyed in the London demi-monde, becoming an arbiter of taste in all matters relating to fashion, art, culture, and even interior decoration. This avidity for the surface of life, its manners, foibles, snobberies, and affectations, is a source of great delight in his comedies, but there is also, at their heart, a stony, basilisk stare at the emptiness of English society, its complacent frivolity, its self-satisfied indifference. So often, Wilde's acidulous comic wit works because the character making the statement that sends the audience into paroxysms of laughter is utterly heartless and heedless of the fact that what his people say and the way that they say it reveal an utter disregard for anything remotely resembling normal human feeling. These Wilde characters, in plays like *Lady Windermere's Fan* (1891), *A Woman of No Importance* (1893), and *The Importance of Being Earnest* (1895), are charming, monstrous beasts, glittering with wealth and well-being, but without the slightest sense that the chance that has given them the lustrous life they have is just that, pure chance. The plots may hint at dark depths of other kinds of possibility, but these, on the whole, are kept at bay. However, the comic action, in its frantic energy and brilliance, moves restlessly across a surface that has beneath it a vault of terror and sadness, which makes these trivial lives all the more effulgent in their amazing jollity. Wilde's stony eye on English society is an Irish one. What satisfaction he (and his mother too) must have gained from hearing the English audiences howl with delighted laughter at their own shocking triviality and indifference. And pay good money to be ridiculed.

As *The Importance of Being Earnest* opens, we are plunged immediately into a world of shifting meanings and identities as the dialogue crackles with paradox, epigram, and surprising inversions of normality. Ernest Worthing, a JP and man about town, turns out to be not Ernest at all, but actually Jack Worthing, a foundling, left behind in Victoria Station in a handbag; his friend Algernon Moncrieff, similarly positioned on the social scale, claims to have a friend called Bunbury in the country, whom he uses as an excuse to get away from engagements that he wishes not to fulfil. Gwendolen Fairfax, with whom Worthing is in love, has an irrational fixation with the name Ernest, and will marry only a man with that name. Worthing pretends, while in the country, to have a brother called Ernest who lives at the Albany, a prestigious set of bachelor apartments in Piccadilly, London. And so it rattles on. The point of this rigmarole is to show up the farcicality of this world, the conditionality of its personalities. These are beings who express themselves in a line of wit, or a smart comment, or a prejudice breezily aired.

Lady Bracknell, Gwendolen's terrifying mother, is deeply impatient with the continually recurring illness of Bunbury, whose indisposition, and Algernon's visits of mercy to him, disrupt her social arrangements. She says: 'it is high time that Mr Bunbury made up his mind whether he was going to live or to die. This shilly-shallying with the question is absurd. Nor do I in any way approve of the modern sympathy with invalids. . . . Illness of any kind is hardly a thing to be encouraged in others.'[3]

Later in the scene, when Gwendolen and Worthing are alone together, he proposes, and, when he does so, she confesses that she is afraid that he has had little practice in this department of human activity. A little taken aback at this, Worthing declares that he has never loved anyone but her, to which Gwendolen responds: 'Yes, but men often propose for practice. I know my brother Gerald does. All my girlfriends tell me so. What wonderful blue eyes you have, Ernest! They are quite, quite blue. I hope you will always look at me like that, especially when there are other people present.'

During this entire last speech Worthing is on his knees. The phrase 'quite, quite blue' is pure genius, catching, with steely accuracy, the intonation of the English upper classes, with a kind of fascination mixed in with the horror and the mockery. It turns out in the end that Worthing is called Ernest after all, he having been named after his father, General Moncrieff, before he was lost in a handbag at Victoria Station by the sentimental novelist and nanny Miss

Prism; which is just as well, as Gwendolen will not marry anyone other than an Ernest, seeing as she never changes, 'except in my affections'.

The year of the brilliant success of this play on the London stage was also the year of Wilde's disgrace and imprisonment. The tale is well known, but the irony of it never loses its iron horror. It is as if Wilde walks right into the charnel house of misery that society can become for those who openly flout its dictates. One of Wilde's lovers was Lord Alfred Douglas, son of the Marquess of Queensbury; the Marquess defamed Wilde publicly, leaving a card for him at the Albemarle Club inscribed to Oscar Wilde as a 'somdomite' [sic]. Wilde took action against Queensbury for libel, but was torn to pieces in the witness box by the Dublin Unionist Edward Carson, later the architect of the partition that kept Northern Ireland within the United Kingdom. Wilde had sought to engage Carson as his barrister, only to find that his opponent had got to him first. Carson, in cross-examination, brilliantly encouraged Wilde's recklessness and daring, with the result that he was damned out of his own mouth and lost the action against Queensbury. In a separate action he was charged with gross indecency and sentenced to two years' hard labour.

From prison he wrote *De Profundis*, which remained unpublished until after his death. This was a letter to Douglas, an extraordinary document, in which he expresses his deep love for his mother (who died in 1896) and his respect for his father. Of her he says: 'No one knew how deeply I loved and honoured her. Her death was terrible for me. . . . She and my father had bequeathed me a name they had made noble and honoured. . . . in the public history of my own country, in its evolution as a nation. I had disgraced that name eternally. . . . What I suffered then, and still suffer, is not for pen to write or paper to record.' And this even though, as he says, he was once a 'lord of language'.[4]

Wilde goes on to accept the centrality of sorrow as the 'type and test' of all great art, and he has now become a man of sorrow, in disgrace; there are no more masks. There may be, behind joy and laughter, a 'temperament, coarse, hard and callous', but there is nothing behind sorrow other than the thing itself. And this moves him onward to the Christ of the Gospels, the man of sorrows, in the words of Isaiah, who took on his shoulders all our grief and pain. He chose as his brothers, Wilde says, those who 'are dumb with oppression and whose silence is heard only of God'. And lastly, he comes to love, the love of Christ, because in the 'divine order of ideal things eternal love is to be given to what is eternally unworthy. . . . Love is a sacrament that should be taken kneeling', a far cry from the recumbent posture Lady Bracknell finds Worthing in as he proposes to Gwendolen with his 'quite, quite blue' eyes.

What has happened is that Wilde has effectively moved to embrace the Catholicism to which he had always been attracted, the Catholicism of Augustine, as James Joyce pointed out, in which the divine can be reached only 'through that sense of separation and loss called sin'. Declan Kiberd, who quotes this passage from Joyce's essay on Wilde, has sketched, in *Irish Classics* (2000), Wilde's tortuous but, it seems, inevitable progress through suffering to eventual admission into the Catholic church at his death, the faith of the despised peasants of his own country, so greatly loved and admired both by his mother and his father.[5] This is certainly a new kind of departure, a new kind of crossing over.

Other crossings over were taking place at this time, in the political vacuum that opened on the disgrace and death of Parnell, following the split in the Irish Parliamentary Party after his being cited in a divorce petition involving his mistress Katharine O'Shea in 1889. Yeats's first collection of poems was called *The Wanderings of Oisin and Other Poems* (1889), and it introduces an entirely new note into Irish verse, a profound attachment to Irish experience, and a sense that the history and culture of that experience should be decoded and opened out. There is an astonishing freshness in some of these poems, a readiness of temperament, an avid longing to respond to the details of landscape, where place becomes suffused with mood and atmosphere, that is now easily overlooked, distracted, as we tend to be, by the complex harmonics and fluency of Yeats's later majesty. But this is where it all starts:

> Where dips the rocky headland
> Of Sleuth Wood in the lake,
> There lies a sleepy island
> Where flapping herons wake
> The drowsy water-rats. . . .[6]

There was a renewal of the 'Celtic thing' in the 1890s, although it was not as if it had ever really gone away since the time of Macpherson. The Ossianic lays had had a European-wide popularity, and Napoleon is said to have carried the poems with him on his campaigns to lift his spirits. Moore's melodious and melancholy Ireland had remained in vogue for most of the nineteenth century. The French cultural historian Ernest Renan wrote of the poetry of the Celtic races in the 1850s, but the major shift in perception came with Matthew Arnold's lectures on Celtic literature given at Oxford as Professor of Poetry and published in 1867. Arnold's ideas on the impressionistic susceptibility and femininity of the Celt, in contrast with the stolid pragmatism of the Saxon, proved very durable and attractive; he also went so far as to say that the romantic longing and the lyrical beauty of much English poetry came from a Celtic substrate. We are seeing here the tentative formulation of a notion of racial stereotype, where it might become possible to feel that there is a key to what it is to be English, somehow, or German, or Celtic, or Aryan. This longing for some inner code of belonging is obviously the first sign of a modern sense of trouble as to what constitutes who or what you are at all, and it is an impulse that is to have appalling manifestations in populist and deeply compelling racist and tribal fervours. A code of belonging will have the exciting corollary of exclusion and its infinite possibilities for hatred. So that the alluring gentleness of the Celt, as Arnold sees him or her, has, in the mental and emotional simplifications involved in the stereotype, an insidious implication that the Celt is to be easily governed, so pliant is that creature, and that the figure almost ordained for that office of mature responsibility over a wayward but attractive minor is the dull Saxon.

Although the Irish (and the Welsh) were grateful for Arnold's complimentary analysis of a supposedly imaginative temperament, they were, naturally, more than a little resistant to the notion that their racial origin meant that they were subject to an inevitably inferior status, while the old enemy, the English, dull though they were deemed to be in this way of looking at things, held the reins, and therefore the money and the influence. And yet, the stereotype worked its magnetism, even on an advanced nationalist like Wilde's mother, probably because it was difficult to resist the attractions of the Celtic idea as embodying some kind of set of otherworldly values.

Yeats's handling of this thorny issue, with all its political and cultural implications, is most adroit. He does not reject Arnold's compliment; instead, in an essay published in the journal *Cosmopolis* in 1898, he turns it around in a complex, sinewy rhetoric that is also not without humour. While he says that the ideas of Ernest Renan and Arnold have made no difference whatsoever really to those who write about Celtic things with any understanding, nevertheless they should be considered. Otherwise we may, he says, 'go mad', and the enemy of what is truly valuable in Celtic tradition will come along, root out the rose garden, and plant cabbages there instead. We may suspect that Yeats is having fun with the stereotype here, and entertain the notion that the cabbages in questions are Savoys.

Yeats's argument is that (quoting William Blake's disciple, the very English Samuel Palmer), 'excess is the vivifying spirit of the finest art', and that it is the job of the artist to make that excess all the more abundant. Instead of following the Arnold line and saying that English literature gets its pathos and melancholy from a Celtic source, Yeats argues that all real writing gets its force and excess from being 'flooded' with passions and beliefs from ancient worlds. And now comes the Yeats turn: he says that of all the sources of energy that come from ancient times, it is the Celtic, rather than the Finnish or Slavonic or Scandinavian (he omits the classical), that has been 'for centuries close to the main river' of the literature of Europe. He then piles in with a set of Arnoldian illustrations, from Shakespeare, Spenser, Scott, to show the majesty and attractiveness of this source, as he alleges it to be.[7]

This is no argument, of course. It is a new departure on the basis of what evidence he can muster for his absolute conviction that the Celtic source is of European importance, and that an art based on this kind of symbolic system will transform minds and feelings. It is a departure from Arnold, but it is also a departure from the political determinations of Maud Gonne, where poetry and drama (Yeats will shortly co-found what will become the Abbey Theatre) can become an operative means in the actual world, rather than just delectation or entertainment, an alternative to military action and violence.

He was deeply involved with Maud Gonne's political agenda, and kept vacillating about how strong his commitment should be to her extremism. Although no socialist, she was in league with James Connolly, the socialist republican and future central figure of the Easter Rising. She was a key figure in various political and revolutionary movements, involving the IRB (the Fenians), the so-called Wolfe Tone committee (a front for republican activism), and another committee for the celebration of the centenary commemoration of the United Irishmen rebellion of 1798. There was, as seems always to be the case with revolutionary movements, incessant in-fighting and unremitting distrust, with supposed colleagues frequently wondering if those whom they thought allies were in reality in the pay of Dublin

Castle. It was exhausting and frightening for almost everyone, except for those like Frank Hugh O'Donnell (a great enemy of Yeats's) who revelled in conflict and suspicion. Around this time Yeats's friendship with Lady Gregory took root, and on his first trips in the summers of 1897 and 1898 to Coole, her estate near Gort in County Galway, he found her companionship and considerateness a source of healing and peace after the agitations and constant turmoil of the Dublin (and London) arenas of political activism. And it was while staying at Coole in 1897 that the idea for an Irish literary theatre took shape, with Lady Gregory typing up (on a typewriter given to her by Lady Enid Layard, wife of Sir Austen Henry Layard, excavator of Nineveh, and sometime ambassador at Constantinople) the prospectus and the proposal to be circulated to friends and potential supporters.

Meanwhile, the ideas advanced in the essay in *Cosmopolis*, that Celtic mythology and symbolism were deeply attached to the sources of European culture itself, were connected to another new departure that Yeats was seeking to pursue, and this with the enthusiastic support of Maud Gonne. He aimed to establish, on some suitable island in the west of Ireland, an order of Celtic mysteries, devoted to magic, which would become a centre for spiritual and occult leadership in the new world that he, Maud Gonne and his old friend George Russell ('AE') were convinced was about to come into being. This mood of apocalyptic intensity, of something of extraordinary import being imminent in the world, with Ireland as some kind of energy source for a great shift in the nature of being, was to be found in the cultural ferment of the late 1890s in Dublin, and it affects the atmosphere of the poetry of Yeats's *The Wind Among the Reeds* (1899), which takes up the old story of the valley of the black pig, where the enemies of Ireland will be defeated once and for all in a final and violent consummation. This legend, and Yeats's redeployment of it, takes us back to the aisling dream of a liberated Ireland, and the traditional prophecies of the defeat of the foreigner, and gives them a new, theosophical and magical twist.

A rational and comic intellect, which had no patience whatsoever with any of this Madame Blavatsky-type voguish mumbo-jumbo, was George Bernard Shaw, a disciple of Ibsen's realism, and a very unlikely recruit to the cultural nationalism that Yeats and Lady Gregory were seeking to advance for the good of Ireland's soul.

And yet. Shaw, a Dublin Protestant and 'downstart' (his own term), had, by the late 1890s, achieved very significant success on the London stage with a series of plays attacking English middle-class complacency and the social and economic structures, which he believed to be thoroughly rotten, that underlay late Victorian prosperity. Like Wilde, Shaw delighted in using comedy, and the way that it manages its effects—by making circumstance collide with expectation, and by showing character and certainty as subject to change and even whim— to compel his audiences to a fresh appraisal of their most cherished assumptions. They were both upsetters of the English apple-cart. But while what drove Wilde's comedy was a relentless sense of there being a vacuum beneath all the vain frippery, in Shaw there is always a feeling that the issue is, at bottom, a political one, and that his own political views are rooted in a never-diminishing longing for social justice.

Such a mind-set is not one that would easily fit well with the apocalyptic visions of Yeats, but there was a greater degree of common ground between Shaw and Lady Gregory, whose impulses had more than a touch of social reform in their make-up. In any case, by century's end Shaw's interest in the Irish literary theatre movement had been engaged, and he promised he would write a play for it. This was to be one of Shaw's masterpieces, *John Bull's Other Island*. It was, he said, to be 'frightfully modern—no banshees nor leprechauns', and it could have been staged as the inaugural performance of the Abbey Theatre, the home of the National Theatre Society from 27 December 1904.[8] It was not to be: the play was beyond the resources of the fledgling company at this stage, but, on top of that, its merciless stripping away of a romanticism that both the Irish and the English use about themselves and each other had an intellectual temper and a remorseless analytic edge that sorted not at all well with the kind of vision that the Irish National Theatre Society was seeking to create for a new imagining of Ireland. It was not until 1916 that the play was produced at the Abbey, where it had a great success, Shaw's reputation in Ireland being very high at the time because of his unambiguous criticism of British policy after the Easter Rising in that year, in particular the execution of the Easter leaders, among them Patrick Pearse and James Connolly.

The play, like so much Irish writing of these years, works against the stereotypes of English and Irish. Instead of the Irishman being depicted as dreamy and ineffectual, it is the Englishman, Broadbent, who turns out to be the hopeless romantic, susceptible to the cunning charm of the stage-Irishy Haffigan in a brilliant opening scene, mainly because it suits Broadbent to believe in the myth that the Irish are feckless and winning, though a bit too fond of the drink. Larry Doyle, the gimlet-eyed Irishman, knows how poisonous all this seemingly attractive guff about the soft and easy Irish can be, and hates the way in which the Irish have subjected themselves to this captivating simplicity and nonsense. As he works himself up into a rage of despair at the useless-ness of so much that goes on in Ireland, Doyle himself starts to acknowledge the terrible reality that the stereotype may indeed be based upon: '... the dreaming! the torturing, heart-scalding, never-sat-isfying dreaming, dreaming, dreaming.... An Irishman's imagination never lets him alone, never convinces him, never satisfies him; but it makes him that he cant face reality.... If you want to interest him in Ireland youve got to call the unfortunate island Kathleen ni Hoolihan and pretend she's a little old woman. It saves thinking. It saves work-ing. It saves everything except imagination....'[9]

This is romantic Ireland as a torment, a place from which Doyle is glad to have escaped. However, they are returning; there is an undertaking afoot, involving English investment and Broadbent's engineering and business skills, which are formidable, in spite of his sentimental and romantic impulses. As the play proceeds we see Broadbent conforming to type, with his English pragmatism sweeping all before him in Roscullen in Ireland, including Nora, Doyle's child-hood sweetheart, a seat at Westminster, and a controlling interest in the land and property which will enable him to build a golf links and a set of tourist attractions, a polytechnic, gymnasium, and so forth, a veritable garden city with every amenity and convenience.

Doyle, the critical Irish intelligence, subjects himself in the end to the practical energies of his English business partner, energies to a great degree sustained by a sentimental attachment to a country Broadbent has not come close to understanding. Doyle understands it only too well, but is cynically resigned to a role that is dictated by progress and profit, just as Broadbent cannot escape the imperatives of capital. Each of them, at last, is compelled by circumstance and necessity. There is one voice in the play which rises beyond the traps of stereotype, money, sentiment, self-delusion, and hatred based on old oppositions, and that is the strange voice of Keegan, a kind of semi-Buddhist defrocked Catholic priest, who sums up the two of them, 'the Eng-lishman, so clever in [his] foolishness, [the] Irishman, so foolish in his cleverness', helplessly admitting that he cannot reject either of them. As the play ends, and as the two partners go off to look over the site of a new hotel, there is a sombre sense that the whole activity of seeking to differentiate between the two cultures is a tiresome and ultimately futile business, when the real issues are those of money and what its power can do to those who have it and those who are without it. Shaw knew his Marx.

In May 1899 the Irish Literary Theatre (known in other formulations as the Irish National Theatre Society, eventually evolving into the Abbey in 1904) staged Yeats's *Countess Cathleen*, along with Edward Martyn's *The Heather Field*. At the end of the week the Dublin *Daily Express* gave a dinner in honour of the new theatrical movement at the Shelbourne Hotel. Yeats spoke, as did many others, Yeats saying that this new theatrical movement had as its aim the spiritualization of the patriotism and drama of Ireland, declaring, in other words, a desire to make a theatre that would transcend the internecine strife and crossed purposes of militant action. Another speaker that night was the novelist and mythographer Standish James O'Grady (1846–1928). O'Grady's influence in shaping the view of the mythological materials of Ireland, in his tales of Cú Chulainn, and in his 'bardic' history of Ireland, can scarcely be exaggerated. That night in the Shelbourne he had had, according to Yeats's account, quite a lot to drink when he stood up to speak in a 'low, penetrating voice', positioning himself between two tables, 'touching one or the other for support'. What he had to say went deep with Yeats, exciting him, but also confirming his worst fears that he would lose Maud Gonne to the active struggle. O'Grady said, referring to the theatre movement and its literary origins, that 'we have now a literary movement, it is not very important; it will be followed by a political movement, that will not be very important; then must come a military movement, that will be very important indeed'.[10]

By the time Shaw's *John Bull's Other Island* was staged in London in 1904, the military movement was gathering momentum. Maud Gonne married Major John MacBride in February 1903, converting to Catholicism to do so, much to Yeats's horror, he seeing it as a descent in status and honour on her part. MacBride had fought with the Boers in the Boer War, and was a member of the IRB (the Irish Republican Brotherhood, antecedent of the IRA). The honeymoon in the south of Spain was partly spent, it is said, on reconnoitring possible assassination strategies and tactics for a forthcoming visit by King Edward VII to

Gibraltar; and a photograph exists of the wedded couple, seated at a table on which is displayed various weaponry. At around this time the young Patrick Pearse had taken over the editorship of the journal of the Gaelic League, *An Claidheamh Soluis* ('The Sword of Light'). In the coming years Pearse was to move more and more towards military action, joining the IRB, eventually becoming commandant-general of Óglaigh na hÉireann, the republican forces that occupied the GPO during the Easter Rising, at the outset of which he proclaimed the institution of an Irish Republic. The IRB had always maintained that its constitution of 1873 had asserted its authority to be the lawful government of the island of Ireland, and Pearse's proclamation was intended to be in continuance of that assertion and legitimacy.

Pearse's personal identification of his own destiny with that of his country was absolute, and he gave it expression in a memorable poem written in the year before his death by execution in Kilmainham Gaol after he and the rebels surrendered to the British in 1916. In this piece he recalls the Hag of Beare and Cú Chulainn:

> I am Ireland:
> I am older than the Old Woman of Beare.
> Great my glory:
> I that bore Cuchulainn the valiant.
> Great my shame:
> My own children that sold their mother.
> I am Ireland:
> I am lonelier than the Old Woman of Beare.[11]

10

The West's Awake

In 1908 Patrick Pearse founded St Enda's, a high school for boys, in Ranelagh in the Dublin suburbs. It was a bilingual school, run on very progressive lines, and Pearse's correspondence with parents, and the painstaking attention he gave to everything relating to the holistic development of his pupils, reveal him to have been an outstanding headmaster and a radical educational reformer. When the school moved to Rathfarnham in 1910 Pearse laid the gardens out in such a way as to give free play to the imagination of the boys, and they were encouraged to imitate and re-enact the heroic stories of Fionn and Cú Chulainn in the shrubberies and the little grottoes he had constructed for them. They were inculcated with what he believed were the ancient Gaelic virtues of honour, courage, and always carrying out what they had said they would do. Summer pageants at Ranelagh and at Rathfarnham were based on the theme of Cú Chulainn's or Fionn's boyhood deeds, taken from the sagas.

He also had built for himself, and for the boys from the school whom he hoped to take with him, a cottage near Ros Muc in the Connemara Gaeltacht. There the pupils would improve their Irish and experience at first hand what greatly mattered to Pearse: Irish Gaelic life, and the language which had a literary and cultural history that extended back close on two thousand years.

For Pearse and for many progressive Irish people at the turn of the century the Irish language was a badge of new confidence, a symbol of a determination to create an Ireland free from the yoke of Britain, ready to assume a position amongst the nations of Europe. Arthur Griffith's Sinn Féin (which means 'Our Selves') looked, initially, to Hungary as an example of a country which had achieved equal status with Austria in the Austro-Hungarian Empire; this was what Griffith argued Ireland should achieve vis-à-vis Britain, although Sinn Féin moved to a more separatist position as time went by, leading to the insurrection of 1916. The Irish language (as had been the case with Hungarian) was an animating force in this freshening impulse towards self-government and self-respect that began to make its presence felt in Ireland. The Gaelic League (Conradh na Gaeilge), founded in 1893 by Douglas Hyde and others, was, by 1900, a hugely popular movement with an ever-expanding membership. This was drawn predominantly (though far from exclusively: there were some Unionist members, in particular the notable editor of Gaelic verse Rose Maud Young from Galgorm outside Ballymena, County Antrim) from the urban Catholic middle classes. It was, in effect, a mass movement, with thousands of men and women enrolling in Gaelic classes in the cities and towns, then spending part of their summers in the Gaeltachts of the west of Ireland, in Ballingeary, west Cork, Ros Muc in Connemara, and Gortahork or Glencolumcille in County Donegal. Their idealism about the language and the cultural history of Ireland to which it gave access fused in their minds with the landscape and the community of what were desolate and beautiful places, where people could still sing the ancient sean-nós songs, and recite tales of Fionn or Cú Chulainn. The west had come awake once more in their minds and hearts. Added to this popular movement and strengthening it was the impetus gained from the revival in literature in English that was now in full swing, with Yeats, Lady Gregory, and Synge drawing the attention of the anglophone world of culture and ideas to the new writing that was coming from Ireland in poetry, prose, and drama. Central to this new literature and to the ideals of the Gaelic League was the west of Ireland, as a locale of ancient beauty, legend, folklore, magic. Yeats and his friend AE considered the west as a realm still alive to the vital energies of the world, energies to which they thought to gain access by ritual and symbolic invocations. There was discussion of the establishment of an order of Celtic Mysteries, along the lines of the Order of the Golden Dawn, something Maud Gonne interested herself in as well as her more revolutionary activities. Knocknarea, Ben Bulben, Nephin, Errigal, Mount Brandon, the Blaskets, the Aran Islands: these places, and many others, began to recover the otherworldly and numinous associations they already had in Gaelic literature and folklore in the writings of the poets and scholars of the literary and cultural revival of the late nineteenth and early twentieth centuries. They had begun to be important places for a newly revitalized culture.

In December 1896 John Millington Synge, then aged 25, met W. B. Yeats in Paris. Synge was in Paris trying out his craft as a writer, studying Breton language and culture, and attending the lectures at the Sorbonne of Henri d'Arbois de Jubanville on Old Irish tales and sagas. Yeats's advice, as Yeats recalled it in his Olympian way, was that Synge should go to Aran, and give expression to a life there that had never found expression. Yeats was not long back from the islands himself, where he found himself frustrated by his lack of knowledge of the Irish language. Synge had studied Irish at Trinity College (where the language was taught in the divinity school, so that its graduates could, if ordained, preach in Irish to their flock), and his notebooks reveal a scholarly interest in Gaelic literature and a sustained attempt at mastering its earlier phases.

Synge did go to Aran, but not until May 1898, having, the year before, suffered the first attack of the Hodgkin's disease that was to kill him. Before coming back to Ireland, and before he settled in Paris, Synge had travelled widely in Europe, often playing the fiddle (as Goldsmith had done in the eighteenth century) for the people with whom he stayed. Synge was a kind of anthropologist, an enquirer into culture and its meanings, and into how its specifics reflected the attitudes and mores of the people and communities who created it. He brought this same inquisitive mind (Yeats describes him as 'that enquiring man',[1] a steady and incisive appraisal of the man's character and temperament) to the Aran Islands, where he visited on five occasions and which had a profound effect on his mind and the approach he took to his art.

The houses on Inishmaan, where he spent the greatest part of the eighteen weeks he lived on the islands, were tiny, so that Synge would have been in very close contact with the people amongst whom he boarded. He studied their language and their customs, with the result that his knowledge of Irish greatly deepened, as did his understanding of the relationship between the spoken English of the west and of rural Ireland in general, and the grammar and syntax of Irish, the linguistic underlay for those varieties of Hiberno-English. The tension that existed between these two linguistic forms created opportunities for speech of great vitality and rhetorical energy (qualities of Gaelic oral culture in any case), a potential he released in his own dramatic work.

Synge came to love the dynamic and declarative eloquence of the island people, their dignity, their instinct for formality and respect, their mischievousness and Rabelaisian humour. He admired their physical courage, their sense of the preordained nature of life, of its being useless to complain too much about anything, given the frailty and brevity of human life, how it hangs by the slenderest threads of fate. All this is analysed and set forth in his *The Aran Islands* (1907), a classic anthropological study, which nonetheless took six years to find a publisher.

Synge travelled throughout a good deal of the west of Ireland and Wicklow (where he had spent much time in his childhood), writing descriptive sketches of the places he visited for the *Manchester Guardian*, which were illustrated by Jack Yeats, the painter brother of the poet. This immersion in the west, and in the Irish countryside in general, was quite different in nature from the search for mystical and symbolic forms that animated writers and artists such as Yeats and Russell. Here was a realist for whom the actual had in it enough mystery as it was, without seeking in it symbols of anything else. Synge's realism, his attention to the ways things are, was so intense as to make the ordinary deeply strange, and often terrifying in its ferocity. The openness he brought to experience, and which the Aran people recognized, admired, and liked in him, makes his work startling in its alertness, utterly surprising in its capacity to catch the shock of events begetting circumstance according to the laws of their own dynamics. He can, with a weird accuracy, capture the frightening shifts from humour to violence, tedium to sheer horror, that happen in life, as only dramatists of the first rank can do.

The Aran Islands was the place where Synge set himself to school to learn about its way of life, but also to learn about himself. His study of the people with whom he stayed became also an enquiry into the ways in which he might read experience. Life on these islands was harsh (he was often asked by the islanders if he had ever seen anywhere poorer than where they lived), and highly formalized because of the utter predominance of the family as an institution. And yet perhaps because of the strict rigour of this life and its emotional and physical demands, there were frequent outbursts of extraordinary hilarity and/or abuse, sometimes at his expense. One such moment occurs after the men get some twenty screaming pigs into the curraghs for picking up by a jobber on Inishmaan. The animals howl with fear, their mouths foaming, as they try to tear at each other with their teeth. Their legs have to be bound with waistcoats to stop them from holing the canvas of the boats with their feet. All this terror creates huge excitement amongst the women on shore. When the men get the pigs on board the curraghs, Synge is left on the shore with the women, who, in their agitated state, crowd around him and start jeering at him because he is not married, which they consider a comical and ridiculous state for someone his age (he would have been around 28 at this time): 'A dozen screamed at a time, and so rapidly that I could not understand all they were saying, yet I was able to make out that they were taking advantage of the absence of their husbands to give me the full volume of their contempt. Some little boys who were listening threw themselves down, writhing with laughter among the seaweed, and the young girls grew red with embarrassment and stared down into the surf.'[2]

As well as revealing much about the culture of Aran life (female dismissal of what appears to be a useless male, the importance of family and reproduction, the suddenness and unpredictability of collective feeling: all matter that gets into his plays), this episode also reveals Synge's approach to his material. There is an absolute clarity to the scene as he describes it, and an unflinching faithfulness to the actualities of behaviour, including the wildness and savagery of the Aran women as they enjoy themselves hugely in the absence of their husbands by letting themselves rip at someone whom they would see and talk about as he mooched around the island with his notebook and his camera, apparently doing nothing, a wastrel of his class. In fact it is his photographs that alter this very situation: he sits down on the slip and takes out his wallet of pictures, and in an instant he has the whole crowd clambering around him, restored immediately to their settled mood.

Synge's first play for the Irish National Theatre Society was produced at the Molesworth Hall in 1903. *In the Shadow of the Glen*, though set in Wicklow, was based on a story told him by the Inishmaan *seanchaí*, or storyteller, Pat Dirane, about events that befell him while travelling on foot on the mainland. He came upon a house deep in the country and, seeing as it was raining hard and very late at night, he stopped to get some shelter and perhaps food. He found that the man of the house, an aged person in comparison to his young wife, has died and is laid out on the table. She goes out to tell the neighbours, she says, but when she does the corpse sits up and tells Pat that his young wife is up to all sorts of tricks, including adultery, and this is his way to catch her out. The play diverges from the story at this point, Synge introducing a shocking detail which outraged audiences, when the girl goes outside to whistle for her lover who comes down from the mountain. There is some fierce comedy when the old man startles the lovers by rising up. The young man whom the girl loves fails in courage and will not stand up to her husband, but the Pat Dirane character, here a tramp, offers to take her with him on the roads, leaving behind them, in the shadow of the glen, the old man and the gutless adulterer, who turn to the drink as soon as the tramp leaves with the young wife. The tramp's evocation of the itinerant life is full of poetry and romance: 'It's fine songs you'll be hearing when the sun goes up, and there'll be no old fellow wheezing, the like of a sick sheep, close to your ear.'[3]

'The like of'—one of Synge's favourite phrases—is used continually in his plays. It is a direct translation of a very common Gaelic idiom—*cosúil le*—and one much used in Irish English (or Hiberno-English, as it has come to be called). The 'likes of him', 'it's like I'm saying', and so on—this phraseology surfaces all the time, and connects to a very deep preoccupation in Synge as a writer: what resemblance is there between the world figured on the stage and the actuality of the life he, Synge, is immersed in? The concern with 'likeness' and the truth of what may be depicted on the stage is part of the enquiry that drives Synge's dramatic art. What sort of a likeness is he creating of Ireland, of the west?

The nationalists hated Synge's first play. What sort of a likeness of Ireland and of the west was this? Arthur Griffith savaged it; Maud Gonne thought it was 'horrid' (though she had not read it).[4] This was a country of adulterers, young wives going off with tramps, drunkenness to escape from dreariness, enforced and loveless marriages, cruelty (the aged husband shows his wife the door, which is when the tramp comes in with his offer). Such a world as this bore no likeness (Griffith asserted) to the true nature of rural Ireland, with (it was argued) its innate heroism, chastity, moderation. To show such an Ireland as Synge's was an insult to the Irish people, and only to be expected from someone of Synge's class and religion. Synge was able to point out that the play was based on a true story told to him by a man of Aran; he could also have argued that the theme of this play is not far from the critique of Irish society made by Brian Merriman in *Cúirt an*

Mheán Oíche ('The Midnight Court') in 1780, sharing in some of the wild gaiety of Merriman's attack on inflexible social attitudes and marriages of financial convenience.

Synge's next play gave the Irish theatre movement its first classic. This was *Riders to the Sea*, set on one of the Aran Islands, and based on events that occurred during Synge's stays on Inishmaan in 1900 and 1901. It was staged at the Molesworth Hall in February 1904: the Abbey itself would not open its doors until December of that year. *In the Shadow of the Glen* envisions a pagan release from the hidebound lives in the glen by taking to the roads, whereas *Riders to the Sea* creates an iron Sophoclean world of fate, where human action is futile in a world of harsh doom and material and financial absolutes.

The play is a masterpiece of concentration and structure. Maurya is awaiting news of her son Michael, who has not returned from a fishing trip he undertook alone. However, a body has been washed up in Donegal a hundred or so miles away, and a shirt and a stocking from this body has been sent to Aran: the play focuses intently on such particulars throughout, making of them a desolate human poetry. Nora, one of the daughters of the house, carries this bundle into the house as she enters at the start of the play. We are in the living room of a tiny cottage, with a hearth, a few sticks of furniture, a loft above the fireplace. Against the wall are plain boards ready for Michael's coffin. Nora half-closes the door, but suddenly it is blown wide open by a surge of Atlantic wind, establishing immediately the frailty of this life lived in a tiny dwelling beaten by the oceanic gales, and where boats are smashed to pieces by terrible seas, and where men are continually being drowned, so that the islanders do not learn to swim, because this would only prolong the process of drowning. Maurya, in her dire and moving dirge and keen later in the play, tells the audience that she has lost her husband, her husband's father, and her six sons to the sea: eight men in all: 'There does be a power of young men floating round in the sea', she says,[5] a horrific phrase, hovering on the edge of farce, as with the blind Gloucester in Shakespeare's *King Lear*, who thinks he is throwing himself off Dover cliffs to his death when in fact he is, through the good offices of his son who is trying to save him from despair, only pitching himself forward onto the solid ground before him.

The play brings before us the drowning of her last son, Bartley, who will be buried in the boards for Michael's coffin. Michael will be laid to rest in Donegal. Fate cannot be averted, and the market too is inexorable. Maurya's first words, when she enters and sees Cathleen, her other daughter, hiding the bundle containing Michael's clothes in the turf-loft above the fire are concerned with unnecessary expense. She thinks her daughter is getting more fuel for the fire: 'Isn't it turf enough you have for this day and evening?', a line emphasizing the harshness and parsimony of the life on Aran, very far removed from the idealizations of nationalists, or the dreams of the occultist Celts.[6]

Cathleen tells her mother that she needs the extra turf she pulls down as she hides the bundle to make sure the bread is baked for her brother Bartley before he crosses over to the mainland to sell the red mare and the grey pony. Continually throughout this play, and in general in Synge's writing, there is an intense use of the definite article, advancing the particular into a more prominent position than would be normal: 'the red mare', 'the black cliffs', 'the half of a red sail'. It is as if Synge wants to bring into intensely clear focus the things of life to emphasize our fellowship with them, but also their pressure on the nature of our fated existence.

The bread for the journey, in a kind of bleak parody of the *viaticum*, the eucharist for the dying, leads to an acrimonious discussion as to whether Bartley should make the boat trip to Connemara with the wind rising up from the north-east, a bad sign. But in this strict and exiguous economy Bartley has to go to the market where he will get a good price for the horses: it is not just fate and chance and the sea that rule these lives, it is money too, and the shortness of it. Nothing prevails against the bleak laws of this universe; neither the priest, nor blessings, nor the family. Maurya is so preoccupied with the danger her last son is submitting himself to that she does not bless him as he goes out the door, and the sisters forget to give him the bread they have baked. Again there is a deliberate evocation of a failure in the eucharist and in the blessing, emphasizing the (to Synge) ineffectuality of such rituals against the harsh actualities of existence.

In a futile attempt to put right her omissions Maurya goes down to 'the spring well' (a hopefully auspicious but, in the end, doomed site) to bless her son and give him the bread as he rides past, but instead this ritual act is once again aborted by the terror of what she sees, which is, as she tells her daughters, 'the fearfulest thing any person has seen, since the day Bride Dara seen the dead man with the child in his arms'. What could be worse than such a sight? She saw the riders to the sea, not *a* rider; she saw Bartley on the red mare (red is the colour of the other-world, of the sídhe, the fairies, indicating he is not long for this life) and behind him his dead brother Michael, on the grey pony, with new shoes on his feet. Bartley is lost to the sea even before he sets sail. When his body is carried in on a plank with a bit of sail over it, one of the women who come in tells Cathleen that the grey pony (ridden, we now know, by the ghost of Michael) knocked him into the sea, and 'he was washed out where there is a great surf on the white rocks', the ominous surf that has been mentioned already.

While the critics were lukewarm about this play in 1904, the audiences loved it, and on 26 February there was total silence when the final curtain fell, the audience moved and shocked beyond applause.

Audiences hated *The Playboy of the Western World* when it was staged at the Abbey three years later in January 1907. There were riots in the theatre, because, once again, Synge used his dramatic and linguistic powers to confront reality, and render it in scenes, transactions, inter-changes that focus on the way things really are in the west, not what his audience, many of whom were motivated by the pieties of nationalism and the church, would like them to be. The play is set in County Mayo; the playboy, Christy Mahon, is on the run from his native Kerry, where he has left his father for dead. The Mayo people are thrilled by the thought that they have amongst them a killer, and even better, a killer of his father. They love the idea of lawlessness and wildness. They are drunks and shiftless, and take easily to betrayal when the danger presents itself that they might get into trouble for harbouring a murderer. They are priest-ridden, hypocritical, and capable of extreme violence themselves, when they think it is safe for them to inflict it. At one point, towards the end of the play, when they have tied up Christy, they try to torture him with a sod of turf they have reddened with the bellows, except that Christy wheels round on the floor and bites his torturer's leg. This is the kind of world, comic, strange, utterly violent, that Synge brings to the Abbey in 1907. No wonder there were riots.

It seemed to many Sinn Féin adherents (and others) that Synge had gone out of his way to offer gratuitous insults to the people of the west, the people whom he was supposedly to revere. Seamus Deane, the Irish critic and writer, once said in a seminar at Coleraine, which I chaired, that Synge had, in effect, portrayed the Mayo people as (this was the word he used) 'morons'. In Deane's mind, in spite of the artistry of the play, some kind of slur had been involved, and, in his case, not forgotten.

The Mayo people are keen to have a hero amongst them, and heroism is one of the themes that Synge opens up in this play. Another major one is sex. There is an attraction to violence when it is used against an oppressive force, and Christy's father, Old Mahon (punning on St Paul's old man, who has to be replaced by the new Christ-man in his theology of resurrection and renewal, except that Christy Mahon is a version of a savage Christ), has kept his son in mute, indeed moronic, subjection to his towering will and ferocity.

After rising up against him and, as he thinks, killing his father with a blow to the head with a loy, Christy flees north into the wilds of Mayo. The girls, especially, go crazy for Christy in this dysfunctional community, and Pegeen Mike, the local beauty, is smitten. However, as Synge makes clear, it is all very well to idealize a killer as long as the killing remains in the realm of storytelling (and every time Christy tells the tale it amplifies and grows more exciting), it is quite another thing to have to confront the reality of blood and violence and their consequences in law. Synge here is putting his finger on a very real moral dilemma: Sinn Féin, and the Fenian tradition of armed resistance to British authority which it revered, was prepared to resort to physical force to achieve independence from the old oppression, as they saw it, imposed on Ireland. There was a martyrology of great heroes who had given their lives for Ireland, for Cathleen Ni Houlihan; and there were the stories of valour and courage and undaunted resolve, featuring Robert Emmet, Wolfe Tone, and many others. Synge's play is raising the very uncomfortable question as to how heroism and killing can be accommodated in the human dimensions of actual society: what do these forces let loose? And we see in this play that what they can easily let loose is yet more violence and brutality. Pegeen says at the end of the play that 'there's a great gap between a gallows [brave] story and a dirty deed', and to the men of the village she says, of Christy, the man she has fallen for, 'take him from this, or the lot of us will be likely put on trial for his deed today'.[7] We, she says, will take the rap for what he has done, we will all be implicated, views that would be and were expressed on the streets of Dublin in 1916, nine years later, when the armed struggle once more broke out under the leadership of Pearse.

The sexual dimension in this play is complex. There are the passionate speeches Christy now finds himself eloquent enough to make to Pegeen, so expanded has his character become in the new role of heroic parricide, in speeches, incidentally, modelled on the love poetry collected by Douglas Hyde in his *Love Songs of Connacht*. But these are rhapsodic, if beautiful, set pieces, which ravish Pegeen's sensibility. Much more sinister, even strange, is the playing with sexual identity that is a powerful strand in the disturbing weave of the play. Christy plays at being the 'boy', the 'boyo', but he also plays into other fields. At the opening of Act Two Christy is on his own on stage, looking at himself in a mirror, cleaning a girl's boots, and he says that he thinks that he has begun to change physically; his skin, it seems, has started to grow soft. Now the girls arrive, bearing gifts, but Christy hides, still terrified of their actuality. One of the girls sees his boots, and wonders if the encrustations on them are his father's blood. Another pulls one of the boots on. This theme of cross-dressing, hinted at here, comes back at the end of the play with a vengeance when this girl, Sara, and the Widow Quin, dress Christy up in one of Sara's petticoats so he may escape the crowd who now want to hang him. There is a great deal of 'shifting' about, of playing with identity, sexual and otherwise. Of Pegeen, Sara says, 'her like does often change'. Again, notice the 'like' locution: what is it to be the like of Pegeen, and what are the audience to make of whatever likeness of her was being presented to them on the stage in 1907?

What sort of a west of Ireland was this? To nationalists and to Sinn Féin it was disgusting, so that when Christy says that he would not give Pegeen for a 'drift of chosen females, standing in their shifts itself', there had been so much shifting about and playing around with what people are and what they are like (and what they are not like) that the audience would have understood the pun.

This was a theatre of relentless enquiry, to use again Yeats's word, from 'In Memory of Major Robert Gregory' in *The Wild Swans at Coole* (1919), describing Synge who, Yeats continues, 'dying chose the living world for text'. Synge did not celebrate the west; he analysed it, subjected it to a cold appraisal, while at the same time delighting in its vigour and strangeness, making it a scene of universal human interplay. By 1909 he was dead.

Yeats advised Synge to go to Aran, but the consequences of that advice were to be as significant for himself as they were for Synge. The younger, 'dying' man became for Yeats an example of fearlessly facing the complex nature of reality. The world that Synge created in his plays was not just a portrait of a colourful Ireland and its romantic west; it was much more than that, a rendering of an entire vision that was as much an expression of Synge's personality, his intelligence, his uniquely questioning nature, even his inhumanity with a touch of a brutal streak, as it was some kind of record of an actuality. The personal became deeply implicated in the way in which perception was registered, and in the ways in which shifts of perception as between different points of view were realized. What this meant was that Synge's drama hit a depth and an authority hitherto unrealized in Irish writing; and his example showed Yeats how it might be possible to combine the urgency and rawness of the personal with his many other concerns and preoccupations as an artist and as a man.

Yeats had an ideal of Irish culture, a sustained conviction that it gave access to energies and potential that led the artist back to some of the most ancient fountainheads of European life and thought, and even into a connection with the nature of being itself. He complicated this conviction with occult learning, and researches into psychic realms, the study of magic and its surviving rituals, all of which he linked to Ireland and to that part of it where he grew up, the west, attributing to some of the old women interviewed by Lady Gregory and himself in County Galway knowledge equivalent to cabbalistic insight.

Yeats was also, of course, a committed nationalist, dedicated to the cause of Irish independence (something one could not say about Synge, whose attachment to such things would be at least deeply qualified), and he had, inspired as much by Maud Gonne as the old Fenian John O'Leary, committed himself to the furtherance of a whole set of patriotic objectives that he hoped, as did Lady Gregory, would enhance the quality and dignity of Irish experience. Chief amongst these was the Abbey Theatre, scene of Synge's (and his) rejection in 1907.

Yeats's passions, commitments, and disappointments in the first decade of the twentieth century were part of a life that was full of contradiction. If there had ever been a superficial notion that Ireland and the west offered a simple and satisfying escape from the growling traffic of modern human interaction, then the controversies and angers that he had to deal with after the end of the 1890s cured him of any hope of such consolations. The reaction to Synge, and Synge's own responses to how he was received, taught Yeats a new toughness and resolve, a fierce and cold energy, which enabled him to bring his life and his art into much closer synthesis than ever before. Yet he never lost the 'fanatic heart', as he would later call it in 'Remorse for Intemperate Speech', saying he carried it from his 'mother's womb'.[8] Part of his intransigence and loyalty was a continued adherence to the west of Ireland and its people, amongst whom he counted himself.

The collection *Responsibilities* (1914) reveals a new clarity of focus as well as complexity, where personal, political, and civic issues are rammed together in a strong and harsh cadence and syntax. Joseph Hone, reviewing the volume for the *New Statesman* in April 1915, identified this quality and its debt to Synge: 'It may be that Synge saved Mr Yeats for Ireland when he suggested that poets should use the whole of their personal life for material if again they should be read by strong men and thieves and deacons, and not by little cliques only.'[9] The volume contains an epigram on those who hated the *Playboy* as fierce as anything in Ben Jonson (another exemplar behind this collection), or the Roman poet Martial. The craven sentimentalists, cleaving to pietistic notions of Ireland and the west, are like eunuchs running through hell to stare at the new arrival, who is Don Juan. These terrified, cowed creatures 'rail and sweat | Staring upon his sinewy thigh'[10] (he writes in a poem entitled 'On Those that Hated "The Playboy of the Western World"'), an extraordinary image of a horseman riding through the tumult and chaos of the hell that modern Ireland can become, a rebuke like something out of a painting of the west by Yeats's brother, Jack.

At the heart of the collection is 'Running to Paradise'. The poem comes out of the same longing and intensity that Synge captures in the Tramp's speech in *In the Shadow of the Glen*, where the wanderer of the roads promises a freedom to the young wife consigned to overarching misery and unacted desire. This speech itself draws upon the wildness and unconfined surges of feeling found in Connacht folk-song, which both Synge and Yeats had studied. Here, in the Yeats poem, we see him keeping faith with that tradition while at the same time recognizing that it embodies a mobility and recklessness of force that is in deep opposition to the kind of Ireland and its mind-set that rejected Synge's relentless gaze:

> As I came over Windy Gap
> They threw a halfpenny into my cap,
> For I am running to Paradise;
> And all that I need do is to wish
> And somebody puts his hand in the dish
> To throw me a bit of salted fish:
> *And there the king is but as the beggar*.[11]

This defiance and its delight in the wayward and the extreme is something that Yeats is now beginning to incorporate into the entire system of his thought and feeling.

In 1917 he published *Per Amica Silentia Lunae*, the first outline of the mystical system he was to explicate fully in *A Vision* (1925). He opens his text with a dialogue, a psychodrama, between two aspects of himself, 'Hic' and 'Ille', this and the other, or the given personality and the created willed one. He calls it 'Ego Dominus Tuus' ('I Thy Lord'), taken from Dante's *La Vita Nuova*, where a being who calls himself Dante's 'lord' appears to him with the poet's beloved Beatrice in his arms. The Yeats piece conjures up a shallow stream, an 'old wind-beaten tower' (evoking Yeats's tower at Thoor Ballylee, which he was renovating and where he was going to live with his young wife, Georgie Hyde-Lees, whom he married in 1917), and a lamp burning in the window behind which the poet has been studying. The book still lies open. And now one of the voices in the poem, the 'here' one, the most 'normal', calls to its opposite, its mask, its antithesis. The mask, central from now on to every movement of Yeats's thought and imagination, is that which is opposed to the given; it is the rebuke the imagination offers to the everyday, the slack, the dull; it is that thing, of all things not impossible, which is the most difficult, because that is what strains the mind and the intelligence to maximum intensity. It is the wildness at the heart of the west; it is what Yeats has always sought in the trees and in the woods and in the mountains as he reached a summit to find yet more distance to traverse. The other self, the mask-self, he writes in the prose text that follows the poem, 'comes but to those who are no longer deceived, whose passion is reality'.[12]

Yeats from now on is to go 'antithetical'; that is, his verse and his drama try to leave the things that seem to strike out into radical forms that will, to quote 'Easter 1916', his poem on the Rising, 'trouble the living stream',[13] just as Pearse and Connolly, in their actions, went antithetical to all common sense and received wisdom. This is a poetic credo that is extreme and utterly demanding, requiring every last effort of the will to create an alternative to what is fixed and given. It involves a high formality as well as total passion, fire and ice. As Rainer Maria Rilke wrote in 1908, at the close of the sonnet 'Archaic Torso of Apollo', 'You must change your life'; and likewise Yeats accepted this necessity and challenge. He made himself more and more a man of the west, renovating his tower at Ballylee, making it an emblem of adversity, that is, of adversity to the slack ordinariness of the comfortable and the everyday. The volume called *The Tower* (1928), one of the major collections of verse of the twentieth century, is full of defiance and a rage against circumstance, from the vantage of the tower standing remote from the flow of things, and yet a part of a landscape of the west, full of association, crammed with memory and with thought. The book opens with 'Sailing to Byzantium', with its direct and shattering line, dismissing the Ireland of his time, 'That is no country for old men'. Ireland recedes into the distance in the perspective of the imagination. It is being left behind in the travelling energy that is the poem's speed, as the poetry makes for Byzantium, out of the west.

The poetry is a moving antithesis, a mask, a rebuke to what is the 'common dream', and it gyres out (the gyres were Yeats's figure for how history unfolds and repeats itself) from its locale at Ballylee in the west to drive towards Byzantium, a holy city of the mind. The poem now, crazily, calls out to sages that, he says, are standing in the 'holy fire' of God in Byzantium, to come towards him as he makes this antithetical mask poem, to rotate towards him in an uncoiling gyre, and become the 'singing masters' of his soul. It is the soul's song he now wants to make, and this will be emitted, he tells us in the last stanza, by a golden bird, an artificial thing 'set upon a golden bough to sing | To lords and ladies of Byzantium | Of what is past, or passing, or to come'.[14]

The strange and terrible beauty of this works because of what it pits itself against, the sensual music of what is born and what dies, mortality, growing old and enfeebled. The energy is pure mask, pure antithesis, but it is driven by what it seeks to overcome, the helpless actuality and pity of being alive. And the next poem in the volume, 'The Tower' itself, plunges right back into the encircumstanced heart, the absurdity of getting old: 'What shall I do with this absurdity ... | Decrepit age that has been tied to me | Like a dog's tail?' He is 63. And he does not know the answer. Yeats is dramatizing consciousness, showing us the process whereby the struggle takes place between the crashing weight of the burden of the actual and the impulse towards the wearing of the mask that will enable him to create wild images, out of the west, to rebuke the commonplace.

This poem 'The Tower' now opens out, sending forth from the battlements of the mind standing watch over experience, the imagination. And what does the imagination engage with? The very things of circumstance which tend to impede its action, which contaminate its longing for absolute purity. In the *Per Amica* essay he wrote of an archer, a woman of 'incredible beauty' whom he saw between sleeping and waking, shooting an arrow into the sky, and he has had always this longing to make the straight line, to leave the 'path of the serpent and become the bowman who aims his arrow at the centre of the sun'.[15] But it is not possible for those still implicated in the 'fury and the mire of human veins' as he will call it in the 1930 'Byzantium', to leave the path of the serpent, and this is what the poem now embodies: the intricacies of memory, work done or left undone, things understood or half-understood, impossible passions and longings that he now cannot figure out, ghosts, lechery, the remorse of loving someone who has been lost in an infidelity to the person he has sworn to love. Misery, the sadness of what it is to live and to have bitter regret and self-hate. All that, as Beckett would say.

And all that chaos of what is concludes the second great reach of the poem in a darkness of inarticulacy as memory and remorse put a stop to the enquiry that the poem has become, into what may or may not be lifted into poetry. And then, assuming the mask of the master poet, daring to determine his will in spite of his absurdities, the poem lifts into the song of the soul, transfiguring all the materiality and leadenness of the previous section. Creating a ghost-work of extraordinary exhilaration, he writes of being dead, of rising in death to create out of the soul something he calls a 'Translunar Paradise', claiming that he has made himself ready for that after-death through study, through love, and through all the effort he has put into the act of creativity itself. And then, in the conclusion, the poem climbs into something scarcely credible, an indifference to death itself, and to life, so that everything that appalled or delighted the living man, including those whom he has loved to despair,

> Seem but the clouds of the sky
> When the horizon fades;
> Or a bird's deepening cry
> Among the deepening shades.

It need hardly be said that it is only someone who feels things with a fierce intensity who could long for this remoteness. As he writes in the next poem in this collection, 'Meditations in Time of Civil War', 'only an aching heart | Conceives a changeless work of art'. And it is those last lines from 'The Tower' that are quoted obsessively again and again in Samuel Beckett's TV play ... *but the clouds* ..., broadcast by the BBC in 1977. Incidentally, this use of 'but' as an adverbial qualifier, which acts to reduce the force and effectiveness of action undertaken by the ceaseless strivings of the ego or the social sphere, is one of Yeats's favourite constructions in prose and in verse. It is as if in this tiny particle the world collides with a mind and an imagination that is determined to have its own value, different from what may be ordained; or as if it were a small island of lonely grammar in the sea of language, retaining its remote dignity in the middle of turbulent waters.

Yeats is a master-poet because of his many gifts. He also, by effort of will and commitment of energy, made himself such. He did not know Irish, and so lacked the intimate access to its linguistic world it might have given him, but he achieved something else, in spite of all the odds, something almost impossible, most difficult (in another one of his favourite phrases), and through that challenge raised the will to full intensity: he achieved, somehow, an integration of the most ancient strata of feeling and understanding in Irish and Celtic tradition with his own manifold and changing personality, as well as a relentless focus on the world as it revealed itself to him in his own time. But at the back of it all was Ireland, and the west. In a poem called 'Under Saturn' he tells how a working-man, seeing him back home in Sligo after long absence, says that it is about time for him to be back again where his people came from. Such attachment to a native place is very great in Yeats, but there is no Irish writer, of any consequence, who does not have this feeling: Seamus Heaney's south Derry; John McGahern's Leitrim; Brian Friel's Donegal; Frank O'Connor's Cork; Nuala Ní

Dhomhnaill's Kerry; Ciaran Carson's Belfast; or, moving back, Samuel Ferguson's Antrim; Oliver Goldsmith's Longford; Brian Merriman's Clare; Aodhagán Ó Rathaille's Sliabh Luachra; Dáibhí Ó Bruadair's Cork; Eochaidh Ó hEodhasa's Fermanagh; Tadhg Dall Ó Huiginn's Sligo; and so on it goes.

11

Hearts of Stone

James Joyce once famously remarked that it had been his hope, when writing *Ulysses* (1922), that it would be possible, in the event of some future cataclysm during which all cities and habitations of men were destroyed, to reconstruct Dublin from the pages of his book. It is certainly a remarkable evocation of a day in the life of a city and its inhabitants, and Joyce brilliantly captures the atmosphere of Dublin on 16 June 1904, its sounds, streets, talk, music, drinking, eating, sexual activity, commerce; its arguments, politics, and night-life; its sheer vitality. There is a wonderful sense of the density of Dublin life, as the people in the book make their way around the city, meeting others whom they know, exchanging news, making plans for activities (some of them none too salubrious) that they will be getting up to later, and all the time the writing also records the interior thoughts and feelings of certain key figures.

Joyce was obsessed with Dublin. During the days he spent writing, his mind would wander its streets and suburbs, recalling its voices and intonations, mockeries, swearing, and badinage. One of those voices, and one of the most important of them all to him, was that of his father, John Stanislaus Joyce, an impossible and difficult man with whom he had a very troubled relationship, but someone to whom he was nonetheless hopelessly devoted. John Joyce was a feckless man, a drinker, a good singer (described as the best tenor in Dublin), a charmer, a puller-of-the-devil-by-the-tail, a chancer. He ran through an inheritance, mortgaging properties again and again for ready cash; he failed to take advantage of the opportunity offered him by a university education; and he frequently, not being able to find the rent, had to do a flit from the houses he rented for his large and remorselessly increasing family. He would borrow cash from friends and then, instead of bringing it home to feed his family, would take himself off to some pub or other in the centre of Dublin and stand rounds for his cronies. He is Simon Dedalus in *Ulysses*, unforgettably evoked in the 'Sirens' episode, where he sings Lionel's song from the opera *Martha* as Leopold Bloom, the Jewish Ulysses of the novel, listens to this siren song while (heedless of kosher injunctions) eating his lunch of liver, bacon, and mashed potato.

Joyce re-creates the experience of hearing his father sing as he registers Bloom's reactions to the performance. Bloom is in the dining room of the Ormond Hotel, while the pipe-smoking Simon Dedalus and his friends (among them Ben Dollard, and Bob Cowley, who is playing the newly tuned piano in accompaniment) are in the bar being looked after by the siren barmaids Miss Douce and Miss Kennedy. Bloom asks the waiter to open the door between dining room and bar so he can the better hear Mr Dedalus singing. 'Glorious tone he still has', thinks Mr Bloom, and then, 'Cork air softer also their brogue'.[1] Mr Dedalus is from Cork, as was John Joyce, who was absolutely typical of a certain type of Corkman surviving to this day.

Cork had, still has, a reputation of being a very musical city: visiting singers to the old Opera House, if the discerning audience thought they were not up to scratch, would be interrupted from the Gods and shown how to sing the aria they had mangled. Messenger boys, the musician and composer Seán Ó Riada told me, would, when he was a young man in the late 1940s, compete in the singing of snatches of opera in Italian as they pedalled around the streets on their hefty cycles. Of course Cork was one of the major harbours of western Europe. Sailors and servicemen of all nations and the British Empire would roam the streets looking for entertainment at night while on shore leave, or while provisioning for long-haul voyages to the North American continent or the Far East. There was, when John Joyce was a young man, a thickly populated red-light district (known as the Holy Ground, whence the popular ballad made famous by the Clancy Brothers in the 1960s) near Anglesea Street, where the Joyce household was, a place he did not fail to frequent himself. There were, it seems, in its heyday in the late nineteenth century, some two hundred full-time prostitutes in Cork and a hundred or so part-timers.

At one point Mr Bloom, who has been ruminating over what music is, overhears Simon Dedalus giving his views on the same subject, as he recalls the Italian sailors in Cork Harbour singing at night. 'It was', says Dedalus to Ben Dollard, 'the only language. He heard them as a boy in

Ringabella, Crosshaven, Ringabella, singing their barcaroles. Queens-town harbour full of Italian ships. Walking, you know, Ben, in the moonlight with those earthquake hats. Blending their voices. God, such music, Ben. Heard as a boy. Cross Ringabella haven mooncarole.'

This Cork world, of singing, nightlife, sport, amateur dramatics, having a good time, enjoying life, keeping the ball rolling anyhow,[2] as Dedalus Senior puts it in *A Portrait of the Artist as a Young Man* (1916), John Joyce retained into his adult life in Dublin, with, of course, disastrous consequences for his family. The style of living he enjoyed in his youth was again something of a Cork phenomenon: young men of a certain class and status had a wonderful time, their leisurely lives and relaxed approach to work underwritten by the relatively widely dis-persed wealth of the Cork merchant princes, and by a confident accept-ance of privilege in a city that burgeoned with money and trade. There was also an elaborate and easy system of patronage, so that safety-nets were in place for those scions of the merchant classes who might prove a little inattentive to their own best interests. So that when John Joyce dropped out of University College Cork, he had little difficulty in finding suitable employment, working as an accountant on a kind of freelance basis, walking the city, seeking and securing commissions from business friends of the family. Earlier, when he left school at St Colman's in Fermoy, his father got him work for a time on the pilot boats that guided the big cargo and passenger ships into the various berthings all over the great reaches of Cork's famously capacious harbour, that extended from the city itself down to Queenstown (now Cobh), Haulbowline, Spike Island. Hence the memories of Ringabella and Crosshaven that surface in the bar of the Ormond Hotel.

There is, therefore, a fascinating doubleness at the heart of *Ulysses*: it is a book that conveys, perhaps more than any other novel ever has done, the living sense of what a city, in this case Dublin, is like to be alive in; and yet, one of its dominating characters is a Corkman. Joyce himself went as far as to say to Louis Gillet in Paris, of his father's presence in the book, that 'the humour of *Ulysses* is his; its people are his friends. The book is his spittin' image.'[3] This is a bit puzzling, in that one would be forgiven for thinking that the central character is the Ulysses figure, the Irish wandering man, the Jew Leopold Bloom, not Simon Dedalus. This may be explained by the fact that, in creating his fiction, Joyce diversified the paternity question into both Dedalus and Bloom, so that Bloom becomes the repository of many of John Joyce's traits, and the novel reflects an extended delineation of the nature of the relations between father and son, as well as embodying all sorts of reverberations of this theme, whether in the tortuous exposition of *Hamlet* in the Scylla and Charybdis episode in the National Library ('through the ghost of the unquiet father the image of the unliving son looks forth'[4]), or in the theological speculations on the consubstantiality of the Father and the Son and the Holy Ghost that surface continually.

And what lies at the core of all this intellectuality and elaborate artifice ('Old father, old artificer', Stephen reflects at the end of *A Portrait*, thinking of Dedalus as maker, designer of the labyrinth on Crete that held the minotaur, and of the flying machine through which his son Icarus met his death), all this cunning construction of thought and words? It is something very simple and very straightforward: it is love, the capacity to feel for another, the thing behind the words and the sounds that make music and song affect us. It is the human quality that animates the vitality that Joyce saw and admired and loved beyond words in his own Cork father. So that, when he recorded the speech from Aeolus (the chapter set in the offices of the *Freeman's Journal*), the famous oration made by the barrister John F. Taylor (and friend of John Joyces's) in defence of the Irish language, there are distinct traces of his father's Cork accent, as a kind of tribute. He sent one of the thirty copies of the recording to him. Furthermore, in the Cyclops episode, there is no doubt in my mind that the voice of the person telling the story there of Bloom's encounter with the nationalist Citizen in Barney Kiernan's pub is that of his father, the flow and vehemence of the thing being pure Cork.

As Bloom listens to Mr Dedalus singing Lionel's aria in the Ormond Hotel, marvelling at the effects the singer can create, he wonders how they come about: 'Words? Music? No: it's what behind.' And then he hears Mr Dedalus climb into the passionate close of the song, Lionel crying out to Martha to come to him: 'In cry of lionel loneliness that she should know, must Martha feel. For her only he waited . . . Alone. One love. One hope. One comfort me.'[5]

And then the final shift into the last phrase, 'Come, to me', Joyce now straining everything to capture the beauty of his father singing, bringing to bear all his mastery of language to get at the thing behind the music and the words, the love: 'It soared, a bird, it held its flight, a swift pure cry, soar silver orb it leaped serene, speeding, sustained, to come, don't spin it out too long long breath he breath long life, soaring high . . . all around about the all, the endlessnessnessness.' And with the final '*To me*' there occurs the following word, 'Siopold!', Simon and Leopold united in one love, one being, consubstantial with each other in the artistry of the son's amazing language, the bringer of the word, if that is not too blasphemous.

John Joyce, before he removed to Dublin (where, again through family and business contacts, he was to assist in setting up a distillery) had been, at the very least, a Fenian sympathizer. After settling in Dublin he became a follower of Parnell, who himself made strategic use of an alliance with the Fenians, and their tradition of not excluding the option of physical force in the gaining of political advantage. These sympathies also surface in Simon Dedalus and his friends, as they listen to the 'native Doric' of Ben Dollard's rendition of the patriotic song 'The Croppy Boy', following the singing of the aria from *Martha* in the Ormond Hotel.

Parnell and the Fenians, the role of the Catholic church in Irish politics, a distrust of British policy, a renegade republicanism, are all shadows that darken the atmospheres of Joyce's writings. But it is Parnell in particular, and the memory of his father's loyalty to him, that figure most prominently in Joyce's re-creation of the political life of Dublin. One of the stories in *Dubliners* (1914), Joyce's first major book, called 'Ivy Day in the Committee Room', brilliantly captures the gloom and depression amongst the old followers of Parnell in the aftermath of his disgrace and death, when, to many, it felt as if they were living in an Ireland where any possibility of independence of mind and integrity had faded.

Famously, in correspondence with the (eventual) publisher, Grant Richards (it took nine years for the collection to get into print), Joyce described the stories as having been written in a 'style of scrupulous meanness' to convey a Dublin which seemed to him to be a city which was a 'centre of paralysis'.[6] This has often been taken to mean that these stories are written in a mean and nasty style to eviscerate a Dublin which Joyce holds in contempt because it is in a state of moral and emotional paralysis. Nothing could be further from the truth. The stories are told in a style that is, generally, spare and stark, with very little in the way of authorial intrusion and certainly no comment; they do explore the lives and activities of Dubliners who are venal, self-absorbed, addicted, frustrated, violent, abusive, and so on; but the dominant mood of the collection is one of profound sorrow that men and women (mostly men, it may be said) have, for whatever reasons, become emotionally paraplegic in their lives, habits, terrors, angers. As Mr Bloom would later say, about Mr Dedalus's singing, it is what is behind the words that matters, and what is behind the storytelling in *Dubliners* is Joyce's sorrowing heart, not a flinty, unpitying gaze.

In 'Ivy Day in the Committee Room' the sorrow is over what Joyce's father, and the Ireland from which he came, had lost. A group of canvassers are gathered in the office of a nationalist candidate in an election, waiting to be paid. This was the kind of work John Joyce often undertook. They are far from certain that their man is to be relied upon to come up with the 'spondulics', or indeed to oppose an address of welcome in the forthcoming visit to Dublin of 'Edward Rex', a 'foreign king' to some of these advanced nationalists. If their hero, Parnell, the anniversary of whose death falls on this dismal day in October, were alive, there would be no question of any of this backsliding they now have reason to fear. Some of the men gathered in the room in Wicklow Street are wearing ivy in their lapels in memory of Parnell.

It is cold and dark and cheerless. A fire is lit from a few coals and cinders, emblematic of the failing phoenix flame of the Fenians and what the old caretaker, Jack, calls 'them times' when 'there was some life in it'. So intense is Joyce's authorial concentration that virtually everything in this story and in the other stories in the collection becomes symbolic and charged with implication. The fire is used to warm the bottles of stout that arrive from their man, who is a publican, and the little 'poks' that interject themselves into the story as the corks in the bottles pop out in the heat from the fire (the corkscrew has had to be handed back) are a pitiful and slightly comic fusillade over the memory of the great leader.

One of the men wearing ivy in his lapel is a Joe Hynes, who is vociferous in his denunciation of the idea of Dublin honouring the British monarch. He leaves, and those behind start talking about him, and as they do we learn that he is not, perhaps, entirely to be trusted, for all his professed loyalty to Parnell and republicanism. They suspect him of coming round to spy for the other side in the corporation elections. He has a reputation for being a Fenian and what they call a 'hillsider' (a guerrilla revolutionary, or someone sympathetic to such tactics), yet they also suspect that, like many who pass themselves off as hard republicans, he may secretly be in the pay of Dublin Castle, and the British authorities. Here Joyce is performing what he called his 'vivisective' anatomy of Dublin hatred, suspicion, and anger, and the way people are paralysed by these obsessions. Yet when Hynes returns (we are not told where he has been) he is offered a bottle of stout, and is praised for his steadfast loyalty to the 'uncrowned king', Parnell. Hynes is asked to recite his poem on the death of Parnell, which, after some hesitation, he does. It is a typical piece of rhetorical verse, for recitation, and, again, it is often assumed that we are supposed to smile at its banality, knowingly recognizing its trumpery of feeling. But what Joyce focuses on is the impact such verse can and does have on the feelings, and this is not dismissed:

> They had their way: they laid him low.
>   But Erin, list, his spirit may
> Rise, like the Phoenix from the flames,
>   When breaks the dawning of the day,
>
> The day that brings us Freedom's reign.
>   And on that day may Erin well
> Pledge in the cup she lifts to Joy
>   One grief—the memory of Parnell.

There is silence, then applause. They then all drink, and in that silence Mr Hynes's cork pops from his stout, but he does not get up to fetch it from where he has sat back on the table, 'flushed and bareheaded'.[7] The story registers the power and dignity of loyalty, and of the emotion that unites even these suspicious and mean-minded Dubliners.

'Too long a sacrifice', Yeats wrote in his elegy for the men of 1916, 'can make a stone of the heart.'[8] Joyce's work recognizes this; more than that, he acknowledges the emptiness of hatred, the devastation it can work on the spirit. But continually he urges against such barrenness of soul something else, the thing behind the words, the humanity he saw in his flawed but loving and beloved father. It is there in the story from *Dubliners*; it is everywhere in *Ulysses*, and especially embodied in Leopold Bloom.

One of the episodes in the novel is that known as the 'Cyclops', set in Barney Kiernan's pub, where the diehard nationalist known as the Citizen (recalling Citoyen Tone, as Wolfe Tone was known as in Paris where he went in the 1790s to seek support from the revolutionary authorities for an invasion of Ireland), holds forth from a bar-stool in the corner, his dog Garryowen on the floor beside him. The main narrator of this section, who remains unidentified in the text but who is modelled on John Joyce, meets up with none other than Joe Hynes, the same slightly shady character we have encountered already in 'Ivy Day'. They decide to repair to Barney Kiernan's, which is at the back of the courthouse, near St Michan's, Hynes having something he wants to tell the Citizen, the Cyclops himself, one-eyed in his extreme nationalist fixation. When they arrive Hynes gets in a round, the Citizen ordering the 'wine of the country', Guinness, the narrator naming his poison as 'Ditto MacAnaspey' (a phrase of John Joyce's, meaning 'son of the bishop').

Bloom, who is looking for someone, sneaks a look into the bar ('. . . I saw his physog do a peep in and then slidder off again'), the dog growls at him, and the Citizen asks him to come in. Hynes, who is uncharacteristically in funds, offers to buy Bloom a drink; he politely refuses, and then accepts a cigar. The conversation revolves around applications that have been made for the position of hangman in Dublin, moving on to whether or not capital punishment is justified for its deterrent effect, Bloom taking a liberal view of the issue, complicating it, seeing different sides. Someone chips in with the observation that there is one thing that hanging does not have a deterrent effect on, and that is 'The poor bugger's tool that's being hanged'.[9] We then hear that when they hanged the Invincible Joe Brady (the Invincibles were a Fenian assassination squad who stabbed to death the Irish Chief Secretary, Lord Frederick Cavendish, in the Phoenix Park in 1882), his erection stood up 'like a poker' in the wardens' faces after they cut him down. Bloom, ever the rational scientific man, tells them that this phenomenon can be explained by science. The Citizen, however, seizes his opportunity, and starts to extol the Invincibles, the Fenians, the men of ninety-eight (1798), and all those who gave their lives for Ireland. He knows this is going to upset Bloom, but he ploughs on, deliberately stirring things up. Eventually he raises his glass of stout to 'The memory of the dead . . . glaring at Bloom.'

Frustrated, Bloom tries to say that the Citizen does not grasp his point, which is the humanitarian one, that physical violence, even for a good cause, is always a dangerous path to follow, only to be inter-rupted by the Citizen saying (using Irish): '*Sinn Féin . . . Sinn Féin amháin*! The friends we love are by our side and the foes we hate before us.' Bloom is standing before the Citizen; the Citizen is making a foe of him, whether Bloom likes it or not. The crisis passes, and the talk moves off in other directions, but the contention remains between them, to be opened up again. More drink is consumed, and the Citizen starts into a litany, and a very eloquent litany, of the wrongs done to Ireland, the kind of thing Joyce would have heard frequently from his father: 'They were driven out of house and home in the black 47. Their mudcabins and their shielings by the roadside were laid low by the batteringram and the *Times* rubbed its hands and told the white-livered Saxons there would soon be as few Irish in Ireland as redskins in America. . . . Twenty thousand of them died in the coffinships.'[10]

Hatred of England intensifies. Victoria is described as 'a flatulent old bitch', who before she died had to be carried up to her bed blind drunk every night, pulling at the whiskers of her footman, singing songs in German, one of the 'sausageeating bastards on the throne'. Bloom tries to speak against all this racial anger, and argues that such attitudes breed 'persecution'. The history of the world is full of this poison, he says, which perpetuates 'national hatred among nations'. That does it. The Citizen asks him what his nation is, to which Bloom replies that it is Ireland. The Citizen spits an oyster of phlegm into the corner at this. Bloom, heedless of the danger he is in, or just persistent, goes on to say that he belongs to a race that is hated and persecuted, 'this very moment. This very instant.' Someone else now comes in to say that the Jews should stand up to their oppressors, 'like men'. To which Bloom replies that force is no use, that it is no way for men and women to live: 'everybody knows that it's the very opposite of that that is really life'.

Challenged on this, he goes further, to say that what matters is 'Love . . . I mean the opposite of hatred.' He then leaves, saying he is off to see if the person he is looking for is in the courthouse nearby. While he is away, Lenehan, one of Joyce's Dublin hangers-on, tells the company that Bloom is in fact off to collect his winnings on a horse: this is inaccurate, but it fuels the antagonism against him, as a tight-fisted, money-grabbing Jew who would not share the tip. So that when he comes back he is subjected to outright anti-Semitism from the Citizen, to which Bloom makes the following response: 'Your God was a jew. Christ was a jew like me.' Enraged at this, the Citizen fetches up an empty biscuit tin, ornamented with Celtic motifs, and flings it at Bloom as he makes his escape on a jarvey's horse and car.

Ulysses was published in 1922, the year after the Anglo-Irish Treaty, which created an Irish Free State for twenty-six of the thirty-two counties of Ireland, was signed, giving it dominion status under the crown. Although the novel is set in 1904, it was written in the aftermath of 1916, and during the period of the Anglo-Irish War, also known as the War of Independence. It is quite clear that the 'Troubles' of that period lie behind much of the writing in *Ulysses*, and Bloom's despairing pacifism and his insistent humanity are one aspect of Joyce's attitudes to contemporary events. Bloom's opposition to war and violence would not be John Joyce's view, but Bloom's compassion, in Joyce's writing, takes the humane qualities of the father into a broader realm of general brotherhood, an espousal of a de-racialized spirit, a generous acceptance of difference.

Bloom's confrontation with the Citizen lays bare a nightmare at the heart of Irish life in those years of struggle and revolution. What do physical violence, social upheaval, shootings, bombings, all done in order to free Ireland from what the nationalists would claim, with justice, as British oppression, do to people? May it not be the case that there are many, like the Citizen, who are motivated by pure racial hatred, who may be at heart no better than what would later be known as fascists? Who knows what lies at the heart of such hate? The fact that the Citizen rounds on the Jew exposes something about the passions of nationalism, that a moral poison may be at work in what may appear to be the deepest of convictions and loyalties. Hatred likes to hate, and it opportunistically seizes on all occasions where it can vent itself against those who are weak or vulnerable or despised or feared; and in this case, in Barney Kiernan's pub in 1904 Dublin, the victim is the Irish-Hungarian Jew Virag, or Bloom, as he is now known. Joyce, the moralist (and he is one, not just an aesthete or a manic exponent of elaborate technique), is showing us a harsh and revolting consequence of extreme nationalist conviction (or what masquerades as such). As Yeats wrote, at about the same time, in 'Meditations in Time of Civil War': 'We had fed the heart on fantasies, | The heart's grown brutal from the fare; | More substance in our enmities | Than in our love....'[11]

Bloom's counter-arguments against such fantastic hatred are weak, as all such arguments against the force of racial passion tend to be, because, in the end the side that is driven by hate will always have recourse to what cannot be dealt with by rational exchange, violence. And that violence can be met only by opposing violence; there is no other way, or at least there is none until the passions exhaust themselves, and that takes a long time. The heart grows brutal, and implacable. So Bloom's useless havering, his attempt to claim a space for human value, is seen to be the pathetic thing it is, when confronted by rage.

However, Joyce does an amazing turnabout by means of the style at the end of the episode. After the throwing of the Celtic biscuit tin, the Citizen lets out a 'volley of oaths' and shouts to the dog to chase after the horse and car, the jarvey driving furiously to get away from the scene. And now the prose changes gear, as it has been doing on and off throughout this chapter, into a higher register, moving into the sublime. Because what Joyce now does is to shift Bloom from being a Dublin Jew trying to get away from a bunch of drunken nationalist bowsies into Elijah the prophet, ascending to heaven in a chariot, the transformed jaunting car. It is comical, of course, but it is very beautiful and very moving as well: 'And they beheld Him in the chariot, clothed upon in the glory of the brightness, having raiment as of the sun, fair as the moon and terrible that for awe they durst not look upon Him.... And they beheld Him, even Him, ben Bloom Elijah, amid clouds of angels ascend to the glory of the brightness at an angle of forty-five degrees over Donohue's in Little Green Street like a shot off a shovel.' This is a transformation of mood brought about by the style, but it is also a change of heart, in that our emotions blaze with delight at the prospect of Mr Bloom soaring into his heaven, our new Elijah of the human.

Bloom's humanitarian protestations against violence ('all that') are echoed two years later in one of the famous plays of Abbey Theatre, Sean O'Casey's *Juno and the Paycock* (1924). In one of the most memorable outcries on the Irish stage, Mrs Boyle, the Juno of the title, at the end of the play, when she has to go to identify the body of her son, executed as a traitor by the IRA, says to Mary her daughter, but really to the audience in the Abbey, and to the Irish people: 'Blessed Virgin, where were you when me darlin' son was riddled with bullets, when me darlin' son was riddled with bullets? Sacred Heart o' Jesus, take away our hearts o' stone, and give us hearts o' flesh! Take away this murdherin' hate, an' give us Thine own eternal love!'[12]

This speech, by any standards, is a powerful outpouring of emotion, but if it were to stand alone it would be just that, an eloquent piece of emotional outcry. But O'Casey's technique is such that he takes this moment, and by a dexterous piece of theatrical juxtaposition, deepens it to a level of chill and cold shock that is utterly new and very moving.

Because at this point, when the women go slowly out—Juno to identify the body she has brought into the world—there is a pause in the action. The audience think the play is over, that it is to end on this note of women's suffering and pain, but the curtain does not come down. There is a shuffling sound on the steps outside, and in come Captain Boyle and his drunken sidekick, Joxer. They are both very much the worse for wear. This is now the conclusion of the final Act of the play, during which everything has fallen apart: the Boyle family have learned that the legacy they were to inherit will not come their way, as Bentham, Mary's fiancée, has made a mess of drafting the terms of the will; Bentham has fled to England and cannot be contacted, having made Mary pregnant; Boyle, having borrowed heavily on the strength of the anticipated legacy, is now being dunned for his debts, and bailiffs arrive to take away furniture acquired on credit; the IRA come for the son, Johnny, to take him to his death (they ask him if he has his 'beads' with him); Boyle, when he hears about his daughter's condition, only thinks about how *he* feels and what the neighbours will say when they find out; Joxer slips the last bottle of stout into his pocket while Boyle is still in bed recovering from a hangover; and then the police come to tell Juno that her son has been executed and that they want her to identify the body. Such a pile-up of calamity verges on melodrama, but what saves it is O'Casey's comedic skill, and his ability to juxtapose dereliction of spirit and morale with bizarre and wild humour, even as these disasters unfold.

And at the very end, after Juno and Mary exit, the two cadgers and drunks stagger on stage, rambling incoherently about the world being in a state 'o' chassis', Boyle rehearsing old sayings, such as the incongruous 'Irelan' sober . . . is Irelan' . . . free', given the state they are in; or Boyle claiming he did his bit during the Easter Rising, and saying that now, if the worst comes to the worst, he can always join a 'flyin' column'. Joxer responds by asking if Boyle has ever read the 'darlin' story' of Willie Reilly and his Colleen Bawn. Thus does the play end, in a disarray of confused and drunken indifference and inconsequence.

Boyle, saying he can always join a flying column, is amongst a number of very clear indications that the play is set during the Civil War that followed the signing of the Treaty. The army of the newly founded Irish Free State found itself at war with the Republican wing of the IRA, the 'diehards' of the play. Johnny is on this side, which he betrays. Boyle claims to have been involved in the Rising, and Joxer mimics his patriotic sentiments. The play is bristling with an awareness, at every shift in the action, at every piece of horrific juxtaposition, of the human cost of civil war. This conflict extended from April 1922, when the IRA occupied the Four Courts in Dublin in protest at the Treaty (which had agreed to the six counties of Northern Ireland remaining under the Union, and accepted an oath of allegiance to the British throne), to May of the following year, when Éamon de Valera supported the order of Frank Aiken, IRA Chief of Staff, to the 'soldiers of the Republic, the Legion of the Rearguard', to dump their arms. That year had seen appalling atrocities and a sickening cycle of reprisals as Irish freedom-fighters waded through the blood of their one-time comrades (as de Valera said they would), in an ever-deepening spiral of fury and hatred that was to poison Irish civic life for decades, well into the 1970s. Some of the incidents (many of which remain unspoken of to this day) equal in atrocity some of the most shocking outrages of the 'Troubles' of the last thirty years of the twentieth century in Northern Ireland, the Republic, and Britain; and, there is no question, the origin of these latter-day 'Troubles' lies with the Treaty signed by Michael Collins and the other Irish negotiators in London in their pressurized negotiations with the British prime minister, David Lloyd George, and the mayhem it released in Ireland. Some index of the scale of this horror can be gauged by mention of a single incident, the blowing up of nine Republican (or Irregular) prisoners by tying them to a land-mine in Ballyseedy, County Kerry, one surviving because he was blown clear by the blast. The fighting was especially fierce in Kerry.

What is impressive about O'Casey's Civil War play is that he captures the bleak reality of the consequences of this conflict on the lives of those in the Dublin tenements. He is remorseless in the way he chronicles the violence and its effects, but he sets this bleakly accurate rendition of the war in the context of the hopes and fears and vanities of people trying to survive, and in this he is full of compassion. And all the time he never entirely releases his grip on that inhuman behaviour which is ludicrous. He manages these transitions and mergings through an artistry which holds such disparate elements in constantly shifting variety, where a unity resides in the surety of his moral and humanitarian force. John Osborne, the English dramatist of the third quarter of the twentieth century, said of the Irish drama (he was thinking of Synge, O'Casey, Beckett, Brendan Behan) that whereas American theatre gave you thought and emotion, Irish theatre gave you those, and the solar plexus, the larynx, the cerebral cortex, the lot. O'Casey's two great Dublin plays, *Juno* and *The Plough and the Stars* (1926, his play about the Rising, which caused rioting in the theatre once again, it having been seen, with some reason it may be said, as an insult to the martyrs of 1916) are classics of world drama, and bear out Osborne's comment.

O'Casey is sometimes seen as an untutored dramatist who stumbled almost by accident into greatness. When he left Dublin to live in England after the reception of *The Plough*, and after his famous fall-ing-out with Yeats over *The Silver Tassie*, his next play (which Yeats, rightly, did not rank highly), there was, it would probably now be generally agreed, a falling off in artistic focus, with O'Casey writing fantasies and bleak, cheerless comedies inspired by his somewhat dogmatic communism. But the sheer inventive novelty and contra-puntal structures and interplays of these two Dublin plays should not be underestimated. The ending of the second Act of *Juno* is astonishing in the shocks it administers and in its restless inclusiveness.

The Boyle family are in good spirits, still believing that the legacy is theirs, and there is a singsong under way in the tenement, with Joxer trying (and failing) to sing 'She is Far from the Land', Thomas Moore's song about Robert Emmet and Sarah Curran, the girl to whom the revolutionary was engaged. Mrs Tancred comes in on her way to the hospital to bring home the body of her son, and the mood shifts. Commandant Tancred, Mrs Tancred's only son, has been shot in an ambush which he led; another casualty in the same exchange was the son of Mrs Mannin', Mrs Tancred's next-door neighbour, who was on the Free State side. Mrs Tancred, in an agony of grief, cannot stop thinking of the son she carried lying shot dead, his head 'half hidden in the wather of a runnin' brook'. Another casualty of this ambush is to be Johnny Boyle, the informer, who has lost his nerve, having sustained injuries during Easter Week. The mood shifts again, and this time Captain Boyle sings before he puts a record on the newly acquired gramophone. The song: the Irish-American 'If You're Irish, Come into the Parlour'.

At this point the tailor Nugent comes in to tell them to be quiet, as Tancred's body is being brought down the street. We hear a hymn being sung, 'To Jesus' Heart all Burning', and the people in the room go down to get a better view of the cortège and the hearse, all apart from Johnny, that is. A young man enters. He has been looking for Johnny, who recognizes the caller as the 'Mobilizer', and Boyle is summoned to a battalion staff meeting in two nights' time to discuss the possibility that he knows something about who gave the game away on Tancred from within the Republican ranks. There now follows the curtain to Act Two: Johnny declares he will not go, because he is not told where the meeting is to be held. The young man reminds Quartermaster Boyle of his oath, at which Boyle exclaims in outraged passion that he has done enough for Ireland, having taken a bullet in his hip in 1916, and having lost his arm, only to be answered by the stony and chilling rebuke of the young man, who says: 'Boyle, no man can do enough for Ireland!' before he leaves, without saying another word.[13] Johnny stands alone on the stage, as the audience hears from the street the opening words of the 'Hail Mary'. Curtain, a heartbreaking curtain, pride and furious sorrow mixed. O'Casey was, after all, a member of Connolly's Irish Citizen Army, who knew what it felt like, as a young man, to give everything for Ireland. John Osborne was right.

O'Casey also knew, from his own direct experience, the truth of Yeats's lines in 'Easter 1916', that 'Too long a sacrifice | Can make a stone of the heart.'[14]

12

Matrix of Surds

I t used to be thought that the period from around, say, 1926, the year
the Abbey produced O'Casey's *The Plough and the Stars*, to some
point in the late 1950s, taking perhaps the publication of Thomas
Kinsella's *Another September* (1958) as a marker at the other end, was
one in which very little happened in the history of Irish literature.
These thirty years were seen as a doldrums, a Limbo state, after the
energy of the revolution had funnelled away, and before a new
modernizing attitude had begun to alter the ways in which Irish people
saw themselves as they entered a phase where investment and prosperity began forever to change Irish ways of life and thought, and Irish
writing began to breathe a more invigorating air.

There was, undoubtedly, a narrowing of minds which took place
on, one might say, a national scale. The Catholic church, in reaction
against the modern forces of secularization and materialism (and
indeed the doctrinaire materialism of Marxism which had developed
into a movement of global reach, driven by Stalin's belief in international revolution), secured an ascendancy in the Irish mind, particularly in the Free State, the southern twenty-six counties. De Valera's
Constitution of 1937 (*Bunreacht na hÉireann*), the blueprint for a new
configuration of church–state relations, and a deliberate attempt to fuse
nationalist idealism with a moral and religious probity, recognized
what was termed the 'special position' of the Catholic church in
Irish history and contemporary life. This created profound disquiet
in the North, where a radical free-thinking strain was a crucial element
in Protestant religious conviction and practice, and not just amongst
Presbyterians. Congregationalists, Baptists, Methodists, Unitarians,
the 'wee frees', and the Church of Ireland itself: all had, through a
very strong affinity with the spirit of the covenanting tradition from

Scotland, involving deep distrust of anything remotely resembling papist supremacy (such as bishops), retained a radical streak, issuing straight from Luther himself and Calvin, through John Knox. For many in the North the Republic was now a different country, and in some respects it was. It is generally agreed that Ireland, in the years from around again, say, 1926 to the beginning of the 1970s and maybe even later, was exceptionally devoted to the forms and observances of the Catholic faith as the source for many precepts and structures to guide one through life, such that it would be difficult to think of many other countries internationally where devotion and formal compliance with the dictates of the church laid the basis for public and private life. A possible comparator with Ireland in this context might be Franco's Spain.

It would be fair to say that during these years, from the mid-1920s to the 1960s, Free State Ireland turned in on itself, seeking consolation from the harshness of economic reality in a conception of itself as a Catholic nation united in worship and the observances of piety. De Valera, when he led the newly formed Fianna Fáil into power after the election of 1932, declared economic war against Britain, refusing to pay the annuities due to Westminster whereby Irish tenant farmers had become small landowners some thirty years before. These small farm-ers, innately conservative, distrustful of novelty, found themselves in a natural alliance with the Catholic church in a resistance to openness and to change. Fianna Fáil sought to position itself at the heart of this powerful body of thought and feeling, linking their republican ethos and their loyalty to the ideal of a Gaelic-speaking Ireland to the founding principles of the Irish state, and the values of 1916. There evolved a powerful and sentimental view of Ireland, which combined the following elements: the common sense of the small farmer; the warm intimacy of the family; the faithful observance of church duties; prayer; the Irish language; rural Ireland itself; decent civil servants wearing pioneer pins that proclaimed their abstinence from drink alongside *fáinní óir* (gold rings worn in the lapel) that revealed them to be fluent Gaelic speakers; membership of the Legion of Mary, which sought to aid the poor in the cities; the nightly rosary said in the kitchen, with the family kneeling in prayer. There was a saying of the time that went: 'the family that prays together stays together', which underlines the centrality of devotion to the main social structure in Irish society at this time, the family. Famously, de Valera evoked, in a speech on St Patrick's Day in 1943, this ideal Ireland as a place where comely maidens danced with strapping, wholesome youths at the crossroads of rural Ireland, representing a Catholic fortitude and integrity in a modern world too much given over to sensation and gratification. In this conception Ireland was to be a beacon of hope and piety in a modern and savage dark age. Crucially, too, it was neutral in the Second World War, the conflict that was to shape modern Europe, Ireland's absence from which was seen in some quarters (notably Britain) as a failure to confront a regime, Nazi Germany, that seemed to be an embodiment of evil.

Fianna Fáil's vision was, of course, a kind of frantic ideal; the reality was altogether different. Every week, from the North Wall in Dublin or from the quays in Rosslare and Cork, the ferries carried Irish emigrants to Liverpool or Fishguard, who would then make their way to the building-sites, motorway-construction companies, or factories where they worked as navvies, many drinking themselves into insensibility at the weekends before resuming the grind again each Monday. Irish brute labour in the fifties, especially, contributed a great deal to the reconstruction of Britain after the war. At home there was an utterly inflexible code of social control. Pregnancy outside of marriage was a disgrace, with the girls either spirited away to hostels maintained for these purposes in England, or more or less incarcerated in institutions in Ireland, where their children would be adopted or sent into orphanages or institutional schools throughout the length and breadth of the country. These places, we now know, were, many of them, bastilles of cruelty and violent physical and sexual abuse, with the clergy themselves, or the brothers who often ran these places, committing all kinds of criminal acts of paedophilia and sadism. Priests, all over the country, north and south, inveigled themselves into the intimate trust of families, only to exploit their positions and subject the children whom they professed to love to all kinds of secret degradation.

In some respects this Ireland of secret vices and outer rectitude was a demented place. Form and appearance were everything. Underneath a world of pioneer rallies, sodalities, novenas, first Fridays, the Miraculous Medal, with priests enjoying a lifestyle of comfort and security, housekeepers, lavish teas and dinners, good hotel lunches; with the nuns maintaining a fragrant environment in the convents of beeswaxed luxury and content; with vocations for the religious life showing continuously healthy recruitment—underneath all this there was a seething netherworld of vice, corruption, despair, and emptiness. In some respects this looks like a situation entirely conducive to the creation of great art. And in many ways it was.

Because, although the received view is that the Ireland of these years was an unproductive time for literary achievement, given the introverted nature of Irish society, its falsity, its rigidity, the opposite is actually the case. In all kinds of ways these years, from the late twenties to the late fifties, comprise a period of serious accomplishment, giving the lie entirely to the slack notion that this was a time when the shadow of Yeats held Irish writing in thrall, with Joyce, exiled in Paris, out of the sphere where he might exert an influence.

Let us have a brief roll-call of some of the writers who came to prominence in these years: Liam O'Flaherty, writing in Irish and English; the realist Frank O'Connor, and his inevitable sidekick Seán O'Faolain; Austin Clarke, the tortured stylist; the savage, laconic edge of Samuel Beckett; the demented grotesquerie of Flann O'Brien; the amplitude of Joyce Cary; the fluent elegance and anomie of Louis MacNeice; the psychological finesse of Kate O'Brien; the heartbreak and clarity of Patrick Kavanagh; the Gaelic rage and frenzy of Máirtín Ó Cadhain; the alacrity and finesse of Elizabeth Bowen; the linguistic force and challenge of the translator Pádraig de Brún; the vitality of Seán Ó Ríordáin's poetry of being; the fusion of ancient and modern in Máire Mhac an tSaoi. Looking at such a listing, there can be little doubt but that we are considering a literature, in two languages, of global significance. This is not a writing that is under the shadow of Yeats or anyone else; that there is a church and state which in their alliance are oppressive to the spirit may have done more to create a forcing ground for creative excellence than work to its inhibition.

The early life of Liam O'Flaherty is an epitome of the many disparate and conflicting elements in Irish society in the period prior to, and consequent upon, the revolution and the War of Independence. He was born on Inishmore on the Aran Islands in 1896, the year when Yeats was telling Synge, in Paris, to go to Aran. He originally intended to become a priest, until he abandoned his studies and enlisted in the Irish Guards regiment of the British Army in 1915 as Bill Ganly, using his mother's maiden name, possibly as a means of covering his tracks, a device used by many at this time when volunteers were being sought for the war in Europe. He was sent to the trenches in France and wounded in a bombardment, after which he was discharged, suffering from depression. He returned to Aran for a while before travelling to, amongst other places, South America, where, in Rio de Janeiro in 1919, he heard that the struggle for independence was under way back in Ireland and he headed home, where he was inspired by the socialist ideas of James Connolly.

Now an activist socialist, O'Flaherty befriended Sean O'Casey and began publishing his first novels. O'Casey's *Juno* had, as Declan Kiberd points out in *Irish Classics* (2000), a profound effect on O'Flaherty and became the inspiration for his best-known work, *The Informer* (1925), with the Johnny Boyle character transforming into the incoherent bundle of sensations and impulses that Gypo Nolan becomes in O'Flaherty's primitivist, lurid, and expressionist melodrama. Made into a successful film in 1935 by the Irish-American director John Ford (who was, in fact, a cousin, and to whom O'Flaherty dedicated *Famine* in 1937), the novel reveals O'Flaherty's lack of interest in psychology. He prefers instead to concentrate on action, scene, and surges of emotion. He tends to see people as phenomena compelled by history and by circumstance, and appears to have not the slightest interest in moral choices or dilemmas of indecision. It is as if it is nature and not man that matters, if we think of man and woman as creatures determined by the choices they make and the reasons they give themselves for those choices. This tends to make O'Flaherty a strangely inhuman novelist, whose realism is a realism of circumstance and determinism. It is a bleak world that he creates. This outlook makes him a writer of telluric power when it comes to the natural world, a world rendered with impressive clarity in his short stories in Irish and in English.

'Birth', a story included in *The Mountain Tavern* (1929), does very little more, in a literary sort of way, than describe the calving of a young cow in a remote area, at night, in a rocky place near the sea. A number of men are there, tending her, but they are careful not to interfere too much in the natural process. The cow is calving for the first time, and the onlookers comment that she will be afraid of the night, as is known to be the case when an animal has not given birth before. However, an old man, Red Michael, maintains that she will not be able to stop the process of birth, even though it is night-time, when the tide starts to turn, and this proves to be the case. The cow is in a rocky enclosure where animals are put when their time is come, and Red Michael knows she will make for the 'hollow by the cairn of little stones' when she is ready to calf. This she does, the old man commenting that 'The darkness of night cannot go against nature. It's the moon they feel when the tide's about to turn', so that the process is now placed in a primordial, even cosmic, context, where this birthing event is depicted, in the fiction, as something which is, at one and the same time, powerful, impersonal, irresistible, and beyond human sentiment or comprehension.

O'Flaherty creates a story which registers, with a series of exceptionally subtle images, the implacable beauty and force of nature and of being, its mysteriousness. For instance, he describes the village houses in the distance, their 'dim shapes' rising against the 'starlit sky', human habitations watched over, as the earth itself is watched over, by 'a myriad of wise heavenly eyes'. At the first moment of the turning of the tide, a sheep, one of the flock that has been lying some distance off, rises and begins to chomp the grass. It is the only sound. In this silence O'Flaherty evokes a vivid image of the daisies closed in for the night, yet still functioning as activities of being: 'What silence! The daisies had arched their white leaves inwards over their yellow hearts; many leafy ladders, along which the dewdrops slid to the yellow core.' The daisies, the sheep, the cow, the human, are all part of this mystery. Then the humans hear the low, 'slightly angry noise' of the 'long waves rolling slowly' as the tide starts to shift. And now, adding a female human presence to this atavistic scene, a young woman arrives, with a can of oatmeal and a little bottle of strong drink which the priest's servant has brought from the town that day. The girl is Red Michael's daughter-in-law; meanwhile his son is out fishing, and the girl thinks of him out there, at the mercy of these long, rolling waves and the tides that change. They drink, gratefully.

The cow calves and they scatter the oatmeal over the newly born thing in order to get the cow to clean it so that the mothering instinct can take hold. At first the cow is scared by what she has created, and pulls back when the calf lifts its head. But then Red Michael moves the calf slightly so it makes 'the first sound of life', at which the cow rushes towards its offspring, in the grip of the natural force: 'She put her mouth close to his, glaring at him with dazed eyes. Then she shivered. A low moaning sound came from her suddenly, like a cry of great anguish or of great love that cannot satisfy itself. Then mumbling, she put out her coarse tongue and licked his body savagely.'[1]

It is certain that Aran is the setting here, and it is quite clear that the writing draws upon O'Flaherty's own experience. He has seen cows giving birth many times; he is aware of the strange connectivity between the birth process and the movements of the tides and the changes of the moon. He knows such things, not as symbolic forms full of implication, as Yeats tends to do, but as actualities. And yet, because he is wide awake to the events that take place and the actions of nature, they acquire a significance and a mystery pertaining to themselves; it is as if he has cleansed the mind of any desire to make what is and what happens mean anything other than what it is in itself.

One would not wish to make too much of this, but it is almost as if O'Flaherty is saying that we have had enough of people trying to put all kinds of constructions on events. A period of revolutionary change is one in which, inevitably, there will be a great deal of argument about who is telling the right story, about how you may interpret events and what people say. All kinds of factions and groups as well as individuals will have their own axes to grind, and they will do all they can to make sure that their version of any given event or issue is the one that will prevail. In the end all political action, indeed all military action, comes down to a question of language (as Brian Friel once remarked in an interview), and the interpretation placed upon what has happened and what is taking place. The severity of Synge's intellect brought him directly to that conclusion in *The Playboy*; O'Casey's sorrowing conscience is appalled at what loyalty to or betrayal of a cause (Johnny Boyle's oath to the republican ideal) can do to the vulnerable in *Juno*. In O'Flaherty, Gypo Nolan, the informer, is an automaton driven by blind sensation, as if to say: this is the human consequence of subjection to historical necessity. But O'Flaherty also suspects that it may the case that there is no alternative to this, that the human is overrated, and that what really counts is process itself, irrespective of our longing or our sentiment. His is a brutal world. The story 'Birth', coming at the end of a decade and more of terrible upheaval in Ireland, removes the human from the picture almost completely, to concentrate on the longer patterns, structures, and impulses of nature in which the human element can become negligible.

It was not, of course, as if O'Flaherty was himself immune from the passions and controversies of the 1920s: in 1922 he and a group of socialists occupied the Rotunda and hoisted the red flag over it, demonstrating on behalf of the unemployed; and in 1926, when the

row broke out over O'Casey's *Plough*, he took the side of the nationalists, writing to the newspapers to say that the play, by his one-time
friend, was a travesty of the memory of Pearse and Connolly. In his
writing, however, he developed a brutalist determinism, whereby
human beings are subject to the workings of fate and of history, forces
that remain indifferent to what people suffer. It is a view that is not at
all unlike that of Synge, a harsh outlook that gave his drama a powerful
transfiguring realism; and it is one that is not unlike that found in
Gaelic (and indeed Celtic culture), where a bleak fatalism is never
entirely absent. Growing up on Aran, O'Flaherty would have been
affected by the grim acceptance of the notion that fate is not something
that one can evade, and that its iron rule is to be found at work in the
continual struggle with necessity and the unforgiving laws of the
natural world that is a reality of Gaeltacht life. This outlook,
that there is no law other than the workings of what is determined
for you, that the consolations of faith and belief in a divine justice that
sets all things to rights in the end may be no more than comforting
illusion, is very much a Gaelic world-view, and it is one of the
elements that go to make Irish literature in the modern period feel
entirely contemporary. It is as if this unsentimental Gaelic attitude, that
history is a process that works according to laws outside our compassion and humanity, that people cannot be trusted to behave in any way
other than to their own advantage, is one that is perhaps better able to
cope with what the modern world has revealed about the brutality of
human nature than any comforting notion that life will come good in
the end. O'Flaherty, along with Máirtín Ó Cadhain (and, oddly
enough, Beckett) is one of the great exponents of this bleak, and
utterly modern, Gaelic pitilessness.

With Frank O'Connor and Seán O'Faolain we move into a much
gentler, more intimate, more compassionate emotional atmosphere.
These men, both from Cork city, were active in the Civil War, taking
the Republican side. O'Connor was taught in primary school by
Daniel Corkery, a major short-story writer who introduced his pupil
to Gaelic and English literature, as well as the Russian masters of
fiction. Corkery's attachment to his native city and to the landscape
and culture of west Cork and its Gaeltacht went very deep with
O'Connor, as did the example of Corkery's combination of a refined
literary intelligence with intense nationalist conviction, the latter, in
O'Connor's case, to be as much guarded against as well as respected.

Corkery went on to become Professor of English at University College, Cork (a position for which O'Faolain, another Corkery protégé, applied and was unsuccessful), and produced highly influential books on Gaelic poetry of the eighteenth century (*The Hidden Ireland*, 1924) and on Synge (1931). His example played no small part in the shaping of O'Connor's career as a man of letters, O'Connor writing a novel, as well as studies of Shakespeare, the short story, and the novel, and the short stories for which he is most famous. He also made fine translations of Gaelic poetry and became something of a scholar of Old and Middle Irish. His scholarship and learning are evident in *The Backward Look* (1967), a history of Irish literature, embracing its two traditions, which was based on a series of lectures he gave at Trinity College, Dublin, before his death, and which is an inspiration for this present book.

O'Connor moved to Dublin where he befriended the remote, shy, and difficult Yeats, who ensured that O'Connor became a member of the Irish Academy of Letters which the elder statesman of Irish letters set up, with Shaw, in 1932. One of the Academy's main aims was to oppose the increasingly intolerant official censorship that seemed minded to ban any writing remotely liberal in matters of sex or religion. The Censorship Board, in a mixture of bare-faced idiocy and craven compliance with the narrowest views of an often ignorant Catholic clergy, reflected some of the worst aspects of the narrowing of Irish society that took place in the post-revolutionary era. Its excesses include the banning of O'Connor's translation of Merriman's *The Midnight Court* (1945), the original of which was readily available in libraries (except that, being in eighteenth-century Irish it would not easily be read by many, and was therefore presumably harmless); and of Eric Cross's *The Tailor and Ansty* (1942), a book of folklore based on the sometimes bawdy but entirely innocent stories of Timothy Buckley from Gougane Barra in west Cork, and a friend of O'Connor's.

Yeats made O'Connor a member of the Irish Academy of Letters at the age of 29, and a director of the Abbey after Lady Gregory's death, because he recognized O'Connor's quite exceptional gift as a writer of fiction. It should be said that Yeats's judgement in such matters was not always impeccable, as he often favoured those whom he found congenial for whatever reason, or who were in agreement with him on matters crucial to him, such as the occult or the reality of the spirit world.

O'Connor himself has said that he, O'Flaherty, and O'Faolain wrote 'in the period of disillusionment which followed the Civil War, though with considerable respect for the nationalism that gave rise to it', which describes their context and their attitude towards it exactly.[2] His justly famous short story 'Guests of the Nation', from the collection of the same name (1931), captures that mood of disillusionment. The story is set in the depths of the Irish countryside, probably west Cork, during the war of independence. Two British soldiers, who may be 'Auxiliaries' (ex-members of the British Army recruited to augment the Royal Irish Constabulary during the conflict), are being held by the IRA in a remote farmhouse when word comes that the Englishmen are to be shot in reprisal for the killing of four IRA men in Cork, one of them a lad of 16. The trouble is that the captors and the prisoners have, in the course of the time they have been together, become quite close, the two Englishmen also making friends with the old lady who owns the house where they are being held. The story is told by one of the men who are guarding the prisoners, known as 'Bonaparte', and O'Connor writes the tale in a style of unflinching, unadorned realism which allows him to bring us to the shocking events at the end with a terrible force.

There is one tiny exception to this bleak, realistic focus, and that is the old woman. One day they are talking about the drought they are going through when she says that it is all to do with 'Jupiter Pluvius', a deity that none of them has heard of, save that one of the IRA men thinks he may have something to do with rainfall among the 'pagans'. And when, on another occasion, they are all talking of the 'German war' (this will be the First World War) with one of the Englishmen, Hawkins, maintaining that it was started by the capitalists for their own financial advantage, she cuts in and says that it was caused by 'the Italian Count that stole the heathen divinity out of the temple in Japan. Believe me, Mr Hawkins,' she says, 'nothing but sorrow and want can follow people who disturb the hidden powers.' At which the narrator, Bonaparte says: 'A queer old girl, all right.'[3]

She certainly is, because here, in this unlikely context, in this dirty war of killings and counter-killings, of men being shot down in cold blood, the ancient Hag has reappeared. Here she is again, the *cailleach*, the Hag of Beare, presiding over life and death in this remote place, her landscape, the realm of Ireland, in which profound offence is to be given, in the name of Ireland, to the energies of being over which she has sway.

O'Connor spares us nothing in this classic narrative of political execution. Hawkins, when they take him out to the bog to kill him, in desperation offers to join the IRA, even though he does not believe 'your stuff, but it's no worse than mine'. They shoot him, but do not quite kill him, and Bonaparte has to put another bullet in his head to make sure he's gone. Then they come to the second prisoner, the taciturn Belcher. Donovan, one of those holding the soldiers, and a vicious man, says that he hopes Belcher will understand that he is only doing his duty, to which Belcher replies that he could never really make out what duty was, but that he thinks they are 'all good lads, if that's what you mean. I'm not complaining.'

After they bury the two bodies ('It was all mad lonely') they go back to the house. The old woman asks them what they have done with the prisoners, but she knows, having heard them putting the spade back 'in the houseen'. And then, custodian as she is over life and death, and uniting in herself pagan and Christian, she falls to her knees in the doorway, 'the very doorway . . . and began praying.' One of Bonaparte's fellow-IRA men does the same, but the narrator pushes past her to stand at the door. He looks out at the stars and listens to the birds as their shrieks die out over the bogs. He cannot describe what he feels. But it is as if the bog where the Englishmen are 'stiffening', and the old woman, and his colleague, and the 'bloody stars', are a million miles away, and he somehow feels 'very small and very lost and lonely like a child astray in the snow.'

We must not moralize the fierce writing that concludes this story, an Irish classic of the consequences of violence. But we do have a startling juxtaposition in the emotional force-field of the tale: the old woman, the guardian of being, the creature from whom all life comes, on her knees, mourning her two dead children, English and all as they are (we are told early on in the story that 'you could have planted that pair down anywhere from this to Claregalway and they'd have taken root there like a native weed'); and one of their assassins, standing in the doorway, lost and tiny. Bonaparte has put himself out of connection with the actuality of being; he has offended the creative force of life itself. The doorway has become symbolic with the stress of realization. The old woman and the other IRA man are on their knees in it, a place between the living and the dying; Bonaparte has passed over into some terrible place of cold isolation, a kind of living death, because of the offence he has given to life. He has lost himself. The two Englishmen were guests of the nation, and one of the basic human rules about how you should treat guests has been broken, with the terrible consequence that the breaking of such a rule can bring. The last sentence of the story is masterly: 'And anything that happened to me afterwards, I never felt the same about again.'

You must never turn someone from your door; you must never insult a guest or a visitor. There is a story about the Hag which tells how she turned up one day at the door of a house outside Fermoy in County Cork which overlooked the River Blackwater. She asks for alms, and the man of the house turns her away. She curses him and says that his son will be drowned. The man, terrified, decides to move away from the river, and builds a new house on a hill outside the town. One day he goes to the building-site with his son to look around; momentarily he loses sight of the boy, only to find that he has fallen into a water-butt and is drowned.

The terrible place this man has created for himself in the story from folklore is the place where Bonaparte has also ended up, a place of dereliction and emptiness, out of the way of being and of creativity. It is no exaggeration to say that this place is where Irish life had come to after the blood-lettings, cruelties, hatreds, delighted revenges, sweet angers and rages of the War of Independence and the Civil War that followed. No wonder Irish life narrowed. What other reaction can there be when you are lost and lonely other than to cling for safety to strict laws, enforced sanctities, desperate pieties? John McGahern's father, the sergeant, in McGahern's compelling *Memoir* (2005), is the embodiment of that strict terror, just as his dead mother represents the geniality and blessedness that life can be if not blasphemed against.

The story of the early manhood of the poet Austin Clarke is a harrowing illustration of the emotional and sexual tensions operating on Irish life in the period after the Rising and into the 1920s. It is possible to see, quite clearly, the psychological damage caused by a strict and unforgiving Catholic upbringing on a sensitive nature in the poetry of personal agony and crisis Clarke was to write during the twenties and thirties. He gives, perhaps, the best account of the struggle between a Jansenist longing to purify the mind and will and the natural sensualities of the body that would have been a major part of the inner lives of many young men and women for that long period of time (from say the 1890s to the 1960s) during which the Catholic church exercised its supremacy over southern Irish public and private life.

Clarke's own life was fraught with tensions he found well-nigh impossible to resolve. They seem to have begun in the extraordinary situation that arose during his first confession, a sacrament usually administered at age 6 or 7. The priest questioned the child about masturbation, concerning which the church had a long fixation, inside the confessional and then later in the vestry. Clarke had no idea what the priest was talking about, but he nevertheless confessed to a sin he had not committed to satisfy the urging of his confessor. His mother, a devout and Hell-obsessed Catholic, made sure the young Clarke went to weekly confession and communion, and these observances continued well into his secondary schooling at the hands of the Jesuits and his university education at University College, Dublin. He was taught there by Thomas MacDonagh, one of the leaders of the Rising, who was executed in 1916, to whose position he was appointed at the remarkably young age of 21.

Around this time he fell in love with the poet, playwright, psychic, and feminist Geraldine (Lia) Cummins from Cork (where she was stoned and jeered at when she protested against the conditions of women factory-workers in the city in 1914), who had had plays of hers staged at the Abbey. Clarke's mother profoundly disapproved of Cummins, whose advanced views she considered scandalous. Clarke, in the deepest misery, suffered a nervous breakdown. He underwent electric-shock treatment at the hands of the poet and neurologist George Sigerson and was confined in St Patrick's Hospital. All this while his relationship with Cummins remained unconsummated, and it continued so even after his marriage to her at the Dublin Register Office on New Year's Eve in 1920. The following year he was dismissed from the university, apparently because of his civil marriage. It now seems incredible that a matter of one's private life could lead to disciplinary action, but such retribution for what was perceived to be immoral behaviour or behaviour that could give scandal was a feature of employment practices right into the 1960s and beyond. Young women who got pregnant out of wedlock were frequently summarily sacked from their positions.

For Clarke, this was an Ireland of iron sorrow, unbending rules, parental love barbed with prohibition and demand. His deeply sensual nature could find no outlet, other than through highly mythologized poetry. There is a sense of loneliness and despair everywhere at work in the verse, the result of the working of a post-revolutionary puritan extremism on a mind already frayed by personal stress and trouble. After the shame of losing his good job (one can easily imagine the reproaches of a loving but faith-obsessed mother on this subject) he went alone on a cycling holiday into the west, to Donegal and Connemara, where he seemed to find some consolation in the life there, aspects of which still lay beyond the harsh injunctions of the church. Some kind of release seemed to have occurred for him in Donegal, reflected in the sonorous and beautiful word-music of 'Cei-lidhe' from *The Cattledrive in Connaught* (1925):

> The red Armada of the sun burned down
> From Magheraroarty, melodeons played
> The Waves of Tory and the young girls sat
> Upon the knees of men; I took my sup,
> I kissed the mouth beside me and forgot
> My sorrow on the cold dark tide.[4]

This poem reveals Clarke's unique use of Gaelic metrics to create elaborate and densely worked effects in English. He takes Irish asso-nantal patterns and shapes them into English rhyme and off-rhyme to develop a soundscape that suggests a haze of Gaelic orchestration. In the above there are runs of 'a' sounds, playing against a harmonically related set of 'ay' tones, and these brightnesses are darkened by the 'n' and 'r' sounds that culminate in 'sorrow' and 'dark'. This entire method was viciously made fun of by Beckett in *Murphy* (1938), where Clarke appears as Austin Ticklepenny, but Beckett's hilarious send-up should not blind us to the considerable linguistic and emo-tional subtlety of poems such as 'Ceilidhe'. These elaborate voicings have a distinctly musical element, and it is interesting to recall that Clarke contemplated a career as a violinist, at one time even (before the job at UCD) applying for a position as violinist at the cinema in New Ross, County Wexford. All things considered, he might have been better off had he taken that up as the day job. For one thing it would have got him out of Dublin and away from the constant rebuke of his mother's anxiety about his immortal soul.

The delicacy of the early art of Clarke has been, as Brian Fallon has argued in *An Age of Innocence* (1998)—his outstanding study of Irish culture in this generally underrated period from 1930 to 1960—often underestimated by comparison with the later flowering that took place beginning in the 1950s. A poem like 'The Lost Heifer', also from *The*

Cattledrive in Connaught, is pure magic. It draws upon the old metaphor that Ireland is a white-backed cow, astray from her keeper, lost in a country that has become the place of foreigners. There is a famous, mournful song in Irish on this subject, which is as old as Indo-European culture itself: India is figured as a sacred cow whose milk nourishes her people. Clarke takes this theme and works it into an elegy of absolute longing and devotion to Ireland, capturing the dizzying intoxication dedication to her cause must have been for many young people at the founding of the Irish state, something it is all too easy to be dismissive of now. Passion, longing, technique, even erotic excitement, all get involved in the exquisite word music:

> When the black herds of the rain were grazing
> In the gap of the cold pure wind
> And the watery hazes of the hazel
> Brought her into my mind,
> I thought of the last honey by the water
> That no hive can find.[5]

The poems of *Night and Morning* (1938), in their locked and frantic urgency, their complex interweave of fervid thought and dark elusive feeling, capture the agony of a tormented conscience, a mind unfree of its obsessions and compulsions, yet longing to be. Two lines from the poem 'Tenebrae' show how deep Clarke's attachment to his Catholicism is, and how it also fills him with foreboding and even terror: 'This is the hour that we must mourn | With tallows on the black triangle....'[6] In all kinds of ways, Clarke's reading of what it was like for an Irish Catholic in this period, heading towards war in a neutral Ireland maintaining its desperate independence from its powerful and imperial neighbour, trying to retain a mind capable of unprejudiced thought, and at the same time all too aware of the vanity of human intellect as against the mighty wisdom of revealed truth and tradition, is a much more valuable account of the interior landscape of the time than a more engaged and therefore probably more naive anticlerical rejection of the church and all it stood for could sustain. Clarke's poetry in this collection takes us into the sufferings of the appalled and stricken conscience. The following lines from the poem already quoted, 'Tenebrae', carefully and uneasily register the confusion of faith transfixed by reason, the fear that what you think may be your undoing, and terror at the idea of a sinful death:

> I hammer on that common door,
> Too frantic in my superstition,
> Transfix with nails that I have broken,
> The angry notice of the mind.
> Close as the thought that suffers him,
> The habit every man in time
> Must wear beneath his ironed shirt.

The Protestant gesture of liberty of conscience, of hammering on the
door the articles of independent conviction free of dogma, is 'angry';
men torment thought itself with the vanity of their presumption,
because, Clarke is saying, the truth is that when it comes down to it,
we must all wear the habit of compliance. There is no confident
throwing off of the shackles of confined belief here; Clarke is far too
subtle for any such unthinking trumpeting of easy liberty. The next
(and last) troubled stanza begins: 'An open mind disturbs the soul',
and he tells us he turns away from the sun, the light of the enlightenment, because it 'makes a show I Of half the world'. So much for
free-thinking. Awaiting us all, he ends, is the 'Darkness that man
must dread at last'.

These gestures of troubled submission are themselves straight out of
Gaelic culture. There is a venerable tradition of poems of repentance
which goes back to the seventeenth century, known as the *aithrí*. Every
major poet of the eighteenth century wrote one of these, renouncing
the vanity of the flesh, and praying Christ's and the Virgin's forgiveness
for all sins committed, all transgressions. This collection contains a
poem, 'Repentance', explicitly modelled on this genre of poem, but in
a sense the entirety of *Night and Morning* is such an act of contrition and
rejection of Satan and the mind's vanities. Clarke, like his Gaelic
predecessors Seán Clárach Mac Domhnaill, or Tadhg Gaelach Ó
Súilleabháin, or Raftery (Antoine Ó Raifteiri), is turning away from
the delights of the flesh, from the young woman of Beare, who made
her last appearance (for a while) in his previous collection, *Pilgrimage
and Other Poems* (1929). Here is the Hag of Beare, but appearing in her
most seductive form, as whore, concubine, pure erotic delight. This is
what he now turns away from, because not to do so will very possibly
drive him literally mad (one of the poems in *Night and Morning* recalls a
time Clarke spent in a mental hospital during a nervous breakdown);
she is letting a client see most, but not all, of what it is he has paid for:

> Heavily on his elbow,
> He turns from a caress
> To see—as my arms open—
> The red spurs of my breast.
> I draw fair pleats around me
> And stay his eye at pleasure,
> Show but a white knee-cap
> Or an immodest smile—
> Until his sudden hand
> Has dared the silks that bind me.[7]

After *Night and Morning* Clarke published no more poetry until *Ancient Lights* (1955), a gap of seventeen years. This silence cannot have been other than involuntary; there was nothing he could do about it. The only conclusion possible is that the writing of poetry had become too painful, because it necessitated engagement with that which scared the living daylights out of him, the world of the senses, and in particular the world of Eros, presided over by the Hag, in her manifestation as seductress, sexual being.

When he started writing poetry again, the Hag was to return, in her erotic form, but by then she had lost something of her chokingly powerful grip on his psyche, and he, Clarke, had become something of a Hag himself.

Mischieviously, Samuel Beckett suggested in *Murphy* (1938), published in the same year as *Night and Morning* (though dwelling sardonically on *Pilgrimage* of 1929), that there was something feminine about Clarke in his heartless portrayal of him as Austin Ticklepenny. In a note to *Pilgrimage* Clarke had written of Gaelic assonance that it 'takes the clapper from the bell of rhyme. . . . [B]y cross-rhymes or vowel rhyming, separately, one or more syllables of longer words, on or off accent . . . lovely and neglected words are advanced to the tonic place and divide their echoes'. It is clear that the musician is in evidence here, in the beautiful and meditative manner he writes about how the aural intelligence can function in poetry. These ideas obviously afforded Beckett great amusement, but for a very serious reason. Beckett was at pains to point out, in his essay on *Proust* (1931), that the artist is engaged on something very different from the (to him) frivolous externalities of assonantal frippery and dividing of echoes. Clarke's 'prosodoturfy', as he derisively called it, is utterly beside the point to anyone approaching their work as a writer with any integrity.

This codology of Clarke's was a kind of transgression on the real nature of the relationship between language, the self, and the object, which is a hell of a lot more complicated than prettifying assonance, a technical tangent all the more irritating for calling to mind the lugubrious attractions of the Celtic thing, Yeats, Russell, the Orders of Celtic Mysteries, and a particularly pertinacious gang of cultists from Cork (O'Connor is another target of Beckett's ire in *Murphy*).

In *Proust* Beckett wrote that art is a kind of penance, an 'apotheosis of solitude',[8] and he holds strictly to the idea that it involves a deep 'contraction of the spirit', a refusal of anything remotely like an easy presumption of knowing what the world is like, because, as he wrote in a review of the cerebral, difficult, and elegant poet Denis Devlin (1908–59), whatever reality might be, 'she' (as Beckett terms her) is not 'the kind of girl' that you can presume to move in on easily.[9] In this she is very unlike the Miss Counihan of *Murphy*, a one-time mistress of the protagonist, who 'looks on for anything'. The 'high-breasted' Miss Counihan, evidently a send-up of Cathleen Ni Houlihan, takes comfort in the 'slow-motion osmosis of love's spittle' she transacts in Wynn's Hotel with a certain Wylie, one of the Corkonians, than which, she had, Beckett tells us, 'never enjoyed anything quite so much'. The gratification she has owes not a little to the fact that (and here is the tell-tale phrase) Wylie was 'not one of those lugubrious persons who insist on removing the clapper from the bell of passion'. Far from it; he insists on inserting the clapper on all occasions. A kiss from Wylie was like, Beckett delights in informing us, 'a breve tied, in a long slow amorous phrase, over bars' times its equivalent in demi-semiquavers.'[10] The mockery of Clarke's earnest note with its musical filigree of metaphor could not be more explicit.

However, even though the comedy is broad (and very funny)— Beckett allows himself a little note to the reader after the above kissing passage to say that it is carefully calculated 'to deprave the cultivated reader'—his point remains serious. Negotiating a connection with whatever it is that the object may be is a dangerous exercise, and not one to be presumed upon, the way that Wylie can presume to insert himself into Miss Counihan, an entry to be gained only because she herself is on for anything. It is a transgressive transaction, a usurpation of secrecies, whereas Murphy's mind, which Beckett goes to some trouble to explain to us, is the artist's mind, into which he contracts in his rocking chair, where he somehow contrives to tie himself up. The mind of Murphy is a 'matrix of surds', Beckett tells us.[11]

It is worthwhile pausing for a moment to see what it is that Beckett means by what might seem like a bit of arrogant youthful pedantry. There is a scholastic pleasure in the ostentatious knowingness, but more is going on than a cavorting of bleak intellectual plumage. What is a surd? A surd is an irrational number. The cube root of 8 is 2 ($2 \times 2 \times 2 = 8$): that means that 2 is a rational number, as is 3. The cube root of 9 is 2.080084, with the decimal reaching into an ever-receding infinity. The cube root of 9 is therefore irrational or surd. Murphy's mind, and by implication the mind of the artist, occupies this irrational space of ever-shifting refinements and implications, where nothing can be presumed. It is not an exaggeration to say that the entirety of Beckett's fiction and drama inhabits this matrix of surds, the interstices between our certainties. This is how he describes the Murphy mentality, and in doing so he limns out the space, the surd space, where all the voices emanate from in the work that is to come, the great work that lies ahead. The wording, even, predicts terrible and moving passages in works such as *The Unnamable* (in French, 1953; English, 1958). Murphy's mind is:

a flux of forms, a perpetual coming together and falling asunder of forms.... But the dark has neither elements nor states, nothing but forms becoming and crumbling into the fragments of a new becoming, without love or hate or any intelligible principle of change.... Here he was not free, but a mote in the dark of absolute freedom. He did not move, he was a point in the ceaseless unconditioned generation and passing of line. Matrix of surds.

Beckett's work takes you into the unnamable, the infinite hinterland of surds between the cube roots of 8 and, say, 27 ($3 \times 3 \times 3$), both of which are rational numbers: 2 and 3. Vladimir and Estragon in *Waiting for Godot* (produced in French, 1953) are in a place that is surd (not absurd, oddly enough, given that Beckett used to be thought of as one of the dramatists of 'the absurd'); their voices are excavatory, immersive, in the gap that obtains between what we imagine might be fixed points. The bravery and comedy of their condition are evident in the continually renewed attempts to send out messages to each other in the void, that infinite space of waiting and unceasing deferral. Pozzo appears to arrive from a fixed world of power and certainty and control, with Lucky as his emblem of mastery over reality; but he too is astray and wandering, for all his cruel oppressions.

In some respects *The Unnamable* is the fiction that presents us with the fullest arena of what is surd. It takes us into the irrational spaces inside time, inside narrative, inside personality, inside speaking and writing itself. Voice succeeds voice in a continuous flow of rage and anger and abuse. There is a kind of narrative voice but this cedes to other voices, ones that we recognize: Molloy, Belacqua, Moran, Watt, and so on, previous utterers of what Beckett called his 'miseries' (his term for his writing; it wasn't as if he enjoyed it). Not just that: there really is no clear distinction between these voices and the narrative one; they all dissolve into each other, 'a perpetual coming together and falling asunder of forms', as he put it in *Murphy*. Here is the narrator, raising maximum doubt about who speaks for whom and for what: 'Sometimes I say to myself, they say to me, Worm says to me, the subject matters little, that my purveyors are more than one, four or five. But it's more likely it's the same foul brute all the time, amusing himself, pretending to be a many, varying his register, his tone, his accent and his drivel.'[12]

'The subject matters little.' And who is to say what the object is when she is at home? In fact neither have a home, other than in the words that come from that space (that outer space) that Beckett's fiction opens for us. In all kinds of ways this was an extreme but in some respects definitive response to all the confidence of the revolution, the agony of Civil War, the despairing piety of the Catholic church in post-Treaty Ireland. The Irish, Beckett says, were 'buggered into existence' by the British Empire and the Catholic church. And the buggers were everywhere in evidence to his sorrowing eye. There is no doubt but that Beckett's work is a response to the condition of Europe during and after the Second World War (when he was in the French Resistance, for which he received the medal of the Legion d'Honneur), the dereliction of life created by grotesque and, for a long time, apparently unconquerable evil; but it was also his own reaction in exile to his upbringing in Ireland, and the torments caused him by the memory of acute mental and physical suffering, the after-effects of which followed him all his life. His realization of in-between places is a deep exploration of what Yeats called 'Anglo-Irish solitude',[13] an Irish writer for an Ireland that was definitely not a home for him, but which remained an obsession. Again *The Unnamable*: 'I'm the air, the walls,

the walled-in one, everything yields, opens, ebbs, flows, like flakes,
I'm all these flakes, meeting, mingling, falling asunder, wherever I go
I find men, leave me, go towards me, come from me, nothing ever but
me, a particle of me.'[14]

Beckett's response to the condition of post-war Europe, the Cold
War, the nuclear threat, and to the condition of Ireland, a habitation of
the mind that never left him, with its narrowness, its craven and half-
crazed piety, the monolithic egos of the old revolutionary warriors,
such as de Valera, was the contraction of the spirit he created in his
writing, one of the bravest and most compelling moral and emotional
confrontations with the nightmare that was Europe (and Ireland as a
compromised region of that tormented place) in the sixty-odd years
from the rise of Fascism to the break-up of Communism that began in
1989, the year he died. It is a strange irony to think that some of the
most significant Irish writing of this (or any) period was created in
French before being translated into Beckett's cold-eyed Hiberno-
English, mostly by himself. Not just that, his translation of the French
dramatist Robert Pinget was done into the same idiom, and it is to be
found in some of the epigrams from Sebastien Chamfort: 'Better on
your arse than on your feet, | Flat on your back than either, dead than
the lot.'[15]

The family background and literary career of Flann O'Brien
(pseudonym of Brian O'Nolan) are in marked contrast to those of
Beckett. He was born in 1911 in Strabane, now in Northern Ireland
but then part of an unpartitioned Ireland under the Union, into a
family of convinced nationalists. His father, Michael, was a civil
servant who steadily progressed up the ranks, eventually becoming a
Commissioner in the Customs and Excise under the Free State government. There were twelve children in the family, and they were
brought up speaking Irish in the home, so that English was, to some
extent, a foreign language to them. Being such a sizeable family unit,
they tended to provide for themselves their own society and entertainment. Added to this, the children were educated at home, largely
to postpone until the last possible moment the acquisition of English,
and were not sent to school until comparatively late, some years in
most cases beyond what would be considered normal. O'Brien's Irish
was, therefore, confident and fluent, so that when he went to University College, Dublin (UCD), where he studied German and Irish, he
was, as Anthony Cronin's fine biography, *No Laughing Matter: The Life*

and Times of Flann O'Brien (1989), points out, taken aback to find that the Irish of his professor, none other than the founder of the Gaelic League, Douglas Hyde, was clumsy and grammatically imprecise, as was that of his lecturer, Agnes Farrelly.

The background was Catholic middle class, and O'Brien remained attached to his faith all his life. The family was reasonably well-to-do, and when they finally settled in Dublin they maintained a large house with two maids. There was, as Cronin makes clear, a deeply conservative element in O'Brien's make-up, which sat uneasily beside a radical, subversive, and sometimes rancorous streak. He attended Synge Street Christian Brothers School for a while, where the O'Nolan children, apart from Brian, were bullied because of their strangeness, having Northern accents, and speaking a not entirely certain English. They then attended the Holy Ghost Fathers College in Blackrock, a very different establishment, where the Dean of Studies was the future, conservative (and influential), archbishop of Dublin, John Charles McQuaid. Thus was laid the groundwork in a complicated personality that contained, with considerable strain, a great many conflicting attitudes, deep-seated loyalties, beliefs, discontents. James Joyce, famously, had Stephen Dedalus proclaim that he had flown by the nets of religion, family, and nation, making, as Anthony Cronin, acidulously says, a song and dance about it, even though he 'managed the business'. For all kinds of complex reasons, it was not such an easy matter for O'Brien, and for his contemporaries, to make these breaks, nor would it be for a great many for years after. Nor is it entirely certain that this kind of cutting loose from adherence to the forms of society is easy in a context where that society is one that has been achieved after a great deal of difficulty and turbulence, to put it mildly. Again Cronin puts his finger on the crux of the matter: 'A break with Catholicism [or, I would add, nationalism, family loyalty] would involve questions of your very identity, racial, social, historical. It would also involve questions of your future and your position in the scheme of things: even your ability to earn a living might be in jeopardy.'[16] The harsh truth of the last observation was very clearly in evidence when Austin Clarke lost his lectureship (the one in which he replaced the executed 1916 leader Thomas MacDonagh) at UCD almost certainly because of the perceived irregularity of his (unconsummated) marriage. When O'Brien went on to UCD, one of his close friends there was Donagh MacDonagh, son of the 1916 martyr, from whom he borrowed *Ulysses*, which, though not actually banned, was very difficult to obtain.

This was, as Cronin observes, 'an immensely talented generation'. O'Brien's contemporaries at UCD included not just MacDonagh, who became a serious poet and a judge; but also Niall Montgomery, a man of wit and refinement, who became an architect; and Niall Sheridan, another poet (and gambler), who earned money as a tipster, and was subsequently the person in charge of public relations for Irish television. O'Brien was to enter the Civil Service. When his father died, he took it as read that he should become the mainstay of family. In fact, there was very little else that he could do. Apart from a sister, who worked as a trainee teacher, no one else was bringing money into a household of twelve children. There was no widow's pension, no children's allowance. O'Brien seemed to accept this responsibility with a ready stoicism. There is a moving story of Christmas Eve in 1937, the year in which his father died, of him coming home from the pub at the, for him, early hour of nine o'clock with a large suitcase full of presents for everyone.

It will be evident that the mentality of O'Brien, and that of his gifted contemporaries, was one in which there was a readiness to make peace with a society about which there might be all kinds of misgivings, but it was one to which it was not impossible to offer some kind of allegiance. There would be worse places to live, and in any case there was very little hankering, certainly amongst the Irish Catholic middle classes now in control of the institutions of church and state, after the good old days of British rule. This despite the fact that there was a high level of emigration amongst the rural and the urban poor. In some respects this group of O'Brien's clever associates at UCD constituted a kind of elite in the new Irish society, giving them a freedom and an artistic licence they fully exploited. Drink played a large part in this liberty, and Grogan's pub (at the corner of Leeson Street and St Stephen's Green) became a more inebriated Irish version of a Parisian café.

Meanwhile O'Brien, while steadily advancing, as his father had done before him, within the Civil Service, was also writing one of the masterpieces of modern Irish literature, the novel *At Swim-Two-Birds* (1939), while his brother Ciaran, who was not in a job, toiled away at a novel in Irish. O'Brien was also to publish, in 1941, *An Béal Bocht* ('The Poor Mouth'), a gruesomely hilarious book about Gaeltacht life, which contrives, in the most elegant modern Irish, to be a devastating attack on obsession with that language, and the almost mystical aura with which Gaeltacht life had been imbued by the likes of Daniel Corkery and Frank O'Connor. O'Brien evokes the constant rain, the constant complaining, the begrudgery, which were aspects of this world, but the whole thing is overcast by a deep sorrow, and a sense of human dereliction. The creatures of *An Béal Bocht*, whose names elide into each other, and who have no identity other than through the privations they undergo for Irish, are not unlike the wrecks who inhabit the fictions of Samuel Beckett, in works such as *Watt* (written 1942–3) or *Molloy* (1951).

In *At Swim-Two-Birds* the separate narratives elide into each other, as the characters do in *An Béal Bocht*. To some extent his model here was the Cyclops episode in *Ulysses*, but O'Brien's comic realism connects the interweaving tales to a much more recognizable version of everyday life on the one hand, while the fantastic and legendary elements, of which there are a great deal, are all inhabited by a vernacular energy and an attentiveness to the witty sallies of Irish speech.

O'Brien was fortunate in that he acquired the services of a good literary agent in London, A. M. Heath, who sent the book to Collins at first, where it was rejected; but then, sending it to Longman's, it came to the attention of Graham Greene, the English novelist, then acting as a reader for that firm. He saw the genius of the book and provided an excellent summary of what it was about in his report:

> its amazing spirits do not disguise the seriousness of the attempt to present, simultaneously as it were, all the literary traditions of Ireland—the Celtic legend (in the stories of Finn), the popular adventure novels (of a Mr Tracey), the nightmare element as you get it in Joyce, the ancient poetry of Bardic Ireland and the working-class poetry of the absurd Jem Casey.... We have had books inside books before now, and characters who are given life outside their fiction ... but O'Brien [goes] a long way further; the screw is turned until you have, (a) the narrator writing a book about a man called Trellis who is, (b) writing a book about certain characters who, (c) are turning the tables on Trellis by writing about him ... [L]ooking back afterwards one realises that by no other method could the realistic, the legendary and the novelette have been worked in together.[17]

As a summary of O'Brien's plot and his method this would be hard to beat.

The narrator is a student at UCD, who spends most of his time in the privacy of his bedroom, when he is not drinking in town with his cronies. He is lodging with his uncle, 'Holder of Guinness clerkship the third class', who enquires about his studies: 'Tell me this, do you ever open a book at all?', to which the narrator replies, 'I open several books every day'. His uncle's reply: 'You open your granny . . . O I know the game you are at above in your bedroom. I am not as stupid as I look, I'll warrant you that.'[18]

Where Murphy retires into his 'matrix of surds', O'Brien's narrator, in the privacy of his bedroom, retires into nothing less than the matrix of Gaelic tradition as it survives in the second quarter of the twentieth century. The novel is an astonishing mixture of folklore, the Fionn cycle, the cycle of the Kings (from which comes the story of Sweeney, the mad king of Rasharkin in County Antrim, who is sent mad through the curse of a cleric and doomed to roam all over Ireland exposed to the elements and living in trees, eating raw cress and grass), stories of the fairies and the pookas (malign members of the sídh, or fairy people), cowboy stories, featuring the adventures of one Slug Willard and his 'butty', Shorty Andrews, who have 'the full of two belts of bright bullets as well as a pair of six-guns apiece', and much else.

O'Brien, presenting his young narrator, writes English as if it is a strange and foreign tongue, which of course it was to some degree. This creates a distancing and distorting effect, whereby the everyday is thrown, as it were, into a kind of grotesque parody of itself. At one point, discovering himself becoming 'verminous', he resolves 'to make an end of my dissolute habits and composed mentally a regime of physical regeneration which included bending exercises'. He also starts attending college with more regularity: 'It was my custom to go into the main hall of the College and stand with my back to one of the steam-heating devices, my faded overcoat open and my cold hostile eyes flitting about the faces that passed before me. . . . Clerical students from Blackrock or Rathfarnham, black clothes and bowler hats, would file past civilly and leave the building by a door opening at the back where they were accustomed to leave the iron pedal-cycles.'[19] 'The iron pedal-cycles' is a phrase that could readily occur in Irish, where an object of a clause is often deferred to the end of a complex sentence to heighten emphasis by a kind of syntactic withholding, but in English it seems to confer a dreadful materiality to the circumstances of the ordinary, making it menacing and forbidding.

The comedy is exultant, however, especially so in those places where O'Brien's affection for, and understanding of, the legendary cycle of Fionn tales combine with a wild and reckless invention that itself comes straight out of a Gaelic tradition of intensely literary self-parody and bare-, but also po-faced, exaggeration. One of the classic tropes of the Ossianic tales has to do with the various traits that a warrior worthy of inclusion in the Fionn militia needs to possess, and the tests novitiates to the soldiery had to undergo to show their prowess. Here is a brief extract from O'Brien's version of this:

No man is taken till a black hole is hollowed in the world to the depth of his two oxters and he put into it to gaze from it with his lonely head and nothing to him but his shield and a stick of hazel. Then must nine warriors fly their spears at him. . . . With the eyelids to him stitched to the fringe of his eye-bags, he must be run by Finn's people through the bogs and marsh-swamps of Erin with two odorous prickle-backed hogs ham-tied and asleep in the seat of his hempen drawers.[20]

But the novel is more than a mere literary flight of learned and fantastical fancy. If it were just this, then it would be no more than a curiosity. Instead it is, amongst other things, a meditation on the ways in which it is possible to perceive reality, a concern in Irish literature as old as John Scotus Eriugena, the ninth-century philosopher at the court of Charles the Bald. It is also a book that records a profound sense of estrangement from a society that is nevertheless registered as one that should be familiar and perhaps even congenial. The world as O'Brien sees it is one that should be secure and reassuring; instead, it has a volition of its own that cannot be controlled. All the authorial play-acting, with people writing novels about other people and thereby controlling them, suggests that the way things are in reality have in them something intractable and, in the end, perhaps, danger-ous. There is a sense that the Pooka in this novel, who is a devil, is its presiding genius. O'Brien appears to have retained adherence to his Catholic faith during his life, and that, of course, includes an accept-ance of the reality of evil, and of the devil as a force and agency, and not just as a metaphysical concept.

At Swim-Two-Birds is that comparatively rare thing, an Irish study of evil. And if this is the case with this novel, it is even more so with its successor, *The Third Policeman* (1967), written in 1939–40, but unpublished until after O'Brien's death. So ashamed was he at its rejection by London publishers (it was found that he had become even more fantastic, when he should, the publishers' readers felt, be trying to become more realistic) that he pretended to have lost the manuscript on a train, or in the Dolphin Hotel, or that it was blown out, page by page, from the boot of a car in County Donegal. O'Brien's life and work were, to adopt Anthony Cronin's title for his biography of his friend, no laughing matter. His fictions do have the capacity to make the reader laugh out loud, but a terrible sadness is implicated in the hilarity. He takes us to the heart of his society: duty mixed with contempt, love of country mixed with rage at the authority of church and state, family affection and loyalty mixed with disgust, friendship interinvolved with hate. And at the back of all this sadness, behind the desperate drinking in Grogan's, the frantic speculations that it is possible for a policeman to exchange his molecules with that of his bicycle (those 'iron cycles'), there lurks a dreadful sense that the world is a place of chaotic energy presided over by Evil, with the devil himself as an active agent: the classic heresy of Manicheism.

One of the subtlest, most careful minds in Irish literature is that of Louis MacNeice. Born in Belfast in 1907, into a Church of Ireland family (his clergyman father became a bishop), he spent his early years in Carrickfergus, County Antrim, before attending prep school in England, then Marlborough public school, then Merton College, Oxford. But Ireland haunted him. MacNeice used to be considered one of the 'poets of the thirties', along with W. H. Auden and Stephen Spender, and he was certainly one of that group, sharing, to some extent, their left-wing views, but this association is a long way from defining him. He used also to be considered to lie outside the Irish tradition, mainly because of his immersion in English life and culture (he taught classics at university level in England before working for the BBC in the features department), and because he was felt to be more Anglo than Irish. It is now recognized that MacNeice is a major Irish poet, all the more so because his relations with Ireland were complex and ambiguous.

In *The Strings Are False* (1965), an unfinished autobiography published after his death, MacNeice writes about what he calls 'falling awake'. He tells us that an American friend once said to him that he never seemed to make any deliberate choices, that he seemed just to go along with what happened, and he agrees with this, saying that the things that happen to you may actually be better than what you choose. And he then goes on to say that this accidental factor is the very thing that marks those poems of his that seem to him to be most effective. As if poetry is a kind of falling awake into things, rather than a big design or an act of the will.

Now, it is for this reason that Yeats fascinated him, and fitted him to be the author of what is in fact one of the best critical books ever written about Yeats, *The Poetry of W. B. Yeats* (1941), in that Yeats is mostly a poet of the Titanic will. History (for which read everything that happens in the everyday world of anger, the quick fix, frustration, self-gratification) to Yeats is something to be approached with disdain and the hard-won belief that somehow what is can be shaped by the drive of the artistic will, to make that famous golden bird to sing in Byzantium of the trivia of what happens. This defiance MacNeice saw and admired, but thought differently. He knew that Yeats believed that spirit was the ultimate reality; so-called reality was a shadowy cave of smoky shadows. Or, to put it in a less overtly Platonic way, in the here and now there is only conflict, where the half-realities or the simulacra fight it out in a conflict that the artist uses as his theme whereby he asserts the supremacy of the pride that can make a man whole, he being the high-priest that delivers the shivering intimations of that ultimate unity of being.

This concept is a long way from the 'falling awake' that characterizes the accidental nature of the way MacNeice thinks of the process of the imagination, which involves a surrender to what he calls the 'drunkenness of things being various' in 'Snow' from *Out of the Picture* (1937). It is worth looking a little more closely at this poem. There is a room with a display of roses in a vase in the bay window; outside there is snow. The room is the front living room of the bishop's residence on the Malone Road, Belfast, now home of the Arts Council of Northern Ireland. There is a fire in the grate, and the world is 'crazier' than we think, 'Incorrigibly plural'. The writing is all alertness, all 'falling awake' into the nature of things being various. The last line is haunting: 'There is more than glass between the snow and the huge roses.' MacNeice says the mystery without declaiming it. He allows himself to fall into its graces.[21]

In the autobiography he associates this feeling of utter variety, of the unknown within what we think we know, with coming upon the seeming endlessness of Magilligan Strand on the north Derry coast for the first time. Ireland remained as close to him as that, where a particular locale is intimately connected with the deepest freedoms and releases of his art.

This basic attitude, whereby artistic delight is to be discovered in the variousness and extent of Magilligan Strand, becomes, through the integrity of his vision, his method and his technique. Ezra Pound believed that technique is no more or no less than sincerity. Of course, it is no simple matter to be sincere. *Autumn Journal* (1939) is a long meditative poem of the deepest sincerity. Written during the Munich crisis, when Britain and France agreed that Hitler be allowed to annexe the German-speaking Sudetenland of Czechoslovakia, the poem allows itself to explore the variousness of the emotions and anxieties of the time, as war, which had seemed inevitable, now looked as if it might have been averted by a dubious tactical capitulation on the part of Britain and France to the imperial demands of the Third Reich. MacNeice writes, on the point of the moment, as it were: 'once again | The crisis is put off and things look better | And we feel negotiation is not vain— | Save my skin and damn my conscience.'[22]

In Section XVI of this long poem he turns to Ireland, its attitude towards its own history and to Europe at this time of dread and fear. He has, he tells us, been reading the memoirs of Maud Gonne, and thinking about how Irish history gets to be retold and used. He envies the 'intransigence' of his countrymen (this is what he calls them) who can shoot to kill and never find that another's motives can have the force to 'sabotage' their own. He remembers the fear that Roger Casement would invade Ulster, and, in a magnificent phrase, the 'voodoo of the Orange bands | Drawing an iron net through darkest Ulster'. And then the brio of his seeking and alert imagination is set free to fall awake, and this searchlight of poetic vigilance is now trained on Cathleen Ni Houlihan, King William riding his horse to the Boyne on a banner, all the 'purblind manifestoes, never-ending complaints', until he reflects that he thought he was 'well out of it' through his English life, except 'her name keeps ringing like a bell | In an under-water belfry'. He cannot turn away, not entirely, even though 'she gives her children neither sense nor money | Who slouch around the world with a gesture and a brogue | And a faggot of useless memories.'[23]

MacNeice, a Horace to Beckett's Seneca, creates a poetry of exquisite (because deeply agonized) balance, an interposition between the
world and its variousness and what the self is may be: whatever it is that
is the case between the roses in the living room and the depth of snow
outside. His poetic, if one might call it that, is exceptionally mature
and sane: no hectic outcries of ego, no wailing against fate. The poetry
is schooled in classic tact and decorum, and becomes a space of the free
intelligence, and more importantly, of free and generous emotion.
MacNeice is an exceptional love poet: see 'Déjà Vu' from *The Burning
Perch* (1963), his last volume. He can see his Ireland, the Ireland of his
time, poised between the past and the present; part of Europe, though
fated to be out of the cataclysm that the continent faced in 1939. What
is remarkable about his achievement is the calm with which such
complexity and understanding is embraced.

In this chapter, which is a survey of the literature of the years
between 1926 and roughly 1960, bearing in mind the contexts of
that writing, and its preoccupation with 'ancient things', one is con-
founded by its sheer range and depth. The canvas is very crowded, and
there is a danger of not seeing the wood for the trees. And yet it is
surely of vital importance to give some small attention to Joyce Cary, a
writer now almost forgotten, and yet the creator of a body of work
which must rank him amongst the finest novelists of the twentieth
century. Again, within the sometimes narrow confines of Irish literature, Cary is frequently classed as an outsider: he very much belongs to
the Anglo-Irish tradition, and most of his life, as with MacNeice, was
spent in England or in the British colonial service.

The Carys, a Devonshire family, were granted lands seized by the
crown from Cahir O'Doherty of Inishowen, County Donegal, under
the Ulster Plantation in the early seventeenth century. By the time Joyce
Cary was born in 1888 the family fortunes had undergone significant
decline, in large part owing to the tenant-relief acts of the late nineteenth century, one of which, in 1881, remitting rent owed to landlords,
ruined the Carys, who, as tolerant landlords, had allowed arrears to build
up. The family settled in London, where Cary's father worked as a civil
engineer. Nevertheless, summers back in Ireland, at the family home,
Castle Cary, and with relatives in Donegal, were formative. His sprawling Tolstoyan novel, *Castle Corner* (1938), is based on the familial
experience of the Irish Land War, as well as political movements in
Britain in the early twentieth century, and his own immediate

knowledge of imperial expansion in Africa. After Oxford (where he did not distinguish himself: he was awarded a fourth-class degree) Cary joined the Nigerian Colonial Service in 1913, serving with it, and earning a war commission, until 1920. He was convinced of the need for African independence, and his understanding of Africa, clear-eyed, unsentimental, open, and appreciative, is much in evidence in his African novels, amongst which can be classed *Castle Corner*, but especially the heart-rending *Mister Johnson* (1939).

There is an affinity between the artistic approach and method of Louis MacNeice and that of Joyce Cary. It may be that this has to do with some shared Anglo-Irish heritage, a sense of belonging to Ireland as much as to England, as well as a remoteness from both these places, what Yeats called, in that striking phrase, Anglo-Irish solitude. The kinship between Cary and MacNeice resides in an openness to the complexity of life ('falling awake' as MacNeice put it) and a capacity to find a form or a technique to accommodate that without being overwhelmed by variousness, sheer multiplicity. The open fretwork of the form of *Autumn Journal*, which allows MacNeice to travel at will through experience and shape things according to their pressure and circumstantial weight, is one answer. The Cary approach is not dissimilar. As a novelist he did not work through a fiction from beginning to end; rather did he build up the novels, point by point, around situations and circumstances in a gathering net of accreted apprehension, so that his narratives acquire a feeling of accumulating presence, of life unfolding according to its own laws. The stories have a sense of being like life itself, a feeling of accidentality and surprise (one of Cary's favourite words). Just to emphasize the plurality of his method, a kind of literary pointillism, it should be remarked that not only did he not work from start to finish on a single novel; more often than not he had several novels on the go at once, as he assembled his fiction, which is all one story really, one great novel of the integrating mind. This perhaps is why his reputation languishes at the moment; in the twenty-first century we are inclined to focus on the small instance, the atomic instant, rather than the whole organum of a serious and complex mind.

Cary's novels work by concentrating on the differences between perceptions, points of view, characters, the stories they tell of themselves. But he does not focus on the chasms between things, and perceptions of them, or between different minds, as Beckett does; Cary registers the difference and then, as a storyteller, tries to

coordinate this variousness into an unfolding continuum of felt awareness and presence. He wanted his novels to have the sense of a
comprehended life as he saw and admired it in James Joyce, a writer
with whom he believed he had an affinity through his mother's
people, Joyces from Omagh, who, like all the Joyces, came originally
from Galway. Incidentally, in the northern part of Ireland, it tends to
be a Protestant tradition to name a child after a wife's surname. Cary
was christened Arthur Joyce Lunel, but it was as Joyce he was known.

   A House of Children (1941) draws extensively on memories of
Inishowen, Moville, Quigley's Point, and the summers spent there as
a child, swimming, boating, fishing, free to roam the roads and wild
countryside, the bogs and woods and rocky inlets. The house he stayed
in, Castle Cary, was almost on the water's edge, and he could see the
waves reflecting the sunlight on the shadowy ceiling and walls of his
room. It was a magical place, and the novel has a strange luminescent
quality, a ready stillness, a wondering wakefulness. Cary is, of course,
aware that he, while of this place, is also, quite crucially, not completely part of it. He is different. But this gives him the readiness to see
what that life is like, to appreciate its otherness and completeness, and
the distance also gives him the impulse to integrate this difference into
his story.

   There is a telling moment when the young boy, Evelyn, the Cary
character, gets lost in the back lanes of Moville (Cary calls it Dunville).
There is a mass of material piled up against the rocks in the lane, fish-
boxes, oars, masts; strung up high on ropes stretching from wall to wall
across the lane are ropes with skate wings hung on them, dripping
brown fish-blood onto the rocks below. There is a bad smell of dead
fish. And then he sees a little girl crouched down, looking beneath a
door, and she asks him in her hoarse rough voice if he wants to look.
He bends down beside her and sees what she sees: a drunk man is
chasing two barefoot girls around the yard and is swearing at them
while they evade him easily, laughing all the time. Cary goes on:

I felt an intense curiosity in her, not as a girl, but as a being, a person. Perhaps
this was the first time I realised another person . . . I remember my keen sense
of this other person; a sense neither sympathy nor curiosity nor wonder; but
containing all three in something greater than any, an indescribable feeling of
difference and community in one. It was, I suppose, as if one blade of
grass should touch another and feel it and think: 'It is not me, but it is very
close to me'.[24]

The writing is perhaps a little abstract at this point, but it comes after the vivid evocation of this place of revelation, of epiphany. It is also, quite deliberately, I think, invoking the language of the Holy Trinity, where three inhere in one and one in three. Each entity is separate, but each also is only itself by becoming involved with the others. Each thing is destined to try to seek its own entity, but it does so only in an incorporation with that which is not itself. This is the 'indescribable feeling', the union of differences. It is the love that forsakes individual love to seek a wider incorporation only to return to that which is personal and singular, where all love starts. This is Cary's great theme, the theme of love achieving itself by recognizing that which is different from itself. It is registered here in the moment of community between the Irish girl from the back lanes of Moville, and Cary, the Anglo-Irish Protestant.

This is the vision that informs Cary's two great trilogies, the Gulley Jimson Trilogy (*Herself Surprised*, 1941; *To Be a Pilgrim*, 1942; *The Horse's Mouth*, 1944) and the Chester Nimmo Trilogy (*Prisoner of Grace*, 1952; *Except the Lord*, 1953; *Not Honour More*, 1955). Each of the novels in this set of six is based on a different character in the network of personages in the two trilogies, so that we are given entirely different perceptions of events and people in each of the novels, a technique Brian Friel was to use in *Faith Healer* (1979). As we read each of the trilogies we experience the shock of discovering that what we thought was a reasonably fixed judgement arrived at in one fiction, undergoes change in the community of understanding that the writing and storytelling becomes. Each of the main characters, Sara Monday, Tom Wilcher, Gulley Jimson in the first trilogy, for instance, has a novel to himself or herself. Each one creates a world, and in that world we see them extending their own realm of possibility, only for this to be modified in the unfolding of complexity that the juxtapositioning of different points of view achieves across the three novels. This is not relativism; it is deeper than that. It is an invitation to the reader to share in the realization of difference and communion that is possible through the kind of storytelling Cary practices. This art is one in which a sense of Anglo-Irish difference is transfigured into a method and a technique that allows Cary to embrace the horror of war, and the reality of brute power being exercised by evil men; Gulley, the artist of *The Horse's Mouth* (who prides himself on speaking from that orifice), admires Hitler, seeing in him something of an artist like himself.

In the London *Evening Standard* the English novelist H. G. Wells
wrote of Irish neutrality in the Second World War as follows: 'God, of
course, is Minister without Portfolio in whatever Cabinet happens to
be in power.... Awkward problems can always be referred back to
Christ or Cromwell.... Yesterday is continuously being shoved in
front of the public eye to bamboozle them about the problems of
today.'[25] The story, it is now generally realized, was more complicated
than that. It wasn't just that de Valera regarded England as the old
enemy (though that undoubtedly formed part of the picture, and it was
a view that would have had some support in the country at large);
there was also the fact that Ireland did not wish to see herself being
dragooned into a war from which, as a small nation, she felt she had the
right to distance herself. Nevertheless, the 'Emergency', as the period
of the war was called in Ireland, had the effect of increasing the
country's isolation from the rest of Europe, and its lack of involvement
in what proved to be a decisive conflict in determining the future state
of the continent heightened a sense, at home, of indifference and bland
complacency. This mood, of introspection, indifference, and frustrated
impulse found expression in one of the major poems of these years,
Patrick Kavanagh's *The Great Hunger* (1942).

Kavanagh, born in 1904, the son of a small farmer from Inniskeen,
County Monaghan, came from the rural Ireland romanticized by the
literary revival. However, in his poetry and novels, while the affection
for the land is pervasive, he is also hugely critical of the sentimentali-
zation of the peasant life, and the ways in which de Valera and the
politicians had developed the rural idyll as an icon of what the real
Ireland should be. In *The Great Hunger* Patrick Maguire lives a life of
sterile and loveless misery, the kind of life Kavanagh himself would
have had to endure but for settling in Dublin in 1939. Not that he was
content there, but he knew very well the tedium and small hatreds that
go to make up much of country life, as well as the fiery torments of
sexual frustration that, for Maguire, are frantically relieved by fantasy
and masturbation. The tedium and sadness of this lonely existence are
captured in the various scenes of isolation that the poem reveals:
Maguire at Mass behind a pillar where he can spit; Maguire in front
of the dying fire late at night, masturbating, his sister grunting in bed;
bachelors playing cards into the small hours, reluctant to face their
silent houses; the mother dying and Maguire feeling nothing. This is
an island of the mind, cut off from life in a sea of disappointment, a

condition of the emotions not unconnected to Ireland's position with regard to Europe in 1942:

> And Patrick Maguire was still six months behind life—
> His mother six months ahead of it;
> His sister straddle-legged across it:—
> One leg in hell and the other in heaven
> And between the purgatory of middle-aged virginity—
> She prayed for release to heaven or hell.
> His mother's voice grew thinner like a rust-worn knife
> But it cut venomously as it thinned,
> It cut him up the middle till he became more woman than man....

Occasionally, just occasionally, through all this sterile male-virgin gloom, there shoot sharp realizations of beauty. The goldfinches 'on the railway paling were worth looking at'; seeing them, you might just imagine yourself 'in Brazil', the romance of the Amazon, briefly traced on the schoolroom map, once more vivid.[26]

The Maguire family, locked in their graceless tedium and rancour, are a rendition of Irish dereliction during the 'Emergency'. Cut off from the greater world of feeling and impulse, they are also cut off from mutuality and responsibility. They hanker after the grim satisfactions of bitterness, and of misfortune visiting others. The Maguires are like this; so is pretty much everyone else. We could not be further from de Valera's vision of youths and maidens dancing at the crossroads. When there are dances, they are occasions of resentment, lust, drunkenness, mockery.

Kavanagh's grim vision of a hate-fuelled rural Ireland is surpassed in ferocity by one of the most devastating portrayals, ever, of Irish rural life, that to be found in Máirtín Ó Cadhain's classic novel of hatred and mockery, Cré na Cille ('Churchyard Clay', 1949). Ó Cadhain was born in 1907 in Cois Fharraige in Connemara, and was trained as a teacher in St Patrick's College in Dublin, returning to teach in the Gaeltacht. He joined the IRA in 1932, taking the Fenian oath (the one Johnny Boyle is reminded of in O'Casey's *Juno*) at the door of his house in Camus, becoming a recruiting officer and attaining the rank of captain. He was kept under constant surveillance by the Garda Síochána, the IRA being now an illegal organization, and in 1936 was sacked from his teaching post for his known subversive activities. Eventually, like many members of the IRA, he was interned in the Curragh during the 'Emergency' (1939–45) as an enemy of the state, during which time he began seriously to write. Although he did not confine his subject matter to the Gaeltacht (many of his stories are set in Dublin, one is set in the Holy Land during the Annunciation to the Virgin), no one else writes with such an intimate attentiveness to the particulars of Gaelic life as it survived into the twentieth century. Many aspects of that life are utterly traditional, as old as the Hag of Beare herself, but he is also alive to the contractions of that life as the ice-floe of Gaelic linguistic integrity melts in the heat of the modern world. He knows his culture is in its death throes, and yet, defiantly, he is one of its greatest stylists ever, as elegant a fashioner of Gaelic prose, based on the vitality of its spoken forms, as was Geoffrey Keating, or the author of the seventeenth-century *Pairlement Chloinne Thomáis* ('The Parliament of Clan Thomas'), a satire on the new churlishness which the author believed was then taking control of Irish life.

Reading Ó Cadhain (something, it has to be said, not that many people do; as noted in Chapter 1, he insisted it should not be translated into English), one is struck by how much is missing in Irish writing in English, as well as acknowledging, paradoxically, one of the sources of its power. What Ó Cadhain's prose reveals is the fluency and eloquence of Irish speech, the virtuosity of which the language is capable. This will have to do with its ancient deposits, its store of rhetorical formalisms, its lexical richness, its capacity for incisive brevity, its sonorities, the craziness and wildness of its humour, and the fact that its folkloric traditions carry into their thew and pith a good deal of the learning and sophistication of the bardic academies, as well much of the traditional corpus of myth, legend, and the sagas. In the Gaelic world (and this is not invention) eloquent speakers of the language were admired and made much of. Poets were revered and feared. Monsignor Pádraig de Brún, when he was translating the *Odyssey* in the 1940s, would take the lines he had been working on in the morning along to the fireside at night, and, over a couple of bottles of stout, would try out his Homeric lines on the local people gathered together in the house where he had lodgings in Dunquin, County Kerry. There the auditors would comment on the versions, and refashion them for their rhythm or suggest different words than his, based on their own experience of the sea, or fishing, or the waywardness of the inhabitants of the spirit world. Incidentally, though de Brún's *An Odaisé* remained unpublished until 1990, when the typescripts were rediscovered and then identified by his niece, the poet Máire Mhac an tSaoi, it is one of the essential books of Irish literature, and one of the finest translations ever of Homer's epic.

What this story of the nightly collaborations over the Homer text in Dunquin reveals is the quite remarkable literary and linguistic refinement of the Gaeltacht community, and the manner in which it reveres practitioners who can deploy language to create the finest effects. And although it is the case that Irish writing in the English language undoubtedly draws upon this Gaelic resource, either directly, through a knowledge of the Irish language on the part of the writer, or indirectly, in that Irish has had all kinds of influences on English as spoken in Ireland in vocabulary, syntax, grammar, and rhythm, nevertheless the Gaelic linguistic world is not that of English. That Gaelic world, and its linguistic integrity, can be accessed only through an immersion in the language, something to be attained by an outsider only through what T. S. Eliot called, in another context, 'great labour'.[27]

Ó Cadhain was born into this world, and he knew its value. Indeed, so conscious was he of its importance that the indifference of modern Ireland towards the language drove him to despair. Another reaction of his to this state of affairs was to write down that language in a kind of frenzy of total recall, so that the Gaeltacht people live in his books through their speech, in all its majesty, with a completeness never before attained. Open *Cré na Cille* anywhere and you are overwhelmed by the vehemence and unremitting energy of this speech. And it is a speech mostly of derision.

Synge's version of the west of Ireland may have been unflattering; Kavanagh's grimly realistic account of Monaghan life in the 1940s laid bare a family and a community mostly sterile; but Ó Cadhain's Gaeltacht people are appalling in their nastiness, their meanness, but chiefly in their capacity to hate. Hatred, I have said, is one of the emotions the Irish are very good at; but Ó Cadhain is the master ventriloquist of a vast chorale of hate.

All the voices in *Cré na Cille* are voices of the dead; in fact, the book is nothing else except voice: there are no descriptions, no expositions. Every scene is constructed orally as these dead voices lambaste each other; or, tormented by memory, recall offences and slights. These people hate everyone, and a special rage is reserved for members of one's own family. A possible exception to this unremitting rancour is the feeling a mother may have for her son, but even that, too, often disappears in the welter of anger. At the heart of the novel is a kinship system of blood and marriage relations, each one of which is tormented by hate. The heart of this poison is the feud between the two sisters, Neil and Caitríona. Neil is still living and it is Caitríona's wish that no other 'corpse come to the cemetery before she does'.[28]

The origin of this quarrel lies in the fact that both sisters loved Jeaic, who dies in the course of the novel. Neil, the eldest girl, gets Jeaic because their father, Páidín, insisted that she marry first, and so she has first choice. That appears to leave Caitríona with no other option than to marry Briain Mór, someone she has already turned down; in fact she marries someone else, not named in the novel. However, Neil's good fortune continues, to Caitríona's disgust: Neil's son Peadar marries Meaig, daughter of Briain Mór, and Meaig turns out to be a great housekeeper, whereas Caitríona's son Pádraig marries a useless slattern called Iníon Nóra Sheáinín. This familial tangle of rage and resentment is never-ending. Caitríona drives herself into a frenzy of anger as she imagines Neil walking past her house, delighting in her own good fortune, and in the fact that Caitríona's house has fallen into disorder and filth. She can even visualize Neil giving a triumphant flick of her backside at those who will be watching from Caitríona's window as she strolls back from the fair, confident in her luck, knowing that she has made yet another good profit in the sale of her pigs. This is the intimacy of hate, where every gesture can become pregnant with insult and hurt: 'She'll have a skirl now in her arse going past our house. She'll know the difference with me gone.'

Ó Cadhain knows the minds of his own people in all their fury and resentment. He spares us nothing. There is a lock, a stasis of hatred, a solid geometry of a petrified world. But washing all over this unyielding emotional stasis is the flood of speech, human, ferocious, hellish, but hilariously funny. Yes, we find ourselves saying, we are like this, we know the bleak satisfaction to be gained from the eloquent outpourings of anger and derision, and we are grateful that Ó Cadhain has shown these in all their gruesome splendour.

But at the heart of this testament to the vitalities of hatred lies something else: a pity, a pity that what is human can be reduced to these programmed angers and fixed jealousies. These are people locked into a system that has dehumanized them, and it is a system controlled by money and by fear. They are people whose humanity has been exhausted, over centuries, by poverty and submission to its apparent inevitability. In a world where there is very little to be had, where there is practically no surplus, then everything has to be cajoled, or got at through jobbery, favours, being in the know, or by magic. There is a fearsome episode in the novel, where, we are told, Neil does a deal with God to heal her son Peadar, who has been knocked down by a lorry and has broken his hip. She gets the Gospel of St John from the priest and puts it against his wound, and Peadar is cured; but, the deal is, that for this healing to work, another life has to be given in exchange. The life Neil gives up is that of Jeaic, her husband, and the man whom Caitríona loved. It is Caitríona who tells this story, and she is far from being a reliable narrator, yet Jeaic does die in the course of the novel.

We are here back with the Hag once again. This is not Christianity as promulgated by Rome or Maynooth; this is a Christianity still entangled with primordial forces, the laws of which are inscrutable, and may involve such transactions as Caitríona describes, at the deepest level of consciousness. But we are also in the presence of minds that have as their dominant tone fear: fear of the world, fear of power, fear of losing all that you have, including a son; this is a world whose inscrutable energies have somehow to be placated. The reality is of course that this mind-set engages when a person or a community feels it has no power to influence its destiny, that it is subject to authority and power over which it has no control. Ó Cadhain's eloquence is that of the despised subject trying to find a speech, and then, as it finds it, giving full vent to its fear and dereliction, in a language that he feared was dying, spoken by those who are already among the dead.

During the Emergency Ó Cadhain was interned as a security risk in the Curragh, County Kildare, in what was called 'Tintown' (referring to the corrugated-iron sheeting out of which the huts holding the prisoners were made). The IRA, in some quarters in Ireland, and with some justification, were thought to be sympathetic to Nazi Germany, hence the internment; however, Churchill regarded de Valera with deep suspicion and remained concerned about the possibility of invasion by Germany using Ireland as a base, with the Irish offering no resistance were Nazi stormtroopers actually to move in on Irish soil. British agents were active in Ireland, but one of the oddest of these informants was the novelist Elizabeth Bowen, who made regular trips home to attend to business on the family estate at Bowenscourt, County

Cork, but also reporting on Irish attitudes to the war to the Ministry of Information. She was, in a minor way no doubt, a British spy.

Bowen was Anglo-Irish, inheriting the magnificent family estate in 1930 at the age of 31. Although she spent most of her life in England, her attachment to Ireland was deep, informing many of her writings. It would be generally agreed that *The Heat of the Day* (1949), her novel of wartime London, with some crucial scenes in Ireland, is amongst her finest fictions. It reflects her experience of working on the fringes of espionage, with its codes of loyalty and betrayal. Stella Rodney, the heroine, is carrying out, for military intelligence, 'secret, exacting, not unimportant work'. Her lover, Robert Kelway, who works in the War Office, is, she finds out, passing information to the enemy. Her source for this intelligence is the preposterous and sinister agent, Harrison, who lets her know that he will not release materials he has on Kelway to his controllers if she consents to become his mistress. The exchange in which Harrison creepily negotiates his way towards making it clear what he is after to Stella is a masterly piece of insinuation, bullying, corruption, knowingness, and quick verbal footwork, which both reveals and conceals vital information at the same time. This density of objective, a mist of all kinds of possible misprision, is part of the way Bowen creates the mood of the novel, an atmosphere of concealment, obscurity, sensuality, and a feeling that which side you give your allegiance to is to some degree accidental.

Meanwhile, in the background, bombs are falling on London, the Blitz is underway; there is, from time to time, the sound of gunfire, and fires light up the city sky. It is easy, Bowen is suggesting, to lose your moral compass in these conditions, and such conditions are, she implies, what war will always bring. Stella Rodney, during the visit to the Anglo-Irish 'big house' that has been left to her son Roderick, a visit that lies, strangely, at the heart of the novel, reflects that she has, for these last years, lived 'at the edge of a clique of war', commanding, she thinks, 'a sort of language in which nothing need be ever exactly said'.[29] This obliqueness, this speaking slightly off the issue, deliberately, is made part of the style of the novel, so that Bowen's language itself seems to have this secretive command.

Mount Morris is clearly based on Bowenscourt, which Bowen had inherited in 1930, just as Roderick, Stella Rodney's son in the novel, inherits the estate at an even younger age. The visit there is a kind of escape to a timeless world for Stella, and the beauty of the house and its location above the river are evoked. But it is not as simple as that. These pages, describing the house and its atmosphere, allow Bowen to develop a most complex meditation on her class, the Anglo-Irish Ascendancy, and their role, such as it is, in British and Irish society during the war years and after. There is a sense of finality, in spite of the fact that the estate has been passed to her son by her cousin, Francis Morris; there is also a sense of emptiness, of waste, of futility.

The house is strikingly evoked: 'By anyone standing down by the river looking up, sky was to be seen reflected in row upon row of vast glass panes.' It is an arena of old light and airiness. As she moves about the interior, with the aid of oil-lamps and candles as it gets dark (it is autumn, the month October, so darkness is coming early), she discovers how familiar it is still, even though she has not been back for over twenty years. As night falls, she sits down to write to her son and recalls that he is keen to know if there is a boat on the river, so she calls out to Donovan, the caretaker, and asks him. Yes, he says, there was, but the 'master' sank it because, so Donovan tells us, the master was of the opinion that 'you were not to know these times what might happen presently', so he sent 'the boys' out one morning to load her with rocks and sink her, with Donovan, Morris, and 'the gentleman' standing watching. When was this? Stella asks. The last time the gentleman was here, Donovan tells her. This person used to come over from England quite a lot, and he and the 'master' would stay up 'gabbing' into the night, a distraction for the master. This visitor had, Donovan tells Stella, a 'very narrow look', with 'a sort of discord between his two eyes'.[30]

Harrison. So, thinks Stella, her heart sinking as the boat had done, he has been here, just as he said he had been to her. What does he not know? Why had he been here? Had he been checking up on her? On Cousin Francis? Francis had been to London before he died. What had been going on? She returns to her writing table but finds it difficult to continue with the letter to her son, the new inheritor. She moves into the drawing room, where she starts to touch the physical remnants of Anglo-Irish Ascendancy: veneers, mouldings, silk, the piano. She looks at herself in the mirror, and she sees that she wears the look 'of everything she had lost the secret of being', a phrase deeply attentive to a feeling of emptiness that must have haunted the Anglo-Irish mind at this, one of its final moments in Irish history. Stella feels she is becoming a ghost. As Bowen's writing proceeds in the next paragraphs, she opens out this ghostly solitude and emptiness to create a historical context for these complicated feelings and sadnesses. Stella's thoughts move to embrace the women who held these rooms, the rustle of their dresses, the flashes from their bracelets, the brooches resting on the lace above their bosoms. Her kind, she thinks, 'knew no choices, made no decisions', but even so, subject as they were to what they were, 'knowledge was not to be kept from them . . . they suspected what they refused to prove'. This burden became, for some, unbearable. 'So', thinks Stella, 'there had been the cases of the enactment of ignorance having become too much, insupportable inside those sheltered heads.' But all of them, all these women, suffered the same consequence of the victory of their class, 'virtually, they were never to speak at all', unless perhaps to the little bird lying 'big with death' on the pathway, or to a child being comforted after a nightmare.[31]

These pages, in their relentless and fierce analysis of the consequences of privilege, reveal the terror that can lie at the heart of what seems like good fortune, the futility in which it becomes necessary to act as if you are ignorant of what your comfort is doing to those on whom that ease depends: 'the enactment of ignorance' can, Bowen says, 'become too much'.

Given such dark intimations, what can the future hold? Next morning she is out looking over the river, and feels hopeful thinking of the 'rapture of strength . . . in the rising tree trunks rooted gripping the slope', when she hears a shout. It is Donovan, standing on the parapet of the house, gesturing and declaiming. She hears the word 'Egypt', and then 'Montgomery's through'; and then she learns that Montgomery (Anglo-Irish, with a family estate in County Donegal), the famous general, has broken through Rommel's positions, and is heading for victory. Donovan says that it is the war turning, which Churchill certainly believed 'Monty's' victory to have been. Donovan stands to attention, and, looking down the valley 'gnawing at the distance with his eyes', starts speaking to himself, moving his lips in a kind of trance, until he says, 'we bred a very fast general . . . hasn't he got them on the run?' Bowen leaves it there. She has already shown that victory can be a kind of curse.

Back in London she and Robert 'have it out', as it were, and Robert more or less outlines his position, such as it is. It is not as if it is a well-thought-out and principled stand. Words like 'betrayal' mean nothing to him; he has had to immunize himself against their poison. But the enemy, she says, they are 'horrible', a view with which he agrees; they are grotesque, but then, as he points out, everything in birth is grotesque. The main thing about the Nazis is that they have 'started something'. She may not like it, but it is the beginning of 'a day. A day on our scale'. She cannot forsake the idea of a country as something worth fighting for, and this country includes Mount Morris, for her. Still she wants him to get down to 'brass tacks'. What does he think the enemy has, she wants to know. If they win, he says, the quibbling would stop: 'I want the cackle cut.'[32]

And so, this is it. It will have been the case that for many the attraction of Fascism was precisely as Robert says: such movements, where the strong exercised power over the weak because, by virtue of being strong, they were revealed as destined to be in command, offered a simplicity, attractive in its sheer brutality. It was a kind of relief from the complexity of guilt, moral refinements, conscience. It allowed one to stop thinking. It cut the cackle. And indeed, the atmosphere of clogged judgement, of dubious motive, that Bowen reveals in this novel of war emphasizes a sense that society is constructed out of 'enactments of ignorance', false compliances, unthinking submission to words like country, loyalty, fidelity. So much cackle, according to Kelway, who shortly after this conversation either accidentally falls to his death as he tries to make his escape from Stella's flat by climbing on to the roof, or else kills himself by throwing himself down.

In this novel Bowen, from an Anglo-Irish standpoint, offers an analysis of the confusions of a Britain at war, and in doing so she reveals the strange probity and acuteness such a vantage gives her, as well as conveying the loneliness of being one of the surviving members of a class and a breed that have outlived their time.

Donovan, the caretaker at Mount Morris, carries a name that comes from west Cork (there is a townland and a castle not far from Drimoleague that is called Castledonovan), and the O'Donovans are a Gaelic sept, one of their most illustrious scions being, in the nineteenth century, the scholar John O'Donovan (1806–61), who prepared an edition of the *Annals of the Four Masters*. The Bowen Donovan has, in keeping with his position in an Anglo-Irish household, dropped the 'O' from his name, and has retained a traditional deference towards his employers: the 'master'. By the time she came to write *The Heat of the*

Day, Bowen's own estate was sold up and the big house demolished, so the chapters at Mount Morris are written in the full, clear knowledge that such places have begun to become anachronisms in what is no longer the Irish Free State but the Irish Republic, from 1947, signalling that twenty-six-county Ireland is not anymore attached constitution-ally to the crown.

One of the representatives of this new Ireland was the poet Seán Ó Ríordáin, from Ballyvourney in west Cork, undoubtedly one of the finest poets of modern Ireland, to rank easily with Yeats, MacNeice, and Seamus Heaney, but suffering the obscurity that attaches to any-one who writes in Irish. In 1932, when he was 16, the family moved into Cork city, which tells its own story about what life was like in Gaelic-speaking Ireland during the Depression of the thirties. He went to school in Cork but did not go on to university, since, his father being dead, it became necessary that he get a job as soon as possible. He joined Cork Corporation and worked as a clerk in the Motor Taxation Department in the City Hall, the kind of job that would have been craved by any number of people in the city in those lean years. He was diagnosed as having pulmonary tuberculosis, a feared and killing disease at that time in Ireland, where unpasteurized milk and the climate collaborated to create particularly virulent strains of the illness. He was sent to the sanatorium at Sarsfield's Court outside the city, and it was from around this time that he started to write. He once remarked that he graduated not with a BA, but with TB. In Cork he met and was influenced by the writers and academics Daniel Corkery (who had been the mentor for O'Connor and O'Faolain—the latter, incidentally, became one of Bowen's lovers) and Seán Ó Tuama, himself a dramatist and poet of distinction, as well as a fine and exacting scholar of Irish literature. Partly through their influence, partly out of his own deep reading and intellectual curiosity, Ó Ríordáin familiar-ized himself with the poetry of modernism, especially T. S. Eliot and Rilke, the Irish modernists Yeats and Joyce, and the thought of neo-Thomist Catholic theologians such as Jacques Maritain.

Ó Ríordáin was also a convinced nationalist, with republican lean-ings. His temperament and character were formed by the idealism of the new state and by the moral and emotional structures of the Irish Catholic church of the time. There was a part of his mind that detested the modern world, for which reason he was drawn to the Gaeltacht of his childhood and the survivals of it to be found in Dunquin in west

Kerry. These places became for him a kind of sacred terrain. The world of English (he was a native speaker of Irish from the west Cork Gaeltacht) he tended to find, in some moods, detestable, rotten, an attitude that coloured the way in which he saw the modern world. He was, of course, far from being alone amongst modernists in harbouring such misanthropy with regard to contemporary civilization. In a diary which he began to keep from around 1940 he confesses to feeling at times that perhaps Hitler has the right idea: maybe it is best to tear the whole rotten edifice down than try to remake it in some kind of gimcrack apologetic way. These, of course, are precisely the views that the English traitor Robert Kelway holds in *The Heat of the Day*. But such terrible opinions are also, to some degree, symptomatic of Ó Ríordáin's medical condition: TB frequently drives the sufferer into extremities of desperate feeling, as we see also in the sometimes hysterical writings of D. H. Lawrence.

The other side of this extremity of temperament was, in Ó Ríordáin, an intensely religious outlook that informs every aspect of his poetry. His attitude was what has now come to be called, somewhat disparagingly, essentialist. He was convinced (and his theological searchings all revolve around this central conviction) that each thing has an essence, and that that was connected to its spiritual identity. So that a person would have an essence, related to what his faith would have taught him about the soul, as would indeed a country: hence his nationalism. There would be a spirit of the person inherent in his or her very being, their unalterable entity, and there would also be a spirit of the nation (as Thomas Davis believed, as did Patrick Pearse). Such a being-essence was to be found in all things, and it was the special duty of the poet to find this animation and respond to it with his own life-energy, thereby creating a new entity, alive to both essences. A key influence on Ó Ríordáin's thought here is the poetry and prose of the Jesuit poet-priest Gerard Manley Hopkins, whom he cites in the long preface to his first collection, *Eireaball Spideoige* ('A Robin's Tail', 1952), a strenuous exegesis on the interface between poetry and theology which outlines his aesthetic.

What is remarkable about this aesthetic is that it reflects the political persuasions of the time with regard to nationalism; it responds to the serious call in the Catholic church for a spirituality that will be adequate to the modern world; it recognizes the crucial importance of language as a means of registering the cultural core of a people; and at the same time allows for the surge of individual creativity as the central driving force that binds all this together. The preface is a considerable achievement, and has never had the recognition it deserves, probably because most intellectuals, so-called, are not very well disposed towards a Christological poetics that draws on Thomism, and a body of theory about language that places it at the centre of issues of human identity. The Hopkins quotation in the preface is from the sonnet 'As kingfishers catch fire': 'Each mortal thing does one thing and the same | Deals out that being indoors each one dwells: | Selves—goes itself.' Each thing 'goes itself', and that will include a country, and that going of itself he called *dúchas* ('core') when it came to a nation and its culture. Getting in touch with that core or 'dúchas' of a person or a thing was what poetry did.

Ó Ríordáin has a story to illustrate his point, a story I suspect comes from his childhood in Baile Mhúirne, in which he recalls looking out a window with his father, watching a horse going past the house. A child, he says, and its father, are looking at a horse going down the road. The father says that there goes so-and-so's horse. That, says Ó Ríordáin, is telling. Let us say, he argues, that the horse is a disease. The father does not contract the disease. The father does not 'get' the horse. But the child does: he gets the sound of the horse, its shape and feel, and when he looks at the horse's hindquarters he is awed by their ancientness and their muscular authority. The world now, for the child, fills with a kind of horse-awe, and that is what poetry is. Poetry is not a telling, the father's view; it is a being, the child's transaction of himself into the being of the horse. And Ó Ríordáin says that he would like to call this participation in the self-being of a thing prayer. Prayer is what comes out of the being-essence, and the contact with this being-essence can never be experienced without a thrust of joy. All true poetry, Ó Ríordáin says, is informed with this 'joy-thrust', which makes it an anticipation of the state of being described by St Augustine as pertaining to the resurrection of the body after death in glorious union with eternal life, because then the body and the soul will be in a continuous joy-thrust of prayer for all time.

No wonder this put some readers off. This looks like nationalist piety gone mad. And yet, Ó Ríordáin has captured something very crucial to the nature of creativity and its relation to the spirit, and to tradition. This preface is as coherent a body of poetic thought as anything in modern Ireland, and in all kinds of ways it is infinitely more coherent than Yeats's theories of masks and history and gyres and body of fate. Not only that: it anticipates, in the concept of 'joy-thrust', the idea of *jouissance* developed by Jacques Lacan in a seminar on the ethics of psychoanalysis in Paris in 1959, to convey the psychosexual surge of creative activity.

One poem to illustrate this set of conceptions must suffice, but it is a masterpiece, from *Eireaball Spideoige*, called 'Siollabadh'. We are in the ward of Sarsfield's Court, and a nurse comes in to take the pulses of the patients. It is afternoon and it is bright. All the pulses of the patients are hammering away. She comes and stands over each bed, takes the pulse, then writes down the metric that has been thudding softly into her fingers, 'syllabilizing' into her being. To adapt the language of his preface, she has become infected with the syllabic metre of each of the patients (syllabic metrics were the form of bardic poetry: each line had a set syllabic pattern which had to be followed religiously). She goes out and leaves behind her a chorale of arteries thumping away. Now comes the Angelus and all say the syllables of the prayers together and then the Amens are whispered. After this is finished the psalmody continues in the pulsing of the arteries, like monks syllabilizing the nones in the afternoon. Here is a poor translation:

> A nurse in the hospital
> On a sunlit afternoon,
> Arteries in the bedclothes
> Hammering steadily;
> She stood beside each bed
> And waited while she counted,
> Then she wrote down the metric
> Of those syllables in her fingers;
> After, she slipped out rhythmically
> From the open ward,
> Leaving behind her a chorale
> Of arteries murmuring:
> Then came the Angelus
> And the lips there said the syllables,
> Until the 'Amens' all died in whispers
> In that sunlit sick-room:
> But in the monastery of the flesh
> The chanting still continued,
> The veins like monks reciting
> The syllables of the nones.[33]

A poem, said Ó Ríordáin, is a being, not a telling, analogous to the slogan adopted by Cleanth Brooks, the so-called 'New Critic', from Archibald MacLeish's 1926 poem 'Ars Poetica': 'A poem should not mean | But be.' This poem of Ó Ríordáin's clearly exemplifies this conjuring of the being-essence of an experience, where a moment becomes transformed through poetic intensity so that it becomes a something else, animated with a 'joy-thrust', a *jouissance*. In its collect-edness, its authoritative integration of rhythm and meaning, its daring in metaphor (the veins become little monks reciting the nones), the poem reveals a maturity and confidence of poetic talent in the Irish language which has been absent for some time. To encounter anything like this level of poetic mastery you have to go back two hundred years, to the Clare of Brian Merriman. And it is quite a remarkable thing to contemplate, that after a hundred years of disgrace, Irish, the language of the Famine victims, of those in the holds of the boats carrying emigrants filled with dread and hope, has now recovered enough of itself to be a medium for a poet of Ó Ríordáin's genius and for a novelist of Ó Cadhain's calibre. This resurrection (it is not surprising that Ó Ríordáin was drawn to Augustine in *The City of God* on the resurrection) is a strange phenomenon. Was it the dying efflorescence? The last kick of Gaeldom? The answer is 'no', as we shall see.

But how may this sudden onrush of energy be explained? In spite of the still-continuing economic hard times, the emigration, the unemployment, the sorrow in much emotional life at the time, the grip of the church, and so on and so forth, there was also a sense that Ireland was beginning to make its way in post-war Europe. Money was flowing in from America as families benefited from the extra cash-fluidity and purchasing power that these dollars (often sent in regis-tered envelopes) gave to an Irish economy with a still very low standard of living, so that things were cheap. American industry started to move in to make use of the labour that was to be had at low cost, while at a higher level there was a well-educated section of society, young men and women trained by the nuns and the brothers to good standards of attainment in literacy and numeracy. Repressed and all as it was, it was a society brimming with talent, and, because of the harsh regimes of the Catholic schools, young people were often highly competent, well-trained, mannerly, and responsible citizens. Further-more, even the poorer Irish people of these times believed in the value of education, and would make sacrifices so that a son or daughter could take advantage of proceeding beyond the primary school to secondary level, which, because of the social mission of a now often-derided church, was to be had at relatively low cost. A key part of the syllabus in the Irish schools of the time was Irish, not least because Irish was a compulsory subject at school, and it was an essential requirement for any post in the Civil Service, teaching, local councils or corporations, the gardaí, the armed forces, and in any part of what would now be called the public sector, a major employer at this time. This was government policy, and was resented by some—why should any subject be compulsory?—but in most cases the requirement was accepted as a fact of life, and had the effect of awakening many to the integrity and antiquity of the Irish language who would not have discovered its richness but for this compulsion. There was, therefore, a small readership for Irish literature, and in addition, with more people going to university and taking Irish as a subject at a fairly high level, a certain amount of insight with regard to its culture began to evolve.

One product of this new consciousness of Irish as a literary language, to be deployed artistically and critically, alongside English, and to be read as one might read French literature, say, was an anthology edited by Ó Ríordáin's friend, the young academic Seán Ó Tuama, at University College, Cork. The anthology was called *Nuabhéarsaíocht* ('New Verse'), and was published by Sáirséal & Dill in 1950, two years before Ó Ríordáin's first book. In the introduction Ó Tuama recognizes that a new spirit is abroad in Irish poetry, that this spirit is consciously modern, that it is in touch with the despair of much contemporary existence, and that it is concerned with the interior life of the individual. He also quite explicitly identifies Ó Ríordáin as a major poet (Ó Tuama is 24 at this stage), the most significant in the Irish language for over a hundred years.

This accolade did not, it appears, at all please another of the anthologized poets, a young scholar at the Dublin Institute for Advanced Studies called Máire Mhac an tSaoi, who reviewed Ó Ríordáin's book harshly when it was published, maintaining that his Irish was uncertain and inauthentic. She was, it is now agreed, wrong about this, and her antipathy to Ó Ríordáin's work probably originates in her own attachment to tradition, very evident in the poems of *Margadh na Saoire* ('Holiday Market', although the title is ambiguous, implying a selling off of something precious; 1956). What impresses in

the work of Máire Mhac an tSaoi, niece to the translator Pádraig de
Brún, is how alive and contemporary the traditional forms become in
the way she handles them. A beautiful poem, 'Oíche Nollag' ('Christmas Night'), which Ó Tuama included in his anthology, embraces the
piety and clarity of Gaelic religious verse in the folk tradition, but
fluently turns it to make a poem that captures the reality of an Irish
devotional impulse that still exists (more than exists, thrives) in the
Ireland of the 1950s. The Gaelic world is far from lost; it is beginning
to recover some of its energies:

> The sky is lit up with the candles of angels
> The wind from the mountain has snow in its breath,
> Build up the fire and go to your bed,
> The Son of God will lie here tonight.[34]

13

Astrakhan Ataraxie

I am all too conscious that the previous chapter has been overlong, but as I worked through the materials I realized that the period I was dealing with, from the end of the 1920s through the 1950s, was a time of immense creativity, and one in which Ireland strove to establish its presence in the modern world. The literature reflects the uncertainty of that struggle, its cost, and the eventual coming through of an expansion of confidence. In some respects this present chapter, which will chart the contemporary, or near-contemporary, situation of Irish writing, could become even more unwieldy, and degenerate, as so many attempts at dealing with the recent history of Irish writing have done, into a list of authors, trying (and failing) to offend no one.

Misgivings assemble as I turn to this task, the task of seeking to give an account of the last forty years or so of Irish writing while, at the same time, trying to retain some consciousness of the traditions this literary history has sought to illuminate. There can be little doubt but that this period, of the latter part of the twentieth century and the early years of the new millennium, has witnessed a literary flourishing; however, it must also be the case that we cannot see clearly, as yet, those writers who carry with them the authority that will ensure they will not be forgotten amongst the vast crowds of the literary dead. It is impossible to say how a literary reputation is achieved after death, but there is no doubt but that time conducts its own winnowing processes. Seán Ó Tuama, that exacting critic of Gaelic literature, used to say to his students (amongst whom I was lucky to have been) in the 1960s that a poet would have achieved greatness if even a handful of his or her poems survived. That did not prevent him making big claims for Seán Ó Ríordáin, about which I am sure he was right, but this caution of his, born of a sharp instinct that very little gets heard across the abysm of years and the deep silence of the grave, drew those of us up short as we entertained notions of our own burgeoning pomps.

Two dates, one towards the beginning of this period, the other towards the end, provide what may be convenient markers of the historical atmosphere of this time, one in which there were seismic shifts in the relationship between Ireland and Britain, between Northern Ireland and the Republic, and in the structures and institutions of the southern state itself. The first date is 1966, the year in which was celebrated the fiftieth anniversary of the Easter Rising, a relatively small insurrection that turned out to be the founding act of the new independent Irish state. That year, 1966, witnessed widespread jubilation, and, given that the Republic had begun to enjoy an entirely unprecedented level of prosperity, with inward investment driving the creation of fresh sources of employment, there was a sense of rising hope, and an intimation that the Rising itself of fifty years before had not been the disappointment many had felt it to have been in the preceding decades. Although the film *Mise Éire* was made in 1959, this documentary based on contemporary footage, with the composer Seán Ó Riada's glorious settings of traditional airs as background music to the scenes of revolution and the executions of the rebel leaders in Kilmainham Gaol, encapsulated the reawakening nationalism of the years coming up to the fiftieth anniversary of the Rising. His orchestral version of the patriotic song 'Róisín Dubh', in which Ireland is envisaged as the beautiful 'Dark Rosaleen' (title, of course, of Mangan's apocalyptic nineteenth-century translation, in which the Erne runs red 'with redundance of blood'), was recorded by the recently founded Radio Éireann Symphony Orchestra for the film. Ó Riada made out of the air a tone poem of astonishing passion, full of aspirant hope as the chords ascend through the crashing, luxuriant harmonies, conveying a spirit of revival and retrieval against the odds. We are here, this music seems to assert; we have come through, and we can strengthen our resolve by remembering who we were. *Mise Éire*, 'I am Ireland', is the title of the film, and it deliberately evokes the words of Patrick Pearse's poem, in which Ireland speaks as an old woman, the Hag: 'I am Ireland, | Older than the Hag of Beare.' Great is her pride, she says in Pearse's poem, in that she gave birth to the great Cú Chulainn; but her shame too is great, in that her own family betrayed their mother. But here, in Ó Riada's music, she is in her triumph; she is young again and full of hope.

The film, and Ó Riada's music, had immense impact. There was already at work in the broader culture in Ireland and elsewhere an impulse to go back to origins, to roots, part of a worldwide urge to reclaim authentic forms of life and culture which led to the hippies and the Black Panther movement in the United States. Ó Riada's music, for the film and with his ensemble Ceoltóirí Chualann, captured this drive to origins, and made the traditional utterly modern. He was a creature of charisma and status, but he also accomplished much in the way of work, in spite of his sorrowful early death, creating a mood in Irish culture which revered its Gaelic past; but more importantly than that, it made that Gaelic and Celtic world exciting, full of numinous possibilities, where myth and legend could be, and often were, connected to individual self-discovery.

After graduating from University College, Cork, where he studied music (playing jazz and swing piano at night in the pubs down the docks), Ó Riada moved to Dublin and worked in Radio Éireann for a time, and also at the Abbey as musical director. During this period he befriended writers and artists, but, in particular, he was to have a profound effect on the poets Thomas Kinsella and John Montague, and the publisher Liam Miller, founder of the Dolmen Press. Both poets have written extensively of their friendship with Ó Riada, and his impact on them. In spite of his comparative youth, to them he was a kind of daring maestro, almost a figure out of *Der Rosenkavalier*, Faustian, esoteric, mercurial. Kinsella has written about the time they and their young families spent on holidays in west Kerry, in the Gaeltacht, and he describes Ó Riada throwing himself into its culture, essaying its fluent and complex Irish, almost mimicking a competence, even a mastery, that would very shortly become real.

In 1964, at the age of 33, having been appointed to a lectureship in music at UCC, he settled his young family in Cúil Aodha (Coolea), immersing himself in its communal life, and becoming the organist in the church there, eventually composing Masses for it. This move in itself became symbolic for an entire generation. It was now perceived to be of vital importance to make the turn back to origins, to establish continuity with the Irish and the Gaelic past. It is not as if tradition had ever really lost its aura; Irish culture has always had (it is one of the themes of this book) a preoccupation with ancient things; it is just that in the 1960s, with the rediscovery of a national pride and assurance that was a feature of those years, this traditionalist impulse acquired a new animation. And Ó Riada's music and his brisk, elegant, abrupt Irish-ness, the flamboyant way he recalled ancient dignities as he sat before the harpsichord playing the sometimes lovely and delicate, sometimes martial and strident, airs in a style that showed finesse and assurance, were key elements in this recovery. An early but accomplished poem by Thomas Kinsella, 'Midsummer', from *Another September* (1958), tracks the impulse. It evokes a rapt attention at a magical place, the past, which has now opened up. Something that has been hidden has parted the 'tragic grasses', lifted its 'perfect head', and welcomed the persons who have now dared to enter this place. Why 'tragic'? It is not explicit, Kinsella's decorum is too alert to make the implications too obvious, but the grasses are tragic because of the history, the silences, the suppressions, that have made this place difficult to get to. The poem concludes:

> We have, dear reason, of this glade
> An endless tabernacle made,
>   An origin.
> Well for whatever lonely one
> Will find this right place to lay down
>   His desert in.[1]

The mood is like something out of the late novels of John Banville. It is enraptured by the agonizing extent of the possibility of the past that has been broken through to, but there is here too a self-aware irony, and, even, an awareness of danger. One had better be careful in these environs. This minatory note comes through, faintly, in the phrase, 'well for', as if to say, it will be well for him, that lucky one (or the one who thinks he is lucky), but he is carrying a desert, and it may be that it is all a bit too convenient to lay your burdens of impacted desiccation down in such places. Places like Cúil Aodha can be valleys of death, as indeed that particular *locus amoenus* became for Ó Riada.

Another September was published by Liam Miller's Dolmen Press (for which it was a Choice of the London-based Poetry Book Society), and Dolmen remained the publisher of most of Kinsella's books until the press ceased trading after Miller's death in 1987. Founded in 1951, Dolmen had, by the 1960s, established itself as a producer of some of the world's most finely designed books, and it played a crucial role in fostering the new confidence and achievement in Irish poetry that came about in the late fifties and sixties. It published the work of

Montague, the late work of Austin Clarke, and that of Richard Murphy, Pearse Hutchinson, Michael Hartnett, Eiléan Ní Chuilleanáin, amongst others. Its publishing masterpiece was Kinsella's translation of the *Táin Bó Cúailgne* (1969), with astonishing brush drawings by the artist Louis le Broquy of a Japanese severity, stillness, and ferocity as illustrations. It became immediately a collector's item, and it is one of the great Irish books of the twentieth century.

Kinsella's *Táin* also represents an outstanding example of the deliberate retrievals that were a feature of Irish culture in these years. It is a new translation of the ancient classic Iron Age tale; it does not, as previous versions had done, gloss over the raw violence and implacable rages which are central aspects of the saga; nor are the sexual and other baldly explicit elements to do with bodily functions toned down. The archaic sections written in a very old form of Old Irish accented verse are rendered, with the assistance of Celtic scholars. The undertaking, as a whole, is an act of recovery, of a literary archaeology being explored; and as this exploration takes place the shape of the heritage revealed in that process is restored. There is a wholeness and integrity about the entire enterprise, involving a poet's imaginative intensity, scholarly input, and a publisher determined to make a book worthy of such venerable materials and exemplary effort.

As Kinsella's writing career has shown since the 1960s, his is a difficult and dark vision. There is, as his irony and watchfulness revealed in *Another September*, no sense whatsoever that the immersion in the past, the recovery of ancient deposits of feeling, offers consolatory cheer. Instead, there is a silence and a bleakness that has to be faced into. This dark inner realm, this hinterland of the psyche as much as of the culture, can be, and most often is, a place of trial and of agony. The personal and the familial and the archetypal are interlocked, 'inveterately convolved', as Wordsworth would say.[2] He turns, in *Nightwalker and other Poems* (1968), to Aodhagán Ó Rathaille, Gaelic contemporary of Swift, and he has Ó Rathaille's great elegy and lament in mind, that one in which he records his forlorn dereliction in Kerry, walking the roads, eating dogfish and periwinkle. Kinsella's re-creation of this sorrow is not a translation; 'The Poet Egan O'Rahilly, Homesick in Old Age' is a short, abrupt lyric cry of historical rage, but it is also an outburst of vitriol at contemporary Ireland, as it turns its back on what it is. The monsters that emerge at the end of the poem are the eighteenth-century English (and native Irish) settlers, taking over land that is not theirs by right; but they are also JCBs, smashing through the remnants of the past that now, in the modern world, for all the talk of retrieval of tradition, mean nothing:

> He pressed red eyelids: aliens crawled
> Breaking princely houses in their jaws;
> Their metal faces reared up, eating at light.[3]

With *New Poems: 1973* (1973) Kinsella comes into the full force of his mastery. He achieves this by combining a relentless focus on the intimate, the personal, and the familial with deep searches into the ancestral and the mythic. He has, of course, been immersing himself in the ancient cultures of Ireland and of the Iron Age Celts for the work on the *Táin*, and this has opened access to layers and deposits of feeling and significance that lie at much more hidden levels than the merely personal, levels and deeps of the mind that reflect archetypal patterns in the innermost secrecies of what it is to be Irish, and what it is to be human. His poetic soul-work at this time reflects his interest in the psychology of Carl Jung, but his divinatory probes and searchings are shadowed by distinctly Celtic and Irish elements. The Hag, as one would expect, is everywhere in evidence.

In the section from this collection to which he gives the title 'Notes from the Land of the Dead', the archetypal and the primordial are set alongside the personal in poems that are written in a dark heart's blood of deadly concentration, as if his life depended on getting the words right. And there does come a sense in the reading of these pile-driven phrases and broken stanzaic forms that it was indeed like that, that these poems are amongst those that get written out of absolute need, rather than out of some form of enjoyable venturing into the emotional possibilities of language and sentiment (which, let us face it, a great deal of what passes for poetry is). In any case, as the folklore and the legendary material tell us, you had better not play games with the Hag, for if you do, she will take her revenge upon you; or, as Michel de Montaigne put it, less portentously, in one of his essays, you can play the fool anywhere you like, but not in poetry.

In one of the poems here Kinsella tracks back to the *Lebor Gabála* ('The Book of Invasions'; earliest recensions: late eleventh century, although the text goes back much further), which tells of the different invasions of Ireland. In 'Survivor' a legendary people come 'prowling' the northern part of the known world out of a 'Deep misery' where the self soils itself hidden in the darkness of some doomed cave. There has been a kind of intimation, a 'flame of cold', that there is somewhere some place of paradisal sweetness (we are back again parting the tragic grasses), and so they set forth. Eventually they come upon promontories 'beautiful beyond description', but the currents are savage and by twilight everything is destroyed and the only survivors are a 'shoal of women' and a single male. They have arrived at Ireland, although the country is not named; the time is primordial, anterior to naming; the idea is that all that is to come later. It is a last outpost in the gloom, the 'land of the dead' of the section title. Where they landed, 'the grass shivered in the thin shale'. In the 1973 version (revised for the *Collected Poems* of 2001), below this, in the sea, 'There was a great rock . . . where we went down | —The Hag: squatting on the water, | her muzzle staring up at nothing'.[4] Kinsella is making it quite clear here that this landing is presided over by that ancient creature whose presence these settlers immediately recognize, and who belongs at the interface between life and death.

In the family poems in this collection the same creature is acknowledged as part of the genetic code. She is in the grandmother who has a shop in the vicinity of James Street in the old part of Dublin near the Dublin Union and Dr Steevens's Hospital. The young male is terrified of this presence, with the strings of jet beads that wreathe her neck and 'hiss' on the black taffeta she wears, and 'creep' on the boy's hair. Calling out to him to 'come here', she says, 'You'd think I had three heads', and of course the truth is there is a sense in which she has.[5] In 'Tear' he is sent in to say goodbye to her as she is dying, and he passes through a 'fringe of jet drops'. The black aprons he used to bury his face in are at the foot of the bed; there is a smell of 'disused organs and sour kidney'. Life is breaking up, the body reverting to malfunction and disorder. He is meant to kiss her, he knows that, but cannot, just keeps his head buried in her aprons. And then he hears her voice, a single drop in the dank vault she is now in. She is talking softly to someone about his father, her son, and how 'he cried | big tears over there by the machine | for the poor little thing'. The father cried down upon the wooden lid of the coffin for the young boy's little sister. The child has, briefly, an intimation of terrible sadness, and of how hard life can be, but he then goes back out of the room of death to where his grandfather sits by the fire, waiting. And now the poem concludes with the capacity of the old to digest grief and the struggle that awaits everyone in life:

> How long and hard it is
> before you get to Heaven,
> unless like little Agnes
> you vanish with early tears.[6]

The primordial and the ancient goddess of life and death are embodied in the figure of the dying grandmother Kinsella, as well as the pity and burden of life, and the helpless love a mother and a father may have for a child, which will count for nothing in the machine that fate is, the machine that the father stands by as he cries big tears down on his child's coffin, little Agnes. She is not named until the very end, and, movingly, she is seen as having escaped the harshness of life by getting to Heaven with 'early tears'. Kinsella here magnificently avoids any trace of sentiment or the falsity that always comes with it, by bringing his writing back to the ordinary, to what people have to say when they are confronted with the brute reality of life and death, the realm of the Hag, that it may after all be a merciful release to die young, and that that may be why we say that those whom the Gods love they take from us out of pity for them, for us.

From 1973, and *New Poems*, indeed from the very outset of his work as a poet, Kinsella has kept faith with the kind of responsible action in language that he sees poetry to be. His writing attends to the inner promptings of the instincts, the obscure impulse to venerate what is sacred in life. He is intensely aware that poetry has a civic dimension, that the poet must attempt to speak of what is ill in the body politic, and he has done that consistently throughout his work. In *Citizen of the World* (2000), a short volume inspired by Goldsmith's probity, in a piece called 'Complaint' he writes: 'The times were bad | and we were in bad hands. | There was nothing to be done, | only record.'[7] There is a profound disgust at literary opportunism, at those who take it upon themselves to preside over 'the republic of letters'.

Kinsella holds himself aloof from the craven anxiety to belong, to be well thought of. In 1972 he issued the first of a series of Peppercanister Poems, named after St Stephen's church in Dublin (known as the 'Peppercanister'), with *Butcher's Dozen*, a ferocious attack in the Hudibrastic style on the whitewash that was the Widgery Tribunal of Inquiry into the shooting of thirteen demonstrators by the British

Army in Derry on 30 January of that year. The Peppercanister imprint continued, with the volumes being subsequently collected in books issued by Dolmen, Oxford, and then Carcanet, as if to signify an intent to retain a fidelity to an implacable independence of spirit. Kinsella has also retained an indissoluble alliance with the Gaelic past, issuing, with Seán Ó Tuama in 1981, *An Duanaire: Poems of the Dispossessed*, an anthology of Irish verse from the seventeenth century onwards, with facing literal translations. But more than this, he has, as all poets must, remained focused on the actualities of life while also holding true to the archetypal forms and ancient strata that lie under the appearances of things. He is, in other words, both contemporaneous and vatic. And he is never forgetful either of that unique struggle and integration between pagan belief systems and Christianity that is so much a part of Irish tradition. We see that uncomfortable but crucial nexus in evidence at the end of the poem 'Tear', with Agnes going straight to 'Heaven' (he is careful to capitalize the H); we also see it at work in 'Son' from *Godhead* (1999), a devotional poem on the Virgin and her Son, worthy of Aodh Mac Aingil in the seventeenth century:

> The Head hanging on one side,
> signifying abandonment.
>
> The Arms hammered open,
> signifying acceptance.
>
> The Smile empty,
> signifying passive understanding.[8]

John Montague, one year younger than Kinsella, was born in 1929 in Brooklyn, New York, to Irish parents, but at the age of 4 was sent back to Garvaghey, County Tyrone, where he was initially brought up by his aunts, for one of whom, Brigid, he had a special affection. That place, Garvaghey, became a special location, a force-field, for his work, and he constantly returns to its memory and associations. It means 'rough field', and it gave the title to one of his best-known collections, *The Rough Field* of 1972. That masterly volume comprises various sections, one of which, 'Patriotic Suite', had been published by Dolmen as a booklet in 1966, and was dedicated to Seán Ó Riada, a dedication retained in the 1972 publication, by which time Ó Riada was dead.

The date of the first publication of 'Patriotic Suite' is significant, of course, and shows Montague connecting Ó Riada's musical renovations of the Irish tradition with new impulses that are stirring at the time of the commemoration of the Rising. The 1966 booklet has, as frontispiece, an engraving from the Elizabethan John Derricke's *The Image of Irelande with a Discoverie of Woodkarne* (1581), which depicts a motley assembly of woodkerns (a contemporary term for Irish rebel outlaws), all bearing pikes, all wearing the notorious Irish moustache and long hair, a troop being led, interestingly, by a musician, a piper playing the Irish uilleann pipes, as he leads them forward in their ragged march; one of the troop has his right hand raised and is giving the fingers sign. Whether or not this was recognized as a gesture of insult in Elizabethan times is a matter of dispute, but there is no doubt but that Montague is, mischievously, importing the current meaning of the gesture into his audacious poem. This is his gesture to Britain in 1966, undoubtedly his father's son, who was on active service with the IRA during the Anglo-Irish War, and who left for Brooklyn after the Treaty betrayed 'both South and North', as Montague put it in *The Rough Field*.

Derricke's book was a sensational 'discovery' of the horrific barbarity of Irish rebels, but here Montague and Miller his publisher are delighting in the very thing the original execrated. The piper leads the rebel throng, and Ó Riada (and others too, Seamus Ennis amongst them) had, by 1966, reinstated the uilleann pipes as a major solo and ensemble instrument in the Irish repertoire, where it had lain in obscurity for seventy or eighty years during the ascendancy of the anodyne *céilí* bands (such as the Kilfenora), which had turned Irish music into a freakish Hibernicized version of a respectable tea orchestra, based on some vile conception of what that might have been like in a gloomy hotel in Harrogate in 1904. Such are the glories of colonialism.

But here, in Montague's fierce poem, the music, the old music, is a 'lure', the title of the poem that opens 'Patriotic Suite': 'Again that note!' (This will be a note that will continue to sound throughout Montague's work, a difficult note, of mixed sweetness and memory and rage.) 'A weaving | melancholy, like a bird crossing | moorland. . . .' And now Pearse is evoked, the last letters he wrote to his mother before his execution in 1916; this is a patriotic suite after all. Enter Ó Riada, who indicates that there is a point where 'folk and art meet', as: 'the wail of tin | whistle climbs against fiddle and | the *bodhrán* begins— | lost cry | of the yellow bittern!'[9]

Montague is explicitly connecting with national feeling, and with the power of music to evoke moods; he is also resurrecting the Rising, as well as the lost culture of Gaelic Ireland; and he is remembering the words of another poet, Francis Ledwidge, who wrote an elegy for Thomas MacDonagh, the 1916 leader, himself executed along with Pearse and the others. Montague is recalling that MacDonagh, a poet too, translated 'An Bonnán Buí' ('The Yellow Bittern') by Cathal Buí Mac Giolla Gunna, and that the poem by Ledwidge (who was killed in action at Ypres in 1917) has the lines, 'He shall not hear the bittern cry | In the wild sky where he is lain'. Montague's writing here is not exactly learned or drearily 'intertextual'; what he is doing is taking a whole network of feeling and association, connected with Irish nationalism, and making it current again in a highly organized and intense manner to focus on the potential of revival. In 'Revolution', from the same 'Suite', the music from *Mise Éire* is specifically invoked: 'Symbolic depth-charge of music | Releases a national dream', and it is clear that Montague perfectly understands what is at work in Ó Riada's music, in his own celebration of it and of the 1916 commemorations.

By 1972, when this series of Ó Riada poems is incorporated into the larger and more ambitious fabric of *The Rough Field*, it forms part of Montague's attempt to assemble the mislaid shards from various fields of influence, involving the music, folklore, and topography of Garvaghey itself; family recollections, and especially memories of his flawed and alcoholic father alone in Brooklyn, and of his aunt Brigid; political and sectarian statements from various periods of history; commentary upon recent events, as the old scar of the Northern Troubles erupts again in violence; Hugh O'Neill buried at Rome; and of course the Hag, who puts in an ambiguous appearance at the end of the poem.

'Like dolmens round my childhood, the old people', he writes, and then goes on to name some of them, all, to an extent, emanating from 'Ancient Ireland', with the chant, the rune, the evil eye, feuds, so that they trouble his dreams in childhood, until once, he says, as he stood in a stone circle, he felt them pass away from the living realm into some otherworld, that 'dark permanence of ancient forms'.[10] They have, in his imagination at least, assumed a congruity with some kind of ancient Gaelic or Celtic permanence, and therefore an archetypal authority. In effect he is saying that it is possible to attain a continuity with the past, with all those ancient symbolic forms, in spite of the smashed cottages, the usurped territories, the exiled chieftains, the humiliation of losing

your own language; and he is also implying that this reconnection with
the past, this healing, can come about through the labour and craft that
is poetry.

The aunt, Brigid, is a benign version of the Hag, who presides,
every morning, over an ordinary miracle, as she sifts the 'smoored
ashes' to blow the sleeping fire back to life. He tells us, in the preface
to the section of the poem given to her, that he draws on that fire.
Although the aunt keeps the ancient pagan fire alive, she is also (again
drawing upon the old nexus of Christian with pagan in Irish culture)
devoted, as so many Irish women were (and still are, even in these days
of the post-*ecclesiam*), to the 'Little Flower', the mild St Térèse of
Lisieux. He recalls how she bent over him in the dark when he was
a child, and he remembers her 'scaly tenderness of touch', the skin of
the 'bony arm' roughened with work. Roses, it is said, fell from heaven
on St Teresa's body after death, and once an old French nun threw him
a sack of lavender from the latticed grille of her enclosed convent.
Now, 'from the pressed herbs | of your least memory, sweetness
exudes', the odour of sanctity. This capacity of the poetry to rise to a
clear admission of love sets in train a countervailing force to all the
historical bitterness that the poem does not shirk. There is historical
injury, and personal damage, and sometimes it is difficult to separate
the two. The poem sequence incorporates anger, resentment, bitter-
ness: 'the swarm of blood | to the brain, the vomit surge | of race
hatred, | the victim seeing the oppressor', who has smashed up the
households, used and abused people, and 'flushed' the native women
like game. The oppressed have been raped; this is an imagery that is
familiar in Irish poetry from the eighteenth century onwards—Ireland
figured as a woman who is held in bondage and raped by the churl
who is her captor, Vulcan to her Venus.

The Rough Field concludes with a section called 'The Wild Dog
Rose', in which the poet, as Kinsella does in 'Tear', goes to say
goodbye to the cailleach, the Hag, calling her explicitly that, although
it turns out that this 'terrible figure' who haunted his childhood is a
lonely old woman, a 'moving nest of shawls and rags', and they talk in
ease 'at last', sharing secrets. But as they converse she tells him something that makes his bones melt. She was 'flushed like game', assaulted,
and almost subdued to the will of the interloper. There is no sense that
the assailant is foreign; indeed, it is made pretty clear that this is a
neighbour of some kind, crazed with drink; but the damage being

done to the old woman is poetically of a piece, Montague is making plain, with that done to Ireland: this is why the poem ends with this story, starkly told. She is just a 70-year-old woman whom someone has attempted to abuse; and she is also the Cailleach Bhéara. She resists the onslaught, and, like her pagan antecedent, has recourse to prayer, in this case to help her withstand the attack. She prays to the Virgin for help, and succeeds in breaking his grip on her. He falls off her and goes to sleep; in the morning he lurches away back across the bog.

This story has been told beneath a hedge filled with the wild dog rose, and now she, conforming to her role as goddess of the natural world, traditionally in her care, reaches out and, with her stick, pulls the flowers towards them where they stand. This rose, she says to the poet, is the only rose without thorns, and whenever she sees it, she thinks of the Mother of God, and all she suffered:

>   . . . Briefly
> the air is strong with the smell
> of that weak flower, offering
> its crumbled yellow cup
> and pale bleeding lips
> fading to white
>   at the rim
> of each bruised and heart-
> shaped petal.

The poem lifts out of the distress of suffering, into the sacred realm of nature, and its presiding goddess, damaged and 'rummaged' as she is. And yet somehow also inviolable, and not entirely dissociated from the world of magic and of miracle.

Montague's *Collected Poems* appeared in 1995, and that volume made clear his attentiveness to tradition, his strong nationalist inclination, his gifts as a poet of love. An admirer of Robert Graves and of that poet's concept of the White Goddess as presiding deity of inspiration, the muse, he makes space in his work for the feminine principle, whether as Hag, mistress, or Ireland manifesting herself as beautiful young girl or ancient crone. He accepts his tradition, acknowledging it as a gift, as well as knowing the burden that it represents, a burden that includes the hot and heavy satisfactions of hate and never-forgotten grievance.

But for all his rages (and that emotion is there aplenty in his work) there is in Montague too a very serene form of acceptance, in that he accepts even his own and others' angers in an openness to what is. There is a poem, 'Red Island' in *The Dead Kingdom* (1984), that registers some aspects of this almost surgical calm of Montague's, which underlies the surface stirs of feeling and ragged emotion. We may briefly remind ourselves here that red is the colour of the other-world. The poem recounts a secret, almost sacred, certainly numinous experience: he and some others take out a boat from where it is hidden in the reeds (Wordsworth's famous 'Stolen Boat' is being deliberately invoked in an Irish context); they bale out the dead water from the hull, then they pole it, 'slowly' (one of Montague's favourite words)

> to
> where the current freed
> itself, and the boat
> accepts, rides, floats
> on the oars' pull into
> the brimming full heart
> of the sunstruck lake.[11]

The word 'accepts' points towards the heart of Montague's vision; the floating buoyancy that it implies brings them into the heart of the lake, brimming, filled with the light of the sun. Everything, as in the Wordsworth poem, has become metaphorical.

And what do they find in the lake? A pike, and inside its stomach, like an embryo, an undigested perch, life and death interacting. Also they see a swan. Is it, they wonder, Fionnuala, the daughter of Lir, transformed to a swan through a curse? Lir's granddaughter, according to some tales in the polymorphic possibilities of interconnection that Irish myth releases, is the river Shannon herself (the river is female), into which the river Inny, here expanded to the lake which encircles the Red Island of the title, flows. The poetry becomes a complex nerve centre of acceptance of the past, and of life and death, in its quiet, calm intensity.

This quality of acceptance in Montague is not the Anglo-Saxon fatalism of Hardy, or the Senecan stoicism of Ted Hughes; this is something Gaelic and pitiless, something pagan, which he shares with Máirtín Ó Cadhain on the one hand, and with Seamus Heaney on the other. And of course, Ó Riada. In a poem in *Smashing the Piano* (1999), he returns once again to Ó Riada, who is walking along a country road in the Kerry Gaeltacht beneath Mount Brandon. A little old woman passes him by, singing to herself in the warm sunlight. He salutes her but she does not smile back, and only after she has passed

> does a chill tell you
> that beneath her shawl
> she had no shoes,

> and no feet, but was floating
> a foot above the ground!

Ó Riada looks back, but of course there is no one.[12]

There is a kind of serenity in Montague that one associates with the rolling easy landscape of south Tyrone, the drumlins of the soft fields shaped by the glacial shifts of the Ice Age, which he describes in *Drunken Sailor* (2004). By contrast, there is a contained attentiveness in the work of Seamus Heaney, an arresting sensitiveness that is watchful and intently questioning, which seems to connect with the tense carefulness that one senses in south Derry, in and around Bellaghy, Anahorish, the strangely sunken territory stretching west from the shores of Lough Neagh. It was, and still is, a contained place, a place set apart: you do not go through it on the way to anywhere else; it is a locale that keeps its secrets, and when you go there you make a special trip, unless of course you come from those parts, and you are going home. There is a hidden quality about Heaney, a feeling that people and things have a secret dimension that should not be usurped. A favourite word is 'occluded': that what is worthwhile needs to be searched out, and that the searching is worth it because what is of value anywhere takes very good care to remain elusive, hidden. The art of poetry is a mysterious business, and the craft is one that carries a sacerdotal significance. In one of his essays (he has written a good deal of criticism exploring the art and craft of poetry, its responsibilities, its complex relationship with law and power) Heaney analyses a possible etymological connection between 'mastery' and 'mystery', as if to suggest that the practice of the art of poetry is more than a set of linguistic games, but that the mastery of it (or rather the attempted mastery of it; there can be no final certitude of power in this order of mysteries) ineluctably involves the practitioner in an almost ritual engagement with immense but inscrutable forces that are also, somehow, implicated in the everyday.

Heaney's second collection was called, memorably, *Door into the Dark* (1969), which is what poetry and the mystery of its craft is. The title comes from the poem 'The Forge', which opens as follows: 'All I know is a door into the dark.' In there is found the smith, master of his dark craft.[13] The anvil 'must be' somewhere in the centre of this occluded place, 'Horned as a unicorn', fabulous, 'immoveable', 'an altar', where the practitioner beats out 'real iron'. The blacksmith here is not unlike the bard who, in the tradition, took himself off into darkness to hammer out his lines of syllabic verse; but the crucial thing about the poetic art is that it works with what is real, the iron reality of what is. There is, from the start, something expectant and watchful about Heaney's approach to the arts of language, and he often surprises, too, with his discoveries, as with his special use of the word 'occluded'.

The poem following 'The Forge' is another 'craft' poem, 'Thatcher'. Here the craftsman arrives after weeks of waiting, and then, when all is ready, he climbs onto the roof, and now Heaney introduces a strange word, 'Couchant', from heraldry, meaning 'crouched', 'hidden', with implications too of something in its lair, expectant, watchful but in command: 'Couchant for days on sods above the rafters', the thatcher shaves the straw, stitches it all together into a 'sloped honeycomb', to leave them all 'gaping at his Midas touch'. They are looking with new eyes at something that has been opened to them. And the reference to Midas reminds us that the world that has been made/remade by the artist is a golden one: he is recalling the words of Sir Philip Sidney, the Elizabethan (whose father, Sir Henry, wrote a tract on Ireland and served as Lord Lieutenant, and, it is said, saw that the young Hugh O'Neill received an English education), who maintained that poetry created a golden world out of the brazen actualities of Nature.

To get the Midas touch, though, you have to go through the dark, what Jung (whom Heaney, like Kinsella, was reading at this time) called the 'nigredo'. *Door into the Dark* announces a quest, a theme, that is to preoccupy (another of Heaney's key words, signalling that things and places in the personality have been occupied before) him for years, that of the search into origins, the letting down of a shaft into the hidden nature of what is real in history, in social relations, and in the personality. The volume concludes with a poem, 'Bogland', which opens up a realm he would make his own for a number of years. The turf-cutters find that, as they dig down, every layer has been 'occupied' already (*Preoccupations* (1984) is the title of one of Heaney's volumes of deeply meditative essays); the bogholes might very well be seepage in from the Atlantic, 'The wet centre is bottomless'. You are never going to get at the centre, the origin will always occlude itself, but the search for this core, while ultimately fruitless, is nevertheless what must be engaged upon. And this is what he now sets out to do, to look into the black hole of the origin, to go into it, with all the obvious psychic and sexual dangers involved in this search into the mother-lode. The mother, while in some aspects a nurturing presence, a blessing, as in the 'Clearances' section of *The Haw Lantern* (1987)—'When all the others were away at Mass | I was all hers as we peeled potatoes'[14]—is also, in other modes, none other than the Hag, the fierce tutelary being who keeps the bog, to whom sacrifice is made.

Wintering Out (1972), the collection that followed *Door into the Dark*, heads straight into the search for origin in obscurity, bafflement, and more than a touch of horror. 'Bog Oak', for instance, issues into bleakness, comfortless wintering out, and adopts curt, short-lined stanzas to create tense, bardic-like syllabic quatrains that he will use throughout this volume to make his interrogative probes into whatever it is that the bog holds. This is no easy assumption of traditional authenticity; the whole thing is fearful, unsure, watchful, anxious. It is no easy matter to get back to the 'oak groves' where the druids once enacted their rites, whatever they were; it is just possible that one can see Edmund Spenser, that first exponent of the need to root out the native forms of culture and language: 'Perhaps I just make out | Edmund Spenser, | dreaming sunlight . . . .' But he, whatever his dream, is 'encroached upon' by that which he is there to oppress, the ironically called 'geniuses' who creep out of every corner of the woods to try to feed upon what is left for them after the ruination of Munster, 'watercress' and, horrifyingly, 'carrion', dead meat, perhaps of their own kind.[15]

Another poem recalls Frank O'Connor and *The Backward Look*, Heaney giving it that title, but aware that a hankering backwards too can be not just comfortless but downright murderous. A snipe is rising, a stagger in the air, 'as if a language I failed', and away it flies in the wake of the wild goose and the yellow bittern (all birds heraldic with historical and nationalist significance), through the 'sniper's eyrie', where the gunman looks down through his telescopic lens to find his target on the streets beneath, the target being the inheritors of Spenser's burden, the British security forces. There were those in the 1970s who held that Heaney was a kind of apologist for nationalist and republican violence, but this vapid criticism entirely missed all the complex countervailings and ambiguities that work through his verse, as in this poem, where the wild Irish bird and what it stands for can be seen to be implicated in something, ruthless killing, that is far from being condoned. It is acknowledged that such things are done in the name of something that is far from clear, something obscure, and all the more dangerous for that.

The master-poem of this collection, and one of Heaney's best-known and most controversial pieces, 'The Tollund Man', heads directly into these dark hag-places. The poem is based on images of Iron Age bog victims which Heaney found in a book by P. V. Glob, *The Bog People*. Bodies preserved by the peat were discovered near Aarhus in Denmark; and other such bodies have been discovered in Ireland, Britain, and elsewhere. Some form of ritual sacrifice seems to have been involved, where the victim was killed, then buried in bogland. It is evident that some kind of obeisance was involved to the water-goddess, and to the land itself, the bog being an in-between place, neither land nor water. There is no doubt but that the deity was the ancient female one we find everywhere associated with the land-scape and with water. The Seine and the Shannon are named after the same entity, and both are, of course, female. We are once again in the presence of the Hag.

'Some day', Heaney writes, he will go to see the Tollund Man. He then describes what he knows of him: he was found naked, except for a skin cap, a noose, and a girdle, ready for his ritual marriage, in death, to the old Hag of the Celts, and indeed of other cultures, although it is fairly certain that this part of Denmark was, at the time of the sacrifice, part of the Celtic imperium. The victim is 'Bridegroom to the goddess', who 'tightened her torc on him | And opened her fen', to take him to her 'dark juices'. These are the ancestors alright, but they are involved in terrible ritual, the physical intimacy of which Heaney makes deliberately appalling. In the poem's second section he opens up the notion that he could, perhaps, 'pray' to this victim (as we do to Christ, the victim of the Christian churches) to make fruitful ('germinate' is the word used) the bodies of those killed in the 'Troubles', those which have erupted, again, in the late 1960s, and which have their origin in those of the Anglo-Irish War after 1916, the latter also, fittingly, recalled. As with Kinsella, as with Montague, the old traumas recur, with, it seems, ever-increasing ferocity.

In the third and last section of the poem Heaney imagines he is driving (as he often is in his poetry), in this case through the country around Aarhus, and says that 'Out there in Jutland | In the old man-killing parishes', he will feel 'lost, | Unhappy and at home.'[16] He will feel at home because he knows what such killing-places are like.

North (1975) is the collection which, more than any other of Heaney's, registers the shocks and wrenchings of the conflict in the North, which had, in the early 1970s, entered into a demented phase of night-killings, reprisals, bombings, sheer carnage. The writing in this volume is stricken but it does not lose its way or its temper. The theme of exhumation, of digging up the memory of the past, of exploring the human archaeology of ancient violence, continues in poems such as 'Bog Queen', where the sacrificial victim is no longer just some chosen male given over to the ritual, but female now, as if Éire herself, as she has appeared in the eighteenth-century aisling poems and as the Hag, is herself that which is offered in some blind obedience to terrible compulsion. In the notorious 'Act of Union' Ireland is taken from the rear by a rampant England, and the progeny of this monstrous coupling are the unyielding adherents to the concept of the Union. These poems and those in the preceding volume are penitential and dark; they unflinchingly face into the nightmare of the fractured structure that partition, now in a state of collapse, has been.

It is tempting at this stage to try to chart the clear and definite progress of Heaney's poetic career from *North* onwards, but this would be a study in itself. What can be said here is that a shift takes place after *North*, and that a new light enters the work with *Field Work* (1979). It is hailed quite specifically in 'Oysters', the opening poem, Heaney making it plain that he is well aware that he cannot 'repose' his trust in the 'clear light', a light like poetry or freedom 'leaning in from the sea'. He is angry that he cannot achieve this, he says, and eats 'the day' deliberately, as if it were an oyster, so it might 'quicken' him into 'verb, pure verb'. This is a longing for the kind of language that will not be pulled down into the old oppressions.

And again, remarkably, Seán Ó Riada makes an appearance in this book, but he is a figure of lightness and freedom, he has the 'sprezzatura', the nonchalance that Castiglione and Yeats wrote of, as he conducts the Ulster Orchestra, 'herding them south'. It is clear that Heaney now wants to make a turn towards the light, and, true poet, knows what it is that he needs to do before he actually accomplishes it.

He is starting to write his own history, rather than accepting what it is that would seem to be ordained for him. He is breaking out, making his own way, making his own 'clearances', the title he chooses for a set of poems in *The Haw Lantern* (1987) about his actual mother and her actual death, as distinct from the turbulent and troubled and implacable ancestral creature that the mythical mother can become in minds and emotions that have lost the run of themselves through sorrow or grief too long impacted. Here, her death, surrounded by the loving family, is a space of absence 'emptied | Into us to keep'; clearances suddenly 'stood open.|High cries were felled and a pure change happened'. This is mysterious, but, to allude to a distinction he is to make later, it is not secret. It is love's mystery which accepts the inevitable but keeps faith with the beloved.

Heaney now goes on to try to become his own self, and *Station Island* (1984) charts a further phase in this progress. The poet makes the old traditional penitential rite, as William Carleton had done before him and recorded in 'The Lough Derg Pilgrim', one of the *Traits and Stories of the Irish Peasantry*. And who puts in an appearance in the opening sections of the poem but Carleton himself, and when Heaney admits that he has no mettle for being angry at sectarianism, Carleton tells him that he must remember everything but also keep his head. In the last section James Joyce turns up, and instructs him to 'Keep at a tangent', 'swim|out on your own and fill the element | with signatures on your own frequency, | echo soundings, searches, probes...'.[17] Once again, as in 'Oysters', we see him engaged upon his own instruction, using Joyce as a kind of Virgilian self-tutor.

Heaney is now engaged on a poetic search for command and mastery that will make him a poet of the world. There is the authoritative poem that opens *The Haw Lantern*, called 'Alphabets', in which this ambition and reach is made quite explicit. It is a poem about signs and symbols, about going to school, about study and learning. It is clear that Heaney is fully aware that it is not possible to be a great poet, which he is now becoming, without very serious learning, but the learning is not just the absorbing of information, it is the learning that allows for connections, because if things are taken to a certain depth, they reveal relationships, deep kinships. He recalls first days at school, 'the globe in the window that tilts like a coloured O'. This globe becomes the wooden O of Shakespeare's theatre, that he learns from, as he does from Robert Graves, also drawn in now; and then comes

Marsilio Ficino, the Renaissance 'necromancer', who hung from his 'domed' ceiling in Florence a 'figure of the world with colours in it', so that the universe would no longer be just 'single things', and that this connectivity would 'meet his sight' when he would go out. Just as the astronaut sees from his small window the 'lucent O' of the earth.

Every word here is weighed and freighted with significance. This 'O' is the vaccination mark on the loved one's arm and thigh celebrated and marked in the poem-series 'Field Work' in that volume; but it is also the empty space, the absence, that went into the poet's sensibility as he stood with others at his mother's deathbed. It is an absence filled with intimations of presence, if this doesn't sound too much like something from 'Pseuds' Corner' in *Private Eye*. It is the helpless love that brims over at the thought that what has once been so alive and animate with presence will, one day, be absent, and this surely is one of those realizations that calls the whole soul of the poet into activity, to plagiarize a phrase of Coleridge.

Every word carries its volume of meaning. The Ficino emblem is there to remind him (and us, through Heaney's poem) that to see things properly is a kind of mystery, a miracle, as if you were 'seeing things' in a way that you had not ever seen them before. It is clear that here Heaney is getting to be entirely in command of his material, mastering the mystery. He is becoming what he set himself to be, a world poet, a poet of the world. The next collection, fully orchestrated, fully integrated, entirely in possession now of his own particularity, is called *Seeing Things* (1991), where he has acquired the gift of bringing a sense of the miraculous into the ordinary, making the ordinary extraordinary in the process, while never forsaking a fidelity to the ways things are in the actual.

The title-poem, 'Seeing Things', describes in its opening section a trip by boat from Inishbofin on a Sunday morning. Once again, nothing is by chance here. Or rather, everything is by chance, but the poet sees the order deep down things, to plagiarize another of Heaney's (and Ó Ríordáin's) masters, the Jesuit poet Gerard Manley Hopkins. Inishbofin is the island of the white cow, the same entity that resides in the tumulus at the Boyne (also meaning white cow); it is also none other than the Hag, translated into animal form and into a part of the always sacral topography of Ireland. The poet and those along with him are all scared as they get into the boat, 'nervous' though the sea is calm. When the engine 'kicked' and the 'ferryman swayed for balance', the poet panics. The terror translates into a kind of vision of seeing things: as they cross the deep 'seeable-down-into' (a recall at work here of Anglo-Saxon compounds, that Samuel Ferguson also used in *Congal* in 1872) water, it is as if, Heaney writes, he looks down from *another boat*, sailing through the air, away up, and can see how 'riskily we fared into the morning | And loved in vain our bare, bowed, numbered heads'.[18] This is now his poise, his sprezzatura, the ability to capture an extraordinary feeling about things, that they hover in a place between life and death, absolutely precious, but numbered, as their days are, as fate has ordained, as God has willed it on this Sunday.

Heaney's story continues, the world-poet positions himself at the centre of a field of vision that tracks the known world of the mind and of the senses. He holds true to Bellaghy, and to Mossbawn. At the end of *Electric Light* (2001) he is back in his childhood, staying in a house which has electric light, now seen for the first time. What he sees in this new strange light is another version of the Hag, with a smashed thumbnail in this 'littered Cumae', the place where the Sibyl was to be found in Italy. The child is terrified of the old woman who is looking after him. He has been left to stay in this place of fear and of exposure, the light being kept switched on all night. He 'wept and wept | Under the clothes'; the Hag/Sibyl asks him what ails him, but it is no use. We are not told why he is left there, but there has obviously been some family tragedy, or at least upset. Later, standing on a chair, he can reach the light-switch; he turns on the wireless and he is allowed to roam 'at will the stations of the world', translated now out of, but still retaining connection with, the stations of Station Island. The Hag remains a threatening and difficult presence, and the poem concludes with the thought of the 'flint and fissure' of her nail still there in her grave among the beads and the vertebrae in the 'Derry ground'.[19]

The poetry is a place of in-betweenness, occupying a position between life and death, the ordinary given, and the miraculous. The 2006 collection, *District and Circle*, concludes with 'The Blackbird of Glanmore', recalling the blackbird over Belfast Lough of the early Irish lyric, and the Glanmore in County Wicklow that has figured in so many of Heaney's poems over the years. He and his wife and children went to live there in the 1970s, after they moved south to Dublin. They initially rented the cottage from the Canadian scholar and Synge critic Ann Saddlemyer (who had originally bought it from the Yeats critic A. N. Jeffares), eventually buying it outright. It is a special place for Heaney, a kind of Ithaca, an association he makes explicit in a number of poems. But there, at the end of this later book, a blackbird is on the grass when he arrives, having, as so often in his work, driven to his destination. He thinks of his father, now among the dead, and then of his little brother, the boy, aged 4, killed in a road accident and commemorated in the early poem 'Mid-term Break'. Heartbreakingly, he recalls the lost brother, now gone to the father, 'Cavorting through the yard' because he was so glad to see the young Heaney home from boarding school. A neighbour, long after the accident, said he saw a bird up on the roof of the shed for weeks before the boy was killed, a disturbing omen. The 'automatic lock' of the car clunks shut, the blackbird panics briefly, then Heaney has 'a bird's eye view of myself, | A shadow on raked gravel | In front of my house of life'.[20] The blackbird, on the grass when he arrives, will be in the ivy when he leaves.

The poem is a masterpiece, poised between life and death, seeing things, and knowing that what is seen is seen all too briefly. The door into the dark opens into a further place of seeing, where things stand in their own miraculous light, all the more there, for their being also certain to become an absence. We become capable of thinking, because of the action of Heaney's mature later poetry, of (as he puts it in a poem to W. H. Auden in this collection) 'dark matter in the starlit coalhouse'. Poetry in Heaney is a considered form of thinking action, of deeper involvement in life, so that in reading it (as he so obviously does in the writing of it), you get what he describes in the interviews with Dennis O'Driscoll in *Stepping Stones* (2008) as a 'lift', or as Ó Ríordáin put it fifty and more years earlier, a 'geit áthais', a jouissance of joy.

In 1984 Heaney dedicated *Station Island* to the dramatist Brian Friel (born 1929), an act of recognition of the older man's importance as mentor, goad, and exemplar. Heaney by this stage was a poet of international standing, and he was becoming a great one; Friel by now had produced a number of theatrical masterpieces that were recognized as such, and had had immense artistic and commercial success with plays such as *Philadelphia, Here I Come!* (1964), *Volunteers* (1975), *Faith Healer* (1979), and the celebrated *Translations* (1980). This was already a body of work that showed an assured command of the technicalities of the stage, a complex intellectual and reflective approach to issues of nationality and identity, a unique gift of being able to combine the drive of a closely cadenced vernacular speech with, from time to time, elaborate language to capture difficult and obscure passages of emotion and of thought. And all this Friel was able to do while still retaining a fidelity to a heightened form of realism, where the world the plays reveal is a known and recognizable one. These are people out of history, set into situations very like those which people encounter in their actuality, so there is a definite sense in Friel's drama of the weight of the real world, of the horror and intractability that people have to deal with as they live through their days. So often, in Friel, you are introduced to a world, usually a place in Donegal called Ballybeg, an invented place of his own, where the heart is and its terrors, and things appear calm and fairly unruffled, and then the issues unfold, and the next thing you know, you are looking down into the abyss that human interaction can become; or you are witnessing the prison where it is possible to be deliberately or accidentally misunderstood; or you are compelled to look on at the false romance that allows people to imagine that things will work out alright in the end, when it is evident that time is running out; or that the characters on stage have made a hell for themselves out of wilfulness or weakness of spirit.

Friel can be funny, bitterly funny at times, but principally what the drama compels you to look at is the sorrow of human action, its futility, as people become trapped in history, process, temperament, while the world shifts on its axis and the victims remain stuck, condemned to inanity and repetition, and often, too, fear of what the consequences of history will mean for those destined to victimage. A dominant theme in Friel's work, perhaps *the* dominant theme, is the tendency we all have to become locked into a story or an idea or a conviction which is desperately held onto in spite of the fact that the world no longer corresponds with what is being fixedly retained. The fracture that works its unease in this situation is dramatically realized in Friel's first great success, *Philadelphia, Here I Come!*, where he adopts the device of having the Public and Private aspects of young Gar's personality played by different actors, allowing the Private dimension continually to rebuke the Public one, and all his fabrications and protestations. The twist here is that the story Public Gar is straining to tell to himself is that he will escape, that he'll get away to Philadelphia out of the repetition and emptiness of Ballybeg, but it is certain that the world he will encounter in America will be no less confining than that which he has talked himself into leaving behind.

Faith Healer takes to extremity an idea opened up in *Philadelphia*, that memory cannot be relied upon, that the stories people tell themselves and each other, based on their constructions of the past, can be, and often are, wildly at variance, even when the same event is in question. And not just that, these stories, in the name of which decisions are made that are life-changing and even life-threatening, can be utterly remote from actual fact. The terrible thing is that people will want to cling on to what they think is the case, because that will often be the cornerstone of the house they have constructed out of what they think is real, a house of language for them to live in. The relevance of this to the way history is narrated and retold in Ireland is not far to seek. To be Irish (or indeed to be of any country or place) is to be involved in the making of one kind of story or another, and the irony is that subjection to one kind of narrative or another is not something over which there is necessarily freedom of choice. To be Irish is to be, to some degree at least, compelled into one of a number of narratives. And nowhere in Ireland is this more in evidence than in the North, where the story you subscribe to may end up being, literally, a matter of life and death. Friel once said that the issue at the heart of the Northern Irish crisis was essentially a language issue, because by means of language a world and a set of attitudes are brought into being. *Faith Healer* lays bare the process by which language constructs a reality, or rather realities in the plural, none of which tally at the really crucial points. These gaps are tragic ones, abysms into which the all too vulnerable human creature plunges to death, misery or oblivion.

By the time Heaney dedicated *Station Island* (a volume preoccupied with trying to keep free of the various causes, impulses and persuasions that would try to get you to join up) to Friel, they were both directors of Field Day, a major theatre company and cultural movement, established initially by Friel and the actor Stephen Rea, but very quickly drawing in Heaney, the poet Tom Paulin, the writer and academic Seamus Deane, and the musician David Hammond. Heaney did join this movement, because he felt called to do so by the civic and responsible element in his make-up, but also because it was a bit insouciant, and because it promised to stir things up. To summarize brutally: Field Day set out to challenge the leaden control exercised by

Dublin over the arts by issuing a challenge from Derry (Friel was fed up of being wilfully misconstrued, often as a cultural nationalist, by Dublin liberal critics falling over themselves to show their antipathy to anything other than a revivified cultural unionism masquerading as fair-mindedness); the directors (later joined by the dramatist and novelist Tom Kilroy) wanted to place the nature of language, political and artistic, at the heart of a new type of cultural debate that would be as free as possible from all the old standpoints and justifications, whether nationalist or colonialist; and there was a desire to try to see the Irish case in relation to other colonial or 'post-colonial' experiences.

The Field Day phenomenon had a 'field day' with their first production, Friel's *Translations*, a dramatic masterpiece which had at its core the question of language. Clustered around the nucleus of this issue were all kinds of negatively and positively charged particles: colonialism and the usurpation of indigenous rights; the longing for communication across the divisions that separate people; the almost erotic thrill of violence and of threat visited on those who wield the ostensible power; the boredom of fixated minds; the weariness of spirit that can afflict those who have, understandably, become heartily sick of people always hankering after the good old days; the deep attraction of drink as a quick exit to oblivion; and the sorrow of seeing a culture falling apart.

I always tend to think of Friel not as a philosopher or as a moralist, but as a therapist, a psychiatrist, who takes apart in his theatre all the poisoned tales and stories that are impacted into each other in the collective psyche of his Ireland. *Translations*, like all Friel's drama, is a kind of speculative and analytical talking cure, that is also theatrical spectacle, of the ills that afflict Ireland. In this play, the British Ordnance Survey is mapping the country and recording, also, as much as it can of the lore of place, so that the names of places will be contextualized. The British employ native scribes and scholars to assist in this process, as had been the case in the nineteenth century when Thomas Larcom's Survey (on which this play is based) made use of the services of George Petrie, John O'Donovan, James Clarence Mangan, and others. Much of this work was in the field, field-work, and the character Owen in the play is based on O'Donovan, whose field-work, and the many volumes he filled with it, remains an invaluable source for Irish cultural history.

Friel's Owen is, as O'Donovan was, a cultured and educated man, and is only too aware of the finality of the enterprise he is engaged upon. He knows very well that the lore of places he is recording (the dindshenchas of Gaelic learning) is fading, and that the stories connected with locales are becoming meaningless as the vital connection between language and cultural continuity is being eroded. His father, the alcoholic hedge-schoolmaster Hugh, is torn by contradiction: on the one hand, he is the representative of the old Gaelic culture and way of life; on the other, he is too intelligent not to be unaware of the fact that what he stands for is on the way out, and that the world will belong to the new technologies of the modern British Empire—the survey is a military operation conducted by sappers, the aim of which is related to taxation and the assessment of the economic potential of the country.

The young and impressionable Lieutenant Yolland, an Englishman infected by the romance of Ireland, wants to cross over, to translate himself, into an Irish identity. He falls in love with one of the local girls, and is entranced by the idea of Irish literature. Hugh, speaking an elaborate English for Yolland's benefit (it is one of the achievements of this play that while the entire thing is, of course, in English, we are continually being led to understand that large sections of the dialogue are meant to be taking place in Irish, so that the theatrical scene itself becomes a virtual site of translation, allowing us to reflect on the nature of language and communication) tells him that, yes, Irish is a rich language, with a great literature. He goes on to say that the language is 'full of the mythologies of fancy and hope and self-deception—a syntax opulent with tomorrows. It is our response to mud cabins and a diet of potatoes; our only method of replying to . . . inevitabilities.' At which point he turns to his son to ask him for the loan of a half-a-crown, a little twitch of typical Friel mischief, where he is slyly indicating that when it comes down to it, to the brass tacks, it is the crown that issues and guarantees the currency. There is no gainsaying that, just as there is no gainsaying of the British Army presence; nor can Yolland, for all his romancing, translate himself.

Hugh, flown with drink, makes a remarkable peroration (which Friel drew from George Steiner's eloquent meditation on translation, *After Babel*), in which he lets Yolland know how well he understands the precariousness of the culture of which he is now the spokesman: 'it can happen that a civilization can be imprisoned in a linguistic contour which no longer matches the landscape of... fact. Gentle-men.'[21] The last word being his farewell: the old man knows how to make an exit. Yolland is deeply moved by this; he is aware that the old man knows what he has come to understand now too, that 'something is being eroded' by that of which he is the representative. But that is not to say that there are not defenders of the Ballybeg way of life, of what some would claim is the integrity of the place. These are the shadowy Donnelly twins, who do not appear in the play, but whose absence is more potent than any presence. They are around. Yolland disappears, targeted because he has taken up with Maire, the local girl, whom he courts across the barrier of language. It is suggested that the Donnelly twins are behind his disappearance.

The play ends with Yolland still missing, perhaps dead, perhaps held as hostage; we don't know. The army threatens a series of reprisals of ever-increasing harshness, culminating in the entire clearance of the whole area, unless Yolland is returned. Now Hugh finishes with another peroration, this time a translation from the first book of Virgil's *Aeneid*, which tells of an ancient city, Carthage, loved by Juno the goddess, above all others. Juno wished that this city would become the capital of all nations, but there came forth a race of Trojan blood who would bring about the downfall of Carthage, and of Libya: 'a people, kings of broad realms and proud in war who would come forth for Libya's downfall'. These are the last words of the play, and again Hugh has them. The 'people' in the *Aeneid* are the Romans, of course, who made Carthage, in the words of Derek Mahon the poet, 'a ballroom for the wind'. In the translated realm that the play is, the Romans are, at first sight, the British, and Ireland Carthage, making Ireland a place favoured by the goddess Juno, but also the Hag, Róisín Dubh, Cathleen Ni Houlihan, and so on. But there is another impli-cation at play here, and that is that in Hugh's damaged mind it is the Irish who are the Romans, who will bring about the downfall of the race who appear so favoured, the British. As the theatre plunges into blackness at the end of Hugh's speech, we are left thinking, what if it is the case that the Empire will end where it began, in Ireland? The Donnellys will never be reconciled until they achieve what they are determined to achieve. A terrible prospect, but one that delivers deep theatrical excitement of a kind that is not entirely licit.

Friel's writing career, with *Translations*, is only halfway through. *Making History* (1988), a play about the Great O'Neill, follows, which concerns itself explicitly with how historical narratives are constructed, and with the purposes these stories are made to serve. *Dancing at Lughnasa* (1990), a world-wide success, is a celebration of the indefatigable spirit of the five unmarried Mundy sisters who are the focus of this play. It is a mysterious piece, and the action is placed against a backdrop of pagan rites and ceremonies connected with the feast of Lughnasa, in the harvest month of August. The play is set in the 1930s, but the deity that presides over the action, and to whom obscure obeisance is made (the fires are still being lit on the hills), is the ancient god of the Tuatha Dé Danann, the sun-god Lugh, after whom the month is named. This ritual dimension to the play is amplified by continuous reference to Africa, specifically Uganda, where Father Jack, brother to the sisters, has been a missionary priest, and where he has 'gone native', even participating in the ritual ceremonies and dances to the tribal deities.

The play captures the sorrow and pathos of human striving and effort set against the context of huge and inscrutable forces and energies, recognized in myth, dance, and ceremonial; and yet there is also an unsubduable kindness and generous vitality that erupts onto the stage when the women dance wildly to the music from the Marconi wireless. It is a strange play, where memory and story detach themselves from history and from facts, and where the stage becomes a place of suggestion and ritualized, yet very restrained, movement, as in the tableaux, enigmatic and poignant, that open and close the action. Over it all there broods a sense of the limits to human action, that what people do is fated by character and circumstance.

Friel's theatre work continues all through the 1990s, and into the first decade of the new century. He revisits his old master, Chekhov, in a series of translations, and also Turgenev. Chekhov is an animating presence in the late masterpiece *The Home Place* (2005), which is set in the year 1878, a date that is significant. This is the year before the founding of the Land League, and the so-called 'new departure', the alliance between Parnell, Michael Davitt, and the Fenians, in order to bring about reform in the ownership of the land of Ireland, and in the arrangements and agreements whereby tenants paid rents and held leases. The Land League was a constitutional movement, but it carried with it the threat of possible violence, which sometimes erupted into actual atrocity, a factor that certainly increased its efficacy. With Friel setting his action in The Lodge, a big house in Ballybeg, in the year before the founding of the movement which is eventually to transform the way in which property was owned and rented in Ireland, he is deliberately creating a situation in which the decline of the landed class is well under way. They are not just under threat; they are doomed.

The Lodge's master is Christopher Gore, an ineffective man in his late fifties. He is in love with the woman who runs the house for him, Margaret O'Donnell, daughter of the local schoolmaster, the alcoholic Clement, who trains the best choir in Donegal which consists of his little 'angels' from the school. We hear the choir singing Thomas Moore's 'Oft in the Stilly Night' in 'opulent three-part harmony' as the play opens, and we watch Margaret as she listens, entranced, to the melancholy words and the mournful air. The song is all about the days that are past and the friends who are now dead; what is left to the remembrancer is memory to console a saddened heart. Friel is giving us, with considered irony, the whole Moore thing. We are at the end of the nineteenth century; the sentimental Ireland that Moore (sometimes) evoked is disappearing, if it ever existed. This is now a world where a landlord can be set upon and killed as he is on his way to evict a tenant.

Gore has just come back from a memorial service for Lord Lifford, whose skull has been battered in with a granite rock, attended by a handful of the local Anglo-Irish Ascendancy; they are all terrified that they are on a list of targets which is said to exist. Lifford's assailants are (though this is not mentioned explicitly) Fenians, members of the Irish Republican Brotherhood or some organization in affiliation with them. Con Doherty, a local man, is involved, and we learn that he has just come back from England where he has been addressing various groups, 'whispering defiance', according to Margaret. Doherty, a version in this play of the Donnelly twins from *Translations*, has a huge minder with him, the monosyllabic Johnny MacLoone from Meendoran, whose mere physical presence is a threat. These are Fenian woodkerns, and Friel is quite specific in the stage directions that they should emerge from the 'thicket'.

Meanwhile the confused and etiolated life of the big house goes on, just about. Christopher, a widower, is in love with Margaret, and so is his son, David; Margaret is in love with David herself, but she has to keep repulsing the courteous importunings of her boss. Richard Gore, a cousin from Kent, who has been in the colonial administration in India, is visiting. Richard is by way of being a scientist of the human species, an anthropometrist or, more familiarly, a phrenologist: Friel is deliberately using the contemporary nineteenth-century terminology, and quotes extracts in an appendix from a paper delivered at the Royal Irish Academy in 1892 on 'craniological' experiments and measurements conducted on the Aran Islands. It is a curiosity of Synge's biography that he knew the person who made these experiments and read the paper, a Professor A. C. Haddon; and not just that, Synge's own sojourns on Aran had an ethnographical dimension, though not of the sort exemplified in Haddon's work.

What Richard is engaged upon is research that will allow him to prove that every race has its own distinctive characteristics, in the size of the skull, height, colour of the eys, and 'nigrescence', the degree of their blackness. If he can get to this proof, and develop a reliable method of measuring racial traits, including nigrescence, then this would allow society the capacity to come to understand, on a scientific basis, what a race of people is like, whether they can be trusted, how intelligent they are.

This is all very silly, of course, as Margaret points out when it is explained to her, but it is vicious too: Richard is in the grip of a racist theory, and insists on carrying out his degrading experiments, at the Lodge, before he heads off to Aran to join in with Haddon's field-work there. Richard admires Margaret, Christopher's 'chateleine' (as he calls her), though he is shortly to be 'spliced' to the delightfully named Edith Bloomers back in Kent (Friel's sly mischief at work again).

The second Act opens with Richard conducting his nonsensical experiments on a few locals. MacLoone turns up, Richard mistaking him for one of the volunteers from the village (they will get their photographs taken for their pains), but, as it turns out, he is there to keep a watch on things. Friel does not spare us the brutal reality of poverty that is the background to this racist frivolity: Mrs Sweeney, a widow, has come along to be measured up at The Lodge in the hope of getting a few 'coppers' that will help her feed her family. She will not.

And now we arrive at the heart of the play: Con Doherty enters, and after a little while just tells Richard Gore to stop. There is anger at this, and refusal, but Doherty persists, and when Richard's assistant tries physically to throw Con out, MacLoone steps forward and produces a cudgel. Still Christopher refuses to give in until Con tells him that there are a number of men at the gate who wanted to come up and put an end to the measuring, which they do not like, and that they will intervene if Richard and his assistant do not leave with all their gear. He also lets Christopher know that these men are the same as dealt with Lifford. Christopher now yields, to the fury of his cousin. Doherty says he has done the right thing.

Afterwards, when everyone has gone, Margaret, Christopher, and David are left in the house. It is revealed that David and Margaret are planning to wed, although she lets the father know that she will leave if it helps. There is a confused penumbra of feeling and emotion now developing, and into this Friel brings a mastertouch, the marking of the trees to be cut down in the old forest planted a century back by an earlier Gore. Christopher also recalls again the 'home place' of the title, and this is not The Lodge or Ballybeg, as was revealed to us earlier: it is Kent, it is England. And Christopher, in the grip of sorrow and self-pity, evokes it: 'the great placid fields of wheat and oats and barley. A golden and beneficient land.' Against this there is now the prospect of David, a planter, marrying out of the colony for the first time in four hundred years. Son and father traipse off to mark the trees for felling, a moment of Chekhov, but given an entirely brutal and absurdly Irish dimension: distracted by a falcon, or what he thinks is one, David accidentally daubs his father with the whitewash brush they are using to mark the doomed trees. Yeats is at work here ('The falcon cannot hear the falconer', in 'The Second Coming'), but almost comically; certainly there is grotesquerie afoot. The colonist now breaks down, as the Moore song from the start is being sung again, night coming on. Is Margaret involved in a plot to get back the lands that were theirs, O'Donnell lands, the lands of the earls of Tyrconnell, but before that title, the lands of the Uí Dhomhnaill, one of the most venerable septs, along with that of the Uí Néill, of the North? Maybe it is the case that his own son is 'in cahoots' with Doherty and the gang who killed Lifford.

Christopher 'breaks down totally'; Margaret puts an arm around him. He cannot 'rise above', he tells her, what his father always said was the duty of the colonist, to rise above, to ascend to one's ascendancy. His resilience is gone, he says. Earlier in the play he has used the verb of this word, 'resile', meaning to come back to an original position (Friel's classical training at work here); now this is beyond him.[22]

I have spent some little time on this play because I believe it is a masterwork of Friel's and of Irish theatre. It carries all the thematic complexities of his drama that stretch back almost fifty years, and it is charged with his deep questionings, pursued over that extent of time, on issues of nationalism, identity, violence, the fragility of human affections against these savage backdrops—it carries all these and strips the matter back to its essentials, and that matter resides in the human misery caused by historical forces. This is the bleakest of all Friel's plays because it suggests that when it comes to matters of private pain and political disaster, there may not be any solution attainable by human effort. Such a comfortless vision is presented with not the slightest hint that there may be in some court of the soul or of the heavens an eventual justification and peace.

The play closes with Margaret saying to her doomed boss that her father, the pathetic drunk now conducting the choir, will be coming up for her. We do not know what this means, other than that it belongs to the nature of what happens, the everyday that has to be endured in all its tedium, sorrow, and potential disaster.

John McGahern began to make his presence felt as a writer at around the same time as Friel was becoming known as a serious dramatist. Brought up in Cootehall, County Roscommon, where his father was the local sergeant in the Garda Síochána, McGahern led the lonely if somewhat privileged life that would be the fate of the son of a Guard in those days. Guards were feared, respected, and also somewhat distrusted: recruits to the police in those days (the 1930s) had the reputation, somehow, of being traitors to the 'cause', with no one being very clear as to what that cause was, other than the fact that persons identified with the law, as the Guards were, had, in some obscure way, inherited the taint that always tends to be associated with authority in Ireland. In republican circles, also, the Guards were thought of as amongst those who had, with indecent haste, identified with the institutions of the Free State after the Treaty, in a panic to hang onto the jobs they had held in the Royal Irish Constabulary under the crown. All this indicates that the Guards were a powerful, ambiguous, mistrusted, and enigmatic presence in the Ireland in which McGahern grew up. His father, the sergeant Francis McGahern, who embodies all these qualities and more, is a creature of lowering intensity and brutal force in his fiction, and in the extraordinary *Memoir* (2005).

McGahern was raised in the family accommodation attached to Guards' barracks at that time. This interior and claustrophobic world, often shared with the constables, was without privacy, had little quiet, and, while the role of a Guard was to keep a watch over the security of his territory, he himself was continually under surveillance from a public who feared and needed him. This atmosphere, of angry watchfulness, intrusion, sudden rages, sexual frustration, and oppression, is conveyed in McGahern's two early novels, *The Barracks* (1963) and *The Dark* (1965), the latter of which was banned, a decision that cost McGahern his job as a primary teacher in Dublin, reminding us that the parish priest and the clerical management had the giving and the taking away of such positions in Ireland up to relatively recently; and indeed the practice is still extant in many rural parishes in the twenty-first century. In McGahern's case his firing was probably the best thing that could have happened to him, in that the expulsion freed him into writing, more or less full-time (he also farmed on a modest scale).

McGahern brings a concentrated realism to bear on Irish life. This concentration is of such an intensity that the prose often acquires the awe and slow wonder of poetry. There is an obsession with getting the details of moods and situations exactly right: the look of a driveway in a certain light; the sounds you hear in a house when you are waiting for news that may change the rest of your life; the little thrusts of savage pleasure to be got by keeping someone in the dark when he's dying to know something that you don't want him to know; the crude self-assurance that imposes its will under the mask of bonhomie; such things. McGahern's prose is luminous with a steady alertness to the uniqueness of the moment; he constantly surprises with just the right detail that brings a scene to the mind's eye: a tense silence, say, as for example occurs in *That They May Face the Rising Sun* (2002) between two people trying to deal with a problem, the only sound being the sigh of a water-tank filling in the attic.

This kind of receptive depth, a sort of patient clarity with regard to the minute circumstances of life, informs a style that is a perfect vehicle for the short story, and McGahern is one of its Irish masters, to set beside O'Connor, Bowen, and O'Faolain. But like Bowen, and unlike the others, he is also a novelist of exceptional gifts. In two mature works, *Amongst Women* (1990) and *That They May Face the Rising Sun*, he opens up fictional worlds that, in their slow, cumulative, rapt, even trance-like dwelling on the people he creates and the situations in which they find themselves, have a brooding energy and power that continuously ignite in abrupt flashes of insight and realization. He forges a kind of magical realism of the ordinary, where the world as it is is imbued with a fantastical and sometimes almost manic strangeness; but he never forsakes the way things are: he holds fast to the appearances and achieves what Coleridge once said was the source of Wordsworth's genius, the ability to supernaturalize the natural.

There is in McGahern a kind of pietas towards the normal and the given, and it is entirely characteristic of the man that he went back to his native landscape as soon as he could, became a farmer, and wrote in a shed away from the house. Seamus Heaney, in *Stepping Stones* (2008), the collection of interviews with Dennis O'Driscoll, tells the story of how he invited McGahern and Alan Sillitoe, the English writer, after some literary shindig in November 1976, back to the big Victorian house he had bought on Strand Road in Sandymount, Dublin. They headed to the newly acquired property, a bottle of Bushmills in hand to pour the libation. At the gate McGahern stood, looked up at the huge bulk of the house, and said: 'Well, you've bought the coffin', a remark that reveals a good deal about McGahern's fear of the burden of stepping too far out of the ordinary, the contained, the low-key.[23]

In *That They May Face the Rising Sun*, McGahern sets the action of the novel in the countryside of Leitrim in the north-west of the Republic that he knows so well. The story unfolds around the lake where Joe Ruttledge, who comes from the same type of landscape some distance away, and his wife Kate, have bought a farmhouse overlooking the water, having moved from London to find a different life. There is, clearly, a strong autobiographical element in the novel, especially in the manner in which McGahern evokes a quiet life, lived in bare but beautiful surroundings, and every page bears witness to the man's almost physical love of his native countryside. His pastoral vision of this land is not conveyed in anything remotely like romanticized description; the writing is too intimate and virtually sacred for that. It has more than a touch of that reverence for nature and its ordinary secrets that is a feature of Gaelic tradition from the earliest times, a theme the present book has attempted to chart: from the mystical nature writings of the early monks, to Eriugena, to the Fenian cycle, to the inspired lyrics of mad Sweeney, to the baroque celebrations of it in the eighteenth century, down to the present day. Indeed, the dominant idea, or rather feeling, in McGahern's last novel is that the old Celtic and Gaelic patterns of thought and belief are still vestigially present in the world that he brings to life around this tiny lake, and the town nearby, which still has a bar with a grocery attached, in the old style, so that when a rumbustious idiot of a customer praises Guinness and goes on to say that it would be even better for you with a raw egg, the proprietor says, mischieviously, looking in through the partition to the grocery, that that could be provided too. This attention to the small incidents of life builds into a kind of majestic poetry that has a legendary dimension to it, and McGahern's confined world opens out to the universe and to the ancient density of Celtic tradition.

Here is the way in which the landscape is enacted in the mind of the reader; it is winter, coming up to Christmas: 'The leaves started to fall heavily in frosts, in ghostly whispering streams that never paused though the trees were still. They formed into drifts along the shore.... Traceries of branches stripped of their leaves stood out against the water like veins. Under each delicate rowan tree lay the pale rowan stones, like droppings.'[24] These sentences contain voices, ghosts, the physical human body, defecation: McGahern is making us aware of the interaction between the natural world, death, and that of animate and conscious existence, the very connection that is depicted on the Gundestrup Cauldron, where the god Cernunnos, antlered, is at the centre of an arrangement of being that includes all forms of life.

McGahern is one of Ireland's most central writers, central to the complexity of the tradition, while retaining his pietas to the ordinary, and how it happens. The deliberation of his writing, its slow exactitude, brings his people into this broad association with the possible eternity of the natural. (Seán Ó Tuama, in one his lectures to us, his students in Cork in the 1960s, once said that it was the view of the Celts and of the Irish that it was possibly nature, not man, which is eternal.) Not long after this stripping bare of the trees, the Ruttledge's neighbours and friends, Jamesie and Mary Murphy, are presented with a dreadful situation. Jamesie's brother, Johnny, has been made redundant at the Ford works in Dagenham in England, and he wants to come back to live with his brother and Mary as he had done before leaving. Johnny comes home every Christmas and it is all they can do to put up with him for that time, during most of which Jamesie absents himself in any case. The problem is that this world has all kinds of rules and expectations: 'They could not live with him and they could not be seen...to refuse him shelter or turn him away. The timid, gentle manners, based on a fragile interdependence, dealt in avoidances and obfuscations. Edges were softened, ways found round harsh realities....These manners, open to exploitation by ruthless people, held all kinds of traps....It was a language that hadn't any simple way of saying no.'[25] Like the Irish language itself, where it is not possible to say no (as Ciaran Carson reminded us in his collection of 1987 with the title *The Irish for No*).

The information from Johnny has come by letter, and Kate suggests that Ruttledge ghost the reply for his friend, making the difficult case for his not returning in a way that will not cause offence or scandal. This he does by saying that when Johnny thinks about it a bit more he'll see that this arrangement he proposes would not work, that it would be 'hopeless from his own point of view'. The essential thing he does is give the brother room to change his mind without saying no. That evening he takes the letter around to Jamesie's and Mary's house, where Jamesie is glued to *Blind Date* on the television, ogling the sexy girl who is making her blind choice, and loving the sexual innuendos that get in everywhere. Even this detail, with its underlying theme of blind fate at work in human instinct, is woven into the Celtic pattern that McGahern makes.

They read the letter, or rather Ruttledge reads it out for him, Jamesie superstitiously avoiding the written word when it comes to matters as grave as this. They are impressed at Ruttledge's skill, but when Jamesie accompanies him part of the way back he wonders if it will do the trick, seeing as old bachelors like Johnny are not wanted anywhere, so they 'have to try to get their head in somewhere', to which Ruttledge replies that they may find themselves in the same case themselves. He walks on alone and sees a 'river of beaten copper' that runs 'sparkling from shore to shore in the centre of the lake. On either side of this bright river peppered with pale stars the dark water seethed.' A heron lifts out of the reeds to flap 'lazily' around the shore, 'ghostly in the moonlight'. On a night like this, Ruttledge thinks, 'a man could easily want to run from his shadow'. As it happens, the letter does work.

The title of the book comes from the notion that the Irish were buried standing up and facing east, so that, in death, they could face the rising sun. McGahern's last work, *Memoir*, is a chilling account of a terrible and fearsome father, and the Ireland that produced and was to some degree sustained by this authoritarianism. It is also McGahern standing up, for one last time, against the terror that was his father; he wants, metaphorically, to be buried standing up, since this book was written while he was in the grip of the cancer that would kill him.

When they were small, the sergeant's children came to live in the barracks during the summer months; and when their mother became ill with cancer they moved in from the house some twenty miles away where they lived with her while she worked as a teacher in the local school. The regime Frank McGahern imposed was horrific: no noise, constant checking for cleanliness, continuous interrogations on all manner of things, physical violence. This contrasted bleakly with the sheer gentleness of their mother, who did not have long to live after her operation and radiotherapy. Always preoccupied with money, the father wrote to the consultant surgeon in Dublin asking him should she return to teaching when she came out, saying that it was her relatives that were pressing her to resume; that it was a matter of indifference to him, when it is perfectly clear from the letter that what he is after is the all-clear and the money that will follow from it.

Against this bleakness their mother presents a love and sensitivity that makes McGahern's portrait of her an unforgettable one. She is the goddess Flora, in tune with the world of nature, in which she takes the young boy for long walks, naming the flowers, and praising him, telling him that it will be her proudest day when he says Mass for her: he has said in his youthful innocence that he will be a priest. She is also Éire, Ireland in her magical beauty as the young girl, the other side of the Hag, who seems in this instance to have taken over the father, if that doesn't sound too flippant; it is just that there is a desperation in the man's masculinity, and an aversion to the feminine (in spite of his consuming sexual drive) that makes one suspect an ambiguity about his maleness. But such speculations fade as the *Memoir* concludes with some of the most remarkable sentences in modern Irish prose. Here the mother moves into another identity, that of the saint, of the St Thérèse of Lisieux mode, suffering illness patiently, in touch always with the natural world. She has had perfect health for forty years; now that this has been taken away, '*it is for some inscrutable reason of His own to try and test my faith. In Him and by Him and for Him I live and place my trust and to Him alone I pray, knowing He will bring me safely along.*'[26]

McGahern tells us that without the promise he had made to her that he would become a priest, he would not have been able to resist his father when he wanted to take him out of school to get him earning money. She has, he realizes, been with him all his life. And then comes the passage of luminescent beauty that ends the book, saying that if he could walk with her again he would take her around the lake near his house in County Leitrim, which he has come to know so intimately, after which they would follow the sky back to the place of origin, whence she has been with him all his life. They would

leave the lanes and I would take her by the beaten path the otter takes under the thick hedges between the lakes . . . . The otter whistles down the waters for the male when she wants to mate and chases him back again to his own waters when his work is done; unlike the dear swans that paddle side by side and take turns on their high nest deep within the reeds. Above the lake we would follow the enormous sky until it reaches the low mountains where her life began. I would want no shadow to fall on her joy and deep trust in God. She would face no false reproaches. As we retraced our steps, I would pick for her the wild orchid and the windflower.

It is as if he is readying himself to be with her, which he was to be only three years later.

A very different kind of poetry emerges in the work of John Banville, another stylist, along with McGahern and Colm Tóibín, of Irish prose in the period from the 1960s to the time of writing. Banville, one of the most learned of authors, whose style is intensely self-conscious, studied, and even mandarin at times in a laconic way, seems to have been fortunate in managing to avoid a university education, something, especially if the student is reading an Arts course, which tends to be an impediment to be overcome if there is a desire to be a writer. Born and reared in County Wexford, like Tóibín, Banville was educated by the Christian Brothers, whose then ardent ferocities of discipline have left their mark on his mind and feelings, but the scars are well-sealed over, and lie buried deep beneath the tissue of the writing. He worked for a time as a sub-editor, then as literary editor of the *Irish Times*, where he reviewed regularly (and well) a range of work from all over the world in a variety of genres. He immersed himself in the traditions of Irish fiction, read Joyce and Beckett avidly, but also sought out the great Germans, especially Thomas Mann, and the Russians, in particular Dostoevsky. He read poetry with intensity and a hunger for what its linguistic energy can achieve in the transformation of the everyday, and for a time frequently quoted the 'Ninth Duino Elegy' by Rainer Maria Rilke in essays and interviews, as a kind of statement of credo: 'Are we, perhaps, *here* just for saying: House, Bridge, Fountain, Gate, Jug... but for *saying* remember, | oh for such saying as never the things themselves | hoped so intensely to be.'[27]

It is this fidelity to the actual, as with the pietas with the ordinary in McGahern, that steadies and ballasts the elaborate craft and frequently joyous arabesques of elaboration that are such seductive features of Banville's mordantly humorous tonalities. The interior weather in his novels is a force in itself; there is ferociously engaged detail about domestic interiors, the way food is prepared, what it is like to travel through Renaissance and Reformation Poland and the Czech lands, Sweden, Germany. The early novel *Birchwood* (1973) tackled that museum of the Irish past that is the Big House, and its colonial guilts, in bizarre and unsettling ways. It is set in the nineteenth century and includes nightmare-like accounts of the Great Famine, but it also incorporates into its narrative scenes of a freakish and intriguing kind, set in a circus and travelling show that remind one of Goethe's *Walpurgisnacht* in *Faust*, a key text for Banville. He takes the historical traumas that the big-house theme has come to embody in Irish fiction, and at the same time advances the Gothic elements that this convention also embraces from the examples of Sheridan Le Fanu and Bram Stoker, and shapes these into the weird distortions of the narrative that Gabriel Godkin writes about his own fantastical life that he has returned to Birchwood to set down. And all the time Banville retains a focus on the actualities of nineteenth-century Ireland and doesn't allow the swirling grotesquerie to get out of control.

There is a strong philosophical, or, perhaps more correctly, theological streak in Banville. He interested himself intensively in the philosophy of science for his series of novels on astronomy, beginning with *Doctor Copernicus* (1976), followed by *Kepler* (1981), *The Newton Letter* (1982), and *Mefisto* (1986); but just as important as the discoveries the scientists in these books make in their researches are the moral and theological issues they raise about the structure of matter, the forces that govern existence, and whether or not there can be discerned, in being, a design or an order that is not pure chance or just sheer uncontrolled energy that may be at root diabolic. These bleak novels, and those that followed them (largely concerned with criminality and violence, such as *The Book of Evidence*, published in 1989), reveal the

world of the intellect and of thought as a region of terror and harrowing accidie to those condemned to it, among whom we may number
the writer himself. What saves these books from a leaden torpor of
unremitting misery is the storytelling itself, the surprisingly brisk
transitions of mood, the constantly unexpected shifts, and, very significantly, the self-lacerating wit the narrators constantly deploy, often
jumping familiar words into a kind of freshened hilarity, sometimes
taking the reader aback with some arcane word that conveys exactly,
and wittily, the particular surge of contempt or self-disgust that surfaces
at that point. The storytelling is an adventure in language which brings
the theological questions into urgent and vigorous play.

Banville is drawn to the darker impulses of human nature. *The
Untouchable* (1997) fictionalizes the career of the spy Sir Anthony
Blunt, Keeper of the Queen's Pictures, whose cover was blown by
the Thatcher government in the 1980s. There is desperation here, the
seediness of the homosexual underworld in the 1930s, the idealism that
drew Blunt (here redrawn as Victor Maskell, an Irishman) to Soviet
ideology, and a memorable and disturbing trip back to Ireland to visit
the household of a fictionalized Louis MacNeice. Over all there
broods an atmosphere of hopelessness and doom, a sense that betrayal
is an understandable code in a society where the kind of solidity of
belief and order that produced the work of the French painter Nicolas
Poussin (a favourite of Blunt's and Maskell's, the latter of whom owns
a fictional painting by the master, *The Death of Seneca*) has disappeared.
Existence is reduced to frantic bouts of sex with boys, when they can
be had, frenzied drinking with 'Boy' (the fictionalized Guy Burgess,
who in one unforgettable scene of drunkenness with Maskell is sitting
cross-legged at the end of the bed, his bare feet unspeakably filthy), and
the bleak satisfactions of cheating his superiors by passing codes the
British have cracked during the war to the Russians. In the end he
shoots himself, writing the (ambiguous) last words in the memoir that
the novel purports to be: 'Father, the gate is open.'

The Sea (2005) is another venture into the obsessions and venality of
a late-modern, Irish mind, of a man thoroughly disappointed with
everything, still recovering from the death of his wife. It is, again, in
the form of a memoir, this time by Max Morden, who is attempting
(and failing) to write a book on the painter Bonnard. He goes to stay
near the seaside where he holidayed as a boy, and the memoir recounts
experiences of sexual awakening in the company of a family who came

to the resort at the same time, the Graces. He relates how he became
sexually obsessed with Connie Grace, the mother, and Chloe, her
daughter, whose twin, Myles, is either a mute or chooses not to speak.
After a fraught and terrified episode of sexual fumbling by the sea in a
changing-shed (that, Banville does not fail to mention, smells of urine),
they are discovered by Rose, the nanny (who it is later revealed is
having a lesbian affair with Connie); the twins take off and walk to the
edge of the sea, then wade out, beyond their depth, and drown. Just
like that: appalling in its suddenness. Everything is conveyed with a
nightmare remoteness, the world and the events that it generates are
utterly inscrutable and strange. A golfer on the course above the sea
sees what has happened and comes down the dunes to where Max and
Rose are standing, nonplussed by the 'indifferent world':

high-stepping flurriedly through the sliding sands with comical haste. He
wore a yellow shirt and khaki trousers and two-tone shoes and was brandish-
ing a golf club. The shoes I may have invented. . . . He kept shouting that
someone should go for the Guards. He seemed extremely angry, gesturing in
the air with the club like a Zulu warrior shaking his knobkerrie. Zulus,
knobkerries? Perhaps I mean assegais.[28]

One does not wish to labour this, but that last little flurry of bleak
humour reveals much about the brutal realism of Banville's fiction;
there is something pitiless in the extremity of the exposure that the
writing is prepared to undergo to reveal the terrible frivolity of the
human mind as it tries to cope with the mystery of the ordinary. His is
a theological intelligence but one that seems without belief or consolation, as if the gods are remote, capricious, indifferent, always
interfering but generally up to no good. This is to be the subject of
one of his finest novels, *The Infinities* (2009). *The Sea* ends with Max
recalling, on the night his wife dies, a sea-surge he experienced during
that fatal holiday when the twins were drowned. He was standing in
the water when, 'in a driving heave, the whole sea surged, it was not a
wave, but a smooth rolling swell that seemed to come up from the
deeps, as if something vast down there had stirred itself. . . . Nothing
had happened, a momentous nothing, just another of the great world's
shrugs of indifference.'

'Nothing' is a word Banville favours, but it would be unwise
therefore to think of him as a nihilist. This nothing of his is more
like the nothing in MacNeice (one of his favourite writers, and one of

the closest to him in temperament and mentality), as he describes it in 'Suite for Recorders': 'The windblown web in which we live | Presumes a yawning negative, | A nothing which cries out to see | A something flout its vacancy.'[29]

The Infinities is a deeply unsettling work. The narrator of considerable portions of the book is none other than Hermes or Mercury, the god of communications, the psychopomp, who brings the dead to Pluto's underworld, and who frequently was given the job of facilitating connections between the mortal world and that of Olympus. His father, Zeus, is active here too, and keeps his son busy working out ways and means whereby he can get at Helen, after whom he lusts insatiably. Helen, an actress, is married to Adam Godley. They are visiting the family house, an Irish big house, called Arden, where the father, old Adam Godley, is, it seems, dying. Adam is a mathematical scientist, who has uncovered the infinities in the relationships between things, at the heart of matter; he is world-famous, it appears, but his controversial work has, at times, been greeted with fury and disdain. However, his theorizing has led to important practical outcomes, such as the conversion of salt water into an endless source of energy, to rocket-ships that will soar free of the normal time dimensions.

Banville is creating an alternative universe, and this novel reveals how deeply, but in a kind of secret code, he is involved in the history of Ireland and its obscure tensions and inherited angers. The house is inhabited by Old Adam and Ursula, his second (and alcoholic) wife, and his daughter, the self-harming Petra. They are looked after by a housekeeper, Ivy Blount, who once owned the property, and who now lives in a cottage in the grounds. The reader has a kind of shock (what is going on here?) when we are told of Ivy's lineage: it is said she is directly descended from Charles Blount, Lord Mountjoy, who was sent over by Mary, Queen of Scots, when she acceded to the English throne after beheading her cousin, 'the upstart and treasonous Elizabeth Tudor', to pacify 'this most distressful country'.[30] This is of course exactly the opposite of what happened. Blount was sent over to subdue the Irish rebels, under O'Neill, which he did, most effectively, at Kinsale. In this version, where time and events have somehow reversed themselves (is it Adam Godley who has done this, or the gods, or are we in another Ireland altogether, a parallel one?), Blount comes over to put down the Protestant interest and restore Ireland to its glorious pre-Reformation Catholicism, under Catholic Mary, who now carries the title Gloriana for her endeavours, the name given by Spenser to Elizabeth as the great Protestant Empress, but here usurped by Mary, Queen of Scots.

We are given another shift in our perceptions when we are told that Helen has been ravished in her sleep (or was she asleep?) by Zeus early in the morning, taking on the form of young Adam, but 'how transfigured! . . . .The things he did to her, the things he had her do! Never, never, in all her life.' She goes to the toilet and checks herself (we are spared nothing), and comes back, fully aroused again, and makes frantic love with her husband, this time in his 'real' form. This is all watched over by Hermes, who calls his 'Daddums' to come, 'put on your horns and take a gander at what these your little ones are up to'.[31]

Immediately after this we are taken back to Old Adam's childhood in what is probably Wexford town, Banville's own native place. He is coming home from school and 'wears a tweed coat with a half-belt at the back, and a peaked cap, and thick woollen stockings the tops of which are turned down to hide homemade, soiled white elastic garters.' This chapter, narrated, we presume, by Hermes, now opens into an evocation of things, in the way that Rilke says that perhaps this is what we are here for, the naming of things for the angel. Some of the things that are named surprise, to say the least: a gravedigger emerges from a churchyard, a spade over his shoulder, and 'leans sideways and shuts one nostril with a finger pressed along the side of it and from the other expertly ejects a bolus of snot'. It is the word 'bolus' that connives at the shock: we really see, in the mind's eye, the spherical volume of snot in its livid actuality. There is, even, a touch of social history at work here: such sights as this were common in the Ireland of the 1940s and '50s, when pavements in the towns were bestreaked with such propulsions at a time when tuberculosis was rife. Soon after this homeward journey his father dies, but his mother insists they have Christmas as usual. She makes a cake, and as she does we see Adam's mind expand into its infinities. She is mixing the cake, and he is wondering what is it to be '*completely mixed*'? She has cried tears into the mixture, and where are they now? 'What about the flour itself, no two grains of which were exactly alike—how could that be *completely mixed*, even if there were no other ingredients present in it, making their own pattern. . . . Was everything in the world so intrinsically linked and yet resistantly disparate?' The world is built of such linkages and resistances, the infinities operating between, where the gods preside.

Ireland in this novel is an integral part of a larger entity, part of some imperium, which functions in no less a way than does the (Catholic) Britain across the water, which remains remote. At any rate, first-class science is being done in Ireland, and there are inventions such as the car young Adam drives, which is powered by a tank of sea-water on the floor. It is as if Banville, in some strange and curiously liberating way, is rewriting history with a kind of insouciant, almost loutish, defiance. A kind of Wexford croppy after all the sophistication.

It is a baffling novel, a masterpiece of style and intellect, deliberately turning the history of Britain and Ireland inside out, as Old Adam's research has done with the laws of time and physics, whose inner inscrutability is presided over by the gods. The old man does not die in the end; Helen is pregnant with Zeus's child, from which will come we know not what. In a late twist Roddy Wagstaff (Adam's intending biographer and Petra's dandified boyfriend) leaves because, invaded by Zeus, he made a sexual overture to Helen and was rebuffed. Old Adam does not know the reason for his hasty retreat, but reflecting on the fact that Roddy wants to write his biography he says he 'should change his name to Shakespeare'; in this realm Shakespeare has become a kind of Boswell. At the heart of the novel lie tensions of repulsion and attraction, in which are implicated the fierce sadnesses of Ireland's history, and the unremitting laments indulged in on their account.

Banville is an enigmatic novelist, saturated in the Irish experience, as Beckett (one of his masters) was, but the pain lies unfathomed in the deeps of consciousness, making continually seismic shifts as the planes and strata drive against each other in the fiery core of memory and its inscribed hatreds and remorse.

Banville writes English with a kind of brutal relish, as if he is, often, prying it open to surprise himself with its hidden latencies and secrecies, and, at the same time, taking his readers aback with the degree of strangeness he can bring to the exercise of language. This is a quality remarked upon already in the work of Flann O'Brien and in Joyce, both of whom write English with ferocious, almost vengeful, address, and is to be related to the linguistic substrate in Irish society that is the Irish language itself, which continuously has an estranging and deepening effect on the way English is used in Ireland in all registers, from daily speech to Banville's exacting elegance. We now know, from contemporary language research by scholars such as Theo Venneman of Munich, that it is not necessary for the speakers of a language to be fluent in another, substrate language, for that anterior language to have all kinds of complex effects on the ways in which the surface language is deployed, especially in the matters of syntax, rhythm, and word order. So that it is now possible to say, without being laughed out of court, that writers such as Beckett, Anthony Cronin, and Banville carry, in their style and linguistic presence, a whole set of behaviours that originate in the Irish-language substrate.

But what of the Irish language itself, as a literary medium, in the years since the 1960s? A major renovation began in Cork in the late 1960s under the influence of Seán Ó Tuama, where Irish language poetry, of a new and radical kind, started to be written by the likes of Michael Davitt, Nuala Ní Dhomhnaill, Liam Ó Muirthile, and Gabriel Rosenstock, known as the Innti poets, named after a broadsheet they began to issue in those years. *Innti* means 'into her', a broad enough joke reflecting the jockeying laddishness of the young male poets who were in the majority, but it also implies a getting back into the motherlode, into the origin, a recovery of the ancient female entity, both hag and young queen, of Irish tradition. And this was now perceived as sexy and cool, and the practitioners of this verse read e. e. cummings, Wallace Stevens, T. S. Eliot, the beat poets, haiku, Baudelaire, the *Tibetan Book of the Dead*. This marvellous eclecticism produced much excitement, and much good verse, as well as style and the signatures of style. I recall Michael Davitt dancing a Kerry Set in a long white gabardine with a beautiful girl in the hall in Ballingeary, County. Cork, in around 1971, and thinking, looking at his grave comportment over the surging energy of his dance, that we had entered a completely new phase of what it was to be Irish.

However, between the publication of Ó Tuama's *Nuabhéarsaíocht* in 1950 and the Innti poets some twenty years later there emerged two major writers who, significantly, were bilingual in their practice. These were Eoghan Ó Tuairisc (also known under his English name as Eugene Rutherford Watters) and Pearse Hutchinson. Ó Tuairisc was a poet and novelist of distinction, creating fictions in Irish that were experimental and almost pointillist at times in their capacity to capture instants of intensity; while his verse, in Irish and English, worked outwards from traditional myth and form to embrace the pain and loneliness of mid-twentieth-century anomie in, for example, the long and ambitious poem, *The Weekend of Dermot and Grace* (1964).

Pearse Hutchinson was born in Glasgow in 1927, reared in Dublin, and educated at UCD, where he studied Castilian. A distinction between Castilian and Spanish is crucial here, because, shortly after leaving university, he went to live in Barcelona where he encountered Catalan and learned Galician. What this signals is a central feature of Hutchinson's poetic and linguistic practice, a multilingualism and receptivity to the plurality of world culture that never diminishes his consuming attachment to Irish and Gaelic tradition. He read voraciously the literatures of the world, from South and Central America, Africa, the Middle East, India, Japan, and also, of course, all the European literatures, including Romanian, Russian, and Portuguese. But this openness was not some form of exoticism; it is a crucial part of the questing intelligence that informs his creative process. He is intent on the exploration of the specifics of the widest extent of culture that may be possible because under it all there is an abiding instinct that there inheres in the great variety of being some unifying impulse where things can be seen standing in their own true light. There is a phrase of Ó Ríordáin's that encapsulates this, where he says that the vison of poetry can bring about a situation where things can be revealed *nite ina mbeatha féin* ('washed in their own being').

Everywhere in Hutchinson we see this pressure to have things stand out as they are. Indeed, he tells us that one of the reasons he turned to writing in Irish with *Faoistin Bhacach* (1968) was because Irish afforded him two new kinds of freedom: a grammar that allowed for very fine differentiations of meaning and nuance; and the opportunity to write about certain things (in particular sexuality) with a directness not possible in English. It is strange, but the grammatical complexity he rediscovered in Irish allowed him to be more direct because it enabled him to write an exploratory and interrogative verse that opened up difficult emotions. In 'A Stór Bí Cinnte' ('Love, Be Certain') in *Faoistin Bhacach* he says that what he is attempting in this poem is the creating of a heart that will be more reverent and humbled than any heart he could open to a woman:

> Love, be certain that in this poem
> I do not blame you that it has won;
> this poem is short, and far away from us
> is that mercy that I told you of.[32]

It is as if the writing in Irish allowed him to develop a moral and even metaphysical edge that he then brought over into his English writing.

Very often in his work, in English and in Irish, there is an ever-increasing moral refinement in process so that the poetry becomes an examen of the mind and the impulses, and those motives that prompt them. 'Bright after Dark', from *Watching the Morning Grow* (1972), is an exposition, in three parts, of the search for grace, for the meaning that will stand in its own light. There are three countries invoked—Transylvania, Ireland, and Guatemala—and in each of these places a certain ritual against evil is invoked. The poem builds its strenuous moral structure as each occasion of danger is contemplated, and the means to overcome it explained. In the first country, to overcome a curse you have to climb a certain hill and play the flute; best if it is a silver flute, Hutchinson wittily attests, but any flute will do as long as it is played after dark. Next it is Ireland, and here, to protect a child outside the house at night, you place a burnt-out cinder in its hand: 'The cinder, in this good function, is called aingeal, | meaning angel.' In the third country, if you journey forth at night, when the witches get up to their work what you have to hope for is that 'someone before you has dropped grains of maize | on the ground to light your way', and you, in your turn, must do likewise, to show others the way, because 'only maize can light the way on a dark night'.[33]

This poem, in its panoptic sweep, its readiness to respond to all forms of human understanding, its alertness to evil and to the grace that may avert it, its recognition that what is human needs to be protected and that this is why good magic (and poetry may be a species of such good magic) was invented, and its ability to make things stand clear in their own being—flute-music, the cinder, maize—reveals the kind of radical rediscovery that Hutchinson's bilingual world opens for us.

Another highly significant moment occurred in these years of ferment, during which there was an impetus of recovery profoundly at work in writing in Irish, when Michael Hartnett, by then an acclaimed poet in English, announced his resolve, in *A Farewell to English* (1975), to write no longer in anything but Gaelic. None of these writers, Hutchinson, Hartnett, or Ó Tuairisc, were native speakers of Irish; they had acquired the language under the de Valera policy of Irish being compulsory in schools in the Free State and then the Republic. Proficiency in the language was also a requirement for jobs in the Civil Service and for much of the public sector. It was, for example, possible for a diehard to insist (as we are told the father of the actor Niall Tóibín did in Cork, much to the embarrassment of the young Tóibín) that a bus conductor transact his business with you in the first official language.

By the 1970s there had been launched a scathing series of attacks on the founding ideas of the nationalist Irish state, condemning, for example, the concept of the blood sacrifice that, it was claimed, animated the revolutionary fervour of Patrick Pearse. As the Republic moved into the modern world and strengthened its ties with Europe, there was an increasing dissatisfaction with the old pieties of faith, nationalist politics, patriotism, and the symbols of Gaeldom; and there was some glee to be discerned in the pleasure certain historians (who came to be known as 'revisionists') took in dismantling the reputations of the nation's founding fathers. Influenced, no doubt, by the renewed violence in the North, as the old wounds opened up again, the Rising of 1916 was now often depicted as a bloody, irresponsible, and murderous set of actions carried out by malcontents and emotionally immature men, who used the opportunity for martyrdom as a means of coping (in Pearse's case, in particular) with underlying problems of sexuality and psychology. The historical interpretation was, as is so often the case, driven by contemporary realities, as the conflict in the North began to shatter the order of normal everyday life, and as its repercussions were increasingly felt in the Republic, with the violence crawling into the border areas and even into Dublin itself. These Republican men and women in the North, the thinking went, may lay claim to a tradition of nationalist resistance that goes back to the founding fathers, Pearse and Connolly and Plunkett, but these progenitors were themselves no better than deranged terrorists driven by abstract hatred and their own manias.

So pervasive and influential were revisionist views at this time that the Irish state took many opportunities of silencing apologists for nationalism, banning them from the mass media and adopting the extraordinary stratagem, for a while, of having actors voice-over the words of political activists in order that the populace not be exposed to the actuality of these individuals. These were strange days, but the convulsions of the conflict in the North were deeply unsettling, and there were times when it did seem as if the ordinary passage of everyday life was in real danger of being usurped.

However, while the revisionists were in the ascendancy in the media and in the universities and in the generality of polite and responsible society, there were of course counter-moves against their moral certitudes. The more the nationalist tradition was traduced by neo-Home Rule intellectuals, the more the other side sought to rehabilitate the validity of Irish republicanism and the justifiability of the armed struggle. Irish, too, was an issue. To some it was the badge of recidivism and untutored indoctrination into the inflexible intolerance of hating the British, while to others it had symbolic value as the main repository of an ancient Gaelic world to which it gave unrivalled access. It also opened, as all languages do, its own quite specific world of feeling and thought, different from English, and for that reason carrying a charged significance at this time. This was the ferment in which the new phase of writing in Irish evolved, a newly contested arena, but on a site as old as the hills.

The life and work of the fiction-writer and dramatist Alan Titley is a fascinating case. Born in 1947, Titley grew up in Cork city, learned Irish at the national school he attended in Turner's Cross, where the classes were vast (something like a scarcely credible seventy-five pupils per class). The school was totally Irish-speaking, so that Titley, like most of his many classmates, would be making sure to use Irish as much as he could, to avoid getting flogged by the master. The stick was put to constant use as a learning-aid in this school (I can attest to this, because I was in the same class, but ours was no different to many other schools), the teacher racing up and down the aisles, howling with rage in Irish, slamming the desks with his polished stick—stick?—cudgel really, certainly not a cane. Titley, as the years went by, discovered a quite unusual gift for language, and for Irish in particular. He became a teacher himself, and then immersed himself in research into the novelist Máirtín Ó Cadhain, getting to the heart of that writer's huge linguistic gift. Titley began producing work of his own that is astonishing in the bravura of its eloquence, and in the sheer daring and inventiveness of his imagined worlds.

Ó Cadhain and Titley are probably the two finest prose stylists of modern Irish, but whereas Ó Cadhain was brought up fully integrated into the Gaelic world, Titley, through some kind of astonishing act of retrieval, has managed to translate himself back into what is a complete relationship with that culture and civilization. His prose is capable of impressive variety in the registers he uses, from broad and laconic vernacular, to a stylistic inventiveness and resource that allows him to travel back into the earlier phases of the language and its modes, from the eighteenth century through to Keating and the elaborate flourishes of Ossianic and romantic storytelling. This linguistic mastery is accomplished without pedantry; rather does he do what he does in this way in a kind of savage and delighted glee, relishing the release the language's richness can give him into old, but also strangely modern, methods of perception. He is a learned writer, but he writes Irish in the way that Borges writes Spanish, studiously, comically, but also, frequently, with profound sadness as the world that he brings into being signals its own precariousness by virtue of the lonely fortitude of Titley's voice, one that is taken very little note of because of the demands his work makes on the reader's intelligence and attention, and the fact that the readership for Irish remains very small.

An Fear Dána ('The Poetry Man', or 'The Insolent Man', 1993) is a novel about the bardic poet Muireadhach Albanach Ó Dálaigh, who flourished around 1220. Titley takes the fragments that we have of Ó Dálaigh's wild career, which saw him kill a man, it was said, then travel to Scotland (hence Albanach), to the Holy Land, then back to Ireland and Scotland, and turn these into a series of events that reflects the Europe of our own time. But this is not an allegory; it is a journey inwards to the nature of the human situation now, where existence is crowded with symbols and signs and numbers, and at the same time a journey backwards into the resource of Irish which allows him to bring to light the confusions of the contemporary world. Here is Muireadhach at the inner court of Alan, the great Chief of Leven in Scotland, where he knows, somehow, that this is a place where he was meant to arrive: 'I stood before the master, my people behind me. It was evident that very little of the light of life was reaching those eyes of his. He coughed: the sound of an oak being split by an axe. A weasel bone between his fingers to pick his teeth with. Five spots on his left cheek, one for each of the wounds of Christ.'[34] This quality of strangeness and of sharply realized shock in human encounters never lets up in this remarkable novel. Continuously the reader is being brought up sharply against what he knows is there before him in Gaelic tradition, but which has gone into disuse: hence the melancholy in Titley's sonorous and vital prose, the bravery of the huge effort expended, the sorrow that it may be that the apparatus of knowing and perception he has re-fired is becoming extinct.

Titley's venture into Irish is, as will be evident, a journey to an interior of a culture which, to many at that time in the 1970s, was, in spite of the revival of interest in many aspects of native tradition, in danger of being closed off because of the decline in the Gaelic-speaking areas of the country. The music of Ireland was increasing in popularity all the time, there was an intense curiosity about Celtic and Gaelic tradition in Irish writing in English, but there was more than an element of bravado and desperation in the way in which the Innti poets, for example, paraded their assurance about the language and its sustainability.

One member of that group who stood apart (not least because she was a woman in a fairly laddish company) was Nuala Ní Dhomhnaill. But it was not only on account of her sex that she was different: she was, to all intents and purposes, a native Irish speaker, having been sent by her Gaelic-speaking physician parents back from England to the Kerry Gaeltacht when she was 5, where she was brought up for a time, and where she encountered the linguistic subtlety of Kerry Irish and its great reserves of culture and folklore. Like Tomás Ó Criomhthain, Máirtín Ó Cadhain, and Peig Sayers, she comes straight out of the native oral tradition without pretence or ostentation. It is just natural to her. It is the way her mind works.

She also looked extraordinary when she arrived at UCC. She had flaming red hair, which she wore long; she had alabaster white skin, and full red lips. And she played the harp and sang in Irish. She looked like a literal incarnation of the white goddess of Robert Graves, and of one of the female embodiments of Ireland conjured by Eoghan Rua Ó Súilleabháin or Seán Clárach Mac Domhnaill. She drove many a poet, Gaelic and otherwise, to distraction, but no one expected what it was she was about to unleash: the driving hag energy of native Gaelic tradition, utterly renewed, and now relevant in ways that could not have been foreseen to the conditions of Ireland, Irish, and women.

With Titley one is aware of the anxieties that trouble the very act of writing itself: is it to be the case that all this learning and eloquence is destined to go nowhere? Earlier, in Ó Ríordáin's verse, there is always the sense that the activity of poetry, in spite of its immense importance, is deeply compromised and provisional, by virtue of the fact that it suspires in a minority and declining language in the shadow of the mighty global and all-consuming organism that is English. And Ó Cadhain grew more disillusioned and more enraged as he despaired of the fact that the Irish people seemed to be unaware that who they were was inextricably bound in with something about which they seemed indifferent. With Ní Dhomhnaill (and indeed with the Innti poets in general) the situation alters. There is no longer the resentment and sorrow at the prospect of the disappearance of the language; there is, even, a kind of liberation from history, if history is thought of as a process with unavoidable consequences given certain facts and conditions. The Innti generation, and the new school of poets arising in the North—Ciaran Carson, Paul Muldoon, and Medbh McGuckian—seem a good deal less burdened by the weight of history than their predecessors, such as Kinsella and Heaney. There was a colonial situation, there was (and is) the decline of the native language: well, what are we to do about it? We work with what we can and move onwards to what may come. This nervous exhilaration is per-haps captured in the title of the collection by Hutchinson, *The Frost is All Over*, who was, as ever, ahead in his instinctual augurings. There is an insouciance at work here, a playfulness, a readiness for the game of language, and if the language that one is playing in is mortally chal-lenged, then it may give the entire enterprise that extra frisson of danger and of risk.

This is not to say that everything now becomes 'ludic' and game-some. All these writers—Michael Davitt, Medbh McGuckian, Ciaran Carson, Paul Muldoon, Liam Ó Muirthile, Gabriel Rosenstock, writ-ing in Irish and English (and some occasionally do both, Carson, for example)—have their preoccupations with Gaelic tradition and the angry scars of Irish history, but these are accepted, worked into the fabric of their verse, and have become part of the material it is given to them to work with; there is not in these writers a feeling that there must be a solution to the problem. It may be that there is an acceptance by them that for all kinds of things in human experience and history there just is no solution; you accept the trauma and try to get over it as best you can. Strangely too, in some respects, this is the kind of curious buoyant acceptance that Friel works into *The Home Place*.

Michel de Montaigne, in his essays, has a set of reflections on the work of Raymond Sebond that is pertinent here, perhaps. Mon-taigne makes a distinction between the stoics and the sceptics, saying that the stoics believe that they can come into possession of the truth; the sceptics, however (among whom he numbers Zeno, Democritus, and Pyrrho, saying that the style of thought ultimately derives from

Homer), admit that there can be only continuous seeking after the truth. The follower of Pyrrho has this 'profession': 'ever to waver... never to be assured of any thing, nor to take any warrant of himself.' Such an attitude allows such men and women to be unfixed, a condition that 'leads them into their Ataraxie...exempted from the agitations which we receive by the the impression of the opinion and knowledge we imagine we have of things'. And this knowledge that we think we have of things leads us into all kinds of trouble, and Montaigne proceeds to list them: 'feare, avarice, envie, immoderate desires...rebellion, disobedience', and so forth.[35]

This 'ataraxie'('freedom from worry') is not indifference; it is an acceptance that it is not possible to remake the world according to our desire; and that it is certain that the final state of clear and steady realization of the situation one is in will never materialize. As Heaney put it (for whom one would not think immediately that ataraxy would be a congenial condition), the 'wet centre is bottomless'. As Friel has it, confusion is not an ignoble condition; or as the joke in Northern Ireland goes: 'if you're not confused, it's only because you do not fully understand the situation.'

It is also perhaps not without interest that this word, 'ataraxie', from John Florio's translation of Montaigne, who had it out of Pyrrho, was recovered in Irish literature by none other than Samuel Beckett in his early fiction: Belacqua is subject to this condition. Beckett almost certainly came upon it through his friend the poet Denis Devlin, who wrote an MA thesis on Montaigne; and it comes alive again in Banville, who has a particular regard for this word. It is the term I wish to adopt as a generic descriptor of a condition shared by a school of poets from the 1970s onwards, those following after Montague and Kinsella, and writing in Irish and in English. They tend to be intellectual, somewhat mandarin and mysterious, playful, the opposite of strident; they do not 'do' protest; they are far from irresponsible as citizens, but they have no aspiration to be legislators, acknowledged or otherwise. They have a predecessor in the earlier period, later than Beckett and of a generation with Heaney, though radically different: Derek Mahon, to whom I shall return.

There are two poets, or rather 'men of letters' (if the phrase has not become too tarnished with associations of dilettantism), whose practices and mentalities make them also antecedants of the kind of ataraxian nonchalance and detachment I am seeking to describe here:

Anthony Cronin and Augustus Young. Cronin, one of twentieth-century Ireland's finest biographers, has written works about the lives of a number of people that are classics in the genre: Flann O'Brien, Beckett, Kavanagh, and Brendan Behan. These studies combine immense learning and considerable archival work with a deep sensitivity to his subjects as imaginative writers, and this because he himself is a novelist, a dramatist, and a poet of quite remarkable achievement. The *Collected Poems* (2004) reveal a committed intelligence and a social consciousness that issue in a human sympathy that is extensive and generous. A late poem, for example, entitled 'Boys Playing Football' has a decidedly socialist view of global economics: the ball the kids are playing with is, probably, made in Pakistan by children who work fourteen-hour shifts, enough to appal the 'liberals' when they hear of it, who will then get the factories closed down. But, of course, the manufacture will move elsewhere, Cambodia or Bangladesh, and the liberals will congratulate themselves on their righteousness. This anger is a readiness of the mind always in Cronin, as in the sequence of 1989, *The End of the Modern World*, and it may seem strange that he is enlisted as one of what I call the ataraxians, given his social temper. However, while satire is frequently at work in his verse, there remains a calm steadiness of mind, a relaxed composure, which is in part what permits the outflowing of a never-failing human accord. The modern world, in its perhaps ending phases (as we know it), can be a heartless and terrible place. Cronin acknowledges this, but it is not the function of the poet to howl and weep; it is to see things for what they are, and accept the brief (and not so brief perhaps) remissions of pain that life can give. This makes Cronin a very fine love poet, on the one hand, and on the other a celebrant of its joyous gifts, as when he writes of 'Our pup Butler'. 'You cannot use the story told', he writes in 'Art', 'To have things your own way'.[36] What is the case is the case, something his detested 'liberals' fail to realize, so immense are the presumptions of their egos. 'Meditation on a Clare Cliff-top', which concludes the *Collected Poems*, is a 'Tintern Abbey' for the contemporary world of astrophysics and black holes, while also raising our eyes to Venus, at the end, and to 'evening love', the last words in the book.[37]

Cronin is a Wexford man, and appears to have been imbued with a 'croppy' spirit: his nationalism has a strong republican and radical streak, unlike that professed by many of the patriots of the era he grew up in. Augustus Young (pseudonym of James Hogan) is a Cork-man, son of a well-known and somewhat controversial professor of history at University College, Cork, also James Hogan. The father was deeply and radically conservative; the son has been careful to distance himself from any overt political espousals. There is instead in Young a studious withholding of anything declarative, presumptuous, or 'inop-portune', a word he uses in his memoir and philosophical reflection *The Nicotine Cat and Other People* (2009). The sentence reads: 'Fear of being inopportune runs deep in me', and he explains this cast of mind by telling how, when he was about 6, jumping up and down in front of his mother who was trying to calm him down, he hit her jaw with his head and dislocated it.[38] Ever since, restraint. Hogan qualified as a dentist, but worked as an epidemiologist and advisor to health authori-ties in Britain, maintaining an imaginative and poetic life alongside. Amongst his guiding spirits are Nicolas Malebranche and Bertolt Brecht. He learnt about Malebranche from Brian Coffey (1905–95), whom he met in London, where Coffey, a significant modernist and religious poet, worked as a teacher. Coffey told him of Malebranche's dictum, 'attentiveness is the natural prayer of the soul', and attentive-ness is one of Young's qualities in his work. This is attentiveness to the workings of the mind, as it perceives, as well as paying attention to what it perceives. Like Malebranche, he distrusts our capacity to know what ideas are, although he doesn't go as far as his mentor, who maintains they reside in God. Young's poetic world is one of maximized doubt combined with an unremitting sense of the frivolity of human strain. His is a most discriminating poetic intelligence. It is an exacting poetry, that makes demands, but the voice, troubled, questioning, irreverent, is a testimony to a form of steadfast fidelity to trying to see things as they are. His detached and scrupulous intellect makes the rush of feeling, when it comes, all the more affecting, as when he writes of his parents in *Rosemaries* (2007).

The openness and receptivity we see in these poets and in the ataraxians in general is to be found also in Nuala Ní Dhomhnaill. Is is a kind of spaciousness of temperament that allows her to unite very disparate things: her situation as a contemporary woman, aware of the complexities that that involves (not least among them the need to avoid sloganizing); and her inheritance as a Gaelic-speaking person, steeped in the folkore and culture she was fortunate enough to grow up in. In *An Dealg Droighin* ('The Sloe's Thorn', 1981), her first collection, she travels back to connect with Mór, a tutelary goddess of Munster, and, of course, yet another version of the Hag. She was writing these Mór poems when she was 16 or 17. In one poem Donnchadh Dí sleeps with her, immersing his head into the seaweed of her hair. When he wakes, he finds her skin covered with the gold sand of the seashore, but her mouth contains the rotten molars of the abyss. He gets away from her, fast. In another poem Amergin, the ancient Irish spirit-poet, is a cancer on the skin of a sister; or the mushroom cloud of a nuclear explosion; or thalidomide; or that which matters less to you than the frost (a rejected lover); or space; or history.

It will be evident that there is here quite unusual intensity, but also quite unusual imaginative adventurousness and play; even a wayward delight in extending the reach of the connections as far back as they will go, and as far forward and inward as her urgent contemporaneity can manage. The tradition becomes personal as well, and she tells us from whom the red hair comes, and the poetry: a Seán Ó Duinnshléibhe who left the mainland to go to live on the Blaskets. One day, she says, in the poem from which this comes, 'I mBaile an tSléibhe', a woman went to the well with her cows. A trout leaped from the river into the bucket she was carrying with her at the same time as three ships came into the bay beneath, and as the eagle nested on the mountain that bears its name. These sudden swoops of the mind, shifting from the family inheritance to the legendary, to the otherworld, to the miraculous, to the ordinary and back to the miraculous again, has the effect of transforming our perception of the world by means of the artistry with which she has re-created it. Here again she is assuming a persona such as Mór, or the Cailleach Bhéara, an entity utterly identified with the land. Ní Dhomhnaill knows precisely what she is doing. It is not as if she believes that she is the Hag herself; but she knows that this figure is implicated in the way she feels about the land, and about healing, and about her own fate.

In *Feis* (1991) she devotes an entire section, 'Cailleach', to the Hag, in which she releases, in poem after shattering poem, the devastating energy for creativity and for destruction which this figure embodies. There is, here, a total alignment with one of the central archetypes in Gaelic and indeed Celtic consciousness. However, at the same time, she is finding a release for all kinds of tensions, angers, and repressions that are at work in our present-day unconscious. These have to with violence against children, where the mother ceases to be the protector and becomes the assailant; with obscure but acutely felt guilt and shame at having done something unspeakably wrong and bloody; and with the feeling that our plenty and our greed as we consume all we can is something that we are certainly going to have to pay for. Over it all presides the Hag, in her double-nature, as goddess of tenderness, love and caring, and as destroyer. In 'First Communion' the Christian ritual and Catholic sacrament are seen as a frail and futile gesture against the terrible reality that awaits the children, who are receiving communion for the first time (amongst whom is the poet's daughter), as they venture into the lawless world that awaits them. These children, in their cotton dresses or suits with rosettes and medals, are like a flock of mild farmyard birds being led into the desert with no one to look after them. She now, the poet, the goddess as nurturer, protector, makes a holy show of herself and starts bawling uncontrollably, and when the child asks her why she is crying she tells a barefaced lie, saying it is because her heart is bursting with pride, when what she is seeing is these little innocents going into the world to be 'slashed | and burned by our latter-day foxes | and wolves—greed, drugs, cancer, skulduggery, the car-crash' (Paul Muldoon's translation in *The Astrakhan Cloak*, 1992).[39] How can she tell her child of the world that lies before her, the darkness she must walk through on her own, even though the mother would give everything to prevent it?

In a horrific lightning sketch, called 'An Fáth Nár Phós Bríd Riamh' ('Why Bríd Never Married'), we are told, in a voice straight out of folklore, recounting this as if it were something that needed to be recorded in as factual a manner as possible, the reason Bríd did not marry. At nine in the morning of the day she was to be wed, her father and two members of her family were found 'cold dead' tied to the branches of a tree, hanged by a nylon rope, 'the wind and the sun pouring through them', the bullet wounds visible. The murderer was never found. The poem concludes: 'the result of that, of course, was that Bríd never married.'[40] The Irish, 'dar ndóigh', you can translate as 'of course', but it is also possible to render it as 'needless to say'; it has an air of casual matter-of-factness about it, entirely appropriate as a tonality to capture the awesome forces that are at work here, that cause such destruction, but that remain indifferent to human pleading and fear. The 'dar ndóigh' indicates that there is very little to be done about such things; there is no point in wishing the world were a different place: the human suffering is registered and honoured, but this acceptance does not stray from there to hankerings after amelioration or solution: an 'ataraxie' of the mind.

The next poem, 'Cailleach', is given over directly to the Hag herself. The poet has had a dream in which she became the land itself, the parish of Ventry, her body transposed into the physical landscape, her shanks and backbone the mountains, her feet the two great rocks at the seashore, Rinn Dá Bhárc in *Cath Finntrágha* ('The Battle of Ventry'), a tale from the Ossianic cycle. She has entered into a visionary identification with the land, a temporary departure from the confines of self and intellect, an open field of possibility where things lose their fixedness and stability. The dream, she says, was so vivid that when she awoke she checked if 'by chance, my two feet were wet'. But then she says she went on 'and I forget | what had happened, oh, | it must be two years and | more now, I'd say'. This vernacular storytelling voice is crucial to what is happening, because we are being introduced to these matters in a manner so deliberately casual as to emphasize the perception, which is at the heart of this poem, that the ordinary is charged with miracle and danger and that we had better look out.

What happens next comes as a shock. She had forgotten all about the dream until one day she was walking along the strand at Ventry with her daughter, when the child decides she will go back because she is tired.

> It wasn't long until I heard her
> coming towards me, agitated
> and whimpering as she ran up to me.

When her mother asks her what's wrong, the girl tells her she is frightened: 'I thought the hills were starting to move, | and that they were a giant of a woman swaying her breasts, | and that she'd rise up and eat me.'

This, it must be emphasized, is not Ní Dhomhnaill exploiting the Gothic possibilities in Irish myth for gratuitous entertainment; she is dealing here with significant psychic and psychological formations that come out of Celtic tradition but which connect with contemporary anxieties concerning motherhood, nurturing, the responsibility we carry with regard to nature, and the terrible consequences that face us if we ignore the claim the world of nature must make on our attention if we are to survive. But again I want to make it clear that in Ní Dhomhnaill, as in many of the poets of her generation, there is no soapboxing or sermonizing: there is the steady recognition that we exist in a universe with certain laws, that these laws connect with forces and energies that go outside human volition, and that it is the contemporary duty of the poet, as was the case in ancient Ireland, to remind us of those laws and their ineluctable and unremitting ordinances.

The 'Cailleach' poem is followed by one on Cathleen Ni Houlihan, where she is made fun of, saying that you couldn't take this creature anywhere, because she'd shame you. She has been everywhere in Irish history, naked in Connacht (with Pearse), on the road to Youghal (folk-song), and so on, in a wonderful *jeu d'esprit*, well translated by Muldoon, as 'Cathleen'. The only problem is, she doesn't seem to understand that her days are up, because she has the

> knack of hearing only what confirms
> her own sense of herself, her honey-nubile form
> and the red rose, proud rose or canker
> tucked behind her ear, in the head-band of her blinkers.[41]

The Yeats ('red rose, proud rose') is gamesome and naughty, as is the original (this little cavort of Muldoon's gets over an untranslatable reference), but poet and translator between them are also letting us know that this Hag energy is by no means depleted: what kind of creature is this now who is honey-nubile and wearing some kind of elaborate (and sexy, and dangerous) headgear? The question is left open.

There is an evident affinity between Ní Dhomhnaill and Muldoon, the finest of her translators, because they both have an attitude to Irish tradition that is as attached and engaged as it is complex, while also, at the same time, retaining a vital sense of self-possession. They are not in anyone's historical pocket, neither is Ciaran Carson, for that matter, nor Mahon, nor Marina Carr, the three last figures in this approach to an Irish literary history.

Muldoon was made for fables to do with Irish history and literature. He was born in Eglish (from *eaglais*, meaning church) in County Armagh and raised near what is known as 'The Moy' (meaning plain) in County Tyrone, very much in the borderlands between the Republic and Northern Ireland. An 'in-betweenness' characterizes all his work, which is a realm presided over by what Jung would have called the 'Trickster', the shape-changer, the mischief-maker. He shares the name of the hero of an eighth-century *immram* (voyage tale), *The Voyage of Mael Duin's Boat*, a link that he made the most of, writing 'Immram', a poem based on the tale, in *Why Brownlee Left* (1980). His poetry is at all times, even at its most elegiac, full of language games, jokes, narratives that sweep to a juddering halt, apparently shocking autobiographical teasings, deadpan solemnity that jumps into mirth, send-ups, irreverences, of all kinds, self-mockery, and a continuous driving intelligence, using language like a kind of two-edged scythe to cut every way it can through that which would cancel the art and the activity of poetry: dire certainty and singleness of purpose.

This playful seriousness, which does not preclude intensity, is in evidence in a poem from the collection named above, called 'Anseo'. This word (meaning 'present' or 'here' or—more clumsily but accurately—'in it, the hereness'!) was, he tells us in the poem, the first word of Irish he spoke, at school in Collegelands, in response to the master calling the roll. The last name in the roll-call was that of Joseph Mary Plunkett Ward, whose name is an encapsulation of nationalist commitment, Joseph Mary Plunkett (1887–1916) having been one of the signatories of the Proclamation of Independence and one of the martyrs of 1916. Ward is Mac an Bháird, thus signifying descent from one of the bardic families of the North. Ward (a common surname of the Travelling Community) is hardly ever at school, and in his absence is the object of knowing winks and sarcastic comments from the master. The little tale ramifies: the first time Ward comes back, the master gets him to go out and cut himself the stick he's to be beaten with, after which, each time he is absent, he brings the instrument of punishment unasked, until he finally hands over his masterpiece, a 'hazel-wand' (Yeats again), all nicely sanded and polished, his initials specially engraved on it. That which was the subject of humiliation becomes the author of masterful irony, turning the tables on the law, with an elegant gesture, the pupil refashioning, after his own ends, the tally stick, symbol of linguistic disgrace. All this is in the poem by implication; this somewhat leaden summation undoes, to some extent, the nasty little cut of the poem, a cut like that which the hazel-wand might administer. The story continues: Muldoon, the voyager, has met the same Ward, now Joe Ward, in a pub just over the Irish border; Ward is living 'in the open', like one of the Fianna, or like an old Fenian, and he is in the IRA, 'fighting for Ireland, | making things happen'. He has risen through the ranks and is Commandant, and tells his old schoolmate: 'How every morning at parade | His volunteers would call back *Anseo* | And raise their hands | As their names occurred.'[42]

Ironies and sadnesses and pride and thrill are crossing over each other in this poem. 'Fighting for Ireland' is a phrase that cannot be used outside a highly charged (and very partial) emotional context without some degree of mockery, but the mockery here is attenuated; the phrase, with all the lumber of atrocious and heroic association, is dropped into the poem, and Muldoon is inviting us not, for once, to reach for the weapons of condemnation, but to listen to what this man has to say, and what he has his men to say: they are 'anseo'; they are there, ready to raise their arms, ready to fall for Ireland too. Poetry can be a way of knowing that is freed from certainties, and from the striving to concur. Of course we are also aware that these men are 'here', but that they aren't also; they are somewhere else, across a border, in a territory where Muldoon is only a visitant.

Muldoon's work, from the first collection *New Weather* (1973), strives always for urgency, presence, and at the same time a kind of relaxed style, a looseness of temper that is not slackness, but rather a kind of cool detachment, invariably lit with humour. The novelist Michael MacLaverty's advice to Heaney, quoted gratefully by the latter, might be the kind of principle informing Muldoon's work: 'don't let the veins bulge in your biro.' There is a readiness in Muldoon, a collectedness, which is not at all to imply that there is anything remotely self-satisfied about the mood he creates. The feeling is always sportive, that he is trying to entertain you, tease you, surprise you, but also there is no doubt but that he is far from invulnerable to what comes and goes. He is a poet of eros, of marriage and family; he is an elegist; he is a gnomic philosopher, playing tricks with signs, ideas, everything; he is a master-metrist, who can twist language round all kinds of corners making it double back on itself by becoming something completely different; but more than anything he is a chronicler of the passage of time in his own time, what that feels like. He, Muldoon, is a constant presence in his work, and while he is as Protean as Mangan ever was, he is also always whatever it is that Muldoon is. He may range the wide world's highways, but he always returns to the

Moy, and his own people, as he does in 'Hedge School', a beautiful
and shocking poem for his sister Maureen, who died, aged 52, in 2005,
and to whose memory the collection *Horse Latitudes* (2006) is
dedicated.

It is a poem very much of our time, with Muldoon the chronicler,
there, in the midst of things. He is in St Andrews, where, he tells us, 'in
673, another Maelduin was bishop'; it is raining, and as he takes shelter
in a doorway on Church Street, and thinks, to begin with, of his great-
great-grandmother at a gate on rainy mornings, with a rush mat over
her shoulders, a mat that flashed 'Papish like a heliograph'. He doesn't
explain but it is pretty clear that she is posted outside a hedge school
sometime in the latter half of the nineteenth century. This oblique
flash of oppression now moves, through a strange twist of projection,
into a future Latin class of his daughter's, where, on rainy mornings in
America, they will be taught to conjugate the Latin 'amo' with the
prefix 'Guantan-', so the class can learn, as Britain has had to do, that
imperial power will be lashed with sorrow. He rhymes 'flashed' with
'lashed', a flash forwards and backwards, equal in predestined and
inevitable woe for those who trample others under. And now comes
the terrible and devastating shift (Muldoon is a poet full of transposition and metamorphosis); he is here, in St Andrews, and he thinks
how all past and present mornings 'are impressed' on him, as he
wonders, talking now to his dead 'dear Sis', if there is any way he
can go back to the corner shop, break open the seal on the dictionary
there, and trace the root of the word '*metastasis*'. What was once settled
and orderly (or was it?) has shifted and transformed itself, as is the case
always in history, to become lashed with woe and destruction. Just as
the cancer's original disorder has transformed itself into something
different, and deadly.[43]

Personal sorrow, historical memory, the signs of the times, the pain
of being alive, the waiting in fear and anxiety in the world that contains
cancers and the downfall of what was once the land of the free: all are
carried forward in the chronicle of a person's thought which the poem
shapes into an elegance that is stricken with actual grief.

Muldoon, from the start, goes for an onward impulse, a relentless
push out of the stasis of the fixed idea, the bleak certainty: a kind of
metastasis in fact. This onward rush, carried through always with the
tone of the Muldoon voice telling us the way, and the way of his doing
what he is doing, is invariably connected with the past, so that one has

a sense of contraries working: a recall of the past (and frequently the ancient and antique) working through and in a perception that operates in the here and now ('anseo'). An early poem, 'Good Friday, 1971. Driving Westward', recalls a poem of John Donne's, 'Good Friday, 1613. Riding Westward'.

The Donne connection is mentioned here, because, while the reference to the Jacobean is a bit adventitious in 1971 (when Muldoon was aged 20), the poem in *Horse Latitudes* which follows 'Hedge School' is saturated in Donne, in particular the 'Nocturnall upon S. Lucies Day', but much else besides, including the prose. The poem is 'Sillyhow Stride', and is in memory of Warren Zevon, the rock musician and friend of Muldoon. The poem, written in a frantic *terza rima*, coasts through New York, the Twin Towers, the Everly brothers (except it's the *other* Everly brothers, whom Zevon accompanied), Sunset Boulevard, Jerusalem, Brian Jones (of the Rolling Stones), and so on. It is an extraordinary elegy, in the Dante death-rhyme, that is crammed with life and death, including again that of his sister:

I . . . couldn't think that she had sunk so low
she might not make the anniversary
of our mother's death from this same cancer, this same quick, quick, slow

conversion of manna to gall
from which she died thirty years ago. I knelt and adjusted the sillyhow
of her oxygen mask. . . .

Muldoon, like his namesake, the bishop and the ancient voyager, is a contemporary *peregrinatus*, afloat on the sea of our culture with the detritus of the past all around. There is no caterwauling that things should be different; there is no gainsaying of history; it just was. There is nothing much to be done about how things are; they just are as they are. His task? To give them shape, not meaning, so that we can see them for what they are, without longing for solutions: a true follower of Pyrrho, an ataraxian. And also, obsessed observer of 'The Old Country', where, as the poem has it, 'every resort was a last resort', and where there were those who would not 'budge from the *Dandy* to the *Rover*'.[44]

Ciaran Carson, born in 1948, was raised on the Falls Road in Belfast. His postman father was a committed Irish nationalist and Gaelic-speaker, and Carson was monolingual until he was 4; after which, he tells us, he learned English on the street. He learned it well. Carson is a wizard of language, a shaman of Belfast, who takes us into the nether realms of dream, phantasmagoria, the cracking white noise that lies under our communications, the static crowding the lines of connection. It is as if he is often himself on some kind of walkie-talkie to us, as he roams the streets and back-streets and dives and drinking-dens of paramilitary Belfast, telling, in broken communications that are always urgent and eloquent, of the situation we are in. Belfast becomes the 'unreal city' that we all inhabit, a place of crossings, borders, lines, territories, accents, passageways, mergings, separations. All these crossing points are marked by history, of course, but in Carson's case it is very much the history of Belfast, with its memories of the Crimean War, and the imperial street names that he turns into a kind of forlorn and beautiful poetry of remembrance of a heritage that is and is not his; and that is and is not part of all who call Belfast home: Sebastopol Street, Inkerman Street, Odessa Street. But Carson's dindshenchas of Belfast includes not just the imperial memory (Mountjoy Street is there in his topography), but also the industrial past (the ships, the foundries, the brickworks, the ceramic factories), and the Gaelic understrata: Shankill ('Old Church'), The Falls Road ('The Road of the Hedges').

But the city is a fluid and dangerous place; it is possible 'for even the little piggy who stayed at home . . . to sometimes feel lost', as he has it in 'Question Time', in *Belfast Confetti* (1989), in which he goes on to say that maybe the ideal map of the city is in the eye of the 'helicopter ratcheting overhead, its searchlight fingering and scanning the microchip deviations: the surge of funerals and parades; . . . the wired-up alleyways and entries; someone walking his dog when the façade of Gass's Bicycle Shop erupts in an avalanche of glass and metal forks and tubing, rubber, rat-trap pedals, toe-clips and repair kits.'[45] The accumulation of material, the list, is important to Carson, as it was in the Gaelic world. But this should be qualified: it is not so much the list in itself that intrigues him, it is the irruption of the order that we assume everyday objects should observe that fascinates him as he picks over and catalogues the detritus in the aftermath of explosion. These lists of disorders created by upheaval are the opposite of what lists are meant to do: give assurance that a serenity can be counted upon in the world of things. So that, as often as not, what Carson lists are things in their

displacements, things and places that are blown up, obliterated, transformed. He is perhaps the ultimate poet of the 'Troubles'.

Sometimes the lists are the names of places that the narrator in the
poetry, the voice, has to find a way through, or past, or into: the city
becomes a coded place, the secrets of which you must try to decipher,
although you can never be sure if the code is being cracked. The only
certainty is when you get through or not. Take 'Barfly', in *Belfast
Confetti*. 'Maybe you can figure it', it opens, why two pubs, The
Crown and Shamrock and The Rose and Crown are at opposite
ends of the town: 'Politics? The odds change. The borders move. |
Or they're asked to.' For example, our storyteller tells us, he's 'getting
it from the horse's mouth' this night when two punters walk in,
'Produce these rods, and punctuate the lunchtime menu: there's
confetti everywhere.' This our man takes as a message. Everything's
chalked up, he tells us, and every so often the slate gets wiped clean;
so now he is a 'hyphen' flitting here and there between 'The Gamble—
The Rendezvous—The Cellars—The Crow's Nest—The Elephant . . .',
and so on. Survival is being capable of negotiating the in-between, the
hyphenated state.[46]

In another piece from the same volume, 'The Mouth', the voice
that is talking is someone from a paramilitary group, probably the
Provisional IRA. The voice is telling us that, 'since nothing in this
world is certain and you don't know who hears what | We thought it
was time he bit off more than he could chew. Literally.'[47] Talk is
cheap, talk is dangerous, talk is all there is, talk is language; Carson's
work is all talk. While Muldoon's voice is everywhere in his work (as is
Ní Dhomhnaill's in hers, as is Medbh McGuckian's), Carson retains a
singularity of tone, a pressure of insistence; he does all kinds of
voices—they are all Belfast, but he is the ventriloquist of the city's
tonal variants, from the squawk of the hand-held telephone to the
threatening murmurings in a bar that are not entirely out of earshot.

These voices irrupt into his work from *The Irish for No* onwards,
along with the famously extended line that he took, it is said, from the
American C. K. Williams. But this long line of his, often containing
seven or more beats, comes out of the old 'fourteener' of late medieval
English balladry, or from eighteenth-century anapaestic Gaelic poetry,
as much as from American experiments. What he was looking for,
really, and what he found, was a metric that would allow him to carry
the voice along, twist it, shift it (as a storyteller would), and flex it open

to accommodate the relentless pile-up of materials that he crams into the poetry. Carson was (and remains: his readings always begin with music) a traditional musician of more than ordinary competence, learning from that inheritance about the dramatic effects of tonal shifts and rhythmic metamorphoses, as well as the way it is possible to alter the mood and nuance of an air by the interjection of ornamentation in the delivery of the expected shape of the rhythm. His lines of verse are full of these shifts of tone and alterations of mood. And he never is anything less than entertaining.

He is a supreme artisan of language, and there is a sense in which all his work is, in one way or another, about language itself, reflecting, perhaps, his unusual linguistic background, and the context of his early monolingualism in Irish in the British Belfast of the 1950s. In mockery, in self-disparagement, he recounts for us his own language activism in 'Zulu' that comes at the end of a whole collection devoted to the 'language question', *Opera Et Cetera* (1996). Like a Zulu he danced 'around the typecast phalanxes of English, shielded only by a dustbin-lid'; then he became, he says, a 'redskin, foraging behind the alphabetic frontier', while the pale 'boldface wagons' drew themselves into a circle as they used to do in the movies. The last three lines (long ones again) crackle with self-awareness and irony, the feeling that one side goes over into the other, that there are no purities of motive, no rectitudes; and that what matters is what he (slightly sending up MacNeice) calls elsewhere the 'bagpipe music':

> Mounted on my hobby-horse, I whooped so much, I had to take a slug of orangeade.
> I loved its cold-jolt glug and fizz, tilted bottle upheld like a trumpet
> To the sun; or so it might be, in the gargled doggerel of this dumb poet.[48]

A golden fanfare of the Orange from a dumb poet.

In the introduction he wrote for his translation of Brian Merriman's *The Midnight Court* (2005), Carson tells us how, the night after he finished the translation, he dreamed of Merriman, how he woke up in his dream in a valley, saw a light from a cottage across the way, went to it and there found the poet. Merriman spoke to him, in eighteenth-century Irish, Carson understanding without any difficulty, very different, he says, from the actual competence of his Irish. Whatever we make of the formality of this disavowal (and it is right to be on our guard as Carson, wizard of language, has translated the *Táin* from Old

Irish in 2007, and Dante's *Inferno* in 2002), there is little doubt but that he is recording an experience that reflects a profound involvement with Gaelic tradition. In Carson's account we get to see Merriman in our mind's eye, as no doubt Merriman became a real entity for Carson.

What we do not see, in Carson, as in Muldoon, or indeed in that other ataraxian Ní Dhomhnaill, is any fetishistic 'typecasting' of the Gaelic world or its antagonists. That world careers through Carson's verse in all its specificity, while he crosses it with his own obsessions and histories. It is a complex weave, a fugue, which later becomes a dominant motif in the aptly entitled *For All We Know* (2008): 'I follow the curve of one of its recurrent figures | trying to figure out the resolution that is never | there in any proper fugue of Bach's.'[49] This statement could easily apply to all Carson's work, and to that of Muldoon, and that of Ní Dhomhnaill. Stated aridly, like this, it may sound all too provisional and cerebral, but there is no doubt about the sorrow, the passion, and the loneliness that inheres in the work of these three major poets.

And so I come to that writer who, along with the dramatist Marina Carr, is to close this literary history. He is the predecessor of these poets of 'ataraxie', in that his provisionality and Pyrrhonist 'wavering' was fully formed almost as soon as he started to produce a body of work that looks certain to last. Derek Mahon is also in the direct line from MacNeice, whose dispassionate adherence to the actual and his acceptance of uncertainty have had a significant influence on the poets and writers of the 1980s and 1990s. MacNeice is a reference and inspiration for Heaney, but for these younger poets and for Mahon, who has much in common with them, he is a guide, an exemplar. Here is how Mahon addresses him in 'In Carrowdore Churchyard', from *Night Crossing* (1968): 'This, you implied, is how we ought to live— | The ironical, loving crush of roses against snow, | Each fragile, solving ambiguity.'[50] What this 'implies' is spelt out very clearly in 'Girls in their Seasons', where he implores them to 'be with me now | And keep me warm | before we go plunging into the dark for ever'.[51] There is a resolute turning away from the 'unreconciled' who, somewhat comically, strangle on the lampposts in the dawn rain. Mahon is absolutely distrustful of the big gesture, the oratorical flourish, the exiguous pain. He is, like any poet must be, enmeshed in history, but like MacNeice, and the other ataraxians, he does not use it as a mallet to knock others on the head with; instead, there is an acceptance that things have fallen out the way they have, and there is little to be gained by seeking out objects of historical accusation. (The word Satan in Hebrew means accusation.)

While Mahon (educated at Trinity College, Dublin, and for lengthy periods of time an Irish resident, making Kinsale in County Cork his home) is certainly a citizen of the island of Ireland, north and south, and is receptive to Gaelic tradition (being one of Ní Dhomhnaill's better translators), he retains a Northern iron, a kind of deep recalcitrance that is related to Ulster Protestant dissent. This wariness of the intelligence, this guardedness of the emotions, informs the kind of classical urbanity he brings to form and to language. He is committed to balance and to the order a poem can bring to the flux of time. The first poem in *Collected Poems* (1999), 'Spring in Belfast', concludes with him saying that the things that happen in the 'echoing back streets of this desperate city | Should engage more than my casual interest, | Exact more interest than my casual pity.'[52] There is a density of thought here, as well as a moral self-scrutiny, that is pure Ulster, but it is also in touch with the grave stateliness and convincing probity of Samuel Johnson and John Dryden, the English Augustans.

And there is something Augustan about Mahon, in the sense that he has a strong kinship with the poets of the English eighteenth century (he has, in later work, come to favour the couplet, which he writes with a verve and pliancy that would compare favourably with the technique of Alexander Pope or George Crabbe); he has a similar regard for the marriage of the colloquial with the rigour of form; he embraces a public role for the poet, and exhibits a deep civic engagement; and he is ready, willing, and able to lambaste the shallowness of present-day society with the frustrated contempt and anger we find in Swift, Pope, and Johnson, the last of whom he follows in translating the tenth satire of Juvenal (which, we should also recall, Samuel Ferguson, another Augustan northerner, translated in the nineteenth century).

But there is another side to this Augustan temper: his readiness to accept the surface of things, the actuality of the world as it is, which connects him to the era of Augustus the Roman emperor, and the major poets of that time, Horace and Ovid. He has, in *The Hunt by Night* (1982), a translation of Horace's famous 'Carpe Diem' poem from the *Odes* (I, 11): 'Don't waste your time . . . living in fear and hope | of the imprevisable future; forget the horosocope. | Accept

whatever happens.... Act with zest | one day at a time....'[53] This
fidelity to the surface of things, to the way life happens, is a trait he
has in common with MacNeice (and Carson, Muldoon, and Ní
Dhomhnaill), which derives ultimately from Horace. The poetry
exerts itself to connect with the variousness of things, their plurality,
and it is not to be confused with the superficial, in that the effect is one
of implication, whereby the language resonates with a sense of a
mystery inhering in the actual, and becomes charged with an emotion
that seems to derive from the qualities in things and the perceiving of
them, rather than the direct expression of feeling. The emotion is
there, in great depth, but it is distanced in the finesse of a classical
detachment, which focuses on trying to get right the shape of the way a
thing or a situation is seen, and on the formal requirements of the
language to deliver this refined and clarified feeling. And yet there is
always, as in all serious poets, the sense of a distinct and unique
personality coming through, in the voicing, the rhythm, the intimacy
that gets carried over, in spite of the detachment.

One of his masterpieces, certainly, is the justly famous 'A Disused
Shed in Co. Wexford', from *The Snow Party* (1975). It takes on a highly
emotive subject, the Holocaust, but it does so in such an oblique and
suggestive, even gentle way, that the specifics of the familiar atrocities
fade, and with them also recede the dangers of appropriating a righteous anger to which one cannot easily be entitled if one was not
amongst those directly affected. In writing of subjects like this, the
greatest decorum is required, and not often engaged. One of the
advantages Mahon gains from a rigorous obliqueness is that the Holocaust is released from horrific details of brutal and inhumane destruction and the theme opens out to include all historical victimage: it is as
if he accomplishes an entirely contemporary version of Johnson's great
ability to charge generalized thought and imagery with profound and
heartbreaking feeling.[54] And in doing this he achieves a remarkable
and paradoxical effect: he combines powerful emotion with intense
restraint, generalized thought with intimacy.

'Even now', he says, there are still places where a thought might
grow, such as 'lime crevices' behind rain-barrels, 'Dog corners for bone
burials; And in a disused shed in Co. Wexford'. It is all very strange,
and it gets stranger: in this shed there are a thousand mushrooms crowding to a keyhole, the only star in their firmament. I suspect (though
I cannot prove this) that this image is taken from the medieval poem

by Gofraidh Fionn Ó Dálaigh, to be found in Eleanor Knott's *Irish Syllabic Poetry*, under the title 'A Child Born in Prison'. These mushroom creatures have learned patience and silence, and have been waiting 'for us' since 'civil war days'. Which civil war is not spelt out; the Irish one comes to mind, inevitably, but it is distanced into a remote and possible allusion. There was once a mycologist, but he was 'expropriated', at that time, in a 'gravel-crunching, interminable departure'. He never came back and since then they have been waiting. There have been deaths, nightmares; those that are nearest the door and the tiny trickle of light, grow strong, pushing the others aside, as they look for 'Elbow room!'; the rest have been 'so long | Expectant that there is left only the posture.' This is the eternal posture of all grief, of all suffering, but observe how it is introduced without over-description or rummaging fuss: we know this posture, and it is not necessary to belabour the effect. When the investigators come to these 'Web-throated' prisoners of the old regime, at the 'flash-bulb firing-squad', they 'lift frail heads in gravity and good faith.' They are, he tells us, begging the investigators to do something, to save them, the (and now he introduces the names) 'Lost people of Treblinka and Pompeii!' They plead with them not to let 'the god' abandon us.[55]

There is here, along with the classic reserve, the highly formal meditative syntax, the more than 'casual pity', a something else: a refusal to venture too far into moral outrage or righteousness. Mahon is no soapbox moralizer; there is a Lutheran, even Calvinist, distrust of the efficacy and condition of 'good works' such a poetry might aspire to achieve. There is, in effect, a Northern quality of withholding, which makes the gentleness of the poem all the more powerful, and enhances the intimacy, thereby personalizing the emotion through (ironically) detachment. The range of referents in this poem crowd to the tiny keyhole of the light he throws: there are Treblinka and Pompeii; but there are also, in here, the people whom the Irish Treaty and the Civil War betrayed, amongst whom can be numbered the Northern Irish Catholics and Protestants; but also too, and most importantly, the *Southern* Irish Protestants, a community the busy jostlings of the new Free State tended to ignore, or despise, or pay them the tribute of traditional fawning and reverence, or all these at the same time, in some instances. The location is Wexford, a place traditionally associated with the 1798 rebellion, but it is also a county with a relatively large Protestant population; the poem is dedicated to

J. G. Farrell, the English novelist who drowned tragically in 1979 while fishing in Bantry Bay, and who wrote *Troubles* (1970), one of the finest novels about the post-1916 turbulence. Mahon's poem was published in the 1975 collection, and it should be recalled that these years, from the late 1960s, in Ireland, were ones in which the extreme violence that re-emerged in a new version of the 'Troubles' went on inexorably, with paramilitaries on both sides engaged in tit-for-tat sectarian killings, and bloody campaigns of bombing in which civilians were victims on a regular basis. The mood of exhaustion and resignation in the Mahon poem reflects the sense of helplessness that many felt during that time.

The Hunt by Night (1982) shows us Mahon beginning to reveal the 'extensive view'(Johnson's phrase from 'The Vanity of Human Wishes') that is to characterize his work more and more, as his confidence, his reach, and his relaxation extend themselves. There was a period in the 1970s when Mahon was poet-in-residence at the then New University of Ulster at Coleraine, a sojourn reflected in some of the bleak poems gathered here: it appears not to have been a happy time for him. And yet, as he writes in 'North Wind: Portrush', in spite of the 'wind | On this benighted coast', the shops open at nine, and even though the newspapers arrive late 'the milk shines in its crate.'[56] Another poem, 'Courtyards in Delft', turns to the Dutch realism of the seventeenth-century painter Pieter de Hooch, recognizing an affinity between the scrupulous exactness of the artist and his own temperament: they both share an obsessive concern with paying attention to the actualities of objects, their surfaces; nothing, he says, no 'lewd fish, no fruit', no opportunistic seducer enters here, into this picture of the girl with her back to us who waits for her man to come home to what he calls 'his tea'; there is nothing to mar 'the chaste | Perfection of the thing and the thing made.'[57] From these poems, he opens out to embrace the classic landscape of Ovid (about his exile at Tomis), Horace, Rimbaud, the painters Munch and Ucello, the Russian poet Voznesensky.

Mahon translated Molière, the French poets Philippe Jaccottet and Gerard de Nerval, as well as turning to the work of Nuala Ní Dhomhnaill. And then, from the mid-1990s onwards, comes the flowering of his mastery in three Augustan books: *The Hudson Letter* (1995), *The Yellow Book* (1997), and *Harbour Lights* (2005). A demotic energy is released in these books, combined with a serene formal elegance which can also allow for runs of impatience and indignation. There is a remarkable openness of intellectual spirit and enquiry, and a generous accommodation of all kinds of influence and thematic concern. This is poet of urbanity and catholicity of taste, who also retains a connection with the past of Irish tradition, including Gaelic.

Mahon is intent on writing on the point of the moment, as Sir Philip Sidney put it way back in the sixteenth century, so that his learning and his depth of thought invigorate the observations he makes of the manners and mores of contemporary life, like a modern Martial or a Juvenal. In 'Auden on St Mark's Place' he delights in W. H. Auden's nonchalance and daring, and asks him what he would make of the way things are now: 'our world of internet and fax | an ever more complex military-industrial complex, | situational ethics, exonerative 12-step programs, | health fascism, critical theory and "smart" bombs?'[58] What is impressive here is the way the formality of the verse requires us to look hard at the ready-made jargon and see it for what it is and what it represents about the triviality of 'the culture', as it began to be termed in the 1990s.

The receptivity to the diversity of Irish tradition is very much in evidence in *The Yellow Book*. He captures Elizabeth Bowen at the Shelbourne Hotel in Dublin in 1940, compiling, at an 'Empire writing-table', her reports for British intelligence on the wartime Irish situation—'the Mata Hari of the austerity age, | I feel like a traitor spying on my own past.'[59] He turns to the eighteenth-century poet Cathal Buí Mac Giolla Gunna to translate his song 'An Bonnán Buí' ('The Yellow Bittern'), a poem translated by many before, but not like this. The bird dies of thirst because the waters are frozen over, and in the original Cathal Buí swears that he will take every opportunity to slake his thirst so that he doesn't share the same fate as the bittern, even though his lover pleads with him to give up the drink because it will kill him; but no, Cathal Buí insists that the booze will help him to a long life (he actually seems to have had not a bad innings, living to 76). Mahon's take is entirely different; he would, he tells us, have broken the ice for the bird, and they might both be drinking and singing too, for theirs is the same story. Mahon has had to struggle with the demons of alcohol, and has overcome them (a rare enough achievement). It used to be the case that 'with characters like us' they would let them wander the roads 'in wind and rain . . . but now they have a cure for these psychoses | as indeed they do for most social diseases',[60] so he sits, at peace with his bottle of water, with the bronze of Patrick Kavanagh on his canal-bank seat, and tries 'to go with the flow'. Austin Clarke is a presence here as well, and in the *Collected Poems* there is a poem, 'St Patrick's Day', inspired by Swift. 'Go with the flow'? he queries; is that what Swift did? No: 'going against the grain | he sits in his rocking chair with a migraine'; it is the sort of day 'a man might hang'. The world now is crammed with distraction and superfluity, and confirms, or seems to confirm, Swift's great pitying misanthropy: 'consensual media, permanent celebration, | share options, electronic animation, | wave motion of site-specific daffodils, | and video lenses in the new hotels.' But in the end there is a refusal to mourn, a readiness to go back to the desk, to 'prismatic natural light, slow-moving cloud'.[61]

In *Harbour Lights*, in a poem called 'Resistance Days', he declares a modest resolution for the New Year, to 'study weather, clouds and their formation', a return to 'creative anarchy'. Towards the end of the volume, in the title-poem, he asks himself what he has achieved: 'Oh, little enough, God knows: | some dubious verse and some ephemeral prose'.[62] It would be hard to think of any Irish poet other than Mahon making such a statement. The self-appraisal is as rigorous as it is inaccurate and necessary. As with the poets and writers who have occupied the end of this story, there is here, in Mahon, not just the refusal to mourn (title of an early poem, and a deliberate echo of Dylan Thomas) but a steady refusal to presume; there is an acceptance of life and of process, of the movement of cloud, and an oblique and wistful nod back to Beckett's . . . *but the clouds* . . . and to its predecessor, Yeats's 'The Tower'.

In another poem of process that lies at the heart of this volume, 'The Widow of Kinsale', he turns back to none other than the Hag of Beare, the persona who has figured prominently in this history. He takes the Old Irish poem of sorrow and regret as the ancient mythic figure mourns her pagan past in the new Christian era and makes it contemporary, something Clarke and Brendan Kennelly have done before, but Mahon's dirge has a pity and an elegance that is very much his own. His widow survives into a post-Christian time. But the primeval figure is there, beneath the surfaces of modern life in Kinsale. She pays, as her ancient predecessor did, lip-service to the clergy,

and go to church despite
the new revised liturgy;

but my true guiding spirit
is something I inherit,
a thing dim and opaque,
a lighthouse in the fog,
a lamp hung in a wood
to light my solitude . . . [63]

The best place is the strand (the focus of the Old Irish poem), with its primitive life-forms, and where the 'ebb-tide withdraws | with a chuckle of bony claws'.

Acceptance, detachment, classic reserve, a refusal to get on the high horse, a seriousness of temper, an intimacy attained through a measured sense that things must be appraised and weighed, a sense of trust: these are the qualities that Mahon has acquired and laboured to achieve. It is for this reason that he is placed last but one in this history, in that his has been an exemplary practice for a new generation of writers, the ataraxians, many of whom greatly admire this poet's craft and exacting decorum.

14

Coda: *By the Bog of Cats*

This book announced its major theme by invoking the primordial ice of May Day Monday, and the special role the cailleach, or the hag, has in relation to the forces that preside over the cataclysmic events of creation and destruction. In October 1998, at the Dublin Theatre Festival, there premiered a play of impressive force and energy, carrying with it, in its searing guttural language, its wild imagery, and most appalling action, those 'ancient things' that lie at the heart of the Irish literary and theatrical tradition and that also preoccupied the great Greek tragedians. For this play was an Irish midlands rendering, of sorts, of Euripides's *Medea*.

The play was *By the Bog of Cats*, and it was produced at the Abbey, the theatre of Yeats, Lady Gregory, and Synge. And it is the legacy of Synge that the author of this play, Marina Carr, has rediscovered for the 1990s and the new millennium, as Beckett recovered it for the Europe of the mid-century. By the time the Abbey produced this work, Carr had written a number of successful plays, including searing renditions of tormented family life assailed by surges of lust and fear. Whereas Synge worked his strange wonder with language to show the rifts and breakdowns between people, and what people think of themselves and others, Carr creates with her midlands dialect (a poor word to describe a language that is capable of the revelatory power of Shakespeare's blank verse) a weaponry with which her characters are ready to wound and even destroy themselves and others, driven by relentless and terrible compulsions and passions. Synge created a world of transfigured realism, revealing the ways in which expectations collide with the recalcitrance of the world and of other people; Carr (and how Yeats would have loved this) shows us people who have the ineradicability of creatures of myth and legend, and who behave according to laws that lie way beyond what we may like or dislike, approve or disapprove.

By the Bog of Cats opens onto a white landscape of ice and snow with Hester Swane, a tinkerwoman, trailing the corpse of a black swan across the white stage, leaving a track of blood behind her as she does. She is watched by a man, a 'ghost fancier' is what he calls himself when she asks him who he is. He is in fact a ghost himself, and she is to join him at the end of the play. He asks her where she has got the swan, and Hester tells him that she found her, 'auld Black Wing', in a bog hole the night before while she was walking the marshes and the bogs, and she 'had to rip her from the ice, left half her underbelly'. It turns out that the ghost fancier has come at the wrong time, thinking it was dusk, when it is actually dawn, the morning after Hester has spent the night traipsing the bogs, tormented by what is to happen that day, the marriage of the man she loves and the father of her daughter, the ominously named Carthage Kilbride, to Caroline Cassidy, a girl innocent of the fearful rampagings of which Carthage and Hester are capable. The ghost fancier will return at dusk, by which time the play's convulsive action will have worked itself out, to take her with him, after she has wreaked her terrible revenges.

But, in order that there be no misunderstanding of the play's orchestration of myth and consciousness, the setting of the familial against the cold backdrop of intergalactic time and space, Carr has a neighbour of Hester's, Monica, say immediately after the ghost leaves, that she sees 'no wan, but ya know this auld bog, always shiftin' and changin' and coddin' the eye'. And when Monica remarks on how cold it is, Hester immediately evokes the ancient strata of ice: 'Swear the age of ice have returned. Wouldn't ya almost wish it had, do away with us all like the dinosaurs.'[1]

As in *Medea*, Carr's play is a family nightmare. Hester's mother left her, her father too is gone; she and Carthage have killed her brother for the money left him by their mother; and the play ends with Hester killing her daughter, then herself, in the arms of the ghost fancier. A mysterious blind seer called the Catwoman knows all that is to happen, and talks to the dead, an ability Hester also shares. At the play's end Hester stands lit by the flames of her house which she has set fire to so that Carthage and his new bride will not have what they now rightfully own. As she gets her daughter, Josie, to close her eyes so she can kill her with the knife she used to take her brother's life, she is in the grip of remorseless and implacable forces that reduce human longings and wishes to the nervous tics they are when set against the huge energies of nature and the dark world of the dead. The terrible thing is that here the child wants to be with the mother, wants to die by her hand, and resists her mother's attempts to persuade her to run: 'It's alright, I'll take ya with me, I won't have ya as I was, waitin' a lifetime for somewan to return, because they don't, Josie, they don't. It's alright. Close your eyes.'[2]

Carr was brought up in the midlands, and her work has for its main locale the great flat, wet centre of the country, all lakes and bogs and marshlands. Her father, the novelist Hugh Carr, worked as a clerk of court in County Offaly, but he came from Dunkineely in County Donegal, and grew up a native Irish-speaker. Marina Carr is as intimate with the heritage of Gaelic Ireland as is Nuala Ní Dhomhnaill, with whose work her own has many affinities. In both these writers this inheritance is scarcely a conscious thing: it is a persuasion of the mind and temperament, and, more than that, an unavoidable psychic terrain that they are drawn to because it retains the stories and horrors that provide modes of revelation adequate to urgent and contemporary rages and despairs.

Ancient things, as ever, have a terribly familiar ring.

15

Conclusion

This approach to an Irish literary history sets out to do a number of things. It seeks, as my *Oxford Companion to Irish Literature* sought, to place the two major literatures of Ireland, that in Irish and that in English, in as close an association as possible. It emphasizes the archaic nature of Irish tradition, its tendency always to look back to the past, which it often mythologizes and distorts. But one of the great attractions of this literature is its ancient feeling, a sense that wherever we go there are layers upon layers beneath where we are at any given point.

Dominant thematic elements have been identified: the Hag, that primordial creature of power, of creativity, and destruction, surfaces continually in different manifestations, corresponding with the ancient impulse to figure Ireland as a female entity, a habit of mind that is of course far from being exclusively Irish, and which is shared with many cultures in the Indo-European continuum. This figure has profound associations with the landscape, which is often seen to be in her care, and this book has attempted to reveal the numinousness of place in Irish tradition at all periods, from the earliest lyrics and tales to the most recent writers of poetry and fiction.

Irish literature is saturated with history. All literature is, but in Ireland's case there were particular circumstances which rendered the historical and political dimensions of the literature all the more urgent and pressing. It was the island's fortune (or misfortune) to have had as her neighbour a mighty nation and a great empire, whose conversion to the Reformed faith became an engine of its drive to establish itself as a dominant presence in the world from the sixteenth century onwards. The trouble with Ireland was that it did not always concur with these ambitions, and was inclined to retain a sense of its own destiny, which would be separate from that of Britain. Éamon de Valera once stated that the country never gave in, in spite of the continual colonial efforts of Britain, from the Reformation onwards, to bring her into line.

The colonial experience, as this history also tries to show, has devastating, if unavoidable, effects, once the structures of its governance and attitudes take hold. There is a necessary reduction, in the mind of the colonial, of the human value of that which he subjects to his will; while amongst the colonized there is resentment, hate, rage, all rendered difficult to articulate because the power lies with the person who has taken over. And there are further twists to this nightmare, as these pages have shown: the colonized begin to believe that they are what they are told they are; while the colonist's distrust of his subjects increases, until, as often happens, he becomes caught in a nightmare of fear, expectation of treachery, anticipation of revenges exacted. And these then in their turn become, in a toxic chemistry of fear and hate, means whereby the colonial begins his own regime of self-hate, to match that of those whom he seeks to control. It is, to use the title of a play of 1986 by the major Irish dramatist Thomas Kilroy, a 'doublecross', a word (and a play) that captures this dilemma as effectively as Yeats's *Purgatory* did in 1938.

This entangled set of entrapments in the political sphere brought to Ireland and to Irish literature an awesome capacity for hatred and self-hate, which helps to explain contradictory tendencies in Irish life and culture: there is a desire to obey, to say the thing you think might please your auditors; but there is also a longing to throw over the traces altogether, and blow your opponents out of the water, or into the air. Rage is a speciality of Irish writing.

And then there is also the factor that Irish tradition is a divided one, linguistically speaking. For a thousand years and more Ireland had a literature of European significance, in the Irish language; that literature continued, of course, but, as time went by, the Irish language fell into disuse, and then became the object of sentiment, revival, enthusiasm. For over a hundred years the speaking of Irish was unknown to large segments of the Irish population, and it was often entered into, by learners, with the self-consciousness of the deliberately contrived act of cultural revivalism, with attendant pieties and embarrassments. That is a measure of the effectivesness of the colonial machine, in that the Irish language became something which the Irish themselves rejected as a badge of shame and failure.

And there is the division that followed the Treaty, whereby Ireland was partitioned, and political allegiances consolidated around that artificial creation. Different forms of isolationism developed in the two parts of Ireland, and there was an advancement of structures and symbols that signified those differences. Hence, to some extent, the power of the Catholic church in the South from the founding of the Free State to the 1980s, as it was seen to give a distinct and even sacral character to Irish destiny. In the North, similar attachments grew to the concept of Britishness, and the Presbyterian church seemed to many to embody a steely resistance to the soft and vague blandishments of the South. These differences were complex and manifold, and were exertions of the political mind and mentality to try to resolve the problem that had lain at the heart of Irish experience since the Treaty, the fact that that had been a device to slather the plaster of apparently separate development and identity over deep flaws and fissures that continued to work apart in the decades after the Treaty, until the surface could not hold any further in the late 1960s and the old violence erupted again.

It may be, however, that this condition of division is one of the reasons why Irish literature retains its powerful emotional force, its ancient longings, its passionate voices, its heartbreaking intensity, and its often wild laughter.

Bibliographical Notes

Unless otherwise indicated, all translations are by the author.

I. ANCIENT THINGS

1. Gearóid Ó Crualaoich, *The Book of the Cailleach: Stories of the Wise Woman Healer* (Cork: Cork University Press, 2003), 100–1.
2. Jorge Luis Borges, *Selected Non-Fictions*, ed. Eliot Weinberger (London: Penguin Books, 1999), 458–63.
3. Translation based on various texts. See Eleanor Hull (ed.), *The Poem Book of the Gael* (London: Chatto & Windus, 1913), 57.
4. John Montague (ed.), *The Faber Book of Irish Verse* (London: Faber & Faber, 1974), 100.

2. IRON AGE MARTIAL ARTS AND CHRISTIAN SCRIBES

1. See Eugene O'Curry, *Lectures on the Manuscript Materials of Ancient Irish History* (Dublin: Four Courts Press, 1995; reprint of the 1861 edition published in Dublin by Duffy & Co.), Lectures II and III.
2. P. L. Henry, *Saoithiúlacht na Sean-Ghaeilge* (Baile Átha Cliath: An Clóchomhar, 1978), 125.
3. See David Jones, 'The Myth of Arthur', in *Epoch and Artist* (London: Faber & Faber, 1959).
4. Ciaran Carson, *The Táin* (London: Penguin Classics, 2007), 76–7.
5. R. I. Best and M. A. O'Brien (eds.), *The Book of Leinster*, Vol. II (Dublin: Dublin Institute for Advanced Studies, 1956), 399.
6. See Gerard Murphy (ed.), *Early Irish Lyrics* (Oxford: Oxford University Press, 1956), 46.
7. Murphy, *Early Irish Lyrics*, 74–82.
8. Murphy, *Early Irish Lyrics*, 6.

3. RECITING FROM THE FINGER-ENDS: THE BARDS AND OSSIAN

1. Frank O'Connor, *The Backward Look* (London: Macmillan, 1967), 2.
2. See Robert Graves, *The White Goddess: A Historical Grammar of Poetic Myth* (London: Faber & Faber, 1971; reprint of 1961 edn.), 197–8.

4. THE UNDOING OF IRELAND: CONQUEST
AND RECONQUEST

1. Augustus Young, *Dánta Grádha: Love Poems from the Irish* (London: Menard Press, 1980), 18.
2. See Eleanor Knott (ed.), *The Bardic Poems of Tadhg Dall Ó Huiginn*, Vol. I (London: Irish Texts Society, 1922), 120 ff.
3. *The Bardic Poems*, p. xxvii.
4. *The Bardic Poems*, 108 ff., and see Vol. II for relevant annotations.
5. See Osborn Bergin (ed.), *Irish Bardic Poetry* (Dublin: Dublin Institute for Advanced Studies, 1970), 124 ff.
6. D. J. O'Donoghue (ed.), *Poems of James Clarence Mangan* (Dublin: O'Donoghue & Co., M. H. Gill & Son; London: A. H. Bullen, 1903), 8–9.
7. *Poems of James Clarence Mangan*, 19.
8. John C. McErlean, SJ (ed.), *The Poems of David O'Bruadair*, Vol. I (London: Irish Texts Society, 1910), 130.
9. *Poems of David O'Bruadair*, Vol. III (1917), 180.
10. *Poems of David O'Bruadair*, Vol. II (1911), 264.
11. See Pádraig de Brún, Breandán Ó Buachalla, and Tomás Ó Concheanainn (eds.), *Nua-Dhuanaire*, Vol. I (Baile Átha Cliath: Institiúid Ard-léinn, 1971), 18.
12. See Revd Patrick S. Dineen and Tadhg O'Donoghue (eds.), *The Poems of Egan O'Rahilly* (London: Irish Texts Society, 1911), 18 and 116.

5. IRELAND: A COLONY?

1. R. Morris (ed.), *The Works of Edmund Spenser* (London: Macmillan & Co., 1902), 654.
2. *Works of Edmund Spenser*, 641.
3. Herbert Davis (ed.), *Swift: Poetical Works* (Oxford: Oxford University Press, 1967), 4.
4. Louis Landa (ed.), *Swift: Gulliver's Travels* (London: Methuen & Co., 1965), 206.
5. See Seamus Deane, Andrew Carpenter, and Jonathan Williams (eds.), *The Field Day Anthology of Irish Writing*, i. (Derry: Field Day, 1991), 388.
6. 'Letter to Thomas Keogh', in *The Works of Edmund Burke*, Vol. VIII (London: George Bell & Sons, 1877), 523–6.
7. Deane *et al.*, *Field Day Anthology*, i. 847.

6. ROMANTIC IRELAND?

1. Charlotte Brooke, *Reliques of Irish Poetry* (Dublin: J. Christie, 2nd edn., 1816), cxxxiv.
2. *Reliques of Irish Poetry*, 231.

3. *Reliques of Irish Poetry*, 34.
4. Deane *et al.*, *Field Day Anthology*, i. 1015.
5. Seamus Deane, *Strange Country* (Oxford: Oxford University Press, 1997), 39.
6. 'Ode II' and 'Ode III', from *The Odes of Anacreon* as translated by Moore. I use one of the many nineteenth-century *Collected Poems* of Moore. His verse still awaits a modern editor.
7. Wilfrid S. Dowden (ed.), *The Letters of Thomas Moore*, Vol. I (Oxford: Clarendon Press, 1964), 143.
8. Lord John Russell (ed.), *Memoirs, Journals and Correspondence of Thomas Moore*, Vol. VI (London: Longman, Brown, Green & Longmans, 1853–6), 183.
9. From the section called 'The Light of the Haram' towards the end of the poem.
10. James Joyce, *Ulysses* (London: The Bodley Head, 1954 edn.), 180.

7. THE FOLK TRADITION

1. Ciaran Carson (trans.), Brian Merriman, *The Midnight Court* (Oldcastle: Gallery Books, 2005), 20.
2. Pádraig Ó Canainn (ed.), *Filíocht na nGael* (Baile Átha Cliath: An Press Náisiúnta, 1958), 228.
3. See the present author's *Irish Poetry from Moore to Yeats* (Gerrards Cross: Colin Smythe, 1980), chap. 2, for a discussion of Callanan and of this poem, its origin, and publication.
4. Ó Canainn, *Filíocht na nGael*, 109.
5. Samuel Ferguson, 'The Dublin Penny Journal', *Dublin University Magazine*, 29 (1847), 196.
6. See Welch, *Irish Poetry from Moore to Yeats*, for an account of Ferguson as a poet and translator.
7. See the present author's *A History of Verse Translation from the Irish: 1789–1897* (Gerrards Cross: Colin Smythe, 1988), chap. 9, for an account of Walsh and his translation work.
8. See any number of recordings of this air, especially that by Moya Brennan and Cormac de Barra on *Voices and Harps* (Audio CD, 2011).
9. Douglas Hyde, *Love Songs of Connacht* (London: T. Fisher Unwin; Dublin: Gill & Son, 1893), 30.
10. Pádraig de Brún *et al.*, *Nua-Dhuanaire*, 77–8.
11. John P. Frayne (ed.), *Uncollected Prose by W. B. Yeats*, Vol. I (London: Macmillan, 1970), 294.
12. Eleanor Hull, *Poem Book of the Gael* (London: Chatto & Windus, 1913), 306.
13. W. B. Yeats, *Collected Poems* (London: Macmillan, 1958 reprint), 80.
14. James Joyce, *Dubliners* (London: Jonathan Cape, 1927), 253–5.

15. Richard Ellman, A. Walton Litz, and John Whittier-Ferguson (eds.), *James Joyce: Poems and Shorter Writings* (London: Faber & Faber, 1991), 54.
16. Samuel Beckett, *Collected Poems in English and French* (London: John Calder, 1977), 61.

8. FAMINE

1. Quoted in O'Connor, *The Backward Look*, 137.
2. See Welch, *Irish Poetry from Moore to Yeats*, for an account of Mangan and his verse, its sources, and publication. A modern edition of his poems is available, edited by Jacques Chuto, Peter van de Kamp, Pádraig Ó Snodaigh, and others, which commenced publication in 1996.
3. Timothy Webb (ed.), William Carleton, *The Black Prophet: A Tale of Irish Famine* (Shannon: Irish University Press, 1972), 347.
4. See M. C. Ferguson, *Sir Samuel Ferguson in the Ireland of his Day*, Vol. I (Edinburgh: William Blackwood & Sons, 1896), 250.
5. See Deane *et al.*, *Field Day Anthology*, ii. 119.
6. *Field Day Anthology*, ii. 181.
7. Samuel Beckett, *Waiting for Godot* (London: Faber & Faber, 1968 reprint), 44.
8. Nuala Ní Dhomhnaill, *Feis* (Maigh Nuad: An Sagart, 1991), 27.
9. Cormac McCarthy, *Outer Dark* (London: Picador, 1994 edn.), 236.

9. NEW DEPARTURES

1. Deane *et al.*, *Field Day Anthology*, ii. 199.
2. Horace Wyndham, *Speranza: A Biography of Lady Wilde* (New York: AMS Reprint edn., 1951; first published), 232–3.
3. Oscar Wilde, *The Works* (Leicester: Galley Press, 1987), 328.
4. Wilde, *The Works*, 853–4.
5. Declan Kiberd, *Irish Classics* (London: Granta Books, 2000), 331–9.
6. Yeats, *Collected Poems*, 20.
7. Robert Welch (ed.), *W. B. Yeats: Writings on Irish Folklore, Legend and Myth* (London: Penguin Books, 1993), 198.
8. Dan H. Laurence and Nicholas Grene (eds.), *Shaw, Lady Gregory and the Abbey* (Gerrards Cross: Colin Smythe, 1993), ix.
9. George Bernard Shaw, *The Complete Plays of Bernard Shaw* (London: Odhams, 1934), 411.
10. W. B. Yeats, *Autobiographies* (London: Macmillan, 1970 reprint), 423–4.
11. Deane *et al.*, *Field Day Anthology*, ii. 558.

10. THE WEST'S AWAKE

1. Yeats, *Collected Poems*, 149.
2. Alan Price (ed.), J. M. Synge, *Collected Works*, Vol. II, *Prose* (Gerrards Cross: Colin Smythe, 1982), 138.

3. Ann Saddlemyer (ed.), J. M. Synge, *Collected Works*, Vol. III, *Plays I* (Gerrards Cross: Colin Smythe, 1982), 57.

4. Anna MacBride White and A. Norman Jeffares (eds.), *The Gonne–Yeats Letters: 1893–1938* (London: Hutchinson, 1992), 174.

5. Synge, *Collected Works*, iii. 23.

6. Synge, *Collected Works*, iii. 7.

7. Ann Saddlemyer (ed.), J. M. Synge, *Collected Works*, Vol. IV, *Plays II* (Gerrards Cross: Colin Smythe, 1982), 169.

8. Synge, *Collected Works*, iv. 287.

9. J. M. Hone, Review of *Responsibilities*, *New Statesman*, 24 Apr. 1915.

10. Yeats, *Collected Poems*, 124.

11. *Collected Poems*, 129.

12. W. B. Yeats, *Mythologies* (London: Macmillan, 1977 reprint), 321, 331.

13. Yeats, *Collected Poems*, 204.

14. *Collected Poems*, 218.

15. *Collected Poems*, 340.

II. HEARTS OF STONE

1. Joyce, *Ulysses*, 260.

2. James Joyce, *A Portrait of the Artist as a Young Man* (1960), 91.

3. John Wyse Jackson and Peter Costello, *John Stanislaus Joyce* (London: Fourth Estate, 1997), 378.

4. *Ulysses*, 183.

5. *Ulysses*, 261.

6. See many sites for the dating of these quotations.

7. *Dubliners*, 152.

8. Yeats, *Collected Poems*, 204.

9. *Ulysses*, 289.

10. *Ulysses*, 314.

11. Yeats, *Collected Poems*, 230–1.

12. Sean O'Casey, *Two Plays* (London: Macmillan, 1926), 111.

13. O'Casey, *Two Plays*, 77.

14. Yeats, *Collected Poems*, 204.

12. MATRIX OF SURDS

1. Liam O'Flaherty, *The Mountain Tavern and Other Stories* (Leipzig: Tauchnitz, 1929), 47–54.

2. Frank O'Connor (ed.), *Modern Irish Short Stories* (Oxford: Oxford University Press, 1964 reprint), xiv.

3. O'Connor (ed.), *Modern Irish Short Stories*, 173.

4. Austin Clarke, *Collected Poems* (Dublin: Dolmen Press, 1974), 117.

5. Clarke, *Collected Poems*, 126.

6. Clarke, *Collected Poems*, 183.

7. Clarke, *Collected Poems*, 165.

8. Samuel Beckett, *Proust and Three Dialogues with Georges Duthuit* (London: John Calder, 1965), 64.

9. See Ruby Cohn (ed.), *Disjecta: Miscellaneous Writings and a Dramatic Fragment by Samuel Beckett* (London: John Calder, 1983), 70–6, for Beckett's 1934 piece on Devlin.

10. Samuel Beckett, *Murphy* (London: Picador, 1973 edn.), 69.

11. Beckett, *Murphy*, 66.

12. Samuel Beckett, *The Beckett Trilogy* (London: Faber & Faber, 1979 edn.), 332.

13. W. B. Yeats, *Pages from a Diary Written in 1930* (Dublin: Cuala Press, 1944), 21.

14. *The Beckett Trilogy*, 355–6.

15. Beckett, *Collected Poems, etc.*, 127.

16. Anthony Cronin, *No Laughing Matter: The Life and Times of Flann O'Brien* (New York: Fromm International, 1998 edn.), 49.

17. Cronin, *No Laughing Matter*, 89.

18. Flann O'Brien, *At Swim-Two-Birds* (London: MacGibbon & Kee, 1966 edn.), 13.

19. *At Swim-Two-Birds*, 61.

20. *At Swim-Two-Birds*, 20–1.

21. Louis MacNeice, *Collected Poems* (London: Faber & Faber, 1966), 30.

22. MacNeice, *Collected Poems*, 61.

23. MacNeice, *Collected Poems*, 134.

24. Joyce Cary, *A House of Children* (London: Michael Joseph, 1951 Carfax edition), 11.

25. See Michael Foot, *H.G.: The History of Mr Wells* (New York: Doubleday, 1995), 284.

26. Patrick Kavanagh, *Collected Poems* (London: Martin, Brian, & O'Keeffe, 1977 reprint), 45–6.

27. T. S. Eliot, *Selected Essays: 1917–1932* (London: Faber & Faber, 1932), 14.

28. Máirtín Ó Cadhain, *Cré na Cille* (Baile Átha Cliath: Sáirséal & Dill, 1949), 25.

29. Elizabeth Bowen, *The Heat of the Day* (London: The Reprint Society, 1950), 164.

30. Bowen, *The Heat of the Day*, 162–3.

31. Bowen, *The Heat of the Day*, 166–7.

32. Bowen, *The Heat of the Day*, 273.

33. Seán Ó Ríordáin, *Eireaball Spideoige* (Baile Átha Cliath: Sáirséal & Dill, 1952), 111.

34. Seán Ó Tuama, *Nuabhéarsaíocht* (Baile Átha Cliath: Sáirséal & Dill, 1966 edn.), 100.

13. ASTRAKHAN ATARAXIE

1. Thomas Kinsella, *Collected Poems* (Manchester: Carcanet Press, 2001), 5.
2. 'Yew-Trees', in Thomas Hutchinson and Ernest de Selincourt (eds.), *Wordsworth's Poetical Works* (Oxford: Oxford University Press, 1969), 146.
3. Kinsella, *Collected Poems*, 73.
4. Thomas Kinsella, *New Poems 1973* (Dublin: Dolmen Press, 1973), 37.
5. Kinsella, *New Poems 1973*, 20.
6. Kinsella, *New Poems 1973*, 25–8.
7. Kinsella, *Collected Poems*, 342.
8. Kinsella, *Collected Poems*, 338.
9. John Montague, *Collected Poems* (Oldcastle: Gallery Books, 1995), 62.
10. Montague, *Collected Poems*, 13.
11. Montague, *Collected Poems*, 140.
12. John Montague, *Smashing the Piano* (Oldcastle: Gallery Books, 1999), 59.
13. Seamus Heaney, *Door into the Dark* (London: Faber & Faber, 1969), 19.
14. Seamus Heaney, *The Haw Lantern* (London: Faber & Faber, 1987), 27.
15. Seamus Heaney, *Wintering Out* (London: Faber & Faber, 1972), 15.
16. Heaney, *Wintering Out*, 48.
17. Seamus Heaney, *Station Island* (London: Faber & Faber, 1984), 57.
18. Seamus Heaney, *Seeing Things* (London: Faber & Faber, 1991), 16.
19. Seamus Heaney, *Electric Light* (London: Faber & Faber, 2001), 80–1.
20. Seamus Heaney, *District and Circle* (London: Faber & Faber, 2006), 75–6.
21. Brian Friel, *Selected Plays* (London: Faber & Faber, 1984), 419.
22. Brian Friel, *The Home Place* (Oldcastle: Gallery Books, 2005); quotations from the beginning and the end of the play.
23. Dennis O'Driscoll, *Stepping Stones: Interviews with Seamus Heaney* (London: Faber & Faber, 2008), 228.
24. John McGahern, *That They May Face the Rising Sun* (London: Faber & Faber, 2002), 183.
25. *That They May Face the Rising Sun*, 186.
26. John McGahern, *Memoir* (London: Faber & Faber, 2005), 271–2. Italics in text: this is a letter of Mrs McGahern's quoted by her son.
27. Rainer Maria Rilke, *Selected Poems*, trans. J. B. Leishman (Harmondsworth: Penguin Books, 1967), 64.
28. John Banville, *The Sea* (London: Picador, 2005), 245.
29. MacNeice, *Collected Poems*, 286.
30. John Banville, *The Infinities* (London: Picador, 2009), 39.
31. *The Infinities*, 61 ff.
32. Pearse Hutchinson, *Faoistin Bhacach* (Baile Átha Cliath: An Clóchomhar, 1968), 44.
33. Pearse Hutchinson, *Collected Poems* (Oldcastle: Gallery Books, 2002), 129.
34. Alan Titley, *An Fear Dána* (Baile Átha Cliath: An Clóchomhar, 1993), 38.

35. 'An Apologie of Raymond Sebond', in *Essays of Montaigne Translated by John Florio*, Vol. II (London: J. M. Dent & Son, 1938), 204–5.
36. Anthony Cronin, *Collected Poems* (Dublin: New Island, 2004), 228.
37. Cronin, *Collected Poems*, 333.
38. Augustus Young, *The Nicotine Cat and Other People* (Dublin: Duras & New Island, 2009), 100.
39. Nuala Ní Dhomhnaill and Paul Muldoon, *The Astrakhan Cloak* (Oldcastle: Gallery Books, 1992), 33.
40. Ní Dhomhnaill, *Feis*, 30.
41. Ní Dhomhnaill and Muldoon, *The Astrakhan Cloak*, 41.
42. Paul Muldoon, *Why Brownlee Left* (London: Faber & Faber, 1985 reprint), 21.
43. Paul Muldoon, *Horse Latitudes* (London: Faber & Faber, 2006), 94.
44. Muldoon, *Horse Latitudes*, 39.
45. Ciaran Carson, *Collected Poems* (Oldcastle: Gallery Books, 2008), 166.
46. Carson, *Collected Poems*, 163.
47. Carson, *Collected Poems*, 177.
48. Carson, *Collected Poems*, 348.
49. Ciaran Carson, *For All We Know* (Oldcastle: Gallery Books, 2008), 92.
50. Derek Mahon, *Collected Poems* (Oldcastle: Gallery Books, 1999), 17.
51. Derek Mahon, *Night Crossing* (Oxford: Oxford University Press, 1969 reprint), 1. Omitted from the *Collected Poems*.
52. Mahon, *Collected Poems*, 13.
53. Derek Mahon, *The Hunt by Night* (Oxford: Oxford University Press, 1982), 36. Omitted from the *Collected Poems*.
54. See 'The Vanity of Human Wishes'.
55. Mahon, *Collected Poems*, 89–90.
56. Mahon, *Collected Poems*, 101.
57. Mahon, *Collected Poems*, 105.
58. Mahon, *Collected Poems*, 203. This forms part of 'The Hudson Letter', Part Two of the volume of that title. In *Collected Poems* the title is 'St Mark's Place'.
59. Derek Mahon, *The Yellow Book* (Oldcastle: Gallery Books, 1997), 17.
60. Mahon, *The Yellow Book*, 26.
61. Mahon, *Collected Poems*, 285–8.
62. Derek Mahon, *Harbour Lights* (Oldcastle: Gallery Books, 2005), 17.
63. Mahon, *Harbour Lights*, 43.

14. CODA: *BY THE BOG OF CATS*

1. Marina Carr, *By the Bog of Cats* (London: Faber & Faber, 2004), 5.
2. *By the Bog of Cats*, 75.

A Bibliography of Literary Histories and Related Works

This is a bibliography of literary histories of Irish literature and of other relevant works, such as anthologies, dictionaries of biography, and Companions. No attempt, apart from one exception (see below under 'Foster, R. F.'), is made to provide a bibliographical account of individual writers or discussions of them: such can be found by accessing one or two of the major studies of these writers and by looking up the bibliographical listings in those works; or by accessing, to begin with, any number of electronic databases. This listing is meant to act as a guide to work that seeks to deal with the corpus of Irish writing in either English or Irish. Specialist bibliographies, such as those by Richard Irvine Best on Irish philology and Irish printed literature, are not listed since these are relevant mostly to the advanced scholar and will be quickly found in the bibliographies of the histories and Companions cited below.

Brown, Stephen J., *Ireland in Fiction: A Guide to Irish Novels*, Vol. 1 (Dublin: Maunsel Press, 1919). Provides plot summaries of Irish novels as well as dates of publication and publishers. Volume 2 of this work was edited by Desmond Clarke (Cork: Royal Carbery, 1985).

Cahalan, James M., *The Irish Novel: A Critical History* (Dublin: Gill & Macmillan, 1988). A survey of the Irish novel in English.

Cleary, Joe and Claire Connolly (eds.), *The Cambridge Companion to Modern Irish Culture* (Cambridge: Cambridge University Press, 2005). Essays by various hands on the diversity of modern Irish culture.

Corkery, Daniel, *The Hidden Ireland: A Study of Gaelic Munster in the Eighteenth Century* (Cork: Cork University Press, 1925). Foundational study of poetry in Irish of the period.

Cronin, John, *The Anglo-Irish Novel*, Vol. I (Belfast: Appletree Press, 1980); Vol. II (Belfast: Appletree Press, 1990). Critical and historical readings of the Irish novel in the nineteenth century (Vol. I) and up to 1940 (Vol. II).

Crotty, Patrick, *The Penguin Book of Irish Poetry* (London: Penguin Books, 2010). Extensive anthology with many translations from the Irish.

Deane, Seamus, *A Short History of Irish Literature* (London: Hutchinson, 1986). A narrative and critical reading of Irish literature in English from Swift through to the 1980s. There is a chapter on the Gaelic Background.

—— Andrew Carpenter, and Jonathan Williams (eds.), *The Field Day Anthology of Irish Literature*, 3 vols. (Derry: Field Day, 1991). A major anthology of Irish literature in Irish and English, with introductory essays and bio-bibliograhical commentaries from various hands. It was followed, in 2002, by two further volumes, edited by Angela Bourke, Gerardine Meany, Clair Wills, and others, devoted to women's writing, Deane's response to the criticism levelled at the first three volumes that women were under-represented.

Dillon, Myles, *Early Irish Literature* (Chicago and London: University of Chicago Press, 1948). Classic account of the early phases of Gaelic literature.

Foster, John Wilson (ed.), *The Cambridge Companion to the Irish Novel* (Cambridge: Cambridge University Press, 2006). Account of themes, contexts, and authors by various hands of the Irish novel from the eighteenth century to present day.

Foster, R. F., *Yeats: A Life*, in two volumes, *I: The Apprentice Mage* (Oxford: Oxford University Press, 1997) and *II: The Arch-Poet* (Oxford: Oxford University Press, 2003). The only single-author citation in this bibliography, because not only does it give an invaluable account of its subject, it also narrates the literary history of Yeats's period.

Gillespie, Raymond and Andrew Hadfield (eds.), *The Oxford History of the Irish Book:* Vol. III, *The Irish Book in English 1550–1800* (Oxford: Oxford University Press, 2006). Book history by various hands, the first to be issued in what will be a five-volume series: General Editors, Brian Walker and Robert Anthony Welch. Volume V, *The Irish Book in English 1891–2000*, ed. Clare Hutton and Patrick Walsh, and Volume IV, *The Irish Book in English 1800–1891*, ed. James Murphy, appeared in 2011.

Hogan, Robert (ed.), *A Dictionary of Irish Literature* (Westport, Conn.: Greenwood Press, 1979). Essays on authors by various hands, mostly confined to writers in English.

Hull, Eleanor (ed.), *The Poem-Book of the Gael* (London: Chatto & Windus, 1913). Translations from Gaelic poetry of all periods into English prose and verse from various hands. A fine and neglected anthology.

Hyde, Douglas, *A Literary History of Ireland* (London: T. Fisher Unwin, 1899). The first attempt at a history of Gaelic literature from earliest times.

Jeffares, A. Norman, *Anglo-Irish Literature* (London: Macmillan, 1982). A historical and critical survey by a Yeats scholar and literary historian.

Kelleher, Margaret and Philip O'Leary (eds.), *The Cambridge History of Irish Literature* (Cambridge: Cambridge University Press, 2006). Comprehensive history by various hands in two volumes from the earliest periods of Irish literature in Irish, English, Latin, and Norman French.

Kiberd, Declan, *Irish Classics* (London: Granta Books, 2000). Analysis of key texts in Irish and English from the seventeenth century onwards, linking them to their historical contexts.

Leerssen, Joep Theodoor, *Mere Irish and Fíor-Ghael: Studies in the Idea of Nationality, its Development and Literary Expression Prior to the Nineteenth Century* (Amsterdam: Rodopi, 1986). The subtitle explains.

——*Remembrance and Imagination: Patterns in the Historical and Literary Representation of Ireland in the Nineteenth Century* (Cork: Cork University Press and Field Day, 1996). A continuation of the above.

Maxwell, D. E. S., *Modern Irish Drama* (Cambridge: Cambridge University Press, 1984). An authoritative critical survey and history.

McCormack, W. J., *Ascendancy and Tradition in Anglo-Irish History 1789–1939* (Oxford: Oxford University Press, 1985). Literary history exploring the problematic nature of 'ascendancy'.

Murray, Christopher, *Twentieth-Century Irish Drama: Mirror up to Nation* (Manchester: Manchester University Press, 1997). A comprehensive critical history, including the story of the Abbey Theatre.

Ó Buachalla, Breandán, *Aisling Ghéar: Na Stíobhartaigh agus an tAos Léinn 1603–1788* (Baile Átha Cliath: An Clóchomhar, 1996). An exhaustive and magisterial study of the political vision poem and its contexts.

O'Connor, Frank, *The Backward Look* (London: Macmillan, 1967). An inspiring history of Irish literary traditions from the earliest times.

Ó Tuama, Seán, *An Grá in Amhráin na nDaoine* (Baile Átha Cliath: An Clóchomhar, 1960). Study of love in Irish folk-song.

Rafroidi, Patrick, *Irish Literature in English: The Romantic Period 1789–1850* (Gerrards Cross: Colin Smythe, 1980). Critical survey and thematic analysis in two volumes.

Regan, Stephen, *Irish Writing: An Anthology of Irish Literature in English 1789–1939* (London: Penguin Books, 2004). A valuable anthology which includes letters, speeches, songs, and travel writing, as well as more conventional literary material.

Richards, Shaun (ed.), *The Cambridge Companion to Twentieth-Century Irish Drama* (Cambridge: Cambridge University Press, 2004). Essays by various hands covering major authors, themes, and contexts.

Vance, Norman, *Irish Literature, A Social History: Tradition, Identity, and Difference* (Oxford: Blackwell, 1990). A literary history exploring varieties of Irishness.

——*Irish Literature since 1800* (Harlow: Pearson, 2002). Readings of Irish authors as representative of variant traditions.

Welch, Robert, *The Abbey Theatre 1899–1999: Form and Pressure* (Oxford: Oxford University Press, 1999).

——(ed.), *The Oxford Companion to Irish Literature* (Oxford: Oxford University Press, 1996).

Williams, J. E. Caerwyn and Máirin Ní Mhuiríosa, *Traidisiún Liteartha na nGael* (Baile Átha Cliath: An Clóchomhar, 1979). A survey of Gaelic literature from earliest times.

A Note on the Author

Robert Anthony Welch was born in Cork in 1947 and was educated there and at the University of Leeds, where he became a lecturer in English. He taught also at the University of Ife in Nigeria. From 1984 to 2009 he was Professor of English at the University of Ulster, where he chaired the department and became Dean of Arts in 2000, a position he held until 2008. He was Emeritus Research Professor from 2009 until his death in 2013.

Robert Welch published poetry, fiction, drama, and criticism. In 1996 he edited the *Oxford Companion to Irish Literature*. His books of criticism included *Irish Poetry from Moore to Yeats* (1980), *A History of Verse Translation from the Irish: 1789–1897* (1988), *Changing States: Transformations in Modern Irish Literature* (1993), and *The Abbey Theatre: 1899–1999* (1999). His poetry included *Muskerry* (1991), *The Evergreen Road* (2006), and *Constanza* (2010). A novel, *Groundwork* (1997), was a *New York Times* Book of the Year, while the *Oxford Companion* was an 'Irish Book of the Month' and topped the Irish bestsellers for three weeks. Drama included *Protestants* (2006), which toured Ireland, Scotland, and the West End, London, and *Static*, for Ransom Productions, which toured Northern Ireland in 2011. He published fiction in Irish, and a critical and biographical book, *Japhy Ryder ar Shleasaibh na Mangartan* (2011), which won the Oireachtas Prize for a work of prose.

He was a Fellow of the English Association and a Member of the Royal Irish Academy, and held visiting professorships and fellowships at Sassari, Sardinia; University College, Cork; and the University of Missouri, St Louis. He was President of the International Association for the Study of Irish Literatures (IASIL), 1988–91. He is survived by his wife, Angela O'Riordan, and three children, Rachel, Killian, and Tiernan. His son, Egan, predeceased him.

Index